Legal Accountability and Britain's Wars 2000–2015

This book discusses the manner in which Britain's wars, which took place between 2000 and 2015, have interacted with the relevant principles of international law and English law for the purpose, primarily, of considering legal accountability.

During a debate in the House of Lords in 2005 a former Chief of the Defence Staff commented that 'the Armed Forces are under legal siege'. The book will discuss the major legal issues that have arisen, ranging from the various votes in Parliament to go to war, the constitutional relationship between ministers and senior commanders, the right under international law to use force, the influence of human rights law, the role of the courts in England (including the coroners' courts), to the legal regime applying to the conduct of UK military operations. It will assess critically whether the armed forces will now have to accept that operations conducted outside the UK are subject to greater legal scrutiny than previously and whether, if this is the case, it is likely to hinder their future military activities.

This book will be of great interest to scholars of international law, the law of armed conflict, military studies and international relations, as well as to those with a professional or other interest in the subject matter.

Professor Emeritus Peter Rowe retired from the University of Lancaster Law School in 2014. He has been chairman of the UK Group of the International Society for Military law and the Laws of War.

Routledge Research in International Law

Available:

International Law and the Third World
Reshaping Justice
Edited by Richard Falk, Balakrishnan Rajagopal and Jacqueline Stevens

International Legal Theory
Essays and Engagements, 1966–2006
Nicholas Onuf

The Problem of Enforcement in International Law
Countermeasures, the Non-Injured State and the Idea of International Community
Elena Katselli Proukaki

International Economic Actors and Human Rights
Adam McBeth

The Law of Consular Access
A Documentary Guide
John Quigley, William J. Aceves and S. Adele Shank

State Accountability under International Law
Holding States Accountable for a Breach of Jus Cogens Norms
Lisa Yarwood

International Organizations and the Idea of Autonomy
Institutional Independence in the International Legal Order
Edited by Richard Collins and Nigel D. White

Self-Determination in the Post-9/11 Era
Elizabeth Chadwick

Participants in the International Legal System
Multiple Perspectives on Non-State Actors in International Law
Edited by Jean d'Aspremont

Sovereignty and Jurisdiction in the Airspace and Outer Space
Legal Criteria for Spatial Delimitation
Gbenga Oduntan

International Law in a Multipolar World
Edited by Matthew Happold

The Law on the Use of Force
A Feminist Analysis
Gina Heathcote

The ICJ and the Evolution of International Law
The Enduring Impact of the Corfu Channel Case
Edited by Karine Bannelier, Théodore Christakis and Sarah Heathcote

UNHCR and International Refugee Law
From Treaties to Innovation
Corinne Lewis

Asian Approaches to International Law and the Legacy of Colonialism
The Law of the Sea, Territorial Disputes and International Dispute Settlement
Edited by Jin-Hyun Paik, Seok-Woo Lee, Kevin Y. L. Tan

The Right to Self-determination under International Law
'Selfistans,' Secession, and the Rule of the Great Powers
Milena Sterio

Reforming the UN Security Council Membership
The Illusion of Representativeness
Sabine Hassler

Threats of Force
International Law and Strategy
Francis Grimal

The Changing Role of Nationality in International Law
Edited by Alessandra Annoni and Serena Forlati

Criminal Responsibility for the Crime of Aggression
Patrycja Grzebyk

Regional Maintenance of Peace and Security under International Law
The Distorted Mirrors
Dace Winther

International Law-making
Essays in Honour of Jan Klabbers
Edited by Rain Liivoja and Jarna Petman

Resolving Claims to Self-Determination
Is There a Role for the International Court of Justice?
Andrew Coleman

The Rise of Tamil Separatism in Sri Lanka
From Communalism to Secession
Gnanapala Welhengama and Nirmala Pillay

The United Nations and Collective Security
Gary Wilson

Justice for Victims before the International Criminal Court
Luke Moffett

Public–Private Partnerships and Responsibility under International Law
A Global Health Perspective
Lisa Clarke

Cultural Diversity in International Law
The Effectiveness of the UNESCO Convention on the Protection and Promotion of the Diversity of Cultural Expressions
Edited by Lilian Richieri Hanania

Incitement in International Law
Wibke K. Timmermann

The Cuban Embargo under International Law
El Bloqueo
Nigel D. White

Resisting United Nations Security Council Resolutions
Sufyan Droubi

The Changing Nature of Customary International Law
Methods of Interpreting the Concept of Custom in International Criminal Tribunals
Noora Arajärvi

The International Criminal Court in Search of its Purpose and Identity
Edited by Triestino Mariniello

Power and Law in International Society
International Relations as the Sociology of International Law
Mark Klamberg

The International Criminal Court and Global Social Control in Late Modernity
International Criminal Justice in Late Modernity
Nerida Chazal

International Law and Boundary Disputes in Africa
Gbenga Oduntan

Means of Transportation and Registration of Nationality
Transportation Registered by International Organizations
Vincent P. Cogliati-Bantz

Reciprocity in International Law
Its Impact and Function
Shahrad Nasrolahi Fard

The Responsibility to Protect in International Law
An Emerging Paradigm Shift
Susan Breau

Seeking Justice in International Law
The Significance and Implications of the UN Declaration on the Rights of Indigenous Peoples
Mauro Barelli

Fragmentation vs the Constitutionalisation of International Law
A Practical Inquiry
Edited by Andrzej Jakubowski and Karolina Wierczyńska

Forthcoming titles in this series include:

Technology and the Law on the Use of Force
New Security Challenges in the Twenty First Century
Jackson Maogoto

International Law and the Rights of those Displaced by Armed Conflict
Elena Katselli Proukaki

International Criminal Law and Sexual Violence against Women
The Interpretation of Gender in the Contemporary International Criminal Trial
Daniela Nadj

Fighting and Victimhood in International Criminal Law
Joanna Nicholson

Legal Accountability and Britain's Wars 2000–2015

Peter Rowe

Routledge
Taylor & Francis Group
LONDON AND NEW YORK

First published 2016
by Routledge

2 Park Square, Milton Park, Abingdon, Oxfordshire OX14 4RN
711 Third Avenue, New York, NY 10017

Routledge is an imprint of the Taylor & Francis Group, an informa business

First issued in paperback 2018

British Library Cataloguing in Publication Data
A catalogue record for this book is available from the British Library

Library of Congress Cataloging-in-Publication Data
Names: Rowe, P. J. (Peter J.) author.
Title: Legal accountability and Britain's wars 2000–2015 / Peter Rowe.
Description: New York : Routledge, 2016. | Series: Routledge research in international law | Includes bibliographical references and index.
Identifiers: LCCN 2015048455 | ISBN 9781138846241 (hbk) | ISBN 9781315727578 (ebk)
Subjects: LCSH: War and emergency powers—Great Britain. | Government accountability—Great Britain. | War (International law) | Military law—Great Britain. | Great Britain—Politics and government—21st century. | Great Britain—Foreign relations—Law and legislation. | Criminal liability (International law) | Peacekeeping forces, British. | Conflict of laws—Great Britain. | Political leadership—Moral and ethical aspects. | Great Britain—History—21st century.
Classification: LCC KD6004 .R69 2016 | DDC 342.41/0412—dc23
LC record available at http://lccn.loc.gov/2015048455

ISBN: 978-1-138-84624-1 (hbk)
ISBN: 978-1-138-61382-9 (pbk)

Typeset in Galliard
by Apex CoVantage, LLC

This book is dedicated to the memory of my parents

Contents

Table of cases

A

B

C

I

J

K

L

M

N

O

P

Q

R

Y

Z

Table of statutes and treaties

STATUTES

TREATIES

List of abbreviations

AJIL	American Journal of International Law
AGE	Anti-Government Elements
APC	Armoured Personnel Carrier
AsocIL	American Society of International Law
BYIL	British Yearbook of International Law
CJIL	Chinese Journal of International Law
CMLR	Common Market Law Reports
Crim LR	Criminal Law Review
CSROF	Coalition of Syrian Revolutionary and Opposition Forces
Daesh	See ISIL below
ECHR	European Convention on Human Rights and Fundamental Freedoms, 1950
EctHR	European Court of Human Rights
EHRR	European Human Rights Reports
EJIL	European Journal of International Law
FOI	Freedom of information
FRAGO	Fractional order
ICC	International Criminal Court
ICCPR	International Covenant on Civil and Political Rights, 1966
ICJ	International Court of Justice
ICLQ	International and Comparative Law Quarterly
ICRC	International Committee of the Red Cross
ICTY	International Criminal Tribunal for the Former Yugoslavia
ICTR	International Criminal Tribunal for Rwanda
IED	Improvised Explosive Device
IHAT	Iraq Historic Allegations Team
IHL	International Humanitarian Law
IMT	International Military Tribunal
IRRC	International Review of the Red Cross
ISAF	International Security Assistance Force
ISIL	Islamic State in Iraq and the Levant
JoC&SL	Journal of Conflict & Security Law
LJIL	Leiden Journal of International Law

LOAC	Law of Armed Conflict
MJIL	Melbourne Journal of International Law
MNF	Multinational Force
MoU	Memorandum of Understanding
NATO	North Atlantic Treaty Organisation
NILR	Netherlands International Law Review
NILQ	Northern Ireland Law Quarterly
NTC	National Transitional Council (Libya)
PII	Public Interest Immunity
PL	Public Law
PTSD	Post-Traumatic Stress Disorder
RAF	Royal Air Force
RMP	Royal Military Police
RN	Royal Navy
RoE	Rules of Engagement
RPA	Remotely Piloted Aircraft
RUSI Jo	Royal United Services Institute Journal
UAS	Unmanned Aerial Systems
UAV	Unmanned Aerial Vehicle
UNAMA	United Nations Assistance Mission in Afghanistan
UNCAT	United Nations Convention Against Torture 1984
WMD	Weapons of Mass Destruction
YBIHL	Yearbook of International Humanitarian Law

Foreword by Major General His Honour Gordon Risius

Attacks of terrorism are not infrequently portrayed in the media, and sometimes even by government spokesmen, as 'acts of war', when in reality only criminal law is likely to be engaged. In such circumstances, books by Peter Rowe are particularly welcome and valuable, because they set the record straight. The present volume is the latest in an authoritative series, beginning in 1987 with *Defence: The Legal Implications*, in which he has set out with clarity and concision the complex nature of numerous aspects of the law of armed conflict. The present volume concentrates on the armed conflicts in which this country has been involved over the last 15 years. Peter Rowe's observations will be of the greatest value to lawyers practising in this field, especially those within the Services, as well as to a wider readership. Given that a convention is now emerging for debates and votes in the House of Commons on the deployment of our military forces, this book should be required reading for members of parliament.

I began learning about the law of armed conflict from Peter Rowe in 1988, when I attended his first course for Army legal officers. We then collaborated on a number of presentations and publications together, and for some years we ran the UK Group of the International Society for Military Law and the Law of War. While the parent Society was already well established, Peter Rowe played a leading role in bringing together academics and Service lawyers in this country, each benefitting from the expertise and experience of the others without jeopardising either academic independence or security constraints. It is a privilege and a pleasure to be invited to contribute this brief Foreword.

As a military lawyer concerned with the legal aspects of British military operations over the final years of the last century, I would have been greatly assisted by a book such as this. It demonstrates that despite his recent retirement from full-time academic life at Lancaster University, Peter Rowe still has a great deal to offer in these uncertain and difficult times.

Preface

This book tries to show how the armed conflicts, in which UK has been involved between 2000 and 2015, have interacted with the principles of international law and English law applicable to them for the purpose, primarily, of considering legal accountability.

A deliberate decision has been made to consider the armed conflicts from the standpoint of one of the states concerned, the UK, in order to be able to take an holistic view of the legal environment applicable to modern armed conflicts in a way which can explore, in depth, the impact of national law, along with international law, on its military activities. When considering the law applicable during an armed conflict, particularly one which involves a coalition of states, it is the national law that will be the main variable, but it is this body of law that will usually be invoked, in terms of legal accountability, by those who seek to challenge state acts or the acts of individuals acting on behalf of the state. The application of the law to these armed conflicts must also be seen in its political context and, in order to do so, I have made considerable use of ministerial statements and other parliamentary material.

It should not be thought, however, that in modern armed conflicts international law is somehow to be relegated into second place to national law in importance. International humanitarian law remains the main body of law dealing with the conduct of armed conflict and the protection of those, such as civilians, the wounded and sick and prisoners of war who require its attention, and most of the obligations derived from it apply in a similar way to all states and to non-state actors in the same way. The British government has stated on a number of occasions that its armed forces are trained in the requirements of it and, in the overwhelming number of occasions, they have complied with it during the course of armed conflicts. The International Committee of the Red Cross/Red Crescent (ICRC) has a pivotal part to play in disseminating this law and has considerable power to influence state behaviour in favour of compliance with it. In adopting a diplomatic approach to potential breaches of international humanitarian law, in which it normally does not make public its concerns about particular cases, it cannot take on the mantle of holding states or individuals accountable in the same dramatic way in which national law or an international criminal trial can.

Anyone writing about particular armed conflicts soon after they have taken place will be faced with the problem of determining the facts, upon which any legal analysis can be grounded. I have used parliamentary material extensively for this purpose, primarily in the form of ministerial statements and evidence given at, or in response to, parliamentary select committee sessions. I have also relied upon the findings of fact in various court proceedings and evidence given to public inquiries.

This book is not intended to deliver an account of international humanitarian law or of human rights law applicable during an armed conflict or, indeed, a narrative of the separate topics contained with it. For reasons of space, reliance on scholarly writing has had to be severely curtailed. It is hoped, however, that this book will prove to be helpful to those involved in the practical application of the law relating to armed conflicts of the type described within it. Recognising, however, that all armed conflicts will be distinct, in which different challenges will arise, it does not propose to be a 'lessons to be learned' manual, applicable to any future conflicts, although it is hoped that the experience of the applicability of the law to the Iraq and Afghanistan conflicts will provide, at least some, basis for further thinking in this area. Those with specialist knowledge of the areas of law dealt with in the following pages, whether as legal practitioners or as scholars, may find the detail contained within the footnotes to be of some assistance to them.

This book was written, and delivered to the publishers, some time before the publication of the report of the Iraq Inquiry, but it has been able to rely on the publicly available evidence given to it.

I am very grateful indeed to Major General His Honour Gordon Risius for writing the Foreword. I would like to thank Sebastian Payne, Michael Gordon and Mark Butler, and in particular, Catherine Deering. I should also like to record my appreciation for the professionalism displayed by all involved with this book at Routledge, especially, Katie Carpenter, Olivia Manley, Marie Roberts, Hayley Kennard and the compilers of the list of cases, statutes, treaties and the index. Responsibility for any remaining errors, or inaccuracies, lies with me.

I am, as always, very grateful to my wife, Anne, for all the support she has given me over the long period of writing.

Peter Rowe
7 December 2015

1 Introduction

The year 2000 was not merely the beginning of a new millennium, it also marked a time when two significant legal developments were either waiting to come into force, or were being debated in Parliament, each of which had the potential to have profound effects on the conduct of an armed conflict, although how they would actually do so would only become clear as the various conflicts, to which the UK became a party, developed. These were the Human Rights Act 1988, which had implemented into English law most of the rights set out in the European Convention on Human Rights (ECHR),[1] and the International Criminal Court Act 2001, which performed the same function for the crimes established by the Rome Statute 1998 of the International Criminal Court (ICC).

From a legal point of view, therefore, the year 2000 marked the beginning of a new era, as the following chapters will attempt to show, and it thereby presented a sensible starting point for this book. Although lessons from the past can never be ignored, any future conflict in which the UK is involved is likely to reflect a legal environment more similar to its wars after 2000, than to those previously.

In addition, the courts in England have shown, since 2000, a greater willingness to hear and determine what might be termed foreign policy issues, which in an earlier age they would have eschewed.[2] Claims for judicial review of decisions made on behalf of the Secretaries of State for Foreign and Commonwealth Affairs and for Defence, and touching directly or indirectly with Britain's armed conflicts have become commonplace with, at times, far-reaching consequences on government policy.

1 Article 13 of the ECHR, referring to a right to an effective remedy, was not specifically implemented since English law would perform this function. The Scottish Parliament passed its equivalent, the International Criminal Court (Scotland) Act 2001.

2 See generally, Lord Sumption, 'Foreign Affairs in the English Courts Since 9/11', Lecture at the Department of Government, London School of Economics, 12 May 2012 https://www.supremecourt.uk/docs/speech_120514.pdf. See further discussion in Chapter 5.

i The wars, 2000–2015

From 2000 to 2015 the UK was involved in armed conflicts,[3] of varying lengths of time and intensity, in Sierra Leone,[4] Afghanistan 2001–2014,[5] Iraq 2003–2011,[6] Libya 2011[7] and Iraq 2014 (against ISIL) which is continuing, and was extended into Syria in 2015.[8] A proposal by the government to carry out air

3 Whether a series of incidents amounts to an armed conflict is discussed in Chapter 6. Although 15 RN personnel from *HMS Cornwall*, then situated in the mouth of the Ahatt al-Arab waterway between Iran and Iraq, were captured by the Iranian Revolutionary Guard on 23 March 2007 and detained for 14 days this did not lead to armed action by UK armed forces. See *The Iran Hostages Incident: the Lessons Learned*, House of Commons Select Committee on Defence, 4th Report, Session 2007–08, HC 181; *Foreign Policy Aspects of the Detention of Naval Personnel by the Islamic Republic of Iran*, Sixth Report of the Foreign Affairs Committee, Session 2006–07, HC 880 (2007). This could not be considered to have been an armed conflict between the UK and Iran, although it had the potential to develop into one.

4 See the statements of the Foreign Secretary, HC Debs 8 May 2000, vol 349, col 518; HC Debs 6 June 2000, vol 351, col 161 and the Secretary of State for Defence, HC Debs 5 June 2000, vol 351, col 14. See also J Bailey, R Iron, H Strachan (eds), *British Generals in Blair's Wars* (Ashgate 2013), Chapter 4. The rules of engagement 'differ in several respects from those used in Northern Ireland', HL Debs 29 November 2000, vol 619, col 133W.

5 UN Security Council Resolution 1368 (2001) condemned the 'terrorist attacks' of 11 September 2001 on New York, Washington DC and Pennsylvania and, in the preamble, it referred to the inherent right of individual or collective self-defence in the UN Charter. As part of the Coalition Against International Terrorism, UK armed forces participated, alongside US armed forces, in the attack on Afghanistan on 7 October 2001, see HC Debs 8 October 2001, vol 372, col 811 (Prime Minister). A detachment of Royal Marines was deployed to Bagram to secure the airport, HC Debs 26 November 2001, vol 375, col 662. See also *Keesing's Record of World Events* (2001), November, [44448]. A total of four UK service personnel were wounded during the campaign, HC Debs 29 November 2001, vol 375, col 1055W. NATO had previously invoked Art 5 of the North Atlantic Treaty 1949 (see further, Chapter 2). The Bonn Agreement, which set up the Afghan Interim Authority, was signed on 5 December 2001, see UN document S/2001/1154 and the UN Security Council established ISAF by Resolution 1386 (2001), the mandate for which was further extended and renewed. The UK participated in ISAF operations for which a minister stated they 'have robust rules of engagement that are entirely appropriate for their mission', HC Debs 14 January 2002, vol 378, col 4. The UK deployment to Helmand Province was announced by the Secretary of State for Defence on 26 January 2006, HC Debs 26 January 2006, vol 441, col 1529 and complete withdrawal from Helmand occurred at the end of 2014.The official end of Operation Herrick was 31 December 2014, FOI, Ministry of Defence, release 23 February 2015.

6 Patrolling of the no-fly zones was being conducted prior to the commencement of the military campaign against Iraq. 'Military operations officially began at 0234GMT on 20 March 2003, although some preparatory air operations had been undertaken in the southern no-fly zone on 19 March', *Parliamentary Approval for Deploying the Armed Forces: Briefing Paper*, House of Commons Library, 7166, 12 May 2015, note 26. Military operations against the Iraqi armed forces ended on 1 May 2003, see HC Debs 15 July 2003, vol 409, col 194W. For the date of the commencement of the occupation, see Chapter 6. United Kingdom operations in Iraq ended by 31 December 2008, *Al-Waheed v Ministry of Defence* [2014] EWHC 2714 (QB), [1], although some UK armed forces remained for training purposes and were withdrawn by 31 July 2009, *Al-Saadoon and Mufdhi v United Kingdom* [2010] 51 EHRR 9, [36].

7 For details, see Chapter 4.

8 For details, see Chapter 4.

strikes against Syria had been defeated by the House of Commons in a vote on 29 August 2013.[9]

The term 'war', is used in the title of this book and, in places, as a generic term to refer to armed conflicts. While it does have a specific meaning in English law,[10] the same can no longer be said of its understanding in international law, given the desuetude by states of the practice of declaring war and its virtual absence from the Geneva Conventions 1949 and related treaties.[11] The term does, however, convey to most people an image that is much more realistic and better understood than its alternatives of 'armed conflicts', 'insurgency' or 'counter insurgency'.[12]

The classifications drawn by the Geneva Conventions 1949 and their two Additional Protocols of 1977, between an international and a non-international armed conflict, set the conditions for the applicability of international humanitarian law (IHL) in each of these two types of conflict. The UK was involved in international armed conflicts in Afghanistan from 2001, which marked the beginning of the invasion by a coalition of states, until the Bonn Agreement[13] in December of that year, in Iraq from 20 March 2003 until the occupation ceased on 28 June 2004[14] and in Libya in 2011.[15]

In the case of Afghanistan and Iraq, the conclusion of the international armed conflicts resulted, in one way or another, in the UK being engaged in non-international armed conflicts with the consent of the governments of these states.[16] That non-international armed conflicts should exist is hardly a change in the pattern of armed conflicts. What was, however, noteworthy, was the involvement of the UK (along with other states) in a foreign conflict of this type, where its ground forces were used in relatively large numbers for lengthy periods of time. By way of comparison, the large-scale involvement of UK ground forces in each of Iraq and Afghanistan lasted for a period longer than that for World War I.

Apart from the difficulties thrown up as to when a situation on the ground amounts to an armed conflict (or 'merely' terrorism), the UK, like its allies, has been faced with problems over legal classification of the conflicts and the

9 For details, see Chapter 4.

10 See *Amin v Brown* [2005] EWHC 1670 (Ch), [34]–[37].

11 See C Greenwood, 'The Concept of War in Modern International Law' (1987) 36 ICLQ 283 and see the Attorney General, HL Debs 19 February 2003, vol 644, col 1139.

12 A good example of this is given by General David Richards in a BBC documentary, 'Afghanistan: The Lion's Last Roar?' (episode 2, 2 November 2014) who rejected attempts to 'downgrade' the fighting in Afghanistan to something less than 'war'. For discussion of 'counter-insurgency' see below.

13 S/2001/1554, adopted by UN Security Council Resolution 1383 (2001).

14 UN Security Council Resolution 1546 (2004), which stated it would end by 30 June 2004.

15 UN Security Council Resolution 1973 (2011) authorised states to take all necessary measures to protect civilians and to create no-fly zones.

16 This was reinforced by authorisation by the UN Security Council resolutions of the multinational force in Iraq, see Resolution 1511 (2003) until expiry of the authorisation on 31 December 2008, Resolution 1790 (2007). The International Security Assistance Force (ISAF) was authorised by Resolution 1386 (2001) and by subsequent resolutions.

consequences of one determination compared with the other, under IHL.[17] It has also been faced with interpretations of the ECHR by the European Court of Human Rights (ECtHR) and of English law by the courts in England during the course of these conflicts, which makes their legal background look quite different from pre-2000 days. The first substantive motion ever put to the House of Commons prior to the UK taking part in an armed conflict, in the case of Iraq in March 2003, and the practice subsequently hardening into a parliamentary convention, has led to even greater public debate about the rights, wrongs and the national interest in a proposed involvement. It is, perhaps, no coincidence that the government of the day established a number of public inquiries to look into the background to the UK involvement (the Iraq Inquiry) or the conduct of British soldiers in Iraq (the Baha Mousa Inquiry, 2011 and the Al-Sweady Inquiry, 2014). As might have been expected, select committees of both Houses of Parliament have held their own investigations into various aspects of the conflicts. In addition, there has been a striking increase in the number of claims for judicial review, or for compensation, brought before the courts in London by Iraqi (and to a lesser extent, Afghan) civilians. Since British armed forces personnel killed in Iraq or Afghanistan have been repatriated, the coroners' courts have also been active in making reports, in appropriate cases, to the Ministry of Defence on the circumstances of individual deaths and the issues involved in how similar deaths could be prevented.[18]

It is not difficult to see how these events have led to a greater atmosphere of accountability, not only of the politicians concerned, the government (particularly the Ministry of Defence) but also of senior and middle-ranking service officers. What has been of significance has been that calls for some form of accountability have occurred when British forces have been operating, particularly in Iraq and Afghanistan, and not merely after these conflicts have ended. A long-standing mantra that it is somehow 'unpatriotic' to criticise the armed forces when they are taking part in the conflict has been carefully laid aside in appropriate cases in favour of greater transparency and accountability, particularly of ministers and of the most senior military leaders. It may well be that this has been due to a lack of overwhelming public support for these wars and, to some extent, the vision of the ordinary British soldier in Iraq or Afghanistan as a 'victim' of the political events that led him or her to be there at all.[19]

ii The link with terrorism

The link between terrorism and an armed conflict is nothing new. During non-international armed conflicts, and in occupied territory, those who fought

17 For discussion of the meaning of this term, and its variants, see below.

18 The reports were made under Rule 43 of the Coroners Rules 1984, see Chapter 5.

19 Public support for British soldiers is discussed in Chapter 8. The idea that soldiers were seen as 'victims' is discussed (and rejected) by General Sir David Richards in the BBC documentary, 'Afghanistan: The Lion's Last Roar?', 2 November 2014.

governmental forces were often categorised as 'terrorists', whether this was used as a pejorative term, or in want of a better one. The events in New York and Washington on 11 September 2001 ('9/11') led to the creation of a new phrase, 'the war on terror', the effect of which was to lead to a blurring of the two separate legal regimes concerned with, on the one hand, the laws of war, developed through international law, and, on the other, the law relating to terrorism, which has been derived principally through national laws.[20] The consequence could, and did on occasions, lead to confusion as to which of these bodies of law applied, which manifested itself most starkly in the ill-treatment of some detainees, and in 'intelligence-led' attacks against particular individuals suspected of being involved in serious acts against various government forces.

Although the phrase 'war on terror' was used even by government ministers[21] a change seems to have come about by 2007 when a government minister was asked for a written answer to the question 'how will they [the government] respond to the advice of the Director of Public Prosecutions on the need to avoid "war on terror" phraseology in public statements?'[22] The concern went beyond discarding a particular phrase, which had been used by some with 'a long pair of tongs',[23] merely with the hope of finding a better one. The real issue was formulated by Lord Steyn, a former Lord of Appeal in Ordinary, who drew attention to the 'endless excesses and acts of lawlessness committed in the name of the war on terror'.[24]

In the absence of a definition of terrorism under international law[25] it is left to individual states to determine its meaning within their own jurisdictions and, in doing so, very little uniformity of approach can be seen.[26] In the UK terrorism is defined as:

> the use or threat of action designed to influence the government or an international governmental organisation or to intimidate the public or a section

20 One of the principal aims of the British government in its attack, as part of a coalition of forces, against Afghanistan in October 2001 was 'to damage, disrupt and destroy al-Qaeda's terrorist network', HC Debs 15 October 2001, vol 372, col 963W; HC Debs 6 November 2001, vol 374, col 131W.

21 See, for example, the Foreign Secretary, HC Debs 7 January 2008, vol 470, col 21 (who was drawing attention to the Report of the Foreign Affairs Committee, Fourth Report, 2005–06, 'Foreign Policy Aspects of the War Against Terrorism', session 2005–06, HC 573 (2006)); Minister for the Armed Forces, HC Debs 19 April 2004, vol 420, col 14W.

22 The minister's response was that 'phraseology is carefully considered in the Government's communications around counterterrorism', HL Debs 19 February 2007, vol 689, col 167W.

23 The Bishop of Peterborough, HL Debs 16 May 2007, vol 692, col 183.

24 HL Debs 8 July 2008, vol 703, col 686. See also his article, 'Guantanamo Bay: The Legal Black Hole' (2004) 53 ICLQ 1.

25 Although see UN Security Council Resolution 1566 (2004) operative [3].

26 See generally, *R v Gul (Mohammed)* [2013] UKSC 64, [44]; B Saul, *Defining Terrorism in International Law* (OUP, 2006), 68.

> of the public . . . for the purpose of advancing a political, religious, racial or ideological cause . . . including action outside the UK.[27]

Within these terms, terrorism can take place even during an armed conflict occurring outside the UK, although acts creating terror in one form or another are also specifically prohibited under IHL.[28] On the other hand, the mere fact that acts of terrorism are taking place is not sufficient by itself to establish an armed conflict.[29]

What is, perhaps, new about Britain's wars since 2000 is that, although they have involved armed conflicts, a significant feature has been the perceived threat of terrorism being imported to the shores of the UK as a result of the instability of various governments, leading to this becoming the primary, or at least a significant, justification for Britain's involvement.[30] Thus, the Minister for the Armed Forces stated in 2012 that, 'we are in Afghanistan for one overriding reason: to protect our own national security by helping the Afghans to take control of their own'.[31] It must be assumed that this perceived threat to the security of the UK is based upon possible attacks in the UK itself by individuals rather than by any organised non-state group operating in, for example, Afghanistan. Not all will accept this argument. Indeed, one MP questioned the minister and asked him to explain 'precisely what the threat to our constituents is from the Taliban in Afghanistan'.[32] In an attempt to dispel the idea that involvement in Iraq or Afghanistan might actually increase the risk of terrorist attacks in the UK, through the radicalisation of some individuals, the Prime Minister addressed the issue in his speeches to the House of Commons on the votes to conduct an air campaign in Syria 2013 and over Iraq in 2014.[33]

27 Terrorism Act 2000, s 1 (as amended). Whether this definition could be narrowed is a matter referred to in *R v Gul (Mohammed)* [2013] UKSC 64, [62].

28 The definition of 'terrorism' in the 2000 Act is not excluded by the fact that it relates to the existence of a non-international armed conflict, *R v Gul (Mohammed)* [2013] UKSC 64, [49], although the acts of which the defendant were convicted occurred within the UK. See also the specific prohibitions on creating acts of terror in Additional Protocol I, Art 51(2) and Additional Protocol II, Art 4(2)(d), along with more general acts contained within IHL which could have the same effects as terrorism. The form in which the UK imposes sanctions, discussed in Chapter 2, does not distinguish between an armed conflict and acts of terrorism.

29 See the reservation made by the UK to Additional Protocol I, 1977, International Criminal Court Act 2001 (Reservations and Declarations) Order 2001/2559, art 1, Sched 1, (d).

30 Added to this has been the fact that a number of British nationals have gone from the UK to take part in armed conflicts, particularly in support of ISIL operating in the territories of Iraq and Syria. The principal concern has been the perceived risk of terrorist acts being committed within the UK on their return. For the decision to prosecute individuals in this situation see the former Attorney General, HC Debs 26 September 2014, vol 585, col 1318.

31 HC Debs 7 November 2012, vol 552, col 241WH, Minister for the Armed Forces.

32 HC Debs 7 November 2012, vol 552, col 242WH, Paul Flynn, MP. No direct answer to the question appears to have been given.

33 HC Debs 29 August 2013, vol 566, col 1439; HC Debs 26 September 2014, vol 585, col 1256. The issue does not appear to have been addressed directly in the Iraq vote on 18 March 2003.

Whilst the events involved in the Falklands war in 1982 could be seen as being quite separate from those arising from the terrorist issues in Northern Ireland at the same time this cannot be said to be the case, at least from the government point of view, in relation to the link between terrorism on the streets of the UK and the armed conflicts in Iraq, Afghanistan and Syria. From a practical point of view, the legal limits on trying to obtain information from suspected terrorists, or from civilians taking an active part in hostilities, is always likely to be more difficult to determine than trying to do the same from, say, prisoners of war during an international armed conflict. One major difference between the two groups is that the limitations set down by Geneva Convention III, 1949, in relation to the questioning of prisoners of war, is clear and reasonably well-understood, whereas for other detainees it is anything but. In this lacuna have crept practices of interrogation which, in the cold light of day, states involved in them are likely to have cause to regret.

These practices have ranged from long-term loss of liberty to the ill-treatment in a variety of different forms of detainees during interrogation, and to unlawful rendition. In so far as there is a connection between these events and the way in which the UK fought its wars they are discussed in later chapters.[34]

In a similar way, the targeting of individuals who are acting on behalf of ISIL and are taking part in the armed conflicts in Iraq and Syria, after 2014, display a distinct characterisation, depending on whether they were attacked from the air by UK armed forces in Iraq or in Syria. Where these events occurred in Iraq, the UK government considers its targeting rules to be those encompassed by IHL. Where they occurred in Syria in 2015, they were characterised as 'counter-terrorism', no doubt because, at the time, the House of Commons had not been given an opportunity to vote on the use of air strikes over Syria.[35]

iii Judicialisation of armed conflict

There can be little doubt that since 2000 the involvement of the courts in some of the issues raised by Britain's wars has increased to unprecedented levels, causing a former chief of the defence staff to use the colourful phrase that 'the Armed Forces are under legal siege'.[36] Others have adopted the terms, 'judicialisation

34 The treatment of detainees is discussed in Chapter 9, the detention of suspects in Iraq in Chapter 7 and the allegations of unlawful rendition in Chapter 5. Whether the government knew of US renditions through UK airspace is discussed in the House of Commons Foreign Affairs Select Committee, 4th Report, session 2005–06, *Foreign Policy Aspects of the War Against Terrorism*, session 2005–06, HC 573, [47]–[58].

35 See HC Debs 7 September 2015, vol 599, col 23. For discussion of the requirement to debate in the House of Commons British military involvement overseas and the attack, on 21 August 2015, carried out by a UK remotely piloted aircraft, against two individuals in Syria, and for the vote on air strikes in Syria on 2 December 2015, see Chapter 4.

36 Lord Boyce, HL Debs 14 July 2005, vol 684, col 1236.

of war'[37] or the juridification[38] of war or 'lawfare',[39] which, if stretched to their extremity, can conjure up an impression that judges in court rooms, rather than military commanders, make the decisions about how an armed conflict is to be fought.

It may be attractive to some to adopt the view that judges should not be involved in any decisions about the conduct of armed conflict since, it is argued, this should be for professional military officials and appropriate government ministers alone.[40] Others may take a less strident view but, nevertheless, see too much judicial involvement. There are certainly dangers to the ability of the armed forces to perform their tasks during an armed conflict in over-judicialisation and there is much to be said for the view that such a result must be avoided.[41]

There are, however, at least two good reasons why the courtroom should not be excluded when issues relating to the conduct of an armed conflict are concerned. First, it is now beyond reasonable argument that individual members of the armed forces who transgress IHL or their own national law may be answerable in a criminal court for their actions. Secondly, few would dispute that the British armed forces should, like all other public bodies within the UK, conduct their activities within the limits of the law, which in this case are IHL and UK law, including the Human Rights Act 1988.[42]

Although there may be disagreement over the range and extent of 'judicialisation', few are likely to argue now that members of the British armed forces should not be accountable for their actions in some way. Evidence that a war crime might have been committed by a British soldier does tend to emerge in unexpected ways, such as by the discovery of so-called 'trophy photographs', or from body cameras or mobile phones, and prosecutions may need to be brought. Popular support is unlikely to be forthcoming for a change in the current practice of repatriating the bodies of soldiers who have been killed in overseas armed conflicts, nor for a change in the law to treat them differently from anyone else

37 Both Lord Hope, in *Smith v Ministry of Defence* [2013] UKSC 41, [98], with whom the majority agreed and Lord Mance, who dissented on some issues, at [150] used this term but both stressed that the judicialisation of war should be avoided.

38 A Forster, 'British Judicial Engagement and the Juridification of the Armed Forces' (2012) 88 International Affairs 283. See also HC Defence Select Committee, *UK Armed Forces personnel and the Legal Framework*, 12th Report, session 2013–14, HC 931, [14], where the question raised was whether 'the law had been used or misused by adversaries'.

39 See C Waters, 'Beyond Lawfare: Judicial Oversight of Western Militaries' (2008–09) 46 Alberta Law Review 885, 890; C Waters, 'Is the Military Legally Encircled?' (2008) 8 Defence Studies 26, 28, who describes the term as one which involves the 'use of law to hamper a state's military power'. An MP referred to the 'real risk that legitimate warfare will be replaced with "lawfare"', HC Debs 17 December 2014, vol 589, col 1413.

40 See generally, T Tugendhat and L Croft, *The Fog of Law, An Introduction to the Legal Erosion of British Fighting Power* (Policy Exchange, 2013), discussed further in Chapter 10.

41 See Chapter 10.

42 For discussion of the attempt to limit the reach of the ECHR to the UK only see the discussion of the proposed Bill of Rights in Chapter 10.

by excluding the jurisdiction of the coroner.[43] In a democracy there will be calls for investigations of specific issues through public inquiries, or by parliamentary select committees, and there have been a number of these since 2000. The application of the law during the course of Britain's wars from 2000–2015 lies at the heart of this book and some attempt to assess whether a balance has been struck between too much, or too little, judicial involvement is made in Chapter 10.

iv Legal accountability

Two of the hallmarks of a parliamentary democracy, as in the UK, are the rule of law[44] and the idea of accountability of those acting in the public service. They are often spoken of in general terms but, when it comes to an armed conflict, they take on a very practical importance. The rule of law will include the UK's obligations under international law. Moreover, this law can change at any time and, as a consequence, the way in which a military operation is conducted may, itself, have to change to reflect the new legal position. Accountability, on the other hand, is a much more slippery term. Does it mean that politicians who voted for or against a proposed military involvement can be held accountable by the electorate when an election is called,[45] or that individuals can be expected to account for their actions before Parliament itself or one of its select committees or before a civilian court? It can, of course, mean all, or any of, these things but this book is concerned specifically with legal accountability. This is perhaps just as well since few will be likely to disagree with King and Crewe who argue that 'the almost total lack of ministerial accountability in the strong sense – of ministers being held to account for their actions and being penalised for their more egregious misjudgements and errors – is one of the most striking features of the British system of government'.[46]

In the context of an armed conflict, 'the notion that the lawful application of power imports accountability for its use',[47] can encompass judgment being passed by others on an individual's conduct, resulting in personal consequences under a system established by law. Where it takes this form it can properly be

43 The role of the coroner is discussed in Chapter 5.

44 See generally, Lord Bingham, 'The Rule of Law', the Sixth Sir David Williams Lecture, 16 November 2006 https://www.google.co.uk/url?sa=t&rct=j&q=&esrc=s&source=web&cd=3&ved=0ahUKEwiGn7bfiafJAhUDNxQKHdnxAhQQFggoMAI&url=http%3A%2F%2F www.cpl.law.cam.ac.uk%2Fsir-david-williams-lectures&usg=AFQjCNHbrN2J1Hhh6KHBy8f8zDfSqtYcNw&bvm=bv.108194040,d.ZWU.

45 For discussion of the accountability of MPs following a vote in the House of Commons to take, or not to take, military action, see Chapter 4.

46 A King and I Crewe, *The Blunders of our Governments* (Oneworld Publications, 2014), 352.

47 See T Gill and D Fleck (eds), *The Handbook of the International Law of Military Operations* (OUP, 2010), p 629; M Shaw, *International Law* (Cambridge University Press, 7th edn, 2014), 954–5. Although Shaw was discussing the accountability of international institutions the underlying reason for accountability is one which, at the personal level, few would dispute.

called 'legal accountability'. In its most understandable form, it involves the bringing of criminal or disciplinary charges against a member of the armed forces in respect of his or her actions or inactions during an armed conflict. It could also encompass a medical practitioner in the armed forces who is alleged to have failed in his medical responsibility and is disciplined by the General Medical Council,[48] or a commander whose actions are analysed by a service inquiry[49] or by a coroner.[50] It could even cover the acts of ministers and those acting under them, who will be 'accountable to the courts for the legality of their actions'.[51] An inquiry, established by the government but which is conducted under a system of law, may also involve criticism of named individuals but, although it will not be capable of imposing sanctions on them, it may still amount to a form of legal accountability.[52]

It is not an essential ingredient of legal liability that a person is at fault, although it usually is.[53] What is also important is that those who are involved in activities concerned with armed conflict (or in any other activity in the public service), understand their legal obligations. In referring to the request in March 2003 from the Chief of the Defence Staff, Admiral Boyce, for a statement of legality of the proposed action in Iraq, the Attorney General, at the time, concluded that there was a 'growing interest, belief, in legality, and the individual responsibilities of people who are actually involved'.[54]

Although members of the British armed forces will be accountable to the criminal or disciplinary systems established by English law, they will not normally be liable for a breach of the law of the state in which they are operating and, in

48 The role of medical officers is discussed in Chapter 8. The fitness to practise procedures are currently contained in the Medical Act 1983.

49 The provisions applicable to discipline in the armed forces and a service inquiry are provided by the Armed Forces Act 2006 and regulations made under that Act. See also the major and minor administrative procedures which may be taken against service personnel and their importance in Iraq, House of Commons Select Committee on the Armed Forces Bill, 2005–06, Report, HC 828 (25 April 2006), [44].

50 The role of the coroner is discussed in Chapter 5.

51 See also *Halsbury's Laws of England*, Vol 20 (Lexis, 5th edn, 2014), [229].

52 The law concerned is the Inquiries Act 2005. For examples see the report of the Baha Mousa Inquiry, Sir William Gage, HC 1452 (2011); Report of the Al Sweady Inquiry, Sir Thayne Forbes, HC 818 (2014). Both were conducted under s 26 of the 2005 Act. The Iraq Inquiry was established as a committee of privy councillors, as was the Review of Intelligence on Weapons of Mass Destruction, HC 898 (2004) Lord Butler, on which Sir John Chilcot was a member. The Report of the Inquiry into the Circumstances Surrounding the Death of Dr David Kelly, CMG, HC 247 (2004), was established by the Secretary of State for Constitutional Affairs.

53 The captain of a Royal Navy ship may be brought before the court martial as a result of his ship going aground even though the fault may lie elsewhere. See F Ledwidge, *Losing Small Wars* (Yale University Press, 2012), [109].

54 Lord Goldsmith, evidence to the Iraq Inquiry, 27 January 2010, 186. He attributed this to the personal liability of individuals as a result of the fact that the UK had become a party to the Rome Statute of the International Criminal Court. For further discussion of this episode, see Chapters 4 and 10.

this sense, they will be unaccountable for their actions.[55] The issue may be more theoretical than real if the sending state, the UK in this case, is methodical in conducting investigations where local civilians are killed or injured by members of the British armed forces. It may, however, be real where a state does not possess criminal jurisdiction over civilian contractors employed by it in that foreign territory.[56]

There may be a natural human tendency to clothe all, or many, military activities during an armed conflict in secrecy for reasons of perceived interests of national security, but to do so could lead to a 'lack of transparency [which, in turn] creates an accountability vacuum'.[57] It would be difficult to argue that there has been a serious lack of transparency in relation to British military operations since 2000. Members of Parliament have put down a large number of questions addressed to relevant ministers, various select committees have delved deeply into specific issues, public inquiries have been held, criminal proceedings brought, disclosure made by the Ministry of Defence (in particular) of information to claimants in civil actions, and in FOI releases, all of which illustrate a very high level of transparency from which some form of accountability can flow.[58]

Shrouding facts in secrecy or in confidential reports therefore can, either intentionally or unintentionally, lead to a lack of accountability. The nature of the access by the International Committee of the Red Cross (ICRC) to, and their reports concerning the detention of, civilians during the armed conflicts in Iraq and Afghanistan are discussed in Chapter 6. The principle followed by the ICRC over many years, that their reports are confidential to the governments concerned, whilst sound from the point of view of the ICRC, can have the unintentional effect of limiting the accountability of government ministers, whose responsibilities cover the detention of civilians abroad. Just such a report was compiled by the ICRC, concerning the conditions of detention in Iraq, and sent to the British government in February 2004. On a number of occasions MPs sought information from relevant ministers but were met with the response that the report was

55 It is normal practice in situations of armed conflict for sending and receiving states to enter into a status of forces agreement or a memorandum of understanding to ensure that the visiting forces will come within the exclusive jurisdiction of the sending state. For further discussion, see Chapter 8.

56 Civilian contractors employed by UK armed forces abroad will come within the jurisdiction of the Armed Forces Act 2006, see s 370 and Sched 15, and the trial in 2010 by the court-martial sitting in England of two British civilian contractors who had been working in Basra where the alleged offence had been committed, http://www.dailymail.co.uk/news/article-1319861/Two-civilians-jailed-court-martial-vicious-attack-Iraq.html.

57 N Pillay, UN High Commissioner for Human Rights speech at the UN Security Council, 19 August 2013, http://www.ohchr.org/EN/NewsEvents/Pages/DisplayNews.aspx?NewsID=13642&LangID=E. Ms Pillay was referring to drone strikes.

58 There may be some conflict between the need to call individual service witnesses before a public inquiry and a criminal prosecution of those who give evidence to the public inquiry. For undertakings against self-incrimination, given by the Attorney General, to potential witnesses that their evidence would not be relied upon in any criminal prosecution, see Chapter 5.

confidential.[59] Although ministers could seek the consent of the ICRC for, at least parts, of the report being released,[60] this is considered unlikely to be forthcoming for the reasons discussed in Chapter 6. The risk of unaccountability will increase if ministers use the report not as a sword to enable them to force through necessary changes, but as a shield against further questioning. It may take the authority of the Prime Minister to adopt a proactive approach, as seems to have been done in May 2004,[61] although by then excerpts of the ICRC report had been leaked, causing the ICRC to give a press conference on the matter.[62]

A further consequence of the confidentiality of ICRC reports on their visits to detainees during an armed conflict is the difficulty it may cause, for example the UK, in putting pressure on one of its allies when the report will be sent only to the state concerned. The UK will not have sight of it and can only learn of any mistreatment of detainees from other sources. Any pressure put by the UK on a coalition partner is likely to take place through informal channels.[63] The UK cannot, of course, be held accountable for the actions of a coalition partner but, certainly at a political level, ministers can be expected to answer difficult questions in Parliament or in the media about facts that have come to light in this way.

Some form of legal accountability, particularly of individuals, whilst uncomfortable for them, is likely to produce structural benefits to the activity concerned. Accountability has been recognised, for example, not only by the Secretary of State for Defence in relation to the obligation to conduct investigations required by the ECHR, Articles 2 and 3 but also by the Secretary-General of the UN, as a means of making 'national interests stronger and more legitimate'.[64]

Being held responsible may be little different from the idea of accountability but taking 'responsibility'[65] for one's actions is quite different, since it operates

59 The detail is discussed in Chapter 6.
60 HC Debs 13 May 2004, vol 421, col 514.
61 HC Debs 12 May 2004, vol 421, col 347.
62 The press conference was conducted by the Director of Operations at the ICRC, on 8 May 2004, see Chapter 6.
63 See, for example, HC Debs 4 May 2004, vol 420, col 1216. See also the discussions with the US authorities over the presence of British nationals in Guantanamo Bay, HC Debs 4 November 2004, vol 426, col 15WS. In a similar way the UK would not have had sight of any ICRC report on the detention by US authorities of Saddam Hussein, see HC Debs 8 February 2005, vol 430, col 1464W.
64 HL Debs 7 November 2013, vol 749, col 413; 'A Vital and Enduring Commitment: Implementing Responsibility to Protect', S/2015/500, 13 July 2015, [20].
65 See A King and I Crewe, *The Blunders of our Governments* (Oneworld Publications, 2013), 348. See also the statement by the Secretary of State for Defence that he took responsibility for the decision to permit some RN personnel, who had been captured in 2007 by the Iranian Revolutionary Guards, to sell their stories to the press, *The Iran Hostages Incident: the Lessons Learned*, House of Commons Select Committee on Defence, 4th Report, Session 2007–08, HC 181, [22]. The Select Committee saw the difference between taking responsibility and being held accountable. In *R (Al-Sweady and Others) v Secretary of State for Defence* [2009] EWHC 2387 (Admin) the court referred to a Royal Military Police (RMP) senior officer who 'must shoulder a considerable proportion of the responsibility for the lamentable disclosure failures by the RMP', [51].

at the discretion of the individual concerned and, by itself, does not entail legal consequences and nor does it necessarily entail an acceptance of blame or fault. So, Jack Straw MP, as the Foreign Secretary at the time of the decision to take military action in Iraq in 2003, has stated, 'I accept my responsibilities fully for what happened in Iraq.'[66] Others may take the view that, on any particular issue, blame lies elsewhere, the effect of which is that they do not accept any form of accountability or responsibility for their actions that have led to some form of failure.[67]

Were the law to provide in time of an armed conflict that those acting on behalf of the UK, whether as members of the armed forces or of the government, were not to be held accountable for their actions it would, in effect, permit power to be exercised without legal restraint. Some other form of controlling action may, of course, be available, such as by an individual's superiors (including in the case of a government minister, the Prime Minister), professional regulators or parliamentary investigations, which may have an equal deterrent effect to prevent rogue behaviour, but in a democratic society it would be expected that the rule of law would govern and control those acting on behalf of the UK. The law of armed conflict was designed specifically for this purpose and, in its modern form, has a history spanning about 150 years.[68] The horrors of being affected, in one way or another, by an armed conflict that is unregulated by law need only to be imagined to be decisively rejected. To those actually carrying out the military operations, the law may appear to be unnecessary and burdensome and there may be legitimate argument as to whether English law should, or should not, seep into certain military activities but, except in a very limited number of situations, legal unaccountability is likely to bring many more hazardous problems in its wake.[69]

Accountability before the law may arise at the individual level, as discussed above, concern by many others that they could also face the same consequences will, no doubt, act as a powerful deterrent to them to act within the law.[70]

It is a common refrain for government ministers, in particular, to state that an individual suspected of some egregious act abroad will be held 'to account'

66 HC Debs 29 August 2013, vol 566, col 1451.

67 In referring to the *Nimrod Review, An Independent Review into the Broader Issues Surrounding the Loss of the RAF Nimrod MR2 Aircraft XV230 in Afghanistan in 2006*, HC 1025, (2009), D Bowen, concluded that 'the report itself was occasioned by the absence of anyone in the MOD willing or able to stand up and accept responsibility', in J Bailey, R Iron, H Strachan (eds), *British Generals in Blair's Wars* (Ashgate, 2013), 278. For successful claims for damages by the families of some of the Nimrod crew, see http://www.brodies.com/node/1570.

68 The start period for this purpose is the first Geneva Convention, for the Amelioration of the Condition of the Wounded in the Armies in the Field, 22 August 1864.

69 See Chapter 10 for discussion as to whether the balance is about right or whether there has been too much 'judicialisation'.

70 This is one of the justifications given by the ECtHR in requiring investigations conducted under Arts 2 or 3 of the ECHR. See further, Chapter 7.

or be 'brought to justice'. Before anyone can be brought to justice,[71] it will be necessary to have evidence that he or she has committed a particular crime, that a court has jurisdiction over it and has the individual within its custody. A foreign national who commits a crime abroad is generally outside the jurisdictional range of a court in England, or indeed, the UK court martial sitting abroad.[72] If, as is likely, the egregious act consists of a crime within the jurisdiction of the ICC, there may be difficulty if that court itself has no jurisdiction over it because, for example, the state in which the crime has taken place is not a party to the Rome Statute 1998 of the ICC.[73] So, holding a person to account may not be as easy as it would appear.

The opposite is true where members of the British armed forces are concerned. They will be subject to service law abroad, in addition to English criminal law, and can be tried by the court martial or by a civilian court in England.[74] They will also be liable for any crimes under the ICC Statute that they commit and they could be tried by the ICC, although the complementarity provisions in that statute have the effect of passing jurisdiction to the English courts. Whilst some soldiers have been charged before a British court-martial none has been tried by the ICC.[75]

Where, however, accountability is focused at a higher level, whether it is the UK itself or a government department, it may be that others will judge the individuals, who actually made the impugned decisions, to have escaped personal attention and thus personal accountability. Placing accountability solely at the government department level would include the decision made by ministers to permit the detention of some Afghan nationals beyond the 96 hours agreed by NATO for ISAF. Leggatt J concluded that 'the consequence of those decisions is that the MOD has incurred liabilities to those who have been unlawfully detained'.[76] As far as the claimant is concerned he was able to hold the UK government accountable for, what was adjudged to be, his unlawful detention, but as for the government ministers concerned their accountability would have to come, if at all, through some parliamentary process.

The practice of parliamentary select committees investigating issues relating to Britain's wars since 2000 has included the calling of serving or former senior officers to give evidence before them. To some extent, this reflects the practice also with some serving civil servants being called to give evidence in order to 'give effect to the constitutional principle of proper parliamentary scrutiny of the

71 This phrase could also mean that 'justice' will be achieved through killing the individual concerned. This possible meaning is not considered further.
72 For further discussion, see Chapter 8.
73 For further discussion, see Chapter 6.
74 For further discussion, see Chapter 8.
75 For further discussion of the ICC, see Chapter 6.
76 *Serdar Mohammed v Ministry of Defence* [2014] EWHC 1369 (QB), [6(xi)], [333], upheld on this point on appeal, *Mohammed v Secretary of State for Defence* [2015] EWCA Civ 843, discussed in Chapter 9.

executive'.[77] It may seem logical to treat senior service officers in a way similar to senior civil servants for the purposes of holding the government accountable to Parliament but, there is, in addition, the important principle that the armed forces of any democratic state should be placed under civilian control, largely because of the actual physical power that they possess and could actually use.[78] The days are long gone when a government could hand the conduct of a war over to the military until its conclusion.

In the course of an armed conflict, there must be a careful balancing act between control exercised by the relevant minister and operational decisions made by senior service officers. In any event, the government will be accountable for their actions and it is, therefore, the responsibility of ministers to assure themselves of the soundness of actions proposed by the service chiefs and to be answerable fully to Parliament for the consequences.[79] It can never be sufficient for ministers to defer to senior military officers in an uncritical, unchallenging manner.[80] In as much as there is a balancing act as between ministers and the chiefs, so there is also a balancing act required of select committees as to whether to hear evidence primarily from the minister or from one or more of the service chiefs. In considering this balance, it may be argued that the accountability of the minister to Parliament is a more important constitutional principle than the accountability of a service chief or a former service chief at a personal level. In any armed conflict uncertainty as to who is actually accountable to Parliament for the conduct of a military campaign can only lead to a weakening of the value of the principle.

Where attention is drawn to the institutional, rather than to the personal, level for the purposes of accountability, another issue arises, namely, the effect on that accountability of legal advice provided by competent lawyers. It seems clear that if the legal advice is against a particular proposed action and it is ignored, the relevant office holder will bear a considerable degree of moral blame and should be personally accountable. Aside from scrutiny of his or her actions by Parliament,

77 House of Lords Constitution Committee, *The Accountability of Civil Servants*, 6th Report, session 2012–13, HL paper 61, 20 November 2012, [60].

78 See, for example, the ministerial answer given to a question concerning a particular training course in the UK for selected members of foreign armed forces, 'it represents the same foundations of rule of law, democratic control of Armed Forces . . . as underpin training to [*sic*] our own Armed Forces', HL Debs 4 June 2013, vol 745, col 163W.

79 Evidence to the Iraq Inquiry, 27 January 2010, Lord Goldsmith, QC (Attorney General) [5]–[6]; the pressure placed by the Minister for Procurement and Defence Equipment and Support on senior service officers to acquire additional helicopters, written evidence of Lord Drayson to the Iraq inquiry, 18 January 2011, [7]; enquiries made by the minister prior to sanctioning the British presence in Helmand Province, Afghanistan in 2006, Dr Reid, evidence to the Iraq Inquiry, 3 February 2010, [55]; the role of ministers in approving rules of engagement (see Chapter 8). Compare M Parris, *The Times*, 3 January 2015 who, when writing about British military campaigns in southern Iraq and in southern Afghanistan, argued that 'the Ministry of Defence is in charge here. Don't blame the politicians.'

80 This issue is discussed further in Chapters 3 and 10.

by a parliamentary committee, or by a public inquiry, it is not clear how this could be achieved in practice.[81] It is more likely, however, that the legal advice will be followed but is shown to be erroneous by a subsequent decision of a court. In these circumstances, the degree of blame is considerably less, or even at vanishing point, and accountability may be limited to the questions of who made the decision and why?[82]

The effect of the Human Rights Act 1998 and its applicability to military operations in Iraq and in Afghanistan has intensified the quest for accountability following the death of a British soldier, or where an Iraqi, or an Afghan national is killed in custody, or on the basis of an allegation of torture, inhuman or degrading treatment caused by British soldiers. This follows from the obligation on a state under Articles 2 and 3 of the ECHR to investigate such incidents and to hold those responsible to account.[83] With the increased reach of the Human Rights Act to military actions abroad since 2011 the obligation to conduct these independent investigations has increased substantially.[84]

An individual, or the state, is much more likely to have been held legally accountable for their acts or omissions during UK military actions from 2000–2015 under the English legal system and procedures, than under international law. In many instances a failure by British soldiers to comply with procedures, such as maintaining accurate records of capture or of detention, compiling of serious incident reports and the like, all of which will be enforceable through service discipline procedures, will be the essence of a possible breach of national or international law obligations.[85] It is for this reason that this book deals with both systems of law in an attempt to assess legal accountability as a whole. It is a striking conclusion to be drawn from the following pages that national law, in this

81 Criminal liability could arise if the consequence of ignoring the legal advice is that a crime under the International Criminal Court Act 2001 is committed by another and the office holder, whether a civilian or a member of the armed forces, bears command responsibility under s 65(3) of that Act.

82 See, for instance, court decisions as to whether the Human Rights Act 1998 applied to activities of the British armed forces in Iraq other than where an individual is held in British military custody, discussed in Chapter 7.

83 In *R (Long) v Secretary of State for Defence* [2014] EWHC 2391 (Admin) the Divisional Court was asked to decide that individual officers and not merely the chain of command should be held accountable as a result of an investigation under Art 2 of the ECHR. The court refused to do so on the basis that there was a distinction to be drawn between an 'unlawful killing by British soldiers and incompetence or a lack of care in ensuring compliance with an order', Leggatt J, [53], [107]. Although the acts of individual soldiers in using force may not be wrongful, the state itself may be liable for its own breach of an obligation under the ECHR, see *McCann v United Kingdom* (1996) 21 EHRR 97, where the UK was held liable for the acts of those members of its armed forces who had planned the particular operation.

84 For further discussion, see Chapter 7.

85 For a list of the various relevant procedural documents see Joint Committee on Human Rights, *UN Convention Against Torture (UNCAT)*, 19th Report, session 2005–06, HL 185, 26 May 2006, written evidence items 14 and 15.

case the law of England and Wales and the various procedures adopted to ensure compliance with it, provides the effective legal underpinning of accountability of the UK's military actions. National law is not, therefore, merely some incidental factor to take into account in the laws of war, which have often concentrated solely on their international law dimension.

Is one form of accountability better than another? In a claim concerning the 'extra-ordinary rendition of the claimants . . . [Simon J warned that] Parliamentary oversight and criminal investigations are not adequate substitutes for access to, and a decision by, the Court'.[86]

This prioritising of accountability before a civil court may not appeal to everyone since it does depend upon the chance of a claim being launched successfully (with the necessary funds to do so) and the actual involvement of the individual in the case may be in form rather than in substance. On the other hand, criminal investigations (and possibly a criminal trial), along with a parliamentary inquiry, do put the individual, whose actions are the substance of the investigation, right at the heart of the process, so that he or she can, at least, *feel*, and the public see, individual accountability.

For most of the time in which British armed forces have been engaged in Iraq and in Afghanistan they have been fighting various non-state armed groups during a non-international armed conflict. Could those groups be subjected to legal accountability in a way similar to, but distinct from, the UK itself? It is not unusual for a UN Security Council resolution to call upon all sides, including non-state actors, to comply with IHL and international human rights law[87] and to be held accountable.[88] Although there is little doubt that non-state actors, as members of organised armed groups, do have obligations under IHL[89] the position is quite different in respect of human rights obligations.[90] Where these non-state actors are co-operating with the UK, as did the Northern Alliance in Afghanistan in 2001, the UK government is able to urge them to respect the

86 *Abdul-Hakim Belhaj, Fatima Boudchar v Rt Hon Jack Straw (and six other Defendants)* [2013] EWHC 4111 (QB), Simon J, [151]. On appeal, [2014] EWCA Civ 1394, the Court of Appeal made no reference to this point.

87 See for example UN Security Council Resolutions 2175, 2143, 2139, all of 2014.

88 Draft Resolution, S/2012/538, 19 July 2012, [8] in relation to Syria, which the Security Council was unable to adopt. Compare UN Security Council Resolution 2249 (2015), [4].

89 As to who is a participant in a non-international armed conflict, see Chapter 6. A participant will be bound by Common Art 3 to the Geneva Conventions 1949. See also J-M Henckaerts and L Doswald-Beck, *Customary International Humanitarian Law: Volume 1: Rules* (OUP, ICRC, 2005), 497–8; L Zegweld, *The Accountability of Armed Opposition Groups in International Law* (Cambridge University Press, 2002). See also the work of Geneva Call in inviting armed non-state actors to undertake a Deed of Commitment for Adherence to a Total Ban on Anti-Personnel Mines and for co-operation in Mine Action, http://www.genevacall.org/what-we-do/landmine-ban/.

90 See L Zegweld, *The Accountability of Armed Opposition Groups in International Law* (Cambridge University Press, 2002), 38–49, 230. A Clapham, *Human Rights Obligations of Non-State* Actors (OUP, 2006), 58, 280–5.

obligations contained in international human rights law and keep in communication with the ICRC, who will have access to detainees.[91]

A state may be unaccountable for the actions of its armed forces, both at the national and the international level if its acts can properly be attributed to another state or to the UN.[92] This principle led the government to argue before the Supreme Court and the ECtHR that the detention by British armed forces of Mr Al-Jedda in Iraq, following UN Security Council Resolution 1546 (2004), should be attributable to the UN, and that the UK was not accountable under the ECHR for depriving Mr Al-Jedda of his liberty. Neither court accepted this argument[93] and both felt able to distinguish the most relevant authority on the issue, *Behrami v France and Seramati v France, Germany and Norway*,[94] as illustrating a role played by the UN in Kosovo quite different from that which it played in Iraq. The Netherlands also sought, without success, to rely on this principle when it claimed that its operations, in support of the UK in Iraq, should properly be attributed, for the purposes of the ECHR, to the UK as an occupying power.[95]

Any suggestion that the UK was attempting to argue, through this principle, that it should not be held accountable for the acts of its armed forces was met by the riposte of a government minister that 'the Government in no way dispute the need for the legal accountability of our Armed Forces'.[96] The minister drew attention to the investigations into the activities of various soldiers, including the death of Baha Mousa, to show that the 'Armed Forces will be held to the highest standards of conduct'.[97] In doing so, he did not draw a distinction between the clearly accepted individual accountability of the soldiers for their own conduct, and the accountability of the UK itself under the ECHR.

Legal accountability can, of course, have consequences, whether to those individual members of the armed forces whose conduct has been judged unfavourably to them, or to the state itself. The non-acceptance, by the ECtHR in individual cases, that the actions of the armed forces of the UK and the Netherlands should properly be attributable elsewhere has meant that the UK has been placed under an obligation to provide a remedy to the individual applicants and

91 Ministerial statements, HC Debs 11 June 2002, vol 386, col 1175W; HC Debs 5 March 2003, vol 400, col 1055 W. See also discussion in Chapter 7.

92 See the International Law Commission, *Draft Articles on the Responsibility of International Organizations* (2004), Art 5, as applied in *R (Al-Jedda) v Secretary of State for Defence* [2007] UKHL 58; *Al-Jedda v United Kingdom* (2011) 53 EHRR 23. It is now Art 7 of the 2011 version, http://legal.un.org/ilc/texts/instruments/english/draft%20articles/9_11_2011.pdf. See also Chapter 7.

93 *R (Al-Jedda) v Secretary of State for Defence* [2007] UKHL 58; *Al-Jedda v United Kingdom* (2011) 53 EHRR 23, [84].

94 (2007) 45 EHRR SE 10.

95 *Jaloud v The Netherlands*, Application No 47708/08, Judgment, 20 November 2014. See also Chapter 7.

96 HL Debs 7 November 2013, vol 749, col 416. See also HC Debs 7 November 2005, vol 439, col 21 (Minister for the Armed Forces).

97 HL Debs 7 November 2013, vol 749, col 416.

compensation to others who had also been detained by UK armed forces in Iraq or Afghanistan.[98]

v Importance of the law as a factor in the willingness to fight

The fact that the Chief of the Defence Staff, Lord Boyce, sought confirmation from the Attorney General in April 2003 that the proposed military action in Iraq would be lawful was not merely for his own comfort, but to enable him to assure members of the armed forces, who were to take part in the campaign, that they would be acting in accordance with the law.[99]

For the overwhelming majority of members of the British armed forces, who have served in Iraq or Afghanistan or in any other of the other armed conflicts since 2000, the legal basis for their actions must have been considered to have been satisfactory, even though they may not have articulated it in this way. The legality of a particular military engagement is not therefore merely a matter for politicians and the most senior military officers. It has been brought much more into the limelight by the parliamentary convention that before military action is taken, the House of Commons is presented with a Government motion (and possibly one from the opposition) on which to vote.[100] Prior to the vote, it has become the practice for the Attorney General, or the government, to set out a summary of the legality of the proposed action for MPs to read before being called upon to vote. Certainly, one of the reasons for the motion proposed by the government in September 2014 to join in the coalition by contributing RAF aircraft and their crews to attack ISIL in Iraq and not in Syria was the difference in the legal basis of each of these proposed actions.

vi The role of law in a practical world

The 15 years that have elapsed since the year 2000 present an opportunity to test the actual operation of the law during a wide range of armed conflicts in which UK armed forces have participated. Has its effect been wholly beneficial or has it, to one extent or another, been a millstone around the necks of the armed forces preventing them from completing their various missions?

It is too late to argue that law, whether of an international or a national kind, has no place in armed conflict. Every state in the world is now a party to the four Geneva Conventions of 1949, and a very large number are parties to a wide range of other treaties applicable during an armed conflict, whether they prohibit certain weapons, such as chemical, biological or anti-personnel land mines, or

98 'Compensation has had to be paid to a large number of people who were detained solely because there was a good reason to think that they posed a threat to security in Iraq and to the safety of members of our Armed Forces', *ibid.*

99 See Iraq Inquiry, evidence of Admiral Lord Boyce, 3 December 2009, 88.

100 For further discussion, see Chapter 4.

protect civilians from the effects of hostilities.[101] Knowledge that in an armed conflict war crimes can be committed and individuals can be tried in a court of law in respect of them, is fairly extensive. All these international law provisions were in place before any shot was fired against Iraqi armed forces in March 2003 and the UK is a party to all the relevant treaties. Similarly, that English criminal law travels with the British armed forces abroad is a long-standing principle.

That all this law is in place reflects the fact that states desire that this should be so. The old maxim, ascribed to Cicero, that 'silent enim leges inter armes' ('when arms speak, the laws are silent')[102] is as outdated as the cavalry charge. Instead, many would agree with Judge Barak who commented that, 'it is when the cannons roar that we especially need the laws . . . there is always law which the state must comply with . . . there are no black holes'.[103]

It is not therefore a startling proposition that the UK armed forces should operate according to the law applicable to their actions. Neither is it startling to recognise that this law can alter over time, either through the reception of a new legal principle, or by the interpretation of an existing norm during the course of an armed conflict. There seems little point in complaining about this if the government and the armed forces themselves believe, as they say they do, that they should always act in accordance with the law. Indeed, one former military officer with experience in Iraq has written that, 'for good or ill, the law is as much part of the environment in which soldiers work as the hot weather. It was ever so, but this has never stopped any serviceman griping about it.'[104] An assessment of the role of the law on military effectiveness is provided in Chapter 10.

vii Some comments on terminology

First, a word on the title of the book, which refers to 'Britain's wars'. Strictly, it should have been 'the armed conflicts to which the UK has become a party' since the term 'war', whilst in wide circulation to describe what this book is about, it now has little legal life in it, apart from its use as a collective noun for certain crimes, defined as war crimes and as a legal term used in a few Acts of Parliament.[105] Although the armed forces of the UK may be colloquially styled as Britain's armed forces, the term UK is used throughout the book to reflect the fact that the armed forces are those of the UK of Great Britain and Northern Ireland.

International law dealing with the conduct of warfare is known by a variety of names. The most descriptive is 'the laws of war' followed by the 'laws of armed

101 Customary international law is an important source of law, both at the international level but it can apply also in English law. For further discussion, see Chapter 6.

102 L Epstein, D Ho, G King, J Segal, 'The Supreme Court During Crisis: How War Affects Only Non-War Cases' (2005) 80 New York University Law Review 1, (3, footnote 6).

103 *Public Committee Against Torture in Israel v The Government of Israel* (2005) HCJ 769/02, [61], 'amid the clash of arms the laws are not silent', *Liversidge v Anderson* [1942] AC 206, [244], Lord Atkin (who dissented).

104 F Ledwidge, *Losing Small Wars* (Yale University Press, 2012), 176.

105 See, for example, Trading with the Enemy Act 1939, s 2; International Criminal Court Act 2001, s 50(1).

conflict' (LOAC) but it is also known as 'international humanitarian law' (IHL). There is no difference in substance among these various titles, and different groups tend to prefer one over the other. The British armed forces, along with a number of other states' armed forces, seem to prefer LOAC; the USA prefers 'law of war' or 'the laws and customs of war',[106] whilst UN bodies and the ICRC use the term IHL, which is also used in this book.

'Armed conflict' and whether it is of an international or a non-international character is defined elsewhere.[107] The term, 'the battlefield' is not defined in any of the treaties relating to IHL, but it is one that has come into usage, particularly by the USA, in the wars discussed in this book. When employed by US government officials, or members of its armed forces, it appears to cover the whole area in which an armed conflict is taking place and not merely where fighting is actually taking place. Its imprecision is heightened when used alongside another vague phrase, the 'war on terror', and in which both terms are linked. So, the 'battlefield', can extend to the whole of the area covered by 'the war on terror', which, in theory, could mean any part of the world. The UK tends not to use the term, 'war on terror'[108] and if it refers to the 'battlefield' it does so to mean the area in which actual fighting is taking place, but it will recognise that an armed conflict could be in existence, even though no actual fighting is taking place in a particular area.[109]

The term 'combatant' calls for short discussion here.[110] It has been given a precise meaning by Additional Protocol I (1977) so that 'members of the armed forces of a Party to a conflict (other than medical personnel and chaplains) . . . are combatants, that is to say, they have a right to participate directly in hostilities.'[111] This linking of membership of the armed forces and the right to participate in hostilities applies only to international armed conflicts. In a non-international armed conflict, such as in Iraq after the end of the occupation in 2004 and in Afghanistan following the Bonn Agreement of December 2001, there can be no question of those fighting the government of each of these states having a 'right to participate in hostilities'.[112] They cannot be 'combatants', let alone 'unlawful combatants' since the term 'combatant' goes beyond merely describing what a

106 J Bellinger III and W Haynes II, 'A US Government Response to the International Committee of the Red Cross Study *Customary International Humanitarian Law*' (2007) 89 IRRC 443.

107 Chapter 6.

108 See above, p 5.

109 See *Prosecutor v Tadic, Decision on the Defence Motion for Interlocutory Appeal on Jurisdiction*, IT-94–1, 2 October 1995, [68]–[70]. Compare the use of the term in *Mohammed v Secretary of State for Defence* [2015] EWCA Civ 843, [8], when it was concerned with the custody of Mr Mohammed in a UK detention facility.

110 It is discussed in more detail in Chapter 6.

111 Article 43(2).

112 See generally, A Clapham, P Gaeta, M Sassoli (eds), *The 1949 Geneva Conventions: a Commentary* (OUP, 2015), 933. The possibility of entering into special agreements, as envisaged by Common Art 3 was, in the circumstances of Iraq and Afghanistan, remote. There may be an issue of whether well-organised rebel groups could be styled as 'armed forces', as to which see above and Chapter 2.

person is actually doing. They are not 'soldiers', which is understood generally to mean a member of the armed forces of a state (notwithstanding the phrase, 'child soldiers'). A term that has come into common currency is that of an 'insurgent', which is used throughout this book, even though in modern conditions it has not been defined legally, either under international law or English law. Other terms which are used by some include, terrorists, rebels, anti-government elements (AGEs), illegally armed groups, but all are avoided in this book for the sake of clarity.

The definition of 'enemy' for the purposes of the Armed Forces Act 2006 includes 'all persons engaged in armed operations against any of Her Majesty's forces . . . armed rebels and armed rioters'.[113] It has, however, become common in non-international armed conflicts, such as those that occurred in Iraq and in Afghanistan, to refer to the enemy as 'al-Qaeda' or 'the Taliban'.

The phrase, 'counter-insurgency' has been used extensively during the phases of non-international armed conflicts, particularly in Afghanistan, to describe what British armed forces, operating as part of ISAF in Afghanistan, intended to achieve.[114] The term itself has no boundaries set purely by legal principles[115] and it appears to have been used interchangeably with 'stabilisation operations' or 'low-intensity operations' or even 'law-enforcement operations', and to reflect a form of military operations different from engagement in an international armed conflict or 'war-fighting';[116] a display of 'soft effects' compared with the use of 'hard military power'.[117] Although its aim is to defeat, or at least to minimise, the impact of the insurgent forces it could

113 Section 374. Compare the definition in Trading with the Enemy Act 1939, s 2.

114 The policy is set out in House of Commons Defence Select Committee, *Operations in Afghanistan*, 4th Report, session 2010–12, HC 554-I, 17 July 2011, [68]–[70]. It involves a clear aim of handing responsibility back to the territorial state, see HC Debs 7 November 2012, vol 552, col 242WH (Minister for the Armed Forces), 'as transition progresses, the campaign shifts from an ISAF-led counter-insurgency mission to an Afghan one', *ibid*.

115 The discussion above shows, for instance, that there is no legal definition of 'insurgent' or of an 'insurgency'. Compare the definitions of 'insurgency' given in F Kitson, *Low Intensity Operations: Subversion, Insurgency, Peace-keeping* (Faber and Faber, 1971), 3; A Alderson, 'Too Busy to Learn: Personal Observations on British Campaigns in Iraq and Afghanistan', in J Bailey, R Iron, H Strachan (eds), *British General's in Blair's Wars* (Ashgate Publishing Ltd, 2013), 283, who directed the 'Army's Counterinsurgency Centre (2009–2012)', *ibid*, xi.

116 The contrast between 'insurgency' and 'warfighting' was brought out by A Alderson, 'Too Busy to Learn: Personal Observations on British Campaigns in Iraq and Afghanistan', in J Bailey, R Iron, H Strachan (eds), *British General's in Blair's Wars* (Ashgate Publishing Ltd, 2013), 283. 'Counter-insurgency' is also spoken of as winning the 'hearts and minds' of the civilian population through the defeat of a common enemy. David Kilcullen 'strongly discourage[s] the use of the expression', 'Interview with David Kilcullen' (2011) 93 IRRC 587, 593. At times in Iraq the use of the term 'insurgency' was discouraged, see evidence of General Sir John Kiszely, Iraq Inquiry, 14 December 2009, 9, 40.

117 T Farrell and S Gordon, 'COIN Machine: The British Military in Afghanistan' (2009) 154 RUSI Journal 18, 21.

involve a concentration on avoiding casualties amongst the ordinary civilian population,[118] rather than attacking the enemy with the firepower available to it. Whilst the principle of proportionality[119] applies to all forms of armed conflict, in so-called counter-insurgency operations its significance is heightened, which, in turn, will determine the methods employed by the armed forces to achieve this aim, principally through the adoption of specific rules of engagement.[120] It may mean also that the armed forces will wish co-operate with armed police forces,[121] as in Afghanistan, which they would not do during the course of an international armed conflict, or involve themselves also in training the local armed forces. They will need to co-operate with government ministers and officials of the territory concerned and, possibly, with civilian departments of their own government as part of an overall strategy for the state in which they are operating.

An exaggerated sense of the importance of the whole concept of counter-insurgency seems to have crept into thinking about the campaign in Afghanistan, driven largely by the so-called McChrystal strategy[122] and the fact that UK armed forces were acting with British and Afghan civilian agencies to achieve a variety of objectives.[123] If the term merely means that the armed forces are engaged in something less militarily intensive than an armed conflict, there might be some descriptive value to it. Even then, it was not in wide circulation during the long campaign in Northern Ireland, which as the British armed forces have claimed, provided important experience for their military operations in Iraq

118 In referring to Afghanistan the Secretary of State for Defence commented that it was an 'essential part of counter-insurgency operations . . . that we are seen to protect the population concerned', HC Debs 8 September 2011, vol 532, col 577.

119 The same principles apply during a non-international armed conflict, Additional Protocol II, 1977, Art 13 and under customary international law, *Prosecutor v Kupreskic*, IT-95–16-T, 14 January 2000, [524] (dealing with precautions in attack); J-M Henckaerts and L Doswald-Beck, *Customary International Humanitarian Law: Volume 1: Rules* (Cambridge University Press, and ICRC, 2005), Rules 11–24, [3]–[78]. See also 'targeting' in Chapter 9.

120 The rules of engagement are discussed in Chapter 8.

121 The relationship between the police and the military in 'counter-insurgency' is not clear. Compare 'Interview with David Kilcullen' (2011) 93 IRRC 587, 592 with K Watkin, 'Use of Force during Occupation: Law Enforcement and Conduct of Hostilities' (2012) 94 IRRC 267, 294, who comments that, 'to be consistent with traditional counter-insurgency doctrine, operational planning should rely on the police primacy principle.' It is difficult to accept that this principle applied *de facto* in Afghanistan.

122 For discussion of it see Defence Select Committee, 4th Report, session 2010–12, *Operations in Afghanistan*, HC 554 (2011), [68].

123 For the Stabilisation Unit see HC Debs 31 March 2008, vol 474, col 552W; HC Debs 17 December 2007, vol 469, col 1020W. For the effectiveness, or otherwise, of the strategy in relation to Afghanistan, see Select Committee on Defence, 11th Report, session 2014–15, *Decision-Making in Defence Policy*, HC 682, oral evidence of Sir Sherard Cowper-Coles, Q 8; Mr D Bowen, Q 57; Dr K Howells, Q 76, and for the difficulties of applying it on the ground, Brigadier E Butler, Q 26.

and Afghanistan.[124] The similarity between British military operations in Maysan Province in Iraq in 2003 were, in fact, considerably different from those applying in Northern Ireland, and any declared similarity for the soldiers on the ground was more apparent than real.[125] The very uncertainty of the term, even if confined to something less than fighting during an armed conflict, sets its own problems at the interface between the legal limitations on the use of force and different classifications of disorder in which armed forces are deployed. Does it apply, for instance only to what has been seen as a non-international armed conflict, or to something less intense than this, such as riots or in anti-terrorist activities?[126]

This is no mere search for some form of legal certainty, favoured by lawyers, but an attempt to illustrate the point that the use of armed forces (in this case the British armed forces) will be accountable not for how well they have complied with their own counter-insurgency doctrines but whether they have complied with the law applicable to them.[127] There is, therefore, a real danger created by the use of the term, which is that it might convey to those taking part in it that the normal laws applicable during a non-international armed conflict do not apply[128] or that it contains within it its own limitations on, or authorisation for, the use of force.[129] For these reasons the term, 'counter-insurgency' is not used in this book.[130]

Neither is the term, 'civil war' used in this book since it also does not possess a legal meaning that could be relevant to issues of accountability. The underlying nature of a civil war is encompassed by the classification of an armed conflict as being of a non-international character. Attempts to define it through, for

124 Evidence of General Sir John Kiszely, 14 December 2009, to the Iraq Inquiry, 'we said we were involved in military aid to the civil power rather than counter-insurgency'. Compare the use of the term counter-insurgency in General Sir David Richards, *Taking Command* (Headline Publishing Group, 2014) 85. For the relevance of the experience gained in Northern Ireland see A Alderson, 'Too Busy to Learn: Personal Observations on British Campaigns in Iraq and Afghanistan', in J Bailey, R Iron, H Strachan (eds), *British General's in Blair's Wars* (Ashgate Publishing Ltd, 2013), 81. Compare F Ledwidge, *Losing Small Wars: British Military Failure in Iraq and Afghanistan* (Yale University Press, 2012), 31, 150.

125 See *The Iraq Fatality Investigations: Inspector Sir George Newman, Consolidated Report into the Death of Nadheem Abdullah and the Death of Hassan Abbas Said*, Cm 9023, March 2015, [17.34]; Aitken Report (Ministry of Defence, 2008), [26].

126 NATO saw a distinction in Afghanistan between 'counter-insurgency' and counter-terrorist activities largely because of the separate roles played by the involvement of US armed forces in ISAF and in Operation Enduring Freedom respectively.

127 There is, for instance, no reference to it in *The Manual of the Law of Armed Conflict*, UK Ministry of Defence (OUP, 2004).

128 See D Kilcullen, 'Interview with David Kilcullen' (2011) 93 IRRC 587, 599.

129 It is frequently used in a pejorative sense, such as to describe 'unexplained killings or disappearances', see *Avsar v Turkey* (2003) 37 EHRR 53, [11]; the evidence in *Mutua v Foreign and Commonwealth Office* [2011] EWHC 1913.

130 See, however, discussion in the argument presented in Chapter 10 that it should not be used at all.

example, the number of casualties caused can only contribute to uncertainty as to which body of law applies at any particular time to military operations.[131]

There has been a lack of uniformity over the appropriate term to use to describe the so-called 'Islamic state' operating in parts of Iraq and Syria since 2014. Various acronyms have been used, such as ISIL, ISIS or Daesh (Da'esh). This book uses ISIL predominantly, but does refer to Daesh, where this term is used in parliamentary source material. This was the preferred practice of the British government[132] but, in December 2015, the term, Daesh, appears more frequently to reflect its wider use worldwide.

For convenience only the term 'soldier' is used to encompass members of the British armed forces, although ground force contingents, such as the Royal Marines and air units, the Royal Air Force Regiment, may have their service home in the Royal Navy (RN) or the Royal Air Force (RAF). For the same reason, the male gender is used to reflect both servicemen and women.

131 See also the view of the British government, HC Debs 4 December 2006, vol 454, col 70W.
132 HC Debs 13 July 2015, vol 598, col 580; HC Debs 17 November 2015, vol 602, col 547.

2 The United Nations and NATO

It was not surprising that the victorious allies in 1945 should attempt to create a worldwide structure to try to prevent a repetition of World War II. The previous model, the League of Nations, could be seen by all to have failed in its major purpose of maintaining peace among nations, although the inter-war period did produce some treaties of significance. The Kellogg–Briand Pact of 1928 attempted to prohibit recourse to war as an instrument of national policy and, by the Geneva Gas Protocol of 1925, states party to it agreed not to use poisonous or asphyxiating gases, solids or materials in war, an early example of a weapon of mass destruction.[1] It was believed by many that things would be different under what became the United Nations Charter of 1945, which born out of World War II, came to reflect the world at that time with its horror of another war, particularly after the use of atomic bombs on Hiroshima and Nagasaki, and the pressure to give a much stronger role to human rights in world affairs. Looking back over the years the Charter has led to much improvement, in a variety of different ways, in the conditions of life of most people; but it is to its role in trying to prevent war to which we must look.

i Prohibition on the use of force

The prohibition on the use of force by states is to be found in Article 2(4) of the Charter, which outlaws the 'threat or use of force against the territorial integrity or political independence of any State'.[2] This may sound very much like lawyers'

1 Including the use of bacteriological methods of warfare. See also Review on Intelligence on Weapons of Mass Destruction, Lord Butler, HC 898 (2004), [156], [172], [183], dealing with the alleged capability of Iraq to deploy nuclear, biological and chemical weapons. https://www.gov.uk/government/uploads/system/uploads/attachment_data/file/61171/wmdreview.pdf.

2 The article goes on to include 'or in any other manner inconsistent with the Purpose of the United Nations.' The Purposes of the UN are to be found in Art 1 and they include 'promoting and encouraging respect for human rights'. A real significance to the term, 'purposes of the United Nations' can be seen in the fact that 'acts contrary to the purposes and principles of the United Nations' may lead to a claimant being denied refugee status under the Geneva

language and, in a sense, it has to be, because states had shown themselves perfectly willing to take advantage of any uncertainty in international law to claim that a use of armed force was not 'war' or not otherwise prohibited.[3] Since the territorial integrity of a state includes its territorial sea and its airspace the use of these environments by warships or military aircraft for hostile purposes will have the same effect. It also explains why warships may be subject to compliance with regulations of the territorial state within its territorial sea,[4] and all aircraft (including military aircraft) require permission to enter its airspace.[5] It also explains why one state must grant permission for the armed forces of another to be stationed on its territory, if a breach of Article 2(4) is to be avoided. This need for consent to be granted by the territorial state has been significant in Britain's wars since 2000, particularly where its military aircraft have had to overfly the territory or territorial sea of, or be based temporarily in, another state to carry out their military functions in Iraq, Afghanistan, Libya or Syria.[6] Similarly, the basing of British troops in Iraq and in Afghanistan has required the consent of their respective governments, once they had come into existence. Such an arrangement is often described as a memorandum of agreement or a status of forces agreement. Where troops are to be based temporarily in another state (whether for training purposes or for the conduct of military operations) these agreements will provide for practical matters, such as entry into the country, customs arrangements, the use of military vehicles, carrying of weapons and who is to enforce criminal penalties against members of the visiting force. The question of which state will have jurisdiction to enforce its criminal law against individual British soldiers serving in Iraq or Afghanistan is one of great importance and is discussed further in Chapter 8.

It is not difficult to see some notable examples of the use of force since 1945, in which Britain has been involved, and where it has claimed legal justification for its actions, from Korea (1950), Suez (1956), the Falkland Islands (1982), the Gulf (1991), Kosovo (1999), Afghanistan (2001), Iraq (2003), Libya (2011) and attacks against ISIL in Iraq (2014) and Syria (2015). Another legally acceptable basis for engaging in the use of force is at the invitation of the territorial state, as was the case in many of Britain's wars since 2000.[7] The provision of

Convention on the Status of Refugees 1951, Art 1(F), which has been implemented into English law by the Refugee or a Person in Need of International Protection (Qualification) Regulations 2006/2525, reg 7, discussed in Chapter 5.

3 For discussion of the meaning of the term 'war', see Chapter 1.

4 Convention on the Law of the Sea, 1982, Art 30.

5 An example would be the overflight of Turkey by Russian military aircraft *en route* to Syria, *The Times*, 6 October 2015.

6 Under customary international law each state has exclusive sovereignty over its airspace, *Case Concerning Military and Paramilitary Activities in and Against Nicaragua (Nicaragua v United States of America) (Merits)*, 1986, ICJ Reports p 14, [212].

7 *Case Concerning Military and Paramilitary Activities in and Against Nicaragua (Nicaragua v United States of America)* 1986 ICJ Reports 14, [246]. See generally, C Gray, *International Law and the Use of Force* (OUP, 3rd edn, 2008), 105; M Jamnejad and M Wood, 'The Principle of Non-Intervention' (2009) 22 LJIL 365.

equipment, other than weapons, by the UK to the Free Syrian Army is unlikely, by itself, to amount to a breach of Article 2(4).[8]

In a sense these are easy examples of an intervention. What of a state that allegedly removes all insignia from its armed forces and vehicles, which are then ordered to cross into the territory of an independent state to support rebels against its government?[9] Questions of proof will naturally arise and any state would have to satisfy itself of the actual responsibility of the alleged wrongdoing before taking any military action in response.[10]

The UN Charter 1945 gives the primary responsibility for maintaining international peace and security to the Security Council.[11] The five permanent members, USA, UK, France, Russia and China, which formed the group of victorious allies at the end of World War II and whose number has not been increased since despite serious discussion about so doing,[12] have the power to veto a resolution

8 *Case Concerning Military and Paramilitary Activities in and Against Nicaragua (Nicaragua v United States of America)* 1986 ICJ Reports 14, [247], where the Court stated that the 'supply of arms and other support to such bands cannot be equated with an armed attack [but] may well constitute a breach of the principle of the non-use of force and an intervention in the internal affairs of a State [which is] certainly wrongful, but is of lesser gravity than an armed attack.' It would appear to be the position of the UK government that the supply of commercially available equipment, such as protective clothing, vehicles and medical supplies, does not amount to an intervention in the internal affairs of Syria. See HC Debs 1 May 2014, vol 579, col 63WS, Foreign Secretary. In 2012 the Foreign Secretary stated that 'we are not contemplating arming anybody. We have not been in contact with the Free Syrian Army, which is engaged in a difficult struggle with the Syrian authorities. I would not classify this as an intervention, therefore', HC Debs 6 February 2012, vol 539, col 31. in July 2015, the Secretary of State for Defence indicated that 'the UK is . . . participating in a programme with US and regional partners to train the New Syrian Forces . . . outside Syria', HC Debs 16 July 2015, vol 598, col 32WS. For the position in November 2014 and the possible supply of weapons see discussion below. See also UN General Assembly Resolution 2131 (XX), 21 December 1965.

9 See the statement of the Foreign Secretary, HC Debs 13 May 2014, vol 580, col 584. Compare where a state has an 'embedding' policy. Chapter 4 discusses the embedding of a small number of members of the UK armed forces into coalition armed forces taking part in airstrikes over Syria in 2015.

10 In much the same way as where it believes that it needs to act by way of anticipatory self-defence. The difficulty is compounded by the fact that reliable information as to what is happening on the ground is difficult to acquire in these circumstances, and is not infrequently shown at a later stage to have been inaccurate. Examples include the statement made by Germany on 4 August 1914 that France was about to attack it through an invasion of Belgium and the claims in 2003 of weapons of mass destruction held by Iraq. As to the position regarding Iraq see *Review on Intelligence on Weapons of Mass Destruction*, Lord Butler, HC 898 (2004); *Review of Intelligence on Weapons of Mass Destruction: Implementation of its Conclusions*, Cm 6492 (2005).

11 Article 24.

12 See 'A More Secure World: Our Shared Responsibility, Report of the High-Level Panel on Threats, Challenges and Change' (2004) A/59/565, [250]–[258]. See generally, M Odello, 'Commentary on the United Nations High-Level Panel on Threats, Challenges and Change' (2005) 10 Jo C & SL 231, 242–3. The UK has indicated that it would 'support reform of the UN Security Council, including an expansion of the number of permanent members . . . [but any reform] should not increase the number of states with the right to veto', HC Debs

of the Security Council, which the non-permanent members, of which there are ten elected by the General Assembly for a period of two years, do not possess. The threat of a veto has caused Britain and the USA, in particular, significant problems when attempting to pursue a foreign policy with similar aims. The perceived intention of France to veto a further resolution of the Security Council authorising the invasion of Iraq in 2003[13] was sufficient to cause the British Prime Minister some difficulty in justifying the military action that began in March of that year. The decision of Russia and China in 2012 to veto a draft resolution[14] to compel a ceasefire by all parties in Syria, with the threat of sanctions for non-compliance, has resulted, many would argue, in severe loss of life in that country.[15] On the other hand, the Security Council was able to adopt resolutions concerning Afghanistan (2001) and Libya (2011). It has, of course, adopted a large number of resolutions in respect of Iraq, but none that had specifically authorised the use of force by the USA and UK by 20 March 2003.

Before the Security Council can consider a resolution it needs to determine whether there is a 'threat to, or a breach of, the peace' under Chapter VII of the UN Charter. It is not surprising that the Security Council is sometimes unable to act, even when most of its members see a blatant breach of the prohibition on using, or threatening, armed force. It is, after all, a political body and not a court of law. The language of the resolutions also displays their political nature. The preamble of a resolution is often quite lengthy but its operative paragraphs may authorise 'all necessary measures' to be taken to enforce the decision of the Council. This phrase 'all necessary measures' cannot be taken literally since IHL imposes limits on what the armed forces of a state could do physically.[16] It must also be considered in its context within the resolution. The phrase could not justify, for instance, the bombing of the civilian population indiscriminately to make their government surrender more quickly.

8 June 2010, vol 511, col 103W. In 2014 France confirmed, at the UN Security Council, its proposal 'to limit the use of the veto in the case of mass atrocities', S/PV.7180, p 4/18, 25 May 2014. This concerned a draft resolution (S/2014/348) to refer the situation in Syria to the Prosecutor of the ICC. The UK voted in favour of the resolution, but it was vetoed by China and Russia.

13 Discussed in Chapter 4.

14 S/2012/538, 19 July 2012. See also the veto by China and Russia of draft resolution S/2014/348, 22 May 2014, to refer the situation in Syria to the Prosecutor of the ICC, S/PV.7180, 22 May 2014, p 4/8.

15 See the comments of the UK representative to the UN Security Council at S/PV.680, 19 July 2012, who commented that 'this is the third time Russia and China have blocked the efforts of the Council to address the crisis in Syria . . . it is deeply regrettable that the Council has been unable today to play the role for which it was established and is duty bound to fulfil.' The Russian representative explained that he could not accept the draft resolution since 'it would open the way for the pressure of sanctions and later for external involvement in Syrian domestic affairs'.

16 R McLaughlin, 'The Legal Regime Applicable to Use of Lethal Force When Operating under a United Nations Security Council Chapter VII Mandate Authorising "All Necessary Means"' (2007) 12 Jo C & SL 389.

It is not difficult to see why (British) Prime Ministers like to have a Security Council resolution behind them when they go to war. This will dispel any argument in Parliament or elsewhere that the action is unlawful. In this light, no question of lawfulness or otherwise arose in relation to enforcing a no-fly zone in Libya in 2011, but it certainly did when Britain took part in the invasion of Iraq in 2003, when there was no such resolution. The possession of a suitable resolution is also a key factor in gaining the support of public opinion for a potential armed conflict. Again, the experiences of 2003 and 2011 can be quite clearly contrasted, so much so that many years after the Iraq invasion the lawfulness of that action is still prominent in public debate.[17]

A Security Council resolution may provide the answers to some difficult legal issues that are likely to arise during the conduct of an armed conflict, but not to all. We have seen that it can authorise the use of armed force against another state but it can also, for example, remind states of their international obligations under IHL and human rights law, call upon other states to take various actions, make declarations of fact and authorise some form of military force on the territory. A number of issues, in particular, have arisen in the last few years, which have caused some confusion over the legal effect of certain resolutions. In Resolution 1546 (2004), a power to intern civilians in Iraq without trial was included, which raised the issue of whether the UK could do so in the face of the limitations on the deprivation of liberty contained in the ECHR. The argument in favour was that since the UN Charter, under which a Security Council resolution is adopted, has, in effect, greater authority than any other treaty with which it is in conflict,[18] such as the ECHR, a resolution could prevail over that treaty. We will see in Chapter 7 that the ECtHR decided that Resolution 1546 (2004) was to be understood as being subject to a state's international human rights obligations, even though the most senior court in Britain thought that it had displaced the Convention's right to liberty.[19]

In some situations it may not be clear whether a UN Security Council resolution has the effect of making a state's military contingent an organ of the UN itself, or whether it remains part of the state's armed forces, for the purposes of a breach by it of human rights obligations.[20] Again, it may not be clear whether a resolution has any effect, by itself, on the law which governs the conduct of British soldiers. General principle would suggest that it cannot, and that British soldiers could not therefore rely on a resolution that, expressly or by implication, included a power to detain civilians, certainly for any length of time.[21] To put it another way, a resolution that authorised 'all necessary measures' could never be invoked by a soldier, who seriously assaulted a civilian detainee, on the

17 See Chapter 4.
18 UN Charter, Art 103.
19 *Al-Jedda v United Kingdom* (2011) 53 EHRR 23; *Al-Jedda v Secretary of State for Defence* [2007] UKHL 58, respectively.
20 Discussed in Chapter 7.
21 Discussed in Chapter 9.

ground that it was 'absolutely necessary' to do so in order to obtain information from him.

ii Aggression

The prohibition of force in Article 2(4) of the Charter has been used for another purpose. This has been to provide the basic structure for the international crime of aggression. Something similar, a crime against the peace, led to the convictions of a number of senior Nazi and Japanese leaders who were tried at Nuremberg and Tokyo respectively for their roles in invading other independent states. It has been contentious since 1945, not because there has been any suggestion that it should not remain as a crime,[22] but largely because it could catch the most senior political and military leaders of a state.

In the Rome Statute of the International Criminal Court 1998 (ICC) no attempt was made to define the crime of aggression, and it was left until a later date to do so.[23] At the conference of states party to the Rome Statute, held in 2010, a definition was agreed but, in keeping with the Statute itself, individual states would have to ratify or accede to this amendment.[24] The crime built upon the prohibition on the use of force in Article 2(4) of the UN Charter and General Assembly Resolution 3314 (1974). The UK, like most other states, has not accepted the 2010 amendment to the Statute, and, even if it decided to do so, there is a role for the UN Security Council, where the UK has a right to employ its veto power.[25]

iii Self-defence

It is likely to be the case that every system of national law will provide for self-defence as a defence to a crime that would otherwise be committed, and international law is no different. Article 51 of the Charter recognises the 'inherent right of self-defence'. It was the main ground upon which the UK justified the sending of the task force to re-take the Falkland Islands after the invasion by Argentina.[26]

22 In *R v Jones (Margaret)* [2006] UKHL 16, the House of Lords held that the crime of aggression, invoked at Nuremberg, remained a crime under international law, although without its incorporation into an English statute, it could not form part of English law.
23 Article 5(1)(d) and 5(2).
24 Further discussion is included in Chapter 8.
25 Article 15 *bis* and its relationship with Art 13, both of the Rome Statute. It may be, however, that the belief by senior military leaders that they might be personally liable could have led the chief of the defence staff to request of the Attorney General a 'yes or no' answer as to the legality of the invasion of Iraq, see Lord Goldsmith, evidence to the Iraq Inquiry, 27 January 2010, 186–7.
26 UN Security Council Resolution 502 (1982) demanded the immediate withdrawal of all Argentine forces from the Islands. The British government relied on Art 51 of the UN Charter to justify the despatch of the task force to re-take the Islands, HC Debs 7 April 1982, vol 21, col 960 (Foreign Secretary); HC Debs 27 April 1982, vol 22, col 719 (Prime Minister).

This is, perhaps, the clearest example of a straightforward application of self-defence by a single state under Article 51 in modern times, although the UK did invoke this concept in 2015 concerning the attack by an RAF remotely piloted aircraft on a British citizen in Syria.[27] The Charter also refers to collective self-defence, where a state that has been the subject of an armed attack requests other states to assist it in repelling that attack. The North Atlantic Treaty Organisation (NATO) is based upon the concept of collective self-defence with its easily understood principle of 'an attack on one [state] is an attack on all'.[28] It was invoked for the first time by the NATO Atlantic Council on 12 September 2001 following the attack on New York and Washington on 11 September 2001.[29] The decision to do so did not thereby commit states to taking military action, since it was clear in the discussions beforehand that 'it would be up to each Ally to judge for itself what action needed to be taken . . . [and] that collective consultation would be necessary'.[30] A large-scale Article 5 military mission[31] was, not in fact, carried out, but if there had been a real chance of doing so, the UK would have had to consider whether to make British troops and assets available. It is unlikely that a decision by the NATO Council to invoke Article 5 at the present time would automatically authorise British armed forces to take part in an armed conflict without the intervention of the House of Commons.[32] In this sense an Article 5 'guarantee'[33] to all members of NATO is, in legal terms, little different from one where there is no such guarantee, although Britain's political and national interest will often be quite different. Despite the 'guarantee' it is possible, although unlikely, that the House of Commons would vote in a way that did not support the government's motion to take military action on the basis of Article 5.[34]

27 Letter from the Permanent Representative of the UK to the UN to the President of the UN Security Council, 7 September 2015, S/2015/688. For further discussion of this event, see Chapter 4.

28 Article 5, NATO Treaty 1949.

29 See Edgar Buckley, 'Invoking Article 5', NATO Review, 2006, available at http://www.nato.int/docu/review/2006/issue2/english/art2.html ; HC Debs 28 November 2001, vol 375, col 910W.

30 Buckley, *ibid.*

31 NATO's Airborne Early Warning Force and the Standing Naval Force Mediterranean were deployed, HC Debs 28 November 2001, vol 375, col 910W. For overflight permissions for US military aircraft through the airspace of NATO members following the decision of the NATO Atlantic Council on 12 September 2001 see HC Debs 26 July 2007, vol 463, col 1475W.

32 See Chapter 4.

33 The Foreign Secretary referred to the 'guarantee' of Art 5 in HC Debs 10 April 2014, vol 579, col 368W. The 'guarantee' to Belgium concerning its neutrality based on the Treaty of London 1839 was arguably not a guarantee at all, since the 1839 treaty placed an obligation on the parties to it to respect the neutrality and independence of Belgium and it did not have a provision similar to Art 5 of the NATO Treaty, 1949.

34 An analogy could be drawn with the authorisation of the UN Security Council to take 'all necessary measures' as in Resolution 1973 (2011) in relation to Libya. It was always possible that the House of Commons would not support the government in the vote on 21 March 2011 (although it did). See Chapter 4.

Whether a state could act in collective self-defence with another state through the use of armed force in a third state has been raised over the issue of whether the UK, acting in the collective self-defence of Iraq (through its invitation to do so), could, by way of air strikes, attack ISIL operating in the territory of Syria. The legal basis of any such action is not unequivocally clear.[35]

Despite the wording of Article 51, which requires there to be an 'armed attack', it is accepted by many international lawyers that there is an inherent right of 'anticipatory self-defence', where an armed attack is judged to be imminent, which has survived under the Charter, although 'the actual invocation of the right to anticipatory self-defence in practice is rare'.[36] The related, but wider, idea of 'pre-emption' was raised as a doctrine by President George W. Bush,[37] particularly after the attacks on New York and Washington on 11 September 2001. The claimed right to use armed force on the basis of pre-emption would give a state, which relied on it, a legal justification to act against a possible threat to it, whereas it was always understood that anticipatory self-defence required the threat to be at least highly probable. There is no evidence to suggest that the UK has accepted the pre-emption doctrine[38] and it played no part in the decision

35 For the limits of collective self-defence, see *Case Concerning Military and Paramilitary Activities in and Against Nicaragua (Nicaragua v United States of America) (Merits)*, 1986, ICJ Reports p 14, [195], [229]. The legality of the air strikes on ISIL located in Iraq is based on the collective self-defence of Iraq, see letter from the Permanent Representative of the UK to the President of the UN Security Council, S/2014/851, 26 November 2014. The issue of the RAF air strike in Syria on 21 August 2015, by a remotely piloted aircraft and those carried out in Syria, following the vote in the House of Commons on 2 December 2015, are discussed in Chapter 4. For discussion of the vote on 2 December 2015 for air strikes in Syria, see Chapter 4. *Quaere* whether a state can act in the collective self-defence of other coalition states assisting Iraq.

36 C Gray, *International Law and the Use of Force* (OUP, 3rd edn, 2008), 161 and see generally, 160–5. Gray also draws attention to the fact that 'many commentators and states do not accept a wide customary right of anticipatory or pre-emptive self-defence survives the UN Charter', 'A Crisis of Legitimacy for the UN Collective Security System?' (2007) 56 ICLQ 157, 159. It was used by the UK government in relation to an attack by a remotely piloted aircraft on two individuals of British nationality in Syria, see HC Debs 7 September 2015, vol 599, col 26, and in relation to the legal justification for air strikes in Syria from 2 December 2015, discussed in Chapter 4.

37 The 'Bush Doctrine' is set out in the US National Security Strategy (2002), C Gray *International Law and the Use of Force* (OUP, 3rd edn, 2008), 210. See also C Henderson, 'The Bush Doctrine: From Theory to Practice' (2004) 9 Jo C&SL 3; L Moir, *Reappraising the Resort to Force* (Hart Publishing, 2010), 76–82.

38 It was rejected as a reflection of international law by the Attorney General in his advice to the Prime Minister on 7 March 2003, see 'Attorney General's Advice on the Iraq War. Iraq: Resolution 1441' (2005) 54 ICLQ 767, 768. Both Professors Brownlie QC and Greenwood QC, concluded in their separate memorandums to the Foreign Affairs Committee, *Foreign Policy Aspects of the War Against Terrorism*, 2nd Report, session 2002–03, HC 196, that the doctrine of 'pre-emption' had no basis in international law. The Response of the Secretary of State for Foreign and Commonwealth Affairs, Cm 5739 (2003) makes no specific comment on the Committee's recommendation at their [154], which had pointed out the dangers of such a doctrine. See also C Greenwood, 'International Law and the Pre-emptive Use of Force:

by the British government, or the House of Commons, to take military action against Iraq in March 2003, although the argument that a failure to take action would enable terrorists to acquire some of Iraq's weapons of mass destruction, sounded very like it. In a similar way, so did the rhetoric of ministers to the effect that a reason for UK military involvement in Afghanistan, particularly after 2006, was to defend the UK against attacks on its streets by those who, if not defeated, could form some sort of government in Afghanistan.[39]

iv Authorisation of the UN Security Council

A resolution adopted under Chapter VII of the UN Charter can give a lawful justification for the use of force by states on the terms laid down in it.[40] Resolution 1973 (2011) provided just such a lawful justification for the airstrikes carried out by UK, along with other coalition, aircraft on Libya; its relevance in the debate in the House of Commons is discussed in Chapter 4. The main issue in the legal justification for the UK to take military action against Iraq in March 2003 was whether UN Security Council Resolution 1441 (2002) required a further resolution to permit the lawful use of force in Iraq or was merely desirable politically.[41] On the eve of the debate in the House of Commons it was clear that no such resolution would be adopted and the UK government, on the advice of the Attorney General, took the legal position that one was not necessary in the circumstances.[42] Although it will be difficult to obtain an authoritative ruling by an international court or tribunal on the legal basis of the UK's military action against Iraq in March 2003, it seems clear that the lack of a strong legal position in international law could produce undesirable political consequences.[43]

v Humanitarian intervention

The term, 'humanitarian intervention', is one that has no legally defined meaning under international or in English law. It is really an intervention through armed force, primarily or exclusively conducted for humanitarian purposes, and it should not be confused with humanitarian interventions by the ICRC or any other humanitarian organisation in a state that has permitted their presence, nor

Afghanistan, Al-Qaida, and Iraq' (2003) 4 San Diego International Law Journal, 7, 36, and V Lowe, 'The Iraq Crisis: What Now?' (2003) 52 ICLQ 859, 865.

39 See discussion in Chapter 4.

40 A list of occasions on which the UN Security Council has authorised the use of force in the period 1990–2008, is set out in Report of the Dutch Committee of Inquiry on the War in Iraq' (2010) 57 NILR 81, 88–89.

41 *Ibid*, 84.

42 For discussion of this issue see Chapter 4.

43 The 'Report of the Dutch Committee of Inquiry on the War in Iraq' (2010) 57 NILR 81, 109 describes these as including the 'setting of precedents and, in the long term, an undermining of the principle of the rule of law'.

with the 'right to protect', discussed below. Neither should it be confused with 'just war'[44] as a purported ground for intervention. Although the reasons of humanitarian intervention and a just war for a decision to use armed force may be similar, they may also be different. The latter term has no direct traction in international law and, if it is to be used, it is best employed as a matter of conscience on the part of those who support the use of armed force outside a state's borders.

Apart from authorisation by the UN Security Council and self-defence, humanitarian intervention has been claimed as a third justification for the use of armed force.[45] Unlike self-defence, there is no mention of it in the UN Charter[46] and it cannot be said to be accepted by all states as a part of international law, although its central theme, the protection of human rights, is a core principle of the Charter. It can be a beguiling idea for political leaders, faced with the demand that something should be done to prevent persecution of an ethnic or religious group of individuals by their own state, particularly if footage is shown nightly on TV news programmes of suffering, vulnerable people. This is the idea that a state could use armed force against another state in order to protect the human rights of a group of its inhabitants or, indeed, all of its citizens. The UK has been at the forefront of a small number of states which have shown some inclination to use military force for these purposes.[47] It was the principal legal ground advanced by the Attorney General in August 2013 for an attack on Syria to deter it from using chemical weapons in the future.[48] Humanitarian intervention as a justification has

44 See also Chapter 4. It was referred to by the Archbishop of Canterbury and by Lord Harries, in the debate on conducting air strikes in Syria, HL Debs 2 December 2015, vol 767, cols 1123, 1129, respectively, although rarely mentioned in the House of Commons debate of the same date.

45 It was claimed by the UK as the legal justification for patrolling the no-fly zones in Iraq in 2001, see Secretary of State for Defence, HC Debs 26 February 2001, vol 363, col 620. In *Amin v Brown* [2005] EWHC 1670 (Ch), Lawrence Collins J set the grounds on which the use of force would be permissible under international law and, after dealing with self-defence and authorisation of the UN Security Council, added, '(perhaps) for the purposes of intervention for humanitarian ends', [27]. It is interesting to note that the government did not refer to this ground of justification for the use of force when it gave examples of when an armed intervention could be justified under international law, Government Response to *Remote Control: Remotely Piloted Air Systems-Current and Future UK Use*, HC 772 at HC 611 (2014), [17].

46 The UN Secretary-General's report 'Implementing the Responsibility to Protect', A/63/677 (12 January 2009) stressed that 'the responsibility to protect does not alter, indeed it reinforces, the legal obligations of Member States to refrain from the use of force except in conformity with the Charter', [3]; A/69/981-S/2015/500, 13 July 2015.

47 The understanding of the House of Commons Foreign Affairs Committee is that 'the UK is almost alone among UN member States in holding this view', written evidence from the Foreign Affairs Committee to the Defence Committee, 14th Report, session 2013–14, *Intervention, Why, When, How?* HC 994-II.

48 See Chemical Weapon use by Syrian Regime: UK Government Legal Position, note 51 below. For the reliance on humanitarian intervention by the UK government in northern Iraq in 1991, the no-fly zones in Iraq from 1991 and the Kosovo campaign in 1999 see Government Response, Fifth Special Report, session 2014–15, HC 582, Annex A; *Afghanistan*, HC 994. See also HC Debs 30 June 2005, vol 435, col 1690W (the no-fly zones over Iraq in 2002).

a ring of 'goodness' about it, especially when allied with the idea that RAF air-crew would be risking their lives to protect women and children in a foreign land.

It is not difficult to find strong grounds for humanitarian intervention in a variety of countries at present. Syria and Ukraine spring to mind, but there are many other countries where particular groups are facing egregious breaches of what might be called their human rights. No military action is being taken by powerful states to assist them, but this is hardly surprising given the fact that it will be politics, rather than any legal justification alone, which will determine whether a humanitarian intervention is undertaken or not. Indeed, it can be seen that it is common for states which wish to, or have, used armed force in another state to justify their actions on a number of different grounds simultaneously.[49] Whilst it will be important to argue that what they intend to do, or have done, is justifiable under international law, senior political leaders know that their words need to be directed at a non-lawyer audience, whether other politicians, or the general public. To include a claim to be taking military action to protect women and children, along with any other justification, is likely to play well with the public. The suffering of the Iraqi people under Saddam Hussein, and those affected by the actions of ISIL in Iraq and Syria, were key factors in the arguments of at least some of the MPs who voted to support the government's decision to take military action, although the concept of humanitarian intervention was not the basis of the legal justification or these interventions.

The idea that international law permitted states unilaterally, or within a relatively small coalition of forces, to attack other states for humanitarian purposes, is viewed by many states with some concern, not least because of the perceived risks to world peace through the domination by the militarily strong over weaker states.[50] Following the chemical attack on Eastern Damascus on 21 August 2013, the Attorney General advised that an air attack on Syria would be 'permitted under international law [as an] exceptional measure . . . in order to alleviate the scale of the overwhelming catastrophe . . . by deterring and disrupting the further use of chemical weapons by the Syrian regime'.[51] No equivocation on the claimed

49 See the examples given in Chapter 4.

50 'China, together with many developing states, opposes humanitarian intervention', C Cai, 'New Great Powers and International Law in the 21st Century' (2013) 24 EJIL 755, 788. For the position of Russia and other states opposing humanitarian intervention see C Henderson, 'The UK Government's Legal Opinion on Forcible Measures in Response to the Use of Chemical Weapons by the Syria Government' (2015) 64 ICLQ 179, 193.

51 The Prime Minister spoke about the 'Attorney General's advice', HC Debs 29 August 2013, vol 566, col 1425, but it was published as 'Chemical Weapon Use by Syrian Regime: UK Government Legal Position' see https://www.gov.uk/government/publications/chemical-weapon-use-by-syrian-regime-uk-government-legal-position/chemical-weapon-use-by-syrian-regime-uk-government-legal-position-html-version. It had been formulated in similar terms in the Attorney General's advice on 7 March 2003 as a general legal justification for the use of force, 'Attorney General's Advice on the Iraq War. Iraq: Resolution 1441' (2005) 54 ICLQ 767, [768] using the terms 'exceptionally to prevent overwhelming humanitarian catastrophe'.

right under international law to undertake a humanitarian intervention by armed force was advanced in the précis of his advice to government and made available to MPs, although conditions were set out before it could be invoked.[52] Nor was an attempt made to show *how* this claimed right actually reflects international law as, in effect, a further exception to the prohibition of the use of force in Article 2(4) of the UN Charter.[53] The existence of this claimed right of humanitarian intervention and of the criteria for its application cannot to be found in UK ministerial statements, however many times the right is asserted, or in English law, but in customary international law. To rely on humanitarian intervention as a basis to supply the need for legality, ministers will have to show that a proposed use of force does actually conform to the requirements of customary international law. It follows that if humanitarian intervention is supported by customary international law, it can be relied upon by any state.[54] The fact that all states agreed the basis of the responsibility to protect (see below), with its important requirement of action to be taken through the UN Security Council, would suggest they were unwilling to accept that states could take military action on their own initiative by way of a humanitarian intervention, the grounds for which would be likely to be similar to those for the right to protect.[55] Whilst a right on the part of states to intervene in another state through the use of armed force

52 These were that there was 'convincing evidence accepted by the international community as a whole of extreme humanitarian distress on a large scale, requiring immediate and urgent relief . . . no practicable alternative . . . force must be necessary and proportionate . . . the minimum necessary to achieve that end and for no other purpose'. Although the doctrine of humanitarian intervention is certainly not accepted by the 'international community as a whole', the Attorney General considered that the evidence of extreme distress must be so accepted.

53 Compare the view of the House of Commons Foreign Affairs Select Committee's Fourth Report (2000) on *Kosovo*, HC 28-I, [132], concerning its conclusion that 'the doctrine of humanitarian intervention has a tenuous basis in current customary international law'. The Committee concluded also that it was 'too ambitious [to say] that a new customary right had developed', *ibid*. See the difference in view between Professors Brownlie QC and Greenwood QC in the Report as to whether humanitarian intervention was supported by customary international law. The Committee's conclusion was based to a large extent on the conclusion drawn by Ian Brownlie QC, see HC-28-II, Appendix 2 [47]–[80] and Appendix 3. Even in his 7 May 2003 advice, the Attorney General expressed the view that 'the doctrine remains controversial', 'Attorney General's Advice on the Iraq War. Iraq: Resolution 1441' (2005) 54 ICLQ 767, 768. A similar view was taken in the 'Report of the Dutch Committee of Inquiry on the War in Iraq' (2010) 57 NILR 81, 87, which concluded that 'the lawfulness of a humanitarian intervention in such emergency circumstances . . . is not without controversy'.

54 Although, as far as the UK is concerned as a permanent member of the UN Security Council, it will be able to exercise its influence in proposing, voting on, or exercising a veto on, a draft resolution where another state has exercised this claimed right of humanitarian intervention.

55 The British government has, however, attempted to show that humanitarian intervention and the responsibility to protect are addressing different issues, the latter being concerned with the responsibility of states towards their own populations and the understanding of the members of the UN that it was for the UN Security Council to take action itself. See the Government Response, Fifth Special Report, session 2014–15, HC 582, Annex A.

on grounds of a humanitarian need, with the necessary caveats of proportionality and urgency, may sound attractive, and even desirable, it cannot be asserted with any degree of certainty that such a right does actually reflect customary international law, and is thus available to all states, at the present time, despite the fact that 'the UK has now unequivocally established itself as the norm entrepreneur in the context of humanitarian intervention'.[56] With the development of the parliamentary convention, to put before the House of Commons a substantive motion for the proposed deployment of combat troops into an armed conflict it is not unreasonable to expect MPs to be given an indication by the Attorney General as to whether humanitarian intervention really is firmly based in international law.[57]

Even if a claim to legality cannot be made out there is some political support, at least in the UK, for the 'legitimacy' of humanitarian intervention where the stringent conditions for it are met, 'on the precedent of the NATO action in Kosovo in 1999'.[58] Whilst this might satisfy many it would be difficult for an Attorney General in the future to give advice, a note of which would need to be made available to MPs prior to a vote in the House of Commons to take military action, to the effect that proposed military action was unlawful although legitimate.[59]

vi Responsibility to protect

In an attempt to protect populations at risk of genocide, war crimes, crimes against humanity or ethnic cleansing, the UN advanced the idea that all states

56 C Henderson, 'The UK Government's Legal Opinion on Forcible Measures in Response to the Use of Chemical Weapons by the Syria Government' (2015) 64 ICLQ 179, 194. See also A Henriksen and M Schack, 'The Crisis in Syria and Humanitarian Intervention' (2014) 1 Journal on the Use of Force and International Law 122, 147. The House of Commons Foreign Affairs Committee, 2nd Report, 2015–16, *The Extension of Offensive Military Operations to Syria*, session 2015–16, HC 457, [17] concluded that humanitarian intervention 'is emerging as a . . . justification but it is not yet fully established'. See also HC Briefing Paper 7404, 'Legal Basis for UK Military Action in Syria', 1 December 2015, [21].

57 This is discussed further in Chapter 4.

58 This is the view of the Foreign Affairs Committee, see written evidence from the Foreign Affairs Committee to the Defence Committee, 14th Report, session 2013–14, *Intervention, Why, When, How?* HC 994-II, a view maintained since the House of Commons Foreign Affairs Select Committee's Fourth Report, session 1999–2000, on *Kosovo*, HC 28-I, which concluded that the Kosovo campaign 'was justified on moral grounds', [138]; the Independent International Commission on Kosovo, *Kosovo Report* (OUP, 2000), referred to the 'need to close the gap between legality and legitimacy', [10]. The UK government rejected the conclusion as to legality drawn by the Commission, see Government Response, Fifth Special Report, HC 582, Annex A. See also the comments of the then Foreign Secretary that 'the legal basis for military action contained in the Charter . . . is no longer fully adequate to cope with today's threats', HC Debs 11 November 2003, vol 413, col 155.

59 The House of Commons Defence Select Committee drew a distinction between legality and 'moral legitimacy' through a two-thirds majority of the UN General Assembly that, in its view, 'would fall short of a "green light" ', to take military action, Defence Committee 7th Report 2014–15, *The Situation in Iraq and Syria and the Response to al-Dawla al-Islamiya fi al-Iraq al-Sham (DAESH)*, HC 690 (2015), [20].

had a responsibility to protect them.[60] The doctrine does not, at the current time, apply to any other activities such as natural disasters or ill-treatment, in other ways, by a state of its own population.[61] Ministers have stated that the UK is committed to this concept and this includes the same obligation on a government towards its own population.[62] It is an obligation, primarily on individual states in relation to their own population, but also on the UN Security Council.[63] Its real significance, in the view of the UK government, is to 'make Security Council action more likely and less controversial in future'.[64] The responsibility to protect as developed by the UN, is quite distinct from humanitarian intervention, but it frequently has a hollow sound to it when considered in relation to the very practical question of what can be done to prevent any further civilian deaths in Syria,[65] or in other countries.

Although the term 'responsibility to protect' appears to give some hope to those oppressed by their own country, the reality is quite different. Apart from political pressure on offending states, which would have existed prior to the development of the idea of responsibility to protect, there are few situations where it has had an effect on the ground to do what it appears to promise. One example of its application, however, could be the intervention in Libya in 2011, where the UN Security Council adopted Resolution 1973 (2011).[66] Experience has shown that the aftermath of an intervention could generate similar issues to those that preceded it, and states will need 'to consider what kind of sustained support may

60 2005 World Summit Outcome, A/RES/60/1, 24 October 2005 (General Assembly), [138]–[139]; Implementing the Responsibility to Protect, A/63/677, 12 January 2009 (General Assembly); UN Security Council Resolution 1706 (2006) operative [4].

61 A/63/677, [10(b)].

62 Ministerial statement, HC Debs 13 May 2014, vol 580, col 466W; ministerial statement HC Debs 22 April 2013, vol 561, col 644W; ministerial statement HL Debs 20 October 2012, vol 551, col 110W; Government Response, Fifth Special Report, HC 582, Annex A, to the Defence Committee's 15th Report, session 2013–14, *Afghanistan*, HC 994.

63 This is made plain by A/RES/60/1 and A/63/677, [3] (above) although it has been suggested that 'that initiative was . . . exclusively on the expectation that the Security Council would take action in the face of genocide, ethnic cleansing and crimes against humanity. Unilateral action was not addressed', M Weller, *Iraq and Use of Force in International Law* (OUP, 2010), 101. The conclusion drawn in A/63/677, [14] that 'the international community can at best play a supplemental role' is likely to refer to the ability of individual states to take non-coercive action to prevent or prosecute genocide, war crimes and crimes against humanity or take economic sanctions against a state.

64 Government Response, Fifth Special Report, HC 582, Annex A, to the Defence Committee's 15th Report, session 2013–14, *Afghanistan*, HC 994. Its significance can also be seen in the support which the UK gives to 'training militaries . . . in the law of armed conflict', statement on behalf of the government, HL Debs 16 July 2015, vol 764, col 721.

65 Civilian deaths alleged to have been committed by government and anti-government forces in Syria are documented in Report of the Independent Commission of Inquiry on the Syrian Arab Republic, A/HRC/27/60, 13 August 2014, Human Rights Council.

66 This is suggested in 'A Vital and Enduring Commitment: Implementing Responsibility to Protect', A/69/981-S/2015/500, 13 July 2015, [9].

be required after the use of force'.[67] In 2013 there were calls for states to intervene in some form in Syria to protect the civilian population, based upon a mix of reasons ranging from humanitarian intervention to the prevention of threats to their own countries from terrorism.[68] Although the UN Security Council was not able to pass a resolution to authorise the use of force under the Charter, due to the political stand taken by Russia and China,[69] it did adopt Resolution 2249 in 2015, as discussed in Chapter 4.

vii Economic sanctions

The idea that economic sanctions, in its variety of forms, could replace the need to take forcible action against a state, which had used armed force unlawfully, was shown in the period before World War II to be Panglossian. Modern practice at the UN is now more realistic. Sanctions have been used quite effectively in recent years where the UN Security Council has determined that there is a threat to the peace, breach of the peace or an act of aggression under Chapter VII of the Charter.[70] Economic sanctions have involved a prohibition on member states exporting to the selected country, arms, or other material, which could be used for warlike purposes, and funds. At the sharp end of sanctions, there have been those targeted on selected political or military leaders and even on rebel groups.[71] In a modern twist to the normal practice of sanctions being imposed upon a particular country, the UN has adopted this method of trying to prevent non-state organisations from carrying out terrorist activities.

All member states of the UN are obliged by the UN Charter to accept and carry out the decisions of the Security Council, so each state has to provide some legal structure whereby the sanctions can be enforced at state level, since the UN itself does not possess a police force and neither does it have established courts and prisons to enforce a sanctions regime. The national law of some states will provide that international law automatically applies within their own borders but others, like the UK, require some form of national law to make a defined part of international law part of English law. The UK is, of course, a party to the UN Charter of 1945, an international treaty, but that treaty cannot be part of English

67 *Ibid.* See also the situation in Libya in 2015, 'Report of the Secretary-General on the Protection of Civilians in Armed Conflict', S/2015/453, 18 June 2015, [15].

68 See 'Tony Blair Calls for UK Intervention in Syria Crisis', http://www.bbc.co.uk/news/world-21602723.

69 Defence Committee 7th Report 2014–15, *The Situation in Iraq and Syria and the Response to al-Dawla al-Islamiya fi al-Iraq al-Sham (DAESH)*, HC 690 (2015), [20].

70 See Art 41, UN Charter 1945.

71 See, for example, the possibility of targeted sanctions on rebel groups and individuals who do not cut off all ties to al Qaida in Mali, UN Security Council Resolution 2805 (2012), operative [2]; travel bans on those directly connected with Col Gaddafi in Libya, UN Security Council Resolution 1970 [15], see SI 2011/547 (revoked). For a demand that all terrorist fighters 'disarm and cease all activities', see UN Security Council Resolution 2171 (2014), operative [1].

law unless an Act of Parliament expressly makes it, or parts of it, so. The United Nations Act 1946 is limited in its reach, since it only provides for the sanctions regime envisaged by Article 41 of the Charter. It enables the UK to enact laws, usually in the form of orders in council, to give effect to Security Council decisions on sanctions and thereby to use English law for their enforcement. At any one time there will be a relatively large number of separate statutory instruments applying to a wide range of countries, most of which will provide criminal penalties for breaking them.[72] In addition, one or more ships of the Royal Navy may be deployed to prevent the export by sea of materials subject to a sanctions regime.

By way of contrast EU law is part of English law and the UK must apply it in some form or other.[73] So, if the EU adopts a policy of sanctions against a particular country, this must be applied also in the UK.[74] A range of sanctions are currently in place.[75] A significant difference between the UN and the EU processes is that the courts of the EU can review the lawfulness, at the instigation of an individual affected, of all acts of the EU including his or her inclusion on a sanctions list, whether that body is acting to implement a UN Security Council resolution or not.[76]

Apart from economic sanctions, a state may take steps to control the export of arms, either on its own initiative, or through some international organisation, such as the UN or the EU. The UK ratified the Arms Trade Treaty 2013 in 2014 and, to implement the national control system envisaged by Article 5, it has enacted the necessary secondary legislation.[77] The Treaty prohibits the export of

72 Examples include the Iraq (United Nations Sanctions) Order 2003/1519, which gives effect to UN Security Resolution 1482 (2003) and which, *inter alia*, prohibits the import or export of illegally removed cultural property from Iraq and permits a search of ships suspected of carrying restricted goods; the Libya (Financial Sanctions) Order 2011/548, which gives effect to part of UN Security Council Resolution 1970 (2011).

73 European Communities Act 1972, s 2.

74 It will be directly applicable, although the UK may need to provide for penalties, see *Hmicho v Barclays Bank plc* [2015] EWHC 1757, [16], which referred to European Regulation (EU) No 36/2012 and to the Syria (European Union Financial Sanction) Regulations, 2012/129. The EU Regulation was adopted 'in view of the continued brutal repression and violation of human rights by the Government of Syria', [3].

75 See, for example the Al-Qaida and Taliban (Asset Freezing) Regulations 2011/2742; the Export Control (Syria Sanctions) Order 2013/2012, which imposes export and transport controls on equipment which might be used for internal repression (art 4) while Sched 2 provides a list of the type of equipment.

76 *European Commission v Kadi* [2014] 1 CMLR 24 and see C Gearty, 'In Praise of Awkwardness: Kadi in the CJEU' (2014) 10 European Constitutional Law Review 15. For the opportunity to challenge a listing under the UN Security Council sanctions regime see UN Security Council Resolution 1730 (2006). Sanctions relating to members of the Taliban are in UN Security Council Resolution 2160 (2014), which provides for a statement of case to be prepared by those seeking the listing of an individual, [16].

77 The Export Control (Amendment) Order 2014/1069. See also the *Strategic Export Controls. Her Majesty's Government's Annual Report for 2012, Quarterly Reports for 2012 and 2013, and the Government's Policy on Arms Exports and International Arms Control Issues*, Cm 8935, October 2014.

arms (as defined[78]) which, to the knowledge of the exporting state 'would be used in the commission of genocide, crimes against humanity or war crimes'.[79] Should the UK wish to export any of the arms covered by the Treaty to a non-state armed group, such as the Free Syrian Army,[80] this limitation would only prevent it from doing so in the very unlikely event that it knew that the arms would be used for the commission of the crimes set out in it.[81] It would be expected that any transfer of arms to a particular group operating as part of the Free Syrian Army would need to involve careful scrutiny of the group's declared intent to protect civilians not taking part in the conflict and the more difficult issue of preventing a diversion of the arms to an unapproved group.[82] Nevertheless, the air strikes by the RAF, as part of a coalition, on ISIL in Iraq have led ministers to have to think of how those forces could be defeated on the ground, which may mean actually providing arms and ammunition to those taking part.[83] A ministerial statement in February 2015 indicates that the government 'plan to make a significant contribution to the US-led train and equip programme to help the Syrian moderate armed opposition counter the Islamic State of Iraq and the Levant'.[84] Should this involve arms and ammunition being supplied by the UK to units of the Free Syrian Army to conduct armed action against ISIL, which is itself fighting government forces of Syria,[85] there is likely to be much less concern in the UK than if those same units were to be engaged in fighting the armed forces of Syria.

Whether a sanctions policy has been put in place or not, a piece of World War II legislation remains on the statute book, the Trading with the Enemy Act 1939. It was pleaded in a dispute relating to a property in England purchased in the name of an Iraqi, who was resident in that country, in which the defendant, in England,

78 Articles 2 and 3, which include small arms, light weapons and ammunition, all subject to the export procedures in Arts 6 and 7.

79 Article 6. These acts (including grave breaches of the Geneva Conventions and attacks against the civilian population) are to be defined by the 'international agreements to which [the exporting state] is a State Party.' The definition of crimes against humanity and war crimes under international law is not limited to those definitions set out in the Rome Statute 1998 of the ICC.

80 The Free Syrian Army consists of many different groups, Foreign Secretary, HC Debs 13 January 2014, vol 573, col 590.

81 Non-lethal equipment has been supplied to the Supreme Military Council of the Free Syrian Army consisting largely of commercially available items, Foreign Secretary, HC Debs 1 May 2014, vol 579, col 63WS.

82 See the Foreign Secretary's statements, HC Debs 28 November 2014, vol 588, col 166; HC Debs 13 October 2014, vol 586, col 26W.

83 The Foreign Secretary, HC Debs 28 November 2014, vol 588, col 166. In the same statement the Foreign Secretary stated that, 'we have supplied the Peshmerga with some high calibre machine guns, which they are now deploying to good effect'. See also Defence Committee 7th Report 2014–15, *The Situation in Iraq and Syria and the Response to al-Dawla al-Islamiya fi al-Iraq al-Sham (DAESH)*, HC 690 (2015), [74].

84 HC Debs 16 October 2014, vol 594, col 473 (Foreign Secretary).

85 This appears to be the intended purpose of any supply of arms and ammunition to units of the Free Syrian Army, Foreign Secretary, HC Debs 28 November 2014, vol 588, col 166.

pleaded that the 1939 Act prohibited trading with a person, who was a national of a state at war with the Crown. Lawrence Collins J held that the 1939 Act did not apply since, although the UK was conducting military operations against Iraq, there was no state of war in existence.[86]

viii NATO

The NATO Treaty 1949 came into existence during the Cold War and it reflected the fear of the western allies that the Soviet Union would attack them through West German territory, to which the only realistic deterrent could be the certainty of a response by all the NATO states, which included the USA. With the collapse of the Soviet Union, NATO has found a different role and has played an active part in the armed conflicts in Kosovo, Afghanistan and in the action taken against Colonel Gaddafi in Libya. Its collective self-defence mechanism under Article 5 of the NATO Treaty has been discussed above, but its military operations in Afghanistan and Libya were based on authorisations from the UN Security Council.[87]

Whilst the NATO institutions can play an important co-ordinating role for its members, the organisation possesses no binding legal powers over its individual members, to compel them to join a particular military operation, or of command[88] over parts of the armed forces of individual states. It can, of course, agree policy, such as that detainees in Iraq held by NATO member states be released after a maximum period of 96 hours, but British ministers have felt free to disregard this when they have considered it appropriate in a particular case.[89] The UK has always played a significant part in NATO operations. By the end of October 2011 when the non-fly zone was terminated[90] the RAF had flown 'one fifth of the total strike sorties flown by NATO', over Libya.[91]

86 *Amin v Brown* [2005] EWHC 1670 (Ch), [46]. The principle that enemy aliens cannot sue in the English courts was also held to be part of the 'traditional laws of war, and . . . there is no warrant for extending it to modern armed conflict, not involving war in the technical sense', *ibid.* On this issue see *Porter v Freudenberg* [1915] 1 KB 857, discussed in Chapter 5.

87 Following UN Security Council Resolution 1386 (2001) the UK became the lead nation of ISAF, see S/2001/1217, 19 December 2001. On 11 August 2003 NATO 'assumed strategic command, control and coordination of ISAF', S/2003/970. Following UN Security Council Resolutions 1970 (2011) and 1973 (2011) NATO enforced the arms embargo on Libya from 22 March 2011 and on 31 March 2011 it 'took sole command and control of the international military effort for Libya', http://www.nato.int/cps/en/natolive/topics_71652.htm. The relevant letters from the Secretary General of NATO to the Secretary General of the UN are at S/2011/203.

88 For coordination purposes a commander may be appointed for all the NATO states involved in a particular mission but this individual will not have legal powers of command over participating units belonging to the armed forces of different states.

89 The legality of this action is discussed in Chapter 9.

90 UN Security Council Resolution 2016 (2011), operative [6].

91 Prime Minister, HC Debs 24 October 2011, vol 534, col 25. The NATO operation was code named Operation Unified Protector.

ix Co-operation with France and other EU states

As a significant military power, certainly in Europe, it is not surprising to see that some form of military co-operation should take place with France, the other European nuclear power and fellow permanent member of the UN Security Council. The days of military rivalry and, indeed, war between these two countries have long past and the common membership of the EU, along with financial constraints have led to formal means by which Britain and France could co-operate for military purposes.[92] The Treaty for Defence and Security Co-operation 2011[93] between the UK and France formalises pre-existing military co-operation between the two states, whether through the UN, NATO or the European Common Security and Defence Policy.[94] Should British and French forces be deployed to take part in an armed conflict without the involvement of any other states, they will need to agree beforehand 'the legal basis under international law for such deployment'.[95] In the absence of an appropriate invitation of the government of the state into which they are to be deployed there are likely to be interesting discussions between the UK Attorney General and his or her French counterpart.[96]

Aside from NATO, the UK is involved with the EU on certain issues relating to defence through British contributions to European military initiatives, such as peacekeeping or training missions through the Common Security and Defence Policy of the EU.[97]

x Recognition of non-state actors

It has been a long-standing policy of successive British governments that, whilst they would withhold or grant recognition of statehood, they would not recognise

92 See the House of Commons Library, *Franco-British Defence Co-operation*, Standard Note SN/1A/5750, 8 November 2010.

93 Treaty Series No 36 (2011). The treaty was signed in 2010, but came into force in 2011.

94 It would appear from a ministerial statement that in working with other European partners, it is 'NATO first and foremost but other partnerships where it is expedient to do so', HC Debs 17 March 2014, vol 577, col 547.

95 Article 5 of the 2011 treaty.

96 This may occur over whether both states can agree that international law permits a state to conduct a humanitarian intervention in the absence of a UK Security Council resolution authorising the use of force. The fact that the USA and the UK had different legal reasons for intervening in Iraq in 2003 can be distinguished since there was no treaty provision binding on both states equivalent to the 2011 treaty, Art 5.

97 In a ministerial statement it was stressed that 'it is important that defence co-operation is driven by states themselves, on a voluntary basis, and not by the Brussels institutions', HC Debs 7 January 2014, vol 590, col 173. See generally, A Sari, 'The Conclusion of International Agreements by the European Union in the Context of the ESDP' (2008) 57 ICLQ 53. See also Consolidated version of the Treaty on European Union and the Treaty on the Functioning of the European Union, 2008, Art 42(7) and its significance following the Paris attacks in November 2015; House of Commons Library, Briefing Paper 7390, 18 November 2015.

governments within states.[98] It is not unusual for a government to lose, perhaps for some time, control over part of its territory.[99]

Despite this policy adopted by the Foreign and Commonwealth Office a change to it appears to have developed in which the British government has expressed publicly a willingness to recognise a rebel or insurgent movement.[100] This has certainly happened with Libya in 2011.[101] From a political point of view there are certain advantages in taking this unusual course. No doubt the British government had taken the view that it was only a matter of time until the Gaddafi government would fall and the rebel movement was sufficiently strong and united such that it would ultimately become the new government. The nature and strength of opposition armed groups are not, however, the same. The position at the time of recognition by the UK of the National Transitional Council (NTC) in Libya was different from the Coalition of Syrian Revolutionary and Opposition Forces (CSROF). In the case of the NTC, the reasons for its recognition were set out in a ministerial statement, which indicated that 'the decision reflected the Council [*sic*] increasing legitimacy, competence, success in reaching out to Libyans country-wide and the level of popular support'.[102] It was quite different in respect of the CSROF of Syria where the Foreign Secretary drew attention to the fact that 'they have much to do to win the full support of the Syrian people and to co-ordinate opposition efforts more effectively . . . but it is strongly in the interests of Syria, of the wider region, and of the United Kingdom that we support them and deny space to extremist groups'.[103] Yet he went on to state that 'Her Majesty's Government have decided to recognise the National

98 See, for example, the minister answering a question about recognition of the Taliban government in Afghanistan between 1997–2001, confirmed that 'Her Majesty's Government recognise states not governments or particular regimes', HC Debs 19 October 2001, vol 372, col 1352W.

99 *Quaere* whether the various governments in Iraq and Afghanistan had effective control over the whole of their respective territories at the relevant times.

100 See generally, C Warbrick, 'British Policy and the National Transitional Council of Libya' (2012) 61 ICLQ 247, 250.

101 'On 27 July [2011] the government announced that they would recognise and would deal with the [National Transitional Council] as the "sole legitimate governing authority" in Libya', HL Debs 3 October 2011, vol 730, col 178W.

102 HL Debs 3 October 2011, vol 730, col 178W. No mention was made of the effectiveness (or otherwise) of control over territory achieved by the NTC at the time of recognition. In the previous month UN Security Council Resolution 2009 (2011), [operative 5], encouraged the 'National Transitional Council to implement its plans to protect Libya's population, restore government services'. See generally, H Woolaver, 'Pro-Democratic Intervention in Africa and "The Arab Spring"' (2014) 22 African Journal of International and Comparative Law 161, 172–180.

103 HC Debs 20 November 2012, vol 553, col 445. In these circumstances, *quaere* whether the UK could seek the consent of the government of Syria for air strikes against ISIL on the territory of Syria, see generally, House of Commons Foreign Affairs Committee, 2nd Report, 2015–16, *The Extension of Offensive Military Operations to Syria*, session 2015–16, HC 457, [18]. See also the attack by a UK remotely piloted aircraft of 21 August 2015 directed against two British nationals in Syria, discussed in Chapter 4.

Coalition of Syrian Revolutionary and Opposition Forces as the sole legitimate representative of the Syrian people.'[104]

The recognition of an opposition group as the 'sole legitimate governing authority' (NTC) or as the 'legitimate representative of the people' (CSROF) implies a de-recognition of the previous government of a state only on the assumption that the difference in wording between these two phrases is not significant. There can be no doubt that the TNC replaced the Gaddafi government in Libya, even though the recognition by the UK occurred some months before the capture and death of the previous head of state, Colonel Gaddafi.[105] It had even taken the Libya seat on the UN General Assembly on 20 October.[106] In Syria there is currently an existing government and there cannot be two separate governments recognised (by the UK) at the same time, unless the government of President Assad has 'lost its legitimacy.'[107] The idea of a 'loss of *legitimacy*' is more in the nature of a political flourish than a test by which the lawful government of a state can be determined, since there are no established grounds by which, under international law, a constitutionally appointed government can lose legitimacy,[108] although it can be accused, of course, of infringing basic human rights or of genocide, crimes against humanity or war crimes and should, in consequence, stand down.[109] A particular government may also be considered by political leaders to have lost its legitimacy because it has ceased to represent a sufficiently large percentage of its population but, apart from a general election, or other constitutional process, there is little way of assessing this on an objective basis relevant to any possible rule of international law on the issue.[110] Indeed, the recognition of a rival group and the de-recognition of an existing

104 HC Debs 20 November 2012, vol 553, col 445. Following House of Commons Foreign Affairs Committee, 2nd Report, 2015–16, *The Extension of Offensive Military Operations to Syria*, 2015–16, HC 457, [18], the Response by the Prime Minister, 26 November 2015, indicated that the government anticipated 'the political negotiations [would lead] towards a ceasefire between the Syrian armed forces and the moderate opposition', 20.

105 Colonel Gaddafi's whereabouts were unknown to the British government on 13 October 2011, HC Debs 13 October 2011, vol 533, col 495, ministerial statement. His death was reported by the Prime Minister on 24 October 2011, HC Debs 24 October 2011, vol 534, col 25. Yet on 16 September 2011, UN Security Council Resolution 2009 (2011) encouraged the NTC to 'restore government services', [operative 5].

106 HC Debs 13 October 2011, vol 533, col 495, Foreign Secretary.

107 Ministerial statements, HC Debs 19 July 2011, vol 531, col 870W; HC Debs 11 September 2014, vol 585, col 720W.

108 There is little problem with the term 'legitimacy' if, in its political context, it is taken to refer to a moral position as compared with a legal one. See also the discussion above about the use of the terms 'legality' and 'legitimacy' in relation to humanitarian intervention.

109 See S Talmon, 'De-Recognition of Colonel Qaddafi as a Head of State of Libya?' (2011) 60 ICLQ 759, 765, who comments that 'even gross and systematic violations of human rights by a government . . . do not automatically lead to its loss of status as a government'.

110 The Prime Minister commented that 'what Syria needs is what Iraq needs: an inclusive, democratic Government that represents all of its people', HC Debs 26 September 2014, vol 585, col 1258.

government could be described as an 'unjustified intervention in [that state's] internal affairs'.[111] It is also difficult to accept on an objective basis that an armed opposition movement, recognised by the UK or, indeed any other state, gains the 'legitimacy' that the previous government (which might have been elected) has allegedly lost.[112]

British diplomatic relations with Syria were suspended in June 2012, well before the statement on recognition by the UK government of the CSROF.[113] The breaking off of diplomatic relations is not, of course, a determining factor as to whether, in this case the British government, recognises another entity as the government of the state. It is, however, unlikely that the British government has ceased to recognise the Assad government as the lawful government of Syria, despite is view on its 'legitimacy' or its status as a 'regime', following the UK government's statement about the CSROF. It may at least need its tacit support in the policy of airstrikes against ISIL.[114] It must therefore be assumed that the so-called recognition of the CSROF is not of the same nature as the recognition of the NTC and that the difference in wording between the two statements is of significance.[115] Should lethal weapons be exported by the UK government to units of the Free Syrian Army, the legal relationship between the UK and the Assad government would, as discussed above, change.[116]

The consequences of any recognition by the UK of an organised armed group as 'the sole legitimate governing authority' of the state will mean that it becomes a legal entity and can literally step into the shoes of the former government and so, for instance, assets held by Libya in the UK will fall under the control of this new government.[117] This is clearly not the position, at least at the present time, in relation to the Syrian opposition movements. In addition, where the organised armed group is recognised as a legal entity (TNC) or is merely the sole legitimate representative of the people (CSROF) can be a risky policy, not because it is likely that in time it may be shown that the British government backed the wrong side,

111 C Warbrick note 100, 252. For a full analysis see M Jamnejad and M Wood, 'The Principle of Non-Intervention' (2009) 22 LJIL 345.

112 Compare, however, the legal status which a recognised armed opposition group will gain in relation to the recognising state. In the case of the UK, see *British Arab Commercial Bank v The National Transitional Council of the State of Libya* [2011] EWHC 2274 (Comm).

113 See http://www.telegraph.co.uk/news/worldnews/middleeast/syria/9312490/Syria-expels-British-ambassador.html.

114 That UK military aircraft conduct surveillance over Syria and some UK aircrew are embedded in the air forces of other states conducting airstrikes over Syria, is some evidence to suggest at least some cooperation by that state. See discussion in Chapter 4.

115 S Talmon, 'Recognition of Opposition Groups as the Legitimate Representatives of a People' [2013] 12 CJIL 219, [9]; H Woolaver, note 102, 181–182.

116 Non-lethal equipment has been supplied to the Supreme Military Council of the Free Syrian Army, see HL Debs 27 November 2014, vol 757, col 201W.

117 *British Arab Commercial Bank v The National Transitional Council of the State of Libya* [2011] EWHC 2274 (Comm), in which Blair J held that a certificate from the Foreign Secretary to this effect was conclusive, [25]. See P Capps, 'British Policy on the Recognition of Governments' (Case Comment) [2014] PL 229.

but because its reputation may suffer to some extent if the members of this group commit war crimes. There has been evidence of this both in Libya, when Colonel Gaddafi was killed very shortly after his capture, and in Syria where alleged serious war crimes have been reported.[118] Ascertaining the actual facts from any war zone is difficult, not least when it comes to the attribution of any of the alleged war crimes to members of a group recognised, for one purpose or another, by the UK (or any other government). Unlike a state that is able to control those acting on its behalf, one that supports an armed opposition group will, at best, be able only to persuade those fighters to comply with IHL, without possessing any control over them to enforce its principled stand.[119]

A great deal is spoken about human rights, particularly of innocent civilians in armed conflicts, but the plain fact is that if the British government, or indeed any other government, recognises an organised armed group it is giving the message that the members of that group must secure the human rights of civilians, along with upholding IHL.[120] Whether this obligation on the armed group derives from human rights norms or not is, in practical terms, interesting but largely irrelevant, since it is beyond doubt that they owe obligations under IHL[121] to those not taking an active part in the conflict that would, in the circumstances of Libya and Syria, be similar to the rights of personal protection to be found in a human rights treaty. Whilst rebel groups cannot be parties to treaties, they can agree to abide by certain principles of IHL, such as the non-use of anti-personnel land mines, the protection of children in armed conflict and protection against sexual violence. Geneva Call is very active in this area and it would appear to be in the interests of the UK, if it is considering recognising a rebel group, to insist that such a group signs appropriate deeds of commitment to abide by these principles.[122]

118 See 'War crimes by Syrian rebels must be condemned too', *The Guardian*, 10 August 2012 http://www.theguardian.com/commentisfree/2012/aug/10/human-rights-abuses-syrias-regime-condemned; Amnesty International, 'Syria: Armed groups carries out summary killing of security forces in Idlib' (1 November 2012, http://www.amnesty.org/en/for-media/press-releases/syria-armed-group-carries-out-summary-killing-security-forces-idlib-2012–11; *Geneva II Conference on Syrian Conflict: Amnesty International's Calls*', 16 January 2014, [5 and 6] refer to the Syrian government and armed opposition groups.' Available at http://www.amnesty.org/en/library/asset/MDE24/003/2014/en/4d9a4382-a3ee-4011-ad1a-08c898b341b1/mde240032014en.html.

119 This principle applies also to the activities of allies. See for example, the concern expressed over some activities of the Iraqi Security Forces engaged in fighting ISIL in Iraq, ministerial statement, HC Debs 4 November 2014, vol 587, col 223W. The UK is currently involved with Iraq in this conflict but its combat forces are limited to delivering air attacks.

120 See, for example, the Foreign Secretary, HC Debs 20 November 2012, vol 553, col 445, 20 November 2012.

121 For example, under Common Art 3 of the Geneva Conventions 1949 and supported by the Rome Statute of the ICC, 1998, Art 8(2)(c); Additional Protocol II, 1977.

122 The Geneva Call Deeds of Commitment can be found at http://www.genevacall.org. It reports that the 'Hazzm Movement, a major brigade of the Free Syrian Army signed the deeds of commitment' in October 2014 relating to anti-personnel mines and sexual violence; the Syrian Kurdish armed forces also signed deeds of commitment in June 2014.

xi End of conflicts

At a time when state practice involved a declaration of war it seemed logical to make some form of official statement that the war had come to an end. The UK followed this practice, usually in the form of a declaration or a ministerial statement in Parliament, although it could be by way of a treaty,[123] which may not have matched the date of the cessation of active hostilities.[124] The UN Security Council determined the date of the end of a period of occupation in Iraq[125] and that a Chapter VII action had been concluded, in the case of Libya in 2011.[126] The armed conflicts, as far as the UK is concerned, in Iraq and Afghanistan, came to an end following agreement with the respective governments and the withdrawal of most of the UK armed forces from those states.[127]

Should none of these formal acts take place the International Law Association concluded in 2010, that 'it is rare for parties to end an armed conflict today with a formal agreement. More normal is the cessation of hostilities for a long enough period of time so that parties and the international community recognise that the conflict is at an end.'[128]

The end of an armed conflict by one of the means discussed above does not automatically end the applicability of IHL and international human rights law to the direct consequences of the conflict. Any prisoners of war remain protected by Geneva Convention III, 1949, until their final release and repatriation[129] and the same is true for civilian detainees protected by Geneva Convention IV, 1949,[130] along with those civilians detained during a non-international armed conflict.[131]

123 See, for example, the Japanese Treaty of Peace Act 1951, which gave effect to the Treaty of Peace with Japan 1951.

124 In *Oppenheimer v Cattermole (Inspector of Taxes)* [1976] AC 249, an issue arose as to the meaning of the phrase 'during war time.' Lord Cross stated that 'it appears to have been assumed . . . that the relevant date would be not May 8, 1945, but July, 9 1951 when the government of this country declared that a state of war had ended [with Germany]', 275–6. Compare the Gulf war 1991 which was ended by a 'suspension of military operations at 0500 GMT today', ministerial statement, HL Debs 28 February 1991, vol 526, col 1105.

125 UN Security Council Resolution 1546 (2004), [2].

126 UN Security Council Resolution 2016 (2011), operative [6].

127 In Iraq this occurred by the December 2008 and in Afghanistan, the end of December 2014. These agreements became a practical reality since, at their date, the UK had been involved in the conflict at the invitation of the governments concerned.

128 International Law Association, Hague Conference (2010), *Use of Force*, 31. It is difficult to accept the rarity of their conclusion, unless the UK provides an exception to the normal practice. See also C Bell, *Peace Agreements and Human Rights* (OUP, 2000), 16, referring to resolution of conflicts.

129 Article 5. For an application of this see the ceasefire declaration made in 1991 at the conclusion of the Gulf war, when some 12 RAF aircrew remained in the custody of Iraq, HL Debs 28 February, vol 526, col 1105.

130 Additional Protocol I, 1977, Art 3(b).

131 In relation to Common Art 3 of the Geneva Conventions 1949 see Additional Protocol I, 1977, Art 3(b) and for Additional Protocol II, 1977, Art 2(2).

They could also look to international human rights law as a source to challenge their continued detention, standard of treatment or the standards of any trials.[132] For a state, such as the UK, to implore a former opposition group that has become the government of the state and that it recognises, to comply with human rights generally in its dealing with those who were detained during the conflict, may have less impact than if it were to draw attention to the specific human rights obligations it owes to this group.[133] Any lack of certainty as to the appropriate legal regime that applies to any remaining detainees after the end of an armed conflict does give rise to the possibility of their ill-treatment.[134]

At the end of an armed conflict there may also be a need to clear any mines laid, or unexploded ordnance, from the areas where fighting was taking place and in which some, or all, parties to the armed conflict will have obligations under international law to make the area safe for innocent civilians.[135] Although there may be no legal obligation to do so, some states, including the UK, are likely to give financial aid to assist in the medical treatment of those civilians who were affected by the fighting.[136]

The potential problem of accountability where an amnesty[137] is granted to individuals at the end of an armed conflict has not arisen as an issue for the UK during Britain's wars from 2000. It cannot, of course, interfere with the legal system in Iraq or Afghanistan and, if those states offer an amnesty to convicted fighters, the UK has to accept it.[138] The position would be no different if individuals, granted a pardon by Iraq or Afghanistan, had been convicted of having attacked British soldiers. Legal accountability of individuals, particularly those

132 It will also be important to determine which treaty, if any, concerned with human rights, is applicable to the circumstances of the particular detainees.

133 See, for example, ministerial statement, HC Debs 17 January 2012, vol 538, col 609, relating to the aftermath of the armed conflict in Libya.

134 The issue of uncertainty as to the legal basis applicable to detainees is discussed in Chapter 9.

135 Ottawa Convention on the Prohibition of the Use, Stockpiling, Production and Transfer of Anti-Personnel Mines and on their Destruction, 1997, Arts 5 and 6: Conventional Weapons Convention 1980, Protocol V dealing with Explosive Remnants of War (2003), Art 3; Convention on Cluster Munitions 2008, Arts 4 and 5. Afghanistan, Iraq and the UK are parties all these treaties except Protocol V, the Explosive Remnants of War, to which only Iraq is a party.

136 See, for example, the donation made by the British government to the ICRC to provide medical treatment for those civilians injured by the fighting around Benghazi, discussed in Chapter 6.

137 This may take various forms and may be tacit, such as an unwillingness to prosecute where the evidence is sufficient to do so, or where a minor charge is brought which does not reflect the gravity of the facts. Where this occurs the ICC retains jurisdiction over the crime if the state concerned is a party to the Rome Statute 1998 of the Court. It may also take the form of immunity from prosecution under national law.

138 In referring to nine Iraqi witnesses at the al-Sweady Inquiry, 2014, a ministerial statement reported that 'all nine were committed in 2004 for trial in Iraq. Two were acquitted due to lack of evidence, while those convicted were subsequently pardoned under a general amnesty', HC Debs 14 January 2015, vol 590, Written Question 220126.

who have directed policy at the highest levels, shines through where they are placed on trial. Recent examples of this include the trial of Saddam Hussein, a former head of state before the Iraqi High Tribunal[139] and of Saif Al-Islam Gaddafi, who has been indicted by the ICC, but not yet surrendered to the Court by Libya.[140]

139 Discussed in Chapter 6.

140 *Prosecutor v Saif Al-Islam Gaddafi*, ICC-01/11–01/11, Pre-Trial Chamber, 10 December 2014. The ICC concluded that Libya had failed to comply with the request of the ICC to surrender Mr Gaddafi. Libya's response, 20 August 2015, indicates that the death sentence passed on him will not be carried out since, under Libyan law, Mr Gaddafi's presence in custody in Zintan is not to be equated with his presence before the Court of Assize in Triploi, which sentenced him to death and, in consequence, he has a right to a new trial once he comes into the custody of the Libyan Government. Although Libya is not a party to the Rome Statute of the ICC, the situation in Libya had been referred to the ICC by the UN Security Council in Resolution 1970 (2011), [4]. The ICC also issued an arrest warrant against Colonel Gaddafi but proceedings were discontinued on 22 November 2011, following his death.

3 The armed forces and government ministers

The Secretary of State for Defence expressed his view that 'our armed forces are . . . licensed to use lethal force in the protection of the state, but they also have to operate within the law, both domestic and international. They have also to conform to the highest ethical standards . . . because by operating according to those ethical standards . . . their use of lethal force gains the acceptance of the British public'.[1]

i The constitutional background to the British armed forces

The early forms of what we recognise today as the armed forces began in the seventeenth and eighteenth centuries. Following the Bill of Rights in 1688 it became unlawful to raise or keep a standing army in time of peace without the consent of Parliament.[2] The Bill of Rights reflected the predominance of Parliament, rather than the crown, on raising and maintaining the army. The effect has been that the governing legislation of the army had been renewed each year by Parliament until 1955, when it was put on a five-yearly statutory renewal cycle. By 2006, the logical position of treating all of the armed forces together in a single statute was realised, which brought to an end the need for separate statutes for the Royal Navy and the Royal Air Force.[3] What this unique constitutional arrangement has achieved is clear parliamentary control over the armed forces, which, instead of being a permanent state institution like the National Health Service, would cease to exist unless Parliament passed renewal legislation every five years.[4] It may be thought that this process shows some lack of enthusiasm for the armed forces in the sense that they are trusted for periods of only five years at

1 HC Debs 8 September 2011, vol 532, col 579. Compare, however, the apology made by the Prime Minister following the Saville Inquiry Report on Bloody Sunday, HC Debs 15 June 2010, vol 511, col 740: *Bici v Ministry of Defence* [2004] EWHC 786, [113], Elias J, 'the Queen's uniform is not a licence to commit wrongdoing'.

2 Bill of Rights 1688, 1 Wm & Mar, Sess 2.

3 The Armed Forces Act 2006.

4 In addition, a statutory instrument is required each year for a maximum period of five years, to renew the Armed Forces Act for a maximum period of five years.

a time. In reality this is not, of course, the case, since renewal in some form has occurred since 1689. The procedure does have one very distinct advantage compared with other government departments or other public bodies. The armed forces are guaranteed a legislative slot on this regular basis to bring into law any changes considered necessary and it has become parliamentary practice to establish a House of Commons select committee to consider the Bill every five years.

These constitutional arrangements suggest that civilian control, through government and Parliament, over the armed forces is well established and that any form of intervention by them, which may occur in other countries, is extremely unlikely in Britain.[5] It did actually occur, in Ireland when that country was part of the UK. In December 1920 a proclamation of martial law was issued by the commander-in-chief in Ireland.[6] Specific offences were created by the proclamation and civilians could be, and were, tried by military court, found guilty and sentenced to death by firing squad. Applications for what we now know of as judicial review were made on behalf of those found guilty by court-martial, but the courts generally refused to intervene on the ground that during a period of martial law the civilian institutions were unable to operate and that the matter was entirely within the hands of the general officer commanding in Ireland. In the 'troubles' in Northern Ireland, which broke out in 1969, the army was used extensively over a long period of time to maintain order on the streets of Londonderry (Derry) and Belfast but soldiers remained liable to the law applicable in Northern Ireland, which was virtually identical with that applying in England and Wales. Indeed, a number of soldiers were tried for murder or manslaughter in the criminal courts in Belfast in respect of their actions whilst on duty and the Ministry of Defence was successfully sued in the High Court of Northern Ireland on a number of occasions and was ordered to pay damages to those affected by the acts of individual soldiers.[7] This is a far cry from the effect of the imposition of martial law, which had occurred in the south of Ireland, only 50 years previously. There was a possibility, however, that it could have been declared in Iraq, following the period of occupation and during the time when British armed forces were serving there at the request of the Iraqi interim government. If that government had the constitutional power to impose martial law, which the British government did not have, British troops could have found themselves conducting military operations within that framework. The methods employed in Ireland in the 1920s would hardly be appropriate for the legal environment applicable to Iraq from 2004 onwards. It was, no doubt, for this reason that a

5 S E Finer, *The Man on Horseback: The Role of the Military in Politics* (Penguin Books, 1962), 25–6, 131; letter to *The Times*, 10 November 2015 by Lord Hutton, 32.

6 *Re Clifford and O'Sullivan* [1921] 2 AC 570, 581; *Tilonko v Natal* 1907 AC 93, 94–5; *Ex parte Marais* [1902] AC 109.

7 See, for example, *R v Foxford* [1974] NI 181; *Attorney-General for Northern Ireland's Reference (No 1 of 1975)* [1977] AC 105; *R v Clegg* [1995] 1 AC 482; *Kelly and others v Ministry of Defence* [1989] NI 341; *Magill v Ministry of Defence* [1987] NI 194; *Lynch v Ministry of Defence* [1983] NI 216; *Farrell v Secretary of State for Defence* [1980] 1 All ER 166.

British minister confirmed that, in the event of a declaration of martial law by the Iraqi government, UK armed forces undertaking 'law enforcement activity in support of such a declaration . . . would do so under the UK's extant Rules of Engagement at the time'.[8]

An issue that does arise from the military operations carried out by UK armed forces, particularly since 2003, is whether the commonly expressed view, that the armed forces do as the government directs them, is an accurate statement of the current constitutional arrangements. It could never be literally true since operational decisions could only be made by the armed forces themselves, but it would be very strange if the Prime Minister did not seek the advice of the chief of the defence staff as to whether his or her proposed military option could be achieved or not. It would be difficult for any Prime Minister to go ahead, or to continue, in the teeth of the advice from the chief of the defence staff. The advice that the chiefs,[9] through the chief of the defence staff, give will, to a certain extent, depend upon how they see the constitutional relationship between themselves and the government. They may take the view that, like civil servants, they should try to enable the government to carry through its chosen policy or, alternatively, they may see themselves as a check and balance to it in relation to its military strategy. There is, however, a fine line between the two and it may be that the 'Chiefs will always feel pressured not to challenge political orders to go to war too vigorously, either through loyalty to the democratic process or from institutional conformity.'[10] If Major General Elliott is correct in his view, this 'loyalty to the democratic process' is likely to have become a more significant factor with the advent in 2003 of the substantive vote in the House of Commons on proposed military action.

8 HL Debs 7 September 2004, vol 664, col WA115. Rules of engagement are discussed generally in Chapter 8.

9 The chiefs of the three services do not advise directly the Secretary of State, Government Response, HC 1126, [2], (2015) to Defence Committee, 7th Report, session 2014–15, *The Situation in Iraq and Syria and the Response to Al-Dawla al-Islamiya fi al-Iraq al-Sham (DAESH)*, HC 690, 2015, although see Defence Committee 11th Report of 2014–15, *Decision-Making in Defence Policy*, HC 682, General Lord Richards, [Q 442] and its recommendation at [123]. The 'isolation of the chiefs' is discussed by Major General C Elliott in the Defence Committee 11th Report of 2014–15, *Decision-Making in Defence Policy*, HC 682, [Q 283]. There are two, perhaps, surprising features about the chiefs of the individual services (and the chief of the defence staff). First, they possess, individually, a right to approach the Prime Minister directly, see HC Debs 31 July 1963, vol 682, col 473 (Secretary of State for Defence); Lord Levene, *Defence Reform Report: Independent Report into the Structure and Management of the Ministry of Defence*, June 2011, [75], or the Secretary of State, Defence Committee, 11th Report of 2014–15, *Decision-Making in Defence Policy*, HC 682, [74]. Secondly, the chief of the defence staff 'does not command the Chiefs', Defence Committee, 11th Report of 2014–15, *Decision-Making in Defence Policy*, HC 682, [79]; General Lord Richards, a former chief of the defence staff, *ibid*, oral evidence, [Q 442].

10 C Elliott, *High Command: British Military Leadership in the Iraq and Afghanistan Wars* (Hurst & Co, London, 2015), [230]. See also his comments concerning the actual conduct of military action, in the Defence Committee 11th Report of 2014–15, *Decision-Making in Defence Policy*, HC 682, [Q 285]; Sir Sherard Cowper-Coles, *ibid*, [Qs 8, 24]; General Lord Richards, *ibid*, [Q 445].

Unlike many other aspects of government, the Prime Minister and relevant ministers have no realistic chance of obtaining advice from anyone else on the feasibility of conducting a particular military operation by British armed forces. It is therefore essential that the chief of the defence staff is able to give realistic advice at all stages before, or during, a military campaign and that the Prime Minister and other ministers understand[11] the basis upon which the most senior commanders advise them, and their respective roles.[12] If ministers (and their civilian advisers) are unable, in practice, to get to grips with 'armed forces speak' they will be unable effectively to challenge the advice they are being given. The result could be that the rhetoric of ministerial accountability to Parliament for the operation of the armed forces will not be matched by the reality and its effects would be likely to range from ministerial strategic decisions on whether military action should be proposed to Parliament, to the conduct of military operations, including rules of engagement, targeting policy and ministerial statements to Parliament.[13]

To some extent, the establishment of the National Security Council[14] in 2010, does provide a further opportunity for wider discussion of military advice to the government and the coordination of all other aspects of a particular operation conducted abroad. The first major armed conflict with which it was concerned was the campaign in Libya in 2011 where it was considered 'to have worked well in respect of the situation in Libya, particularly in coordinating the response of Governments Departments. This was important as the mission in Libya had many component parts, not just the military operation.'[15] A significant feature

11 'There were also cases where . . . the papers presented to Ministers were almost incomprehensible to a civilian without knowledge of military acronyms', Sir Sherard Cowper-Coles, *Decision-Making in Defence Policy*, HC 682, [Q 8].

12 See Chapter 1 for further discussion of the accountability of service chiefs and ministers respectively, as to the decision in 2006 to take on responsibilities in Helmand Province of Afghanistan when British troops were already engaged in Iraq, and the control exercised by ministers over the rules of engagement and targeting policy.

13 'Ministers themselves did not appear able to challenge military advice', Defence Committee 11th Report of 2014–15, *Decision-Making in Defence Policy*, HC 682, [62]. Compare the statement of the former chief of the defence staff, Lord Stirrup, that 'they [ministers] usually wound up accepting the military advice they were given. They rarely failed to question it, and rightly so', House of Commons Defence Select Committee, *Operations in Afghanistan*, 4th Report, session 2010–12, HC 554-I, 17 July 2011, Q.657.

14 The permanent members of the Council are set out in HL Debs 14 October 2014, vol 756, col 37W. It is a sub-committee of the Cabinet, HC Debs 28 April 2014, vol 579, col 473W; Baroness Neville-Jones, Defence Committee 11th Report of 2014–15, *Decision-Making in Defence Policy*, HC 682, [Q 359–40]. The 11th Report concludes that it wished to 'seek clarification of the relationship between the National Security Council and the Cabinet', [82].

15 House of Commons Defence Select Committee, Ninth Report, session 2010–12, *Operations in Libya*, HC 950–1, [95]. For further discussion of the role of the National Security Council see Q. 208. For its role in the Afghan conflict see the government's response to the Defence Committee's 4th Report of session 2010–12, HC 1525 (2011), response to recommendation 8.

of its membership is that there is no place for the Attorney General, or other law officer, or, indeed, a senior lawyer from the Foreign and Commonwealth Office, or the Ministry of Defence, to guide it through the international and national law implications of any of its decisions.[16] The Attorney General was, however, invited to attend a meeting to discuss the legal basis of any air strike in Syria against identified ISIL fighters who were believed to be planning attacks in the UK.[17]

ii The chief of the defence staff

At any particular time, the chief of the defence staff may originally have come through the Royal Navy, the Army or the Royal Air Force routes. During Britain's wars from 2000, all three services provided, at one time or another, one of their most senior officers to take on this role. The means of formal consultation between the chief of the defence staff and the service chiefs is by way of the chiefs of staff committee[18] and, since 2011, also the armed forces committee.[19]

The chief of the defence staff will play a central role leading up to, and during, any armed conflict. In January 2003 the chief of the defence staff, Admiral Boyce, requested from the Prime Minister 'an assurance of the legal basis of the conflict' in the form of a 'one liner' from the government Law Officer.[20] This was sent to him, through the legal adviser at the Ministry of Defence, on 14 March.[21] He would have received it even before the Attorney General's written statement in the House of Lords about the legality of military action on 17 March and also before

16 The membership is set out in the Defence Committee 11th Report of 2014–15, *Decision-Making in Defence Policy*, HC 682, [81].

17 HC Debs 7 September 2015, vol 599, col 29. The attack on 21 August 2015 by a remotely piloted aircraft is discussed in Chapter 4.

18 The regularity of the meetings of the chiefs of staff was described by Lord Stirrup, a former chief of the defence staff, at the Defence Select Committee, see 4th Report of session 2010–12, *Operations in Afghanistan*, HC 554, Q 657.

19 For the armed forces committee see C Elliott, *High Command: British Military Leadership in the Iraq and Afghanistan Wars* (C Hurst and Co, 2015), 224 and his oral evidence to the Defence Committee, 11th Report of 2014–15, *Decision-Making in Defence Policy*, HC 682, [283]; General Lord Richards, [Q 442], particularly on the links with the chiefs.

20 Iraq Inquiry, Evidence, 3 December 2011, Admiral Lord Boyce who commented that this assurance 'formed the first line of my Operational Directive which I signed on 20 March', 88. In his Statement to the Inquiry on 27 January 2011 Lord Boyce observed that, 'if [legal authorisation] had not been forthcoming at the end of the day, UK forces would not have engaged in hostilities'. There was no precedent for such a request, Lord Goldsmith, evidence to the Iraq Inquiry, 27 January 2010, 185, although compare evidence of General Sir Mike Jackson, 28 July 2010, 39. The request came in the form of a 'yes or no decision' Sir Roger Lyne, Iraq Inquiry, 29 January 2010 in a question to Mr Blair, and the evidence of Lord Goldsmith, 27 January 2010, 172, 184. The background is discussed by General Jackson, above, at 35–39 and for its link with the Attorney General's advice to the Prime Minister of 7 March 2003, see *R (Gentle and another) v Prime Minister and others* [2008] UKHL 20, [50].

21 Letter, Brummell to Hemming, Iraq, Position of the CDS, 14 March 2003, Iraq Inquiry declassified document.

MPs would have been able to read it. It shows that the chief, on behalf of the armed forces, may feel the need to be assured by the Attorney General, where any doubt lingers, that the proposed military action is actually consistent with national and international law. The significance of this lies in the fact that the chain of command is said to flow from the Prime Minister to the Secretary of State for Defence to the chief of the defence staff.[22] There are no intermediate breaks in it to feed in the advice of the Attorney General. Indeed, it is by no means certain that a statement from the Attorney General is 'crucial' as a means by which the chief of the defence staff receives his 'legal and constitutional authority'.[23] It appeared to be, in the case of the Iraq war in 2003, as a result of 'the speculation in the press about the legality or otherwise' of the proposed military action.[24] Where, however, the legal position is much more clear, as it was in Libya in 2011, based as it was on UN Security Council Resolution 1973, it is difficult to imagine the chief of the defence staff having to obtain, as a matter of constitutional rectitude, a certificate from the Attorney General indicating the lawfulness of the use of force. In that case there would have been little or no time to do so since the resolution was passed on 17 March 2011, with the military action taking place two days later, before the vote in the House of Commons and before a summary of the Attorney General's advice was published, as it was on 21 March 2011.

Indeed, it could be argued that Admiral Boyce did not actually need the assurance he personally sought since the Attorney General had declared the legality of the proposed action in a written statement in the House of Lords on 17 March 2003, the day before the vote in the House of Commons and before any military action actually took place. Admiral Boyce signed his operational directive, containing a statement of the legality of the action, two days after the vote in the House of Commons.[25] From a practical point of view, however, the earlier receipt of the assurance from the Attorney General must have made the military planning for the proposed armed conflict a little easier.

Some may see Admiral Boyce's request for assurance from the Attorney General as an unwelcome involvement of the armed forces in the affairs of government, but his action could be better seen as a healthy development if it encourages the

22 General Sir Mike Jackson, House of Commons Defence Select Committee, Fourth Report, *Operations in Afghanistan*, 4th Report, session 2010–12, HC 554-I, 17 July 2011, Q.505. Compare General Sir Robert Fry, who stated that it went from the Prime Minister to the chief of the defence staff, to the chief of joint operations, to deployed forces in the field, Defence Select Committee 11th Report of 2014–15, *Decision-Making in Defence Policy*, HC 682, [Q 63]; General Lord Richards spoke of it running from the Prime Minister to the chief of the defence staff to the operational commander, Defence Committee 11th Report of 2014–15, *Decision-Making in Defence Policy*, HC 682, [Q 437].

23 Iraq Inquiry, Evidence, 3 December 2011, Sir Kevin Tebbitt, 89.

24 Iraq Inquiry, Evidence, 3 December 2011, Admiral Lord Boyce, 88. He stressed that the need for such an assurance was also necessary for the members of the armed forces and their families so that they would know that 'what they were doing was legal'. See also General David Richards, *Taking Command* (Headline Publishing, 2014), 339, concerning the possible targeting of Colonel Gaddafi.

25 Lord Boyce. *ibid*. For discussion of the vote in the House of Commons see Chapter 4.

chief of the defence staff to satisfy himself, or herself, on behalf of all members of the armed forces who are likely to be involved, that the proposed military action is consistent with national and international law.[26] In reality, the Attorney General's opinion will almost certainly show that the proposed military action is lawful, otherwise a future Prime Minister would be unlikely to wish to pursue such an option. It does mean, however, that on an appropriate occasion, the chief of the defence staff can play an important constitutional role by seeking assurance from the Attorney General rather than merely from the political decision-makers or the Ministry of Defence.

iii Members of the armed forces

It is a traditional practice of UK government ministers, in particular, to pay wholesome tribute to the members of the armed forces prior to,[27] during[28] and after, an armed conflict in recognition of the risks to them that attend military operations. The nature of service in the UK armed forces is relevant to the armed conflicts in which they have been called upon to fight since, although they will be all volunteers, there must be a firm legal background to all their actions.

One of the overarching themes, particularly before the various Armed Forces Bill select committees, has been that of trying to ensure that the conditions of service of members of the armed forces are made as similar as possible to those found in civilian life.[29] They cannot be exactly the same, largely as a result of the various roles that Parliament expects the armed forces to carry out during the armed conflicts that it votes to support. These range from war fighting, engaging in other forms of combat operations overseas, training of foreign armed forces, maintaining no-fly zones and all related activities.

The fact that the UK permits recruitment of soldiers from the age of 16 has caused some to campaign for the raising of this age to 18, but this is a matter that could easily be dealt with in a future Armed Forces Bill, should the government and Parliament wish to do so. In 2011 there were 2,370 members of the army under the age of 18.[30] What has been of international concern, particularly in conflicts in Africa, is the use during combat operations of 'child soldiers'. A number of defendants have recently been tried by the International Criminal Court for recruiting and using children under the age of 15 during civil wars. Those under 18 years of age have also been the subject of a treaty, the Optional Protocol to

26 For the link between the lawfulness of the military action itself and the consequences to the serviceman or woman see *R (Gentle) v Prime Minister* [2008] UKHL 20, Baroness Hale, [50], discussed in Chapter 8.

27 See for, example, the government and any opposition motions before the House of Commons to take part in an armed conflict, discussed in Chapter 4.

28 The practice of reading out on the floor of the House of Commons the names of those killed and expressing sympathy with their families is an illustration of this.

29 This can also be seen as indicative of strong civilian control over the armed forces.

30 Ministry of Defence, Annual Manning Report, Analysis by Rank and Age, 1 April 2011, table 2.

the Convention on the Rights of the Child, 2000.[31] This is directed towards the prevention of those under the age of 18 taking a direct part in hostilities, although they may be recruited into the armed forces. The UK is a party to this treaty and it has issued a declaration that it will take all feasible steps to prevent those members of its armed forces under the age of 18 from taking a direct part in hostilities but that there may be some circumstances where 'there is a genuine military need to deploy their unit . . . to an area where hostilities are taking place'.[32]

A significant difference between working in the armed forces and in any other public body is that the key role of the former is to engage in combat, often with very little notice, so many parts of each of the services must be trained and be kept at a sufficient degree of readiness for action. Apart from training for their various roles, military discipline must be maintained and, to some extent, the needs of the individual must give way to those of the unit to which he or she belongs. As a result, employment rights often look quite different from those employed in other parts of the public service. A soldier is not employed on a contract of service and he or she cannot bring a case to an employment tribunal, except for a claim based on racial or sex discrimination. Unlike a civilian, a member of the armed forces cannot resign at any time and may therefore commit a service offence if he or she refuses to take part in an armed conflict.[33]

In 2006 a review chaired by Nicholas Blake QC into the circumstances surrounding the deaths of four soldiers at the Princess Royal Barracks Deepcut recommended the appointment of a commissioner of military complaints.[34] In the Armed Forces Act of the same year the post of service complaints commissioner was created but suggestions were made recently, including from the Service Complaints Commissioner herself, that the government should go further and establish an armed forces ombudsman, as there is in a number of other European countries. Initially the government resisted this suggestion, arguing that the current system was the most appropriate way of 'maintaining the primacy of the chain of command, which so critically underpins morale and discipline, particularly in conflict'.[35] In a change of mind over this issue in March 2014, the Secretary of State announced that, in due course, an amendment would be made to the 2006 Act to introduce a Service

31 Optional Protocol to the Convention on the Rights of the Child on the Involvement of Children in Armed Conflict, 2000, A/RES/54/263.

32 See the full declaration made by the UK on signature and confirmed on ratification of the Optional Protocol. For the inadvertent deployment of five members of the UK armed forces into combat zones see FOI Release, Ministry of Defence, 8 December 2014.

33 An issue discussed in Chapter 8.

34 https://www.gov.uk/government/uploads/system/uploads/attachment_data/file/228930/0795.pdf recommendation 26. It was announced on 25 March 2014 that the parents of one of the four soldiers who died at Deepcut barracks could challenge in the High Court the decision of the coroner in that case.

35 House of Commons Defence Select Committee, 'The Work of the Service Complaints Commissioner for the Armed Forces: Government's and Commissioner's Responses to the Committee's Eighth Report of Session 2012–13. http://www.publications.parliament.uk/pa/cm201314/cmselect/cmdfence/505/50504.htm.

Complaints Ombudsman who would be able to make recommendations directly to the Defence Council, and that any decisions made by that body would have the effect of 'maintaining the authority of the chain of command'.[36] Reform came in the Armed Forces (Service Complaints and Financial Assistance) Act 2015, where the office of the Service Complaints Commissioner was abolished and replaced by a Service Complaints Ombudsman.[37]

Only time will tell how far the new system, when it comes into effect, will go in meeting the demands of those who argue that the services have a poor record in handling complaints, particularly in relation to bullying and harassment. This is a significant issue since some 10% of the army believed they had been the subject of discrimination, harassment or bullying in a service environment between 2009 and 2010, although only 1% believed they had been discriminated against on grounds of race, colour or ethnic origin.[38]

The effect of their unique employment arrangements is that, although soldiers sign up for a fixed period of time and commissioned officers can expect to serve either for a pre-determined time or until retirement, all members of the armed forces can be dismissed at any time or be made redundant without the normal civilian procedures being applicable.[39] Soldiers who have fought in Afghanistan could find when they return home they are told that they will have to find other employment, although there are some short-term exemptions.[40] It is, perhaps, ironic that those who have borne the brunt of the actual fighting, mostly infantry soldiers, will often find the greatest difficulty in transferring to civilian employment the skills they have acquired. The practical consequences of the armed forces covenant may be more than of passing interest to them.

iv The armed forces covenant

With a large number of soldiers killed in action, let alone those seriously wounded, a high price has been paid for the various combat roles undertaken

36 HC Debs 13 March 2014, vol 577, col 35WS.

37 The Act inserted s 365B into the Armed Forces Act 2006.

38 Armed Forces Continuous Attitude Surveys, 2010 Report, table B4.5. This question was added to the Surveys for the first time for the 2010 Report. https://www.gov.uk/government/uploads/system/uploads/attachment_data/file/280711/2010.pdf. The comparable responses dropped to 8% in each of the Reports in 2011 and 2012, https://www.gov.uk/government/uploads/system/uploads/attachment_data/file/280180/2012.pdf, table B4.3. For discrimination on race, colour or ethnic origin see 2010 Report, table B4.6. The figure for discrimination based on sexual orientation was zero, table B4.11.

39 *Re Tufnell* (1976) 3 ChD 164; *Quinn v Ministry of Defence* [1998] PIQR P387, 395–6. See generally, G Rubin, 'Military Law and the Service Engagement; Some Preliminary Conceptual Observations' HC Select Committee on the Armed Forces Bill 2000–2001, HC 154-II, 2001, App 7. They can bring a complaint in relation to sex discrimination to an employment tribunal only after a service complaint has been made, Equality Act 2010, s 121.

40 See 'Armed Forces Redundancies', Commons Library Standard Note SN 05951, 24 January 2014, p.8: http://www.parliament.uk/briefing-papers/SN05951/armed-forces-redundancies.

over the years since 2000. The government recognised this and, in 2011, introduced the armed forces covenant, which establishes a unique relationship between it and one group of those who work for it, the armed forces. The covenant sets out the main obligations of the government towards the armed forces. It includes, for instance, terms and conditions of service, health care, education, deployment and housing.[41] To the disappointment of some, the covenant is not a legally binding document, but legislation in 2011 does require ministers to provide statements to Parliament from time to time on various matters affecting the covenant.[42]

If it is not a legally binding document does it have any real significance, apart from being an aspirational statement? It could not be relied upon, for instance, to argue that, because of it, the Ministry of Defence is placed under an additional legal obligation to ensure that soldiers have the best training and equipment for the military operations on which they are engaged, including the means to avoid so-called 'blue on blue' or 'friendly-fire' incidents.[43] This should not, however, detract from the increasing practical significance of the covenant to assist veterans.[44]

v Command of the armed forces and the role of government ministers

The command of the armed forces is vested in the sovereign but it will actually be exercised by those acting on behalf of the Defence Council.[45] Although part of the chain of command,[46] neither the Prime Minister nor the Secretary of state for Defence can actually order individual members of the armed forces to do anything, although each may give general directions through the chief of the defence

41 The Covenant can be found at https://www.gov.uk/government/uploads/system/uploads/attachment_data/file/49470/the_armed_forces_covenant_today_and_tomorrow.pdf.

42 The Armed Forces Act 2011 adds s 343A to the Armed Forces Act 2006. The first annual report, published by the Secretary of State for Defence, is at https://www.gov.uk/government/uploads/system/uploads/attachment_data/file/36615/20121210_af_covenant_annual_report_updated.pdf.

43 See, for example, the issue concerning the Challenger tank incident in Iraq, *Smith v Ministry of Defence* [2013] UKSC 41, discussed in Chapter 7.

44 See, for example, *2010–2015 Government Policy: Armed Forces Covenant* (2015) https://www.gov.uk/government/publications/2010-to-2015-government-policy-armed-forces-covenant/2010-to-2015-government-policy-armed-forces-covenant.

45 See generally, House of Commons Defence Select Committee, 14th Report, session 2013–14, *Intervention: Why, When and How?* HC 952, 28 April 2014, [52]. The Defence Council was established by the Defence (Transfer of Functions) Act 1964, s 1. It 'met only twice in my six years in London', Lord Inge, a former chief of the defence staff, HL Debs 11 October 2006, vol 685, col 294. See also Queen's Regulations for the Army 1975 (Amendment No 26), J1.001–003.

46 For the meaning of this term see Defence Select Committee, 4th Report, session 2010–12, *Operations in Afghanistan*, HC 554, Q 621, Lord Stirrup, formerly chief of the defence staff, and discussion above, p 57.

staff, or the chiefs of staff of the individual services.[47] In Britain's wars from 2000 it has been common for ministers to set out, for example, any restrictions on the type of targets that may be attacked from the air, due to their concern about civilian deaths or destruction of civilian homes, which could be caused in the form of collateral damage when a military objective is hit.[48] General directions of this type are likely to find their way into the ROE, or into other standard operating procedures, and will reflect political choices made as to the nature and intensity of the conflict. There is certainly considerable merit in a constitutional arrangement that does not subordinate directly the head of the armed forces to a political body. An example of the opposite arrangement can be seen in *Prosecutor v Krajisnik*, where the ICTY accepted that 'General Mladic was directly subordinated to the Presidency . . . [which] would frequently discuss military-related issues and make decisions on those matters.'[49]

A feature of most of the wars since 2000 has been that they have taken place with allies, which has meant that co-operation with the armed forces of another state has become a necessity. Although, for instance, the US army may have had overall control of a particular operation with which British armed forces were participating, there was no question of US officers giving orders directly to British soldiers. This will be achieved normally through British officers being involved in planning operations which are under US control and British soldiers will end up taking their orders from their own officers within their normal chain of command. From time to time, however, individual members of the British armed forces were stationed with US forces from whom they would have had to take direct orders, simply because they were operating within a specific military unit. Take the example of an RAF officer seconded to a US air base from where he is assisting with US drone strikes in Iraq or Afghanistan. It is clear that as he will not be a member of the US armed forces, he will remain subject to English law and to the ROE applicable to the British armed forces, and not those applicable to US forces, where there is any difference between the two.[50]

The conduct of Britain's wars from 2000 has not been the product of one or more decisions of government ministers, but it has involved their frequent involvement often over a long period of time, not least in answering parliamentary written and oral questions from members of both Houses, giving evidence to select committees, responding to decisions relating to the armed conflicts given in the courts, and being prepared to answer questions from the media and the public generally. Ministers will also have been aware that the establishment of public inquiries of one sort or another are a common feature when a war has

47 Following the request by France for 'limited logistical support [to support operations in Mali] the PM agreed . . . and directed the Chief of Defence Staff to make aircraft available', HC Debs 14 January 2013, vol 556, col 621.

48 See Chapter 9.

49 IT-00–39T, Judgment, 27 September 2006, [194], [205].

50 See discussion of this issue in Chapter 8, and for the issue of embedding British service personnel within the armed forces of an ally, see Chapter 4.

ended, and when their actions may be judged in the cold light of forensic analysis, sometimes long after they have left office. Cabinet decisions result in the collective responsibility of those who made them, whether it is a decision to use military force or decisions concerned with how the armed conflict should be conducted. It was not only Saddam Hussein who was tried by the Iraqi High Criminal Court, but also those who made the decisions with him. The same pattern can be seen at the ICTY, where senior politicians, such as Krajisnik and Plavsic, were convicted of crimes against humanity through the decisions they made and the orders they gave. Indeed, Biljana Plavsic, who pleaded guilty to crimes against humanity, made a rather chilling statement which shows how individuals, even senior politicians, can get dragged into acts which in other circumstances would horrify them. She explained to the Tribunal, 'at the time, I easily convinced myself that this was a matter of survival and self-defence.'[51] She was sentenced in 2003 to 11 years' imprisonment.

Responsibility for collective decisions, whether made in the Cabinet or elsewhere, is not limited to the Prime Minister, although from a political point of view he or she may be seen as *the* person responsible. A Cabinet minister who cannot accept a decision made by the cabinet has no real choice other than to resign from the government. This was the position faced by a former foreign secretary, Robin Cook, who resigned on the eve of the debate in the House of Commons, on whether to support the government's decision (made by the Cabinet) to take military action in Iraq in 2003.[52] One other Cabinet minister, Clare Short, resigned nearly two months later[53] and at least one other minister also resigned from the government. After these events in 2003 no other Cabinet minister has resigned purely on the grounds of decisions to take military action or how any of the armed conflicts have been carried out. No Secretary of State for Defence resigned, for instance, after events came to light of the mistreatment of Iraqi civilians who had been detained by British forces.

vi Legal advice

The wars in Iraq and Afghanistan threw up a myriad of legal difficulties, many of which had not been encountered before. The UK had not been an occupying power since it had ratified the Geneva Conventions in 1957, nor had it been involved in an armed conflict overseas, where the European Convention on Human Rights was applicable to its own military activities, and certainly not since the Human Rights Act 1998 had come into force. Government ministers could look to the Attorney General, the Foreign and Commonwealth Office lawyers and lawyers in the Ministry of Defence for legal advice. In addition, each of the armed services had their own teams of uniformed lawyers. It is not surprising

51 IT-00-39 & 40/1, Case Information Sheet.
52 R Cook, *The Point of Departure* (Simon & Schuster, 2003).
53 See her oral evidence to the Iraq Inquiry, 2 February 2010.

that, given the novelty of many of the legal issues which were being brought forward, opinions amongst these different groups should differ from time to time.[54]

It is noticeable, however, that of the cases brought before the courts or the ECtHR from 2003, which related to one or more of Britain's wars, virtually all were decided against the government.[55] This track record certainly does not lead to the conclusion that government lawyers were poor at their jobs. In the vast majority of cases they will have instructed civilian lawyers, mostly QCs, to advise and to act as advocates in the higher courts and most of the legal issues were novel. It is a strong feature of the rule of law within a democracy that government actions or decisions, like the actions of private individuals, are subject to independent judicial scrutiny. During time of armed conflict it is particularly important that government lawyers are able to maintain their own independence, derived from their professional obligations, so as to provide, if necessary, legal advice to government ministers which they may not wish to hear.[56]

Whilst the importance of the idea that ministers and senior armed forces officers should act within the law during an armed conflict cannot be gainsaid, their understandable lack of knowledge of the legal principles involved may result in their failing to recognise an issue as one calling for legal advice, or their being unable fully to understand the strengths (or otherwise) of the legal advice given. There is much to be said for the provision of additional training on the legal principles involved in the specific type of armed conflict in which they are engaged, for ministers in the Ministry of Defence and for the most senior service officers.

vii Equipment

New helicopters and armoured personnel carriers are unlike other vehicles; there is often no ready market available for the government to buy them for immediate delivery. When a military campaign changes format, for example, from war fighting to occupation of territory or into a non-international armed conflict, experience shows that the threat to soldiers can also change. Afghanistan, in particular, has shown the threat posed by the improvised explosive device (IED) and the need for a sufficient number of helicopters to rescue those who have been injured by them, or to transport soldiers from one place to another, and the essential requirement to provide armoured personnel carriers (APCs) that could withstand their blast. At various times ministers appear to have been told that there were a sufficient number of helicopters and at other times that there were not.[57]

54 See for example, 'Straw reply to Wood', 29 January 2003, in Written Evidence, Iraq Inquiry.

55 As to the perceived legal difficulties involved see Defence Select Committee, 12th Report, session 2013–14, *UK Armed Forces Personnel and the Legal Framework of Future Operations*, HC 531, 2014, [19]–[29].

56 IHL requires 'military commanders at the appropriate level' to have 'legal advisers, when necessary, to advise on the [Geneva Conventions and Additional Protocol I]', Additional Protocol I, 1977, Art 82.

57 Defence Select Committee, 4th Report, session 2010–12, *Operations in Afghanistan*, HC 554, [41]. See also discussion in Chapter 7.

It soon became clear that the 'Snatch' Land Rover, so called because it had been used in Northern Ireland to provide a fast means for soldiers to get into a troubled area and arrest suspects, proved to be quite unsuited to the risks posed by IEDs. Too many soldiers were being killed when their vehicle ran over one. It would clearly take time to produce a suitably protected vehicle and the Mastiff was developed after the invasion of Iraq to achieve this.[58] Even then soldiers were still being killed in the Mastiff; three were killed in May 2013 in one incident alone.

The public can be quite unforgiving of government ministers when they see that members of the armed forces lose their lives because of faulty or inappropriate equipment, whether it arises from the lack of a sufficient number of flak jackets, helicopters or APCs which can withstand IEDs. Ministerial responses referring to the length of time it takes for equipment to arrive at the front line after the order has been placed with a manufacturer, let alone the costs involved, will cut no ice, particularly with headline writers of a number of newspapers. The issues are never as simple as this, since the risks posed to soldiers in combat are constantly changing and are likely to differ from one armed conflict to another. To argue that ministers and senior officers should always be able to foresee that particular forms of equipment would be necessary to meet known risks is to adopt a counsel of perfection.[59]

58 Evidence of the Chief of Defence Procurement, 2003–07, Iraq Inquiry, 26 July 2010, 31. See also the coroner's Prevention of Future Deaths Report of 28 May 2015 into the death of Sergeant Horton and others in a Ridgeback vehicle, discussed in Chapter 5.

59 See discussion in Chapter 7.

4 The role of Parliament in armed conflict decisions

The title of this chapter discloses a difficulty both in terminology and in the respective roles of the government and Parliament. An alternative would have been 'waging war: Parliament's role and responsibility',[1] and, whilst self-explanatory, it suffers from the use of the language of 'war' which, certainly in modern international law, has been replaced with that of armed conflict. Adoption of the phrase, 'armed conflict decisions'[2] appears to solve this problem only to run against a widespread general use of the term 'war'. This chapter will not attempt to decide between them but will address the issue of the respective roles of government, the House of Commons and the courts, based on the experience of the debates in the House of Commons to take military action against Iraq in 2003, Libya in 2011, Syria in 2013 and in support of Iraq in 2014, along with discussion of air strikes over the territory of Syria in 2015.

i The Iraq vote in 2003

On 17 March 2003 Robin Cook resigned as a Cabinet minister amidst a standing ovation in parts of the House of Commons.[3] He had argued that he could not support military action against the Saddam Hussein regime in Iraq without a further resolution of the UN Security Council, and it was clear that this was not going to be forthcoming, since the President of the French Republic, Jacques Chirac, had (it was stated) made plain his intention that France would veto any such resolution[4] and the options available to Mr Blair had become more limited.

1 This is the title of the House of Lords Select Committee on the Constitution 15th Report, session 2005–05, HL 236 (27 July 2006).

2 See Political and Constitutional Reform Select Committee, 12th Report, session 2013–14, *Parliament's Role in Conflict Decisions: a Way Forward*, HC 892, 27 March 2014.

3 A Campbell, *The Burden of Power: Countdown to Iraq* (Arrow Books, 2013), 508; N Robinson, *Live from Downing Street* (Bantam Books, 2012), 370. For the lead up to the resignation speech see R Cook, *The Point of Departure* (Simon & Schuster, 2003), 317–25. For an account of the role of politics in decisions to go to war see C Peevers, *The Politics of Justifying Force, The Suez Crisis, the Iraq War, and International Law* (OUP, 2013).

4 This was reported as occurring on '10 March 2003 . . . the French position was actually more nuanced', M Weller, *Iraq and the Use of Force* (OUP, 2010), 219, as to which see 13 March

At that time many thousands of British forces were in Kuwait waiting for an order to press on with the attack, or to remain there for a limited period, or to come home.

Mr Blair rose in the House of Commons to make his rallying call for a vote in support of military action. It was clear that there was considerable public opposition to war in Iraq, leading to a very large 'anti-war' march in London in February 2003, with many of the marchers carrying banners shouting out 'Not in My Name'. Although the Conservatives had indicated that they would vote with the government and the Liberal Democrats would vote against the motion, it was predicted that many Labour MPs would rebel against the government. In the circumstances there was not a real risk of the motion being lost, but if a large number of his own MPs rebelled, he would have to consider his role as leader of the party and thus his position as Prime Minister.[5]

What may seem surprising is that this vote could have been avoided altogether and Britain could have been led into taking military action without any vote in Parliament. The constitutional practice of the UK was that the decision to go to war (along with the signing of treaties and the deployment of British armed forces) were matters within the royal prerogative. This is a term that hardly falls from the lips of most people, but it does have resonance in English constitutional history and law.[6] In the long transition from an absolute monarchy to a parliamentary democracy, virtually all royal powers had been transferred to Parliament, save for those retained as part of the royal prerogative. The sovereign does not, of course, exercise them personally; they are exercised on his or her behalf by the government of the day.[7] Thus, when the Prime Minister declared in a radio broadcast on 3 September 1939 that 'this country was at war with Germany' he had not done so following a vote in the House of Commons. The House was informed earlier on the same day that HM Government had declared war on Germany.[8] During the course of the war there would be opportunities for debate on adjournment motions and the like. This practice was continued through to

2003 FCO telnote 53 'Iraq-Foreign Secretary's Conversation with French Foreign Minister', Iraq Inquiry, Declassified Documents; Mr Blair, HC Debs 18 March 2003, vol 401, col 767; *Plowden v Information Commissioner*, 1st Tier Tribunal (General Regulatory Chamber) 21 May 2012, which ordered a partial disclosure of information contained in a telephone conversation between Mr Blair and Mr Bush of 12 March 2003. For an interpretation of the French position about a possible veto see *ibid*, [67].

5 See C Mullins, *A View From the Foothills: The Diaries of Chris Mullins* (Profile Books, 2010), 237.

6 See generally, N White, 'International Law, the United Kingdom and Decisions to Deploy Troops Overseas' (2010) 59 ICLQ 814, 815–16; J Gray MP and M Lomas QC, *Who Takes Britain to War?* (History Press, 2014).

7 Compare A J P Taylor, *English History 1914–45* (Clarendon, 1965), 2, who refers to a privy council meeting with King George V at 10.30 pm on 4 August 1914, which 'sanctioned a proclamation of war'. In fact, a declaration of war was mistakenly sent to the Germany Embassy earlier that evening from the Foreign Office, Imperial War Museum Press Information, '4 August 1914. The Lead up to Britain's Declaration of War'.

8 HC Debs 3 September 1939, vol 351, col 292.

the Korean War in 1950, the Suez Crisis of 1956, the Falklands War 1982, the Gulf War 1990–1991, the bombing campaign in Kosovo in 1999, intervention in Afghanistan in 2001, and the subsequent deployment to Helmand Province in 2006.

The decision by the government in 2003 to make any British commitment to military action against Iraq dependent on a vote in the House of Commons drew considerable praise at the time and it continues to do so.[9] We will see later that from 2005 attempts have been made in Parliament to provide that this should occur as a matter of course. Some 12 years later no substantial change has been made and it might be wondered why this should be so if many MPs think it a good idea, in a modern democracy, to give the House of Commons the final say as to whether or not military action should be taken by UK armed forces. At least part of the reason can be seen when the various debates on whether proposed military action should be taken are analysed.

The main part of the motion asserted that the House 'supports the decision of Her Majesty's government that the United Kingdom should use all means necessary to ensure the disarmament of Iraq's weapons of mass destruction'. The government was not merely proposing that the House vote for military action; it was informing it that the government had made a decision, which it had the power to do under the royal prerogative, to take such action. It was for the House to give its support, or not, to that decision. In strict constitutional practice, the Prime Minister could have lost the vote and still have taken action quite lawfully, under the pre-existing constitutional practice of the UK, discussed above.[10]

The Prime Minister drew attention in the motion to the opinion of the Attorney General, which had indicated that military action against Iraq would not be contrary to international law. The Attorney's argument had been that Iraq had failed to comply with UN Security Council Resolution 1441 (2002) and, being in material breach of it, 'the authority to use force under Resolution 678 has revived'.[11] In using this reasoning the Attorney General had drawn upon an established legal justification, the authorisation of the UN Security Council, to use force against Iraq, albeit indirectly and by a construction of different resolutions. Resolutions 678 (1990) and 686 (1991) had provided the legal basis for the force used by a coalition of states, including the UK, in 1991 to drive Iraq from Kuwait, which it had invaded in August 1990. Would the Attorney's summary of the legal position be adequate to convince MPs that, if minded to do so, there was a lawful justification for military action? I stress the word 'adequate'

9 The Foreign Secretary at the time has subsequently explained how this change came about, J Straw, *Last Man Standing: Memoirs of a Political Survivor* (Macmillan, 2012), 375.

10 See the statement made by Mr Cameron when his motion to attack Syria was defeated in the House of Commons in September 2013, discussed below.

11 HL Debs 17 March 2003, vol 646, cols WA 2–3 (Lord Goldsmith). His advice, on the reactivation of UN Security Council Resolution 678, was considered by the Prime Minister of the Netherlands, in addressing his Parliament on 18 March 2003, to be 'definitative', 'Report of the Dutch Committee of Inquiry on the War in Iraq' (2010) 57 NILR 81, 125.

here since the Attorney General's opinion had been challenged by other legal opinions, which had come firmly to the view that military action against Iraq in these circumstances could not be justified under international law.[12] Not only would MPs have to weigh up the arguments for and against war, when they would have known that many of their constituents were against it,[13] but they were faced also with different legal opinions aired inside and outside Parliament. It is unlikely, that MPs would have known at the time of the vote, that the Foreign and Commonwealth Office Legal Adviser and the Deputy Legal Adviser had taken the view that, in the absence of a further resolution from the UN Security Council, the proposed military action would have been unlawful under international law.[14]

It seems almost trite to say that a Parliament that prides itself on the rule of law should act in accordance with the law. The House of Commons is not, of course, a court of law in the modern sense of the term, but it nevertheless should not act in a way that it knows, or believes, to be unlawful. Faced with a clash of legal opinion, individual MPs could choose one opinion over another. Indeed, a Conservative member and a lawyer himself, went so far as to say that the 'Campaign for Nuclear Disarmament commissioned an opinion from a QC and got an opinion that was precisely the opposite of the Attorney General's. How surprising. There is no point in paying one of those expensive people if they are not going to say what one wants to hear.'[15] He went on to conclude that 'there is a strong case that the action is legal, even if the case is not watertight'. He was prepared to vote in favour of the Prime Minister's motion even though he thought the legal case was not 'watertight'.

The Attorney General himself had recognised in his earlier opinion of 7 March to the Prime Minister that there was a reasonable case to be made that the action proposed was lawful under international law.[16] This opinion was released in 2005

12 Contemporary views can be seen in the letter from a number of professors of international law to *The Guardian*, 7 March 2003; R Singh, QC, 'Why war is illegal', *The Times*, 14 March 2003. Compare J Knowles, 'Why war is legal', *The Times*, 14 March 2003. For an assessment of the different arguments over whether Resolution 1441 justified military action, F Gibb, *The Times*, 14 March 2003. Although there have been many opinions on the legality of the military action against Iraq in March 2003, the position for and against its legality are set out respectively by C Greenwood, 'International Law and the Pre-emptive Use of Force: Afghanistan, Al-Qaida, and Iraq' (2003) 4 San Diego International Law Journal, 7 and V Lowe, 'The Iraq Crisis: What Now?' (2003) 52 ICLQ 859, 865.

13 See A Treneman et al, 'Middle England packs a picnic and', *The Times*, 17 February 2003, which discussed the anti-war march in central London on 15 February.

14 The Deputy Legal Adviser resigned over the issue, see the letter of 18 March 2003 of Ms Wilmshurst to the Legal Adviser, Documents, Iraq Inquiry. For the legal opinion on the legality of the military action, see the statement of Sir Michael Wood of 15 January 2010, 15, to the Iraq Inquiry.

15 HC Debs 18 March 2003, vol 401, col 838, Mr Maples, MP.

16 See 'Attorney General's Advice on the Iraq War. Iraq: Resolution 1441' (2005) 54 ICLQ 767. It is also appended to the published written evidence of Professor Philippe Sands QC to the Political and Constitutional Reform Select Committee, 12th Report, session 2013–14,

and its much more equivocal tone was in marked contrast to the apparent confidence of his summary of 17 March, the day before the debate in the Commons, and which would have been available for MPs to read before they voted. Conspiracy theorists could, and no doubt did, argue that the earlier opinion had been kept deliberately hidden by the government since, had it been known, it might have affected the decision to be made on 18 March. There is, however, a legal reason for its non-disclosure at the time. It is an accepted principle of English law that legal advice obtained by a client is privileged in the sense that, in the absence of the client waiving that privilege, it need not be disclosed to anyone else. The traditional view is that the Attorney General's opinion, in this case, on the legal position under international law of an invasion of Iraq, was prepared for his client, the Prime Minister. It was only after pressure from various groups that, in 2005, Mr Blair agreed to disclose it.[17]

Members of Parliament could hardly have failed to have been aware also of the so-called justification for military action against Iraq as formulated by President Bush, that of 'pre-emptive use of force', or 'regime change'. For those MPs who thought seriously about the legal justifications for the military action against Iraq upon which they would be voting, this was, no doubt, troubling. They might be forgiven for asking how it is that we will be going to invade Iraq with our major partner (the USA) justifying its action on the basis of a pre-emptive strike (or regime change), whilst we are using the reactivation of UN Security Council Resolution 678 (1990) to do just the same? They might even envisage other states arguing that their justification was neither of these two grounds, but on humanitarian intervention, to prevent the people of Iraq suffering further under Saddam Hussein. Although Mr Blair had ruled out regime change as a justification, some MPs might have queried why neither self-defence nor humanitarian intervention was the kernel of the legal basis, since the Prime Minister referred in his speech to the possession by Iraq of weapons of mass destruction (WMD) being a 'real and present danger to Britain' and the 'brutality of the regime – the death, the torture camps, the barbaric prisons for political opponents, the routine beatings for anyone or their families suspected

Parliament's role in conflict decisions: a way forward, HC 892, 27 March 2014. It is discussed in N White, *Democracy Goes to War: British Military Deployments Under International Law* (OUP, 2009), 262. For an assessment of the role of the Attorney-General in giving his legal advice in March 2003, see M Weller, *Iraq and the Use of Force in International Law* (OUP, 2010), 250–4, the difference between advice and opinion, *ibid*, 230 and for the role of the Attorney General as principal legal adviser to the government see the *Butler Review of Intelligence and Weapons of Mass Destruction*, HC Paper 898 (2004) [374] *et seq*. At [387] the Review comments that on 17 March 2003 'the Foreign Secretary gave a more detailed statement of the legal position in his letter to both Houses of Parliament which includes a note summarising Iraq's record of non-compliance with United Nations Security Council Resolution 1441'. This is set out in Annex D of the Report.

17 See below for further discussion of the role of the Attorney General in the decision to go to war.

of disloyalty – is well documented'.[18] This sounded like self-defence of Britain if the threat was sufficiently imminent, or a humanitarian intervention. Compared to these relatively simple concepts, the legal justification was, instead, based upon a complex deconstruction of various UN Security Council resolutions. It may be for this reason that the justification for the war relied upon by the government, and expressed by Mr Blair in particular, never really caught on amongst the electorate.[19]

Although the moral case for removing Saddam Hussein from power and thereby releasing a large proportion of the population from his grip seemed extremely strong (indeed, it was voiced clearly by Mr Blair and many MPs who spoke in the debate), there was little mention of the 'just war' concept even by the bishops in the House of Lords debate.[20] It was left to Mr Hogg, MP to discuss the issue. He did not think that 'any of the usual characteristics of a just war have been satisfied . . . I do not believe that what is going on in Iraq is a sufficient moral basis for war'.[21]

The debate concluded eight hours after it had begun with the closing speech made by the Foreign Secretary and MPs then filed into the division lobbies.[22] The motion proposed by the Prime Minister was carried by 412 votes to 149.[23]

ii The Libya vote in 2011

The vote by the House of Commons on Libya on 21 March 2011 gave rise to two unusual features. First, military action by British armed forces actually began on the night of Saturday and Sunday, 19/20 March, with the debate being held on the following Monday. Secondly, the issue before the House of Commons was much more straightforward since Resolution 1973 (2011), which had been adopted by the UN Security Council on 17 March under Chapter VII of the Charter, authorised member states to 'take all necessary measures to enforce compliance with the ban on flights' over Libya for the protection of civilians – thereby establishing the no-fly zone.[24] The Prime Minister had, in his

18 HC Debs 18 March 2003, vol 401, cols 768, 772.
19 For the view of a diplomat see, Sir Sherard Cowper-Coles, *Ever the Diplomat: Confessions of a Foreign Office Mandarin* (Harper Press, 2012), 155.
20 The Bishop of Oxford wrote that the just war 'criteria are not being met' in the Observer, 4 August 2002, http://www.theguardian.com/world/2002/aug/04/iraq. In the debate in the House of Lords on Iraq he commented that 'the war was not yet strictly necessary; and that it is only a strictly necessary war that can be regarded as just', HL Debs 18 March 2003, vol 646, col 150.
21 HC Debs 18 March 2003, vol 401, col 796. J Gray MP and M Lomas, QC, *Who Takes Britain to War?* (History Press, 2014), 84, proposed a statutory codification of 'just war'. *Quaere* how this could be consistent with international law.
22 There were some 52 speeches made by backbench or opposition MPs prior to the winding-up speech by the Foreign Secretary, see HC Debs 18 March 2003, vol 646, col 896.
23 See J Straw, *Last Man Standing: Memoirs of a Political Survivor* (Macmillan, 2012), 409.
24 Operative [6] and [8] of the Resolution.

hand, something that had proved elusive in 2003 and would later be in 2013, namely a UN Security Council resolution directly authorising the use of force. The resulting debate, supported by the government's summary of the Attorney General's legal advice,[25] saw 557 MPs voting for the government motion with only 13 against. It was, no doubt, the existence of UN Security Council Resolution 1973 with its ability to create a 'clear legal basis for urgent action to protect the people of Libya'[26] that had persuaded the vast majority of MPs to support the government. The result of this vote records the highest number of MPs in favour of military action since this parliamentary procedure began.

iii The Syria vote in 2013

It was all quite different when, following the use of a chemical weapon in Syria on 21 August 2013, the Prime Minister recalled parliament a week later to debate a motion in which the House of Commons was invited to agree 'that a strong humanitarian response [was] required from the international community and that this may, if necessary, require military action that is legal, proportionate and focused on saving lives by preventing and deterring further use of Syria's chemical weapons'.[27] The motion made it clear that 'every effort should be made to secure a Security Council resolution backing military action . . . [and that] before any direct British involvement in such action a further vote of the House of Commons will take place'.[28] The Prime Minister was at pains to distinguish the context of this motion from that relating to the Iraq war in March 2003. There was, he argued, no question of regime change, or of invasion, and it was clear that a chemical weapon had actually been used. He also drew attention to the fact that NATO, which had been divided over the Iraq war, was unified on this proposed action, which also had the strong backing of the Arab League.

There were also other important differences between the government motions in 2003 and 2013. In the former the vote of the House was invited to support a decision made by the government, whilst in 2013 no such decision to use force had been made and a second vote would be called. The nature and form of any second government motion is, however, speculative, since, given the result of the first, a second motion was never proposed to the House. The possibility of a second vote was unprecedented, and it would have given the government the opportunity to clarify issues of fact (especially intelligence information) between

25 This is set out in House of Commons Library, Standard Note SN/1A/5909, 24 October 2011, *Military Operations in Libya*, [3].

26 See the government motion, HC Debs 21 March 2011, vol 525, col 806.

27 HC Debs 29 August 2013, vol 566, col 1425. For the practical difficulties over access to papers faced by MPs when Parliament is recalled, see Defence Select Committee, 11th Report, session 2014–15, *Decision-Making and Defence Policy*, HC 682, Q 15 (Mrs Moon, MP).

28 A draft resolution before the UN Security Council, which did not purport to authorise military action, was rejected on 19 July 2012, see S/2012/538, 19 July 2013.

the two votes. Moreover, the legal underpinning of the resolutions differed. In 2003 it was largely a case of upholding earlier UN Security Council Resolutions relating to Iraq, whilst in 2013 the legal basis was stated to be that of humanitarian intervention, a ground that could have been employed by the Attorney General in 2003, but that, as discussed above, was not.[29] In 2013, but not in 2003, the Leader of the Opposition had proposed an amendment[30] to the motion standing in the name of the Prime Minister, which by its very nature was likely to lead to division in the House on such an important matter. A further difference was that in 2013 the Prime Minister drew attention to whether the proposed action would 'risk radicalising more young Muslims, including people in Britain', and to make this a point of difference from the Iraq vote he concluded that the it was 'a vital question, and one that was not asked enough in 2003'.[31]

Despite these significant differences in 2013, the government lost the vote on its motion and it was then faced with the choice of accepting it as the will of the House, or ignoring it and taking its proposed military action on the basis of the royal prerogative. It had, after all, produced an opinion of the Attorney General that indicated that the proposed action would have been lawful under customary international law (by way of the doctrine of humanitarian intervention)[32] and to commit the armed forces to military action under the royal prerogative would itself have been lawful. At the end of the debate, the Prime Minister chose the first option by stating that 'the British Parliament, reflecting the views of the British people, does not want to see British military action. I get that, and the Government will act accordingly.'[33]

iv The Iraq vote in 2014

The advance of ISIL into parts of the territories of Iraq and Syria led to the government proposing a motion to join a coalition of forces in conducting air attacks to 'support Iraq, including Kurdish, security forces' efforts against ISIL in Iraq'.[34] The legal justification for the action was stated by the Attorney General to be based upon the request of Iraq itself for this type of military assistance.[35] What was particularly significant about this government motion was that it stated

29 See note 11 above.

30 HC Debs 29 August 2013, vol 566, col 1440. Other amendments were debated in 2003.

31 HC Debs 29 August 2013, vol 566, col 1439. In fact, the leader of the Liberal Democrats did say that 'the action will simply breed further generations of suicide bombers', HC Debs 18 March 2003, vol 401, col 786.

32 'Chemical Weapon Use by Syrian Regime: UK Government Legal Position' https://www.gov.uk/government/publications/chemical-weapon-use-by-syrian-regime-uk-government-legal-position/chemical-weapon-use-by-syrian-regime-uk-government-legal-position-html-version. See also Chapter 2.

33 HC Debs 29 August 2013, vol 566, col 1556.

34 HC Debs 26 September 2014, vol 585, col 1255.

35 The note of the legal position of the government was published by the Prime Minister's Office on 25 September 2014. It can be found at https://www.gov.uk/government/

explicitly it would 'not endorse air strikes action against Syria', nor would it involve the deployment of 'UK troops in ground combat operations'.[36] The government's motion was approved by 524 votes to 43.[37] The first air strike carried out by the RAF occurred on 30 September 2014.[38]

Although US armed forces were leading the coalition and had accepted the need also to carry out air strikes against ISIL on the territory of Syria, the British government closed down this possibility by expressly excluding it in the motion placed before the House of Commons. This was despite the personal view of the Prime Minister that there were legal grounds available by which such an action could be justified, through the notion of collective self-defence with Iraq against ISIL operating on Syrian territory.[39] The opinion of the Prime Minister on the legal justification for air strikes on Syria, was not addressed by the Attorney General[40] in the summary of his opinion and, in any event, it was expressly excluded in the motion. It was to rise again in July 2015 during the debate in the House of Commons on the position of UK aircrew embedded with US forces conducting air strikes over Syria, discussed below, and also in November 2015, following the attacks in Paris.

It might have seemed clear to MPs that air strikes on the territory of Iraq were justified legally by the consent of the Iraqi government to their taking place and, in the absence of similar consent from Syria (which the British government would be unlikely to seek), no action against ISIL on the territory of Syria would take place without a further vote in the House of Commons. The government stated, however, that 'it would seek further Parliamentary approval before UK aircraft conducted air strikes in Syria, unless there was . . . the need to prevent a humanitarian catastrophe'.[41] This ministerial written answer suggested that should a

publications/military-action-in-iraq-against-isil-government-legal-position/summary-of-the-government-legal-position-on-military-action-in-iraq-against-isil. In a letter of 20 September 2014 to the President of the UN Security Council, the Iraqi government stated that 'the aim of such strikes is to end the constant threat to Iraq, protect Iraq's citizens and ultimately, arm Iraqi forces and enable them to regain control of Iraq's borders', S/2014/691, 22 September 2014 which was included in the note.

36 HC Debs 26 September 2014, vol 585, col 1265, 'the reason for choosing "combat troops" is very important' (Prime Minister). Compare the use of British military helicopters 'to evacuate the Yazidi people from Mount Sinjar [which] involved British forces being in an area of Iraq', *ibid*.

37 For the details of the campaign and for the views of former senior military officers and other commentators see House of Commons Library, *ISIS: the military response in Iraq and Syria*, SN/IA/6995, 17 October 2014.

38 *Ibid*, [3.1]. See also House of Commons Library, In Brief: *Progress against ISIS December 2014*, SN/1A/07063, 18 December 2014 . There does not appear to be any significance in the difference between the use of ISIL by the government and ISIS by the House of Commons Library.

39 HC Debs 26 September 2014, vol 585, col 1263.

40 Compare the view of Mr Grieve, MP, who had held the office of Attorney General a short period before the debate on 26 September 2014, as to self-defence of Iraq against ISIL operating in Syria, *ibid*, col 1319.

41 HL Debs 9 July 2015, vol 763, col WA p 10. For discussion of humanitarian intervention and its status in international law, see Chapter 2.

'humanitarian catastrophe' occur, air strikes by UK aircraft could be carried out in Syria without a further vote, although the probable explanation of it is that the government would call on the House of Commons to give retrospective approval.[42]

The disclosure in July 2015 that a small number of British aircrew, embedded within coalition forces, had taken part in air strikes over Syria, raised a number of separate legal issues. These included whether such participation contravened the terms of the motion on which the House of Commons had voted in 2014, which employed the phrase, 'this motion does not endorse UK air strikes in Syria as part of this campaign'.[43] It also gives rise to the significance of the rules of engagement to which those British aircrew members were subject. Since US (and not UK) combat aircraft[44] were being flown on the mission over Syria, there would appear to have been no technical breach of the motion. There can be little doubt that it was lawful for the government to authorise UK personnel to serve in the armed forces of an ally as part of a short-term exchange 'embedding' arrangement. A legal justification for this action would be one based on the royal prerogative, which has survived the parliamentary convention, and can apply, unless it has been voluntarily curtailed by the Prime Minister, in whose hands it now lies. Since the involvement of British aircrew in this situation neither breaches the convention, nor the motion,[45] attention might be paid to the authorisation

42 The convention stipulates that 'before British troops are committed to military operations, the House of Commons should have an opportunity to debate the matter, except in the event of an emergency', HC Debs 20 July 2015, vol 598, cols 75–6WS (Secretary of State for Defence); HC Debs 31 January 2013, vol 557, cols 1059–60. *Quaere* whether it is an accurate statement of the parliamentary convention, as to which see discussion below. Retrospective approval for action was sought, and granted, during the Libya vote in 2011 and in relation to Syria it was foreshadowed by the Prime Minister, HC Debs 26 September 2014, vol 585, col 1265. Notification of, although no formal approval was sought for, the British air strike against two British nationals in Syria on 21 August 2015, see HC Debs 7 September 2015, vol 599, col 26.

43 The government motion relating to Syria, which was defeated, was based solely upon, and as a response to, the claimed use by Syria on 21 August 2013 of chemical weapons, see HC Debs 29 August 2013, vol 566, col 1426. Following the defeat of his (and that of the opposition) motions, the Prime Minister's assurance that he would not 'use the royal prerogative to order the UK to be part of military action before there has been another vote in the House of Commons', *ibid*, cols 1555–6, must be taken to refer to the substance of the motions, the appropriate response to alleged the use of chemical weapons by Syria.

44 FOI, Ministry of Defence, week commencing 13 July 2015: https://www.gov.uk/government/uploads/system/uploads/attachment_data/file/446281/20150717-FOI2015-03225-03226-03227_IraqSyria_Operations.pdf.

45 The ministerial approval 'required for UK embeds deployed with allied forces on operations', HC Debs 20 July 2015, vol 598, cols 75–6WS, which was granted, must have referred to authorisation 'to deploy with their units to participate in coalition operations against ISIL . . . the USA and Canada are operating in Syrian airspace', FOI, Ministry of Defence, week commencing 13 July 2015: https://www.gov.uk/government/uploads/system/uploads/attachment_data/file/446281/20150717-FOI2015-03225-03226-03227_IraqSyria_Operations.pdf. *Quaere* whether the authorisation, when given, was merely to deploy with the foreign units concerned or whether it was also to participate in strike action over Syria.

of a minister for them to participate in the action. If the aircrew concerned had been authorised by a minister to participate in air strikes over Syria, as compared with action over Iraq, this would have amounted to the use of force against Syria, which, unlike Iraq, had given no consent for it.[46] Although they were flying US combat aircraft, a significant issue would be whether they were in reality, members of the armed forces of the UK, or of the USA. Embedded UK 'personnel operate *as if* they were the host nation's personnel . . . but remain subject to UK domestic law, international and Host Nation law.'[47] It is difficult to conclude that the UK aircrew actually became, for the period in which they were embedded, members of the US armed forces, since, as stated, they remained subject to UK domestic law, which would have included the Armed Forces Act 2006. It may be that the government would have had to rely on the Prime Minister's claimed justification of collective self-defence with Iraq[48] and not therefore the consent, express, or implicit, of Syria, for the action. It is worthy of note that the government did not provide a note of the Attorney General's legal opinion on this, or any related issue, prior to, or during the statement.[49] In the very unfortunate occurrence of a British pilot being shot down and being captured by the armed forces of the Syrian government, he would have been entitled to prisoner of war status, as a member of the 'armed forces of a Party to the conflict'.[50] Had a British pilot been captured by ISIL forces there would be no entitlement to prisoner of war status and his fate, in their hands, would have been extremely dire.

What is also of significance are the rules of engagement (RoE) applicable to the UK aircrew and whether they are those that applied to US forces, within which they were embedded, or were UK rules. This is an issue that had arisen earlier over the involvement of RAF pilots flying remotely piloted aircraft (drones), whilst embedded with US armed forces, and it is discussed in Chapter 9. The requirement on them to comply with UK rules of engagement, where they were more restrictive than those permitted by the USA,[51] would mean either that ministers would have had to approve those RoE for air operations over Syria, or the aircrew would, themselves, have had to adapt the RoE, which applied to UK aircrew engaged in air strikes over Iraq.

The Prime Minister announced to Parliament on 7 September 2015, that on 21 August, an RAF remotely piloted aircraft (a 'drone') had carried out a missile strike on a car travelling along a road in Syria, in which the occupants, British citizens, were killed; that the Attorney General had attended a meeting of the

46 See the discussion in Chapter 2 concerning the 'legitimacy' of the Assad 'regime' in Syria.
47 Ministerial statement, HC Debs, 20 July 2015, vol 598, cols 75–6WS (emphasis supplied).
48 HC Debs 26 September 2014, vol 585, col 1263; HC Debs 20 July 2015, vol 598, col 1249 (Secretary of State for Defence), *ibid*, col 1244, Mr Grieve, QC (a former Attorney General).
49 The Attorney General did not speak on the issue but did sit next to the Defence Secretary during the latter's speech to the House.
50 Geneva Convention III, 1949, Art 4. The international armed conflict would have been between the UK and Syria, unless there was implied consent given by Syria to such action.
51 HC Debs 20 July 2015, vol 598, col 1240 (Secretary of State for Defence).

National Security Council and had 'confirmed a legal basis for action'.[52] This claimed legal basis was the inherent right of individual self-defence under the Charter of the UN, which would be duly reported to the UN Security Council.[53] The Prime Minister explained that 'the individuals were planning and directing attacks against the UK . . . air strikes were the only feasible means of effectively disrupting [them] . . . in this area [Raqqa] there is no Government we can work with; we have no military on the ground to detain those preparing plots'.[54]

Whilst there may, on the evidence, be grounds to justify the action on 21 August 2015 by way of self-defence under international law, this is relevant, primarily, as the legal justification for the use of force by the UK in the territory of another state, Syria.[55] The legal justification for killing one or more individuals, whether of British nationality or not, must be sought elsewhere.[56] It could be found under IHL, since that body of law applies to an armed conflict and there is, undoubtedly, an armed conflict taking place in Syria between its government forces on the one hand, and a range of opposition armed groups, including ISIL, on the other. The UK is not formally a party to that armed conflict, but this action (along possibly with the embedded British aircrew issue, discussed above) demonstrates that it has become, albeit on a very limited basis, a party to that armed conflict and it must, therefore, apply IHL to its targeting decisions.[57] The participation of the UK is a matter of fact and that is all that IHL requires in order to apply to its actions.[58] Whether the parliamentary convention, concerning overseas military action, has been complied with or not is irrelevant to the legality, or otherwise, of this action.

52 HC Debs 7 September 2015, vol 599, col 29.

53 *Ibid*, col 26. The required notification to the UN Security Council is contained in the letter from the Permanent Representative of the UK to the UN to the President of the UN Security Council, 7 September 2015, S/2015/688. It also included the justification based on the collective self-defence of Iraq, which was not referred to by the Prime Minister in his statement to the House of Commons on the same date. The right of anticipatory self-defence can only be invoked if the threat to the UK is imminent, see discussion in Chapter 2.

54 HC Debs 7 September 2015, vol 599, cols 25, 26. See also the reliance upon the 'self-defence of the United Kingdom' in the statement of the Prime Minister, HC Debs 17 November 2015, vol 602, col 540, concerning the air strike against Mohammed Emwazi, in Syria, conducted by US forces on 12 November, where no reference was made to the collective self-defence of Iraq.

55 Suggestions in the debate in the House of Commons on 26 September 2014 that there would be legal grounds under international law for the UK to take part in the coalition against ISIL, through attacking its forces located in Syria, had focussed on the collective self-defence of Iraq. The separate ground put forward for the 21 August attack in Syria made unnecessary any reference to collective self-defence as a possible justification. For discussion of the nature of self-defence and of the UK's attitude to the National Coalition of Syrian Revolutionary and Opposition Forces, see Chapter 2.

56 See generally, House of Commons Library, 'UK Drone Attack in Syria: Legal Questions', Briefing Paper 7332, 20 October 2015.

57 See further discussion in Chapter 9.

58 This point is strengthened further by the undoubted participation by the UK against ISIL in Iraq.

In addition, there will also be issues concerning the reach of English law and the ECHR, given that the remotely piloted aircraft was flown by British aircrew. The Prime Minister told the House of Commons that 'specific rules of engagement' had been applied that 'comply with international law and the principles of proportionality and military necessity'.[59] Even if the right to life under the ECHR[60] applied to those who were targeted, it is possible that, depending on the facts, the killing was 'absolutely necessary . . . in defence of any person from lawful violence'.[61]

v The vote on air strikes in Syria, 2015

A number of unique features of the vote on 2 December 2015 to conduct air strikes against ISIL on the territory of Syria make this particular intervention a possible beacon of parliamentary process for the future, where circumstances permit. The perceived illogicality of the decision to conduct air strikes over Iraq, made in 2014, led to the House of Commons Foreign Affairs Committee calling upon the government to show how any proposed air strikes over Syria would comport with strategic, diplomatic and coalition action in resolving the Syria crisis.[62] This it did in its response.[63] The response also incorporated UN Security Council Resolution 2249 (2015), which although it did not expressly authorise military action, called upon member states 'to take all necessary measures, in compliance with international law, in particular with the UN Charter . . . on the territory under the control of ISIL'.[64] It therefore fell to the Prime Minister to provide the legal justification for the proposed air campaign, which was stated to

59 HC Debs 7 September 2015, vol 599, col 26. For further discussion of rules of engagement, see Chapter 8.

60 It is unlikely that the reach of the ECHR extended, in these circumstances, to the territory of Syria, see Chapter 7.

61 ECHR, Art 2. For its relationship to English criminal law and British soldiers, see *McCann v United Kingdom* (1996) 21 EHRR 97.

62 The Foreign Affairs Committee, 2nd Report of session 2015–16, *The Extension of Offensive British Military Operations to Syria*, session 2015–16, HC 457, [33].

63 Prime Minister's Response, 26 November 2015. The Foreign Affairs Committee decided by a majority vote that the Prime Minister had not 'adequately addressed concerns contained [in its 2nd Report of session 2015–16] in his response provided on 26 November', House of Commons Foreign Affairs Committee, Formal Minutes, Session 2015–16, meeting of 1 December 2015.

64 Unlike UN Security Council Resolution 1973 (2011), relating to Libya, Resolution 2249 (2015) was not stated to have been adopted under Chapter VII of the UN Charter. The use of the term 'threat to international peace and security' does not apply exclusively to resolutions authorising the use of force under Chapter VII of the UN Charter, see, for example, Resolutions 2170 (2014), 2195 (2014). The Russian delegate in the Security Council spoke of his delegation being 'convinced that the Charter of the United Nations should be an important foundation in combating international terrorism as it relates to the use of force. We felt it important that that be reflected in the text, as in fact it now is', S/PV.7565, 20 November 2015. The significance, or otherwise, of the wording in UN Security Council Resolution 2249 (2015), is discussed in 'Legal Basis for UK Military Action in Syria', HC Library Briefing Paper 7404, 1 December 2015.

be action in the collective self-defence of Iraq,[65] and that the appropriate notification had been transmitted to the UN Security Council.[66] Finally, the significance of the relatively detailed legal argument, made by the Prime Minister, in his response to the Foreign Affairs Committee report, and his statement to the House of Commons on 26 November 2015,[67] rather than one made by the Attorney General, could signal an increased awareness of the importance of displaying, at the highest level, the legal grounds for a military intervention, prior to any vote in the House of Commons. A serious issue to consider, however, is whether this practice could provide, in response to questions from MPs, a fully accurate and authoritative account of the legal position.[68] It should be noted that this statement to the House, prompted by the Foreign Affairs Committee, provided an additional opportunity, prior to the debate on the substantive motion, for MPs to question the Prime Minister about the issue.

The debate on 2 December 2015 was won by the government by 397 votes to 223. The first British air strikes occurred the following day.

vi Other military engagements since 2000

It is not surprising that the military intervention in Sierra Leone in 2000 came without a vote by the House of Commons to support the government's decision to do so. Like those in Afghanistan in 2001, the events in Sierra Leone occurred prior to the ground-breaking Iraq vote in 2003 and British citizens, including the safety of a detained British army officer, were in immediate danger. The Foreign Secretary announced in the House of Commons that 'we have taken the precautionary measure of deploying a number of British military assets to West Africa . . . to secure the security of British nationals . . . There is no question of a long-term commitment by the troops that have been sent.'[69] Some five months later the troops were still in Sierra Leone and one soldier had been killed.[70] Their final withdrawal did not take place until July 2002.[71]

65 Including the collective self-defence of 'other allies and partners . . ., where they request our assistance', 17, Prime Minister's Response, 26 November 2015.

66 It was stated to be in a letter of 25 November. See other notifications, Iraq, 22 September 2014 (S/2014) 691; USA, 23 September 2014 (S/2014/695); Canada, 31 March 2015 (S/2015/221); France, 8 September 2015 (S/2015/745).

67 HC Debs 26 November 2015, vol 602, col 1489. During the debate on the government motion the Prime Minister did not refer to the Attorney General, being content with, 'we have taken legal advice', HC Debs 2 December 2015, vol 603, col 339.

68 See, for example, the differences of emphasis placed on the adoption of UN Security Council Resolution 2249 (2015) by the Attorney General and the Prime Minister, HC Debs 26 November 2015, vol 602, cols 1468, 1532, respectively. In addition, the House of Commons Library published its 'Legal Basis for UK Military Action in Syria', HC Briefing Paper 7404, 1 December 2015. For a further example of the Prime Minister dealing with the legal reasons, see HC Debs 7 September 2015, vol 599, col 26.

69 HC Debs 8 May 2000, vol 349, cols 518, 529.

70 HL Debs 10 October 2000, vol 617, col 169 (ministerial statement)

71 http://www.bbc.co.uk/news/world-africa-14094419. For an account of the deployment see General (Retired) Sir Nicholas Parker in J Bailey, R Iron, H Strachan (eds), *British*

It is, however, surprising that in 2006 the House of Commons was not called upon to vote for what turned out to be a major extension to Britain's military commitment in Afghanistan. No such vote had been taken to support the government's decision to commit British forces to Afghanistan in 2001[72] and Parliament's role lay therefore only in the ways in which it could hold ministers to account through select committees or through questions in either House. Casualty figures for British forces increased substantially compared with those envisaged at the start of the war in 2001. So, between 2001 and 2005, there were five UK soldiers killed, but, between 2006 and 2013, the number rose to 442. The same increase can be seen in the number of UK soldiers wounded or seriously wounded. Before 2006 there were ten, but between 2006 and 2013, there were 600.[73] This is often the way since the direction and consequences of military action are highly unpredictable, but in the Afghanistan case MPs could have reasonably expected one type of conflict when British troops were involved initially – to remove the Taliban from power and help establish a government there – but got another when British troops took over Helmand Province in 2006. In 2013 Jack Straw, MP, who was Foreign Secretary in 2006, admitted during evidence before a House of Lords Select Committee that 'my reflection is that that [the intervention in Helmand in 2006] ought to have come to Parliament . . . it is a matter of regret to me but it was led by the Ministry of Defence'.[74] The fact that deployment to Helmand in 2006 was not subject to a vote in the House of Commons meant, of course, that MPs did not have the opportunity to vote on the proposed military action; nor was the Attorney General required to assess the legal justification for such action, as in the case of Iraq in 2003.[75]

Generals in Blair's Wars (Ashgate, 2013), p.132, who commented that 'we had intervened almost by accident: an operation designed to evacuate UK nationals had had considerably greater impact.' See generally General Sir David Richards, *op cit*, 'Sierra Leone 2000: Pregnant with Lessons', Chap 4.

72 Parliament was recalled to enable the Prime Minister to make an announcement that British forces had been engaged in 'destroying and degrading elements of the al-Qaeda terrorist facilities and the Taliban military apparatus that protects them', HC Debs 8 October 2001, vol 372, col 811.

73 The statistics can be found at https://www.gov.uk/government/publications/op-herrick-casualty-and-fatality-tables.

74 House of Lords Constitution Committee, *Constitutional Arrangements for the Use of Armed Force*, Session 2013–14, HL Paper 46, 17 July 2013, Q.39. See also the evidence of Dr Reid, MP to the Iraq Inquiry, 3 February 2010, [57]. That it did not come before Parliament for a vote might have owed something to the possibility of a confusion between an operational and a political decision. On the relationship between these types of decision, see Select Committee on Defence, 4th Report, session 2010–12, *Operations in Afghanistan*, HC 554, Qs 562, 575 (Lord Browne).

75 It is likely that the Attorney General would have put forward the request of the government of Afghanistan as the ground for the legal basis of the deployment or the authorisation of ISAF to 'take all necessary measures' to fulfil its mandate, in UN Security Council Resolutions 1501 (2003), 1563 (2004), 1589 (2005), 1623 (2005), 1659 (2006) and 1707 (2006).

There were, in fact, two significant changes to military operations in Afghanistan after the initial intervention in 2001. There was the nation-building mission in January 2006 and, later in the same year, a change of plan with the establishment of the 'platoon houses' over a larger area of Helmand Province, when British casualties began to rise significantly.[76] In 2009 Dr Reid, MP attempted to dispel the 'myth . . . that at any stage [he] had hoped, predicted, expected, promised or pledged that we would leave Afghanistan without firing a shot'.[77] His statement to the House in January 2006 did not contain this phrase but its development to the status of a 'myth' indicates the dangers of taking on a new military role without a full debate on a government motion in the House of Commons.[78]

The military assistance given to France in Mali (2013) followed the Afghanistan model, with no call by the government for support from the House of Commons, prior to the initial deployment of two RAF transport aircraft to assist French armed forces. This was, no doubt, due to the statement the Prime Minister made in the House of Commons that 'we are not seeking a combat role in Mali. We believe we should be supporting the French, who have taken emergency action to stop Mali being overtaken by . . . an al-Qaeda-based group of rebels.'[79] Although one MP did call upon the government to 'table a votable motion on the increasing deployment and involvement of British armed forces [in Mali]'.[80]

76 The statement about deployment of British armed forces to Helmand Province in Afghanistan was made by the Secretary of State for Defence (Dr Reid, MP) at HC Debs 26 January 2006, vol 441, col 1529. He stated 'their task is not to seek and destroy terrorists-the United States are leading that mission . . . we will provide the security framework within which the reconstruction of Afghanistan can take place', col 1541. The change in plan is discussed by the Defence Select Committee with General Sir Mike Jackson and Air Chief Marshal Lord Stirrup, Defence Select Committee, 4th Report, session 2010–12, *Operations in Afghanistan*, Sessions 2010–12, HC 554 (6 July 2011), Evidence, Qs 505–668. See also Dr Reid, MP's evidence of 3 February 2010 to the Iraq Inquiry, [52]–[59] concerning the decision to deploy in Helmand Province.

77 HC Debs 16 July 2009, vol 496, col 512. The background is referred to in Select Committee on Defence, 4th Report, session 2010–12, *Operations in Afghanistan*, HC 554, Q 553 (Lord Browne).

78 The statement of Dr Reid and the subsequent speeches occupied the House of Commons for just over one and a quarter hours, a much shorter time than it took to debate the various government motions to engage in armed conflict in 2003, 2011, 2013 and 2014.

79 HC Debs 21 January 2013, vol 557, col 29. See generally, House of Commons Library, *The Crisis in Mali: Current Military Action and Upholding Humanitarian Law*, SN06531, 11 March 2013; House of Commons Library, *Parliamentary Approval for Deploying the Armed Forces: an Update*, SN05908, 13 October 2014, [4.1]. A minister stated that he 'could assure the House that the British forces will not undertake a combat role in Mali', HC Debs 14 January 2013, vol 556, col 621. The UK personnel providing technical support for the RAF transport aircraft in Mali 'were armed with side arms for their personal protection. The Government of Mali was informed through diplomatic channels', HC Debs 29 January 2013, vol 557, col 709W. For the call out order made under the Reserve Forces Act 1996, see HC Debs 12 March 2013, vol 560, col 10WS.

80 HC Debs 31 January 2013, vol 557, col 1059 (Mr Corbyn MP).

It is apparent that it is for the government itself to determine whether the parliamentary convention is, or is not, applicable and therefore whether a vote should be held. If the French military involvement was properly characterised as 'emergency action' by the Prime Minister, it was, on this basis, clearly outside the parliamentary convention relating to the deployment of armed forces overseas.[81]

vii How significant is the need for a legal justification for armed conflict?

Whilst the House of Commons is a political body and will make its decisions on what its individual members consider to be in the national interest, or that which is considered to be politically expedient, the legality of the effects of their decisions must remain an operative, although possibly not a decisive, factor in any decision to go to war. In all the debates, many MPs are likely to have concluded that the real issue was whether it was in the national interest of the UK to take military action. The 'national interest' is not, of course, a legally-defined term; it is always likely to be interpreted subjectively, either for or against taking military action. There is, for instance, no getting away from the wide-ranging role that the UK tends to play in world affairs, not only because of its history, but also through its permanent membership of the UN Security Council. To some MPs in 2003, the need to uphold the credibility of the UN Security Council, which had passed many resolutions in respect of Iraq, was imperative. To others, a feeling that this was the 'right thing' to do came to the forefront of their minds, whilst to others the risk of creating a 'recruiting sergeant' for terrorism was a strong argument in favour of at least some delay before making a final decision or, as in the Syria vote, an important issue to be considered.[82] The national interest is clearly not identical with national security, but it is likely that some MPs would have taken the latter variant as the key factor in making their individual decisions.

How important then is the issue of the legality of going to war? It will be recalled (Chapter 2) that international law is not, by itself, part of English law, or indeed, the law of any other of the nations comprising the UK. Treaties do not usually provide detailed definitions of words or phrases and the number of relevant judgments given by an international court or tribunal will be relatively small. It is therefore likely to be much less certain in its application, hence the possibility of honestly held different opinions. There was no need to try and undermine the Attorney General's opinion in the Iraq vote in 2003, by claiming

81 See the statement by the Leader of the House of Commons, HC Debs 31 January 2013, vol 557, cols 1059–60, who drew attention to the exclusion of emergency action from the existing parliamentary convention; statement by the Prime Minister, HC Debs 17 November 2015, vol 602, col 543, concerning the air strike against Mohammed Emwazi in Syria on 12 November.

82 HC Debs 29 August 2013, vol 566, col 1439 an issue spoken of by the Prime Minister was whether the proposed military action in Syria 'will risk radicalising . . . young Muslims . . . in Britain . . . it was not asked enough in 2003'.

that he was really a commercial lawyer[83] and not a specialist in international law, or suggesting in relation to a contrary legal opinion that 'there was no point in paying one of those expensive people [a QC] if they are not going to say what one wants to hear'.[84] Members of Parliament were also aware that Kofi Annan, the UN Secretary General had expressed the view that to go ahead without the support of the Security Council could lead to its legitimacy being questioned.[85] Many will have accepted that there was a genuine division of opinion amongst international lawyers on the legality of that war.

The opinion of the Attorney General, as 'the person charged with the constitutional duty of advising the Government and the House on the legality or otherwise of actions'[86] that military action would be justified under international law did not, of course, compel that action. If MPs accepted the Attorney's opinion, they could weigh up whether it really was or was not in Britain's interests to take the proposed action. Had that opinion in 2003 gone the other way – that the proposed invasion would be likely to be adjudged as contrary to international law – difficult issues would have arisen. Since it had previously been agreed that the House of Commons would be given a vote on the issue, a negative view as to legality, held by the Attorney General, would, it may be hoped, have led to a decision by the government not to proceed further with the proposed motion to take military action against Iraq. In theory, the Prime Minister could have appointed a new Attorney General in the hope of a different legal opinion, argued before the House that other states had taken a different view on the legality issue, that since military action against a state charged with non-compliance with UN Security Council resolutions was unprecedented, there was no international law precluding it. Although the law did not compel military action the legality of the proposed action was, however, an essential pre-requisite to it, not least from a political and operational level.[87]

The existence, on the other hand, of a UN Security Council resolution authorising the use of force goes much further than merely providing a legal justification for military action, since it also displays, on its face, the authority of the UN body with primary responsibility for the maintenance of international peace and security. Its availability for the Libya vote in 2011 can be contrasted with its absence in the Iraq vote 2003 and the Syria vote in 2013. Its presence in

83 HC Debs 18 March 2003, vol 401, col 837, Mr Sedgemore, MP. The Attorney General explained who had drawn up the written answer he gave on 17 March 2003, see HL, vol 670, col WA1.

84 *Ibid*, col 838, Mr Maples, MP.

85 *Ibid*, col 786 Mr Kennedy, MP; K Annan, *Interventions: a Life in War and Peace* (Penguin Books, 2012), 357.

86 *Ibid*, col 893 Mr Ancram, MP, see also note 124 below re Suez.

87 See, for example, the evidence to the Iraq Inquiry, 3 December 2009, of Admiral Lord Boyce, who had been chief of the defence staff in the lead up to, and the attack on, Iraq in 2003, where he explained that he had required a certificate from the Attorney General that the proposed action would be lawful. See discussion in Chapter 3.

the Syria vote in 2015 provided strength to the government motion, despite the fact that it did not refer specifically to an authorisation to use force under Chapter VII of the Charter.

viii Accountability of Members of Parliament

What significance did the votes for military action have? From a political view, a majority vote in favour of the respective motions meant that the government was able to show that the military action was supported, not only by itself, but also by the representatives of the people in Parliament and it was therefore consistent with democratic principles.[88] In terms of responsibility for their decisions following a vote, a line cannot in principle be drawn between some, such as Cabinet members and backbench or opposition MPs. If any accountability exists for the consequences of their support of the government motions it applied to all, or to none. But personal accountability is not so simple. The Prime Minister and some other senior Cabinet members, along with their shadows in the official opposition party, would have received security briefings from allied intelligence services, unavailable to other members of the Cabinet, let alone to backbench MPs.[89] None of this would, or could, be disclosed in the debate in the House of Commons. When events on the ground take a course different from those envisaged, which they most frequently will in armed conflict, it is always open to MPs to allege that they were unintentionally misled by the facts presented by government ministers in Parliament.[90] By its very nature, security or intelligence information concerning activities in a foreign country is subject to a significant risk of inaccuracy as to the primary facts and thus any conclusions to be drawn from them. It is inherent in the nature of such information. No doubt those who passed on the facts to the Prime Minister, that Iraq possessed various types of WMD, that there was a link between Al-Qaida and Saddam Hussein, or that there was a further risk to the UK itself, believed this to be the case.[91]

A line of causation between a vote to take part in an armed conflict and the consequences of it is relatively easy to trace, although there is likely to be dispute

88 The vote is given only to the House of Commons. *Quaere* whether this adds 'legitimacy' to a lawful ground for taking military action, see evidence of Jack Straw, MP to the House of Lords Constitution Committee, *Constitutional Arrangements for the Use of Armed Force*, Session 2013–14, HL Paper 46, 17 July 2013, EV Q 40. The difficulty with this approach is that it appears to suggest that if the government were to order the deployment of the armed forces in an emergency this would somehow be lacking in 'legitimacy' (until a vote in the House of Commons) when such action would, assuming that the grounds under international law for doing so were lawful, be constitutionally proper within the terms of the royal prerogative and the present parliamentary convention. A justification on grounds of 'morality' has been advanced by the Foreign Affairs Select Committee, *Kosovo*, 1999–2000, HC 781, 19 April 2000, but this was where it concluded that NATO's military action was 'of doubtful legality', [138].

89 A point made by Mr J Norman, MP, HC Debs 26 September 2014, vol 585, col 1351.

90 See, for example, Mr Hain, MP, *ibid*, col 1277.

91 See the *Butler Review of Intelligence and Weapons of Mass Destruction*, HC Paper 898 (2004).

as to the proper attribution of causes of particular events on the ground. It is much more difficult to determine the consequences of voting against proposed military action. It is unlikely to be free of consequences and the actual decision as to which way they vote will be as difficult for those who are against a motion as for those who are in favour of it, particularly when the leader of the state to be attacked or, in the case of the 2014 and 2015 votes, ISIL, is seen as being responsible for egregious crimes. The accountability of MPs, who vote against a government motion, is no different in principle from those who vote in favour of it.[92]

Along with accountability of MPs comes some degree of responsibility for the actual conduct of the military operations. The extents of this responsibility is obviously much less than those charged with the executive actions involved, whether as ministers, commanders in the armed forces or civil servants, who will bear, depending on their roles, both personal accountability and personal responsibility.

When it comes to making decisions by governments, or a vote by MPs whether to use military force overseas, it is currently not possible to obtain a definitive ruling as to whether such action would, in the particular case, be permitted by international law. One reason is that any judgment as to legality, or otherwise, could only be given if the facts are established. We have seen above that these will often be far from clear and many of the relevant facts are likely to remain subject to security and intelligence procedures. In reality, the best any government could achieve would be a combination of established and predicted facts. So, at the time of the Iraq vote, whilst some facts were known (for example, Iraq's treatment of the weapons inspectors, and the inspection system established by the UN Security Council), others were merely predicted, such as that in March 2003 it actually did possess WMD in defiance of the UN.

Even if the key facts could be established, it is extremely difficult to find a court or tribunal able to decide the issue. The International Court of Justice, for instance, requires states to accept its jurisdiction and to co-operate with it in order to come to a judgment that could be respected by both states. It cannot hear cases brought by individuals or by non-state organisations.[93] It could not, for instance, hear an application by 'anti-war protesters' and issue a declaration prohibiting a state from taking military action until a full hearing could be held and a judgment given.

It was always a possibility that the UK could be taken before the International Court of Justice by another state on the basis that it had contravened international law through its use of armed force outside its own territory.[94] That this was a foreseeable possibility led the Attorney General to consider appointing leading

92 Those who voted against a government motion to engage in armed conflict were in the majority in the Syria (2013) vote but in the minority in relation to Iraq (2003), Libya (2011), Iraq (2014) and Syria (2015).

93 The Statute of the International Court of Justice (annexed to the Charter of the United Nations 1945), Art 34(1).

94 See, for example, *Case Concerning Armed Activities in the Territory of Uganda (Democratic Republic of Congo v Uganda)* 2005 ICJ Reports 168 [1]; *Case Concerning Legality of the Use of Force (Serbia and Montenegro v United Kingdom)* 2004 ICJ Reports 1307, [1]. This was a

counsel to plead the UK case should it become necessary.[95] No such litigation actually materialised. The Court can, and has, heard cases in which it has been asked to give an advisory opinion but it can only do so if requested by an organ of the UN itself.[96]

None of the international criminal tribunals has any jurisdiction to give such a ruling. Neither could an individual MP, or group of MPs or indeed anyone else, go to the English courts for an application for judicial review in order to test the decision of the government to undertake military action, since this particular power is considered to be a non-justiciable issue and this is likely to remain the same outcome if a vote is actually held in the House of Commons.[97]

The MPs called upon to vote in 2003, 2011, 2013, 2014 and 2015, would have to make up their own minds as to the legality under international law of the proposed military action. It is, of course, impossible to know how high this legal issue came in each individual MP's decision on which way to vote. In any event, those who spoke in the debate could only ever be a minority of those who actually voted.

Members of Parliament were also faced with another difficulty posed by the Iraq motion in 2003, and one which would arise in different forms in subsequent motions for military action. This was that, wrapped within the call for support of the government's decision to take military action, there were three other major propositions. These were that the House supported 'the men and women of Her Majesty's Armed Forces now on duty in the Middle East'; that the government would pursue a further UN Security Council resolution if military operations were commenced; and that the House should also welcome the imminent publication of the Quartet's road map 'as a significant step bringing a just and lasting peace settlement between Israelis and Palestinians'. An MP who decided to vote 'no' to this motion would appear also to be rejecting the other three main propositions contained with it. In the motion, therefore, there was no straightforward single question put to members of the House, such as whether they supported or not the government's decision to take military action against Iraq.[98]

possible risk expressed by the Attorney General in his advice of 7 March 2003 in relation to Iraq, 'Attorney General's Advice in the Iraq War: Resolution 1441' (2005) 54 ICLQ 767, 777. It was also a risk foreseen in the Netherlands as a risk also for that country, see *Report of the Dutch Committee of Inquiry on the War in Iraq* (2010) 57 NILR 81, 112.

95 Lord Goldsmith, QC, evidence to the Iraq Inquiry, 27 January 2010, [193], where he also referred to the 'Kosovo case', see *Case Concerning Legality of the Use of Force (Serbia and Montenegro v United Kingdom)* 2004 ICJ Reports 1307. For alleged actions by the UK in Kosovo see [20].

96 Statute of the International court of Justice, Art 65; 'Attorney General's Advice in the Iraq War: Resolution 1441' (2005) 54 ICLQ 767, 777. See, for example, *Legal Consequences of the Construction of a Wall in the Occupied Palestinian Territory* 2004 ICJ Reports 136; *Legality of the Threat or Use of Nuclear Weapons* 1996 ICJ Reports 226.

97 This is discussed in Chapter 5 and below.

98 See also the amendment, which opposed military action in the absence of a UN Security Council resolution authorising it, but which also gave total support for the armed forces', HC Debs 18 March 2003, vol 401, col 779.

What was omitted from a motion can be as important as that which was included. There was, for instance, no reference in 2003 to a period of occupation of Iraq. Military planning had, however, assumed that there would be a period of occupation (in the Basra area) as early as 24 March 2003.[99] It did not figure as such in the government's 'Iraq: Military Campaign Objectives',[100] although the effect of an occupation appears to have been raised as an issue by Clare Short, MP, International Development Secretary in the 'war cabinet'.[101]

There is little evidence in the debate on the Iraq vote that MPs were aware of, or had taken into account, that once the Iraqi regime had been defeated the UK would become an occupying power with all the consequences of that position.[102] True, there was some discussion of development funds being assigned to Iraq after the fighting had ceased but little recognition that, as an occupying power, the UK would be responsible for, amongst other things, law and order in that part of Iraq over which it was in occupation under the Hague Regulations 1907 and Geneva Convention IV, 1949.[103] Some six weeks or so after the vote the UK found itself (along with the USA) as an occupying power[104] and soon found that the number of troops needed to conduct a swift ground campaign would dwarf the number required to maintain law and order effectively during a period of occupation. It was, no doubt for this reason that Ms Short, MP, gave her opinion that there was a failure of both the US and the UK military command to 'take seriously their Geneva Conventions obligations to keep order [and that] the British military should have said to [the Prime Minister], "we are not ready"'.[105]

Occasionally, individual MPs have been questioned in the media as to why they voted in favour of the Iraq war in 2003, but the general public have seen it largely

99 Report of the Baha Mousa Inquiry, HC 1452-II, 2011, vol II, 853, [9.3]–[9.4].

100 Butler Review (2004) Annex C. This document is dated March 2003. An earlier written statement was made to the House of Commons, HC Debs 7 January 2003, vol 397, col 4WS.

101 Oral evidence to the Iraq Inquiry of Clare Short, MP, 2 February 2010, [92].

102 It had not been referred to as a possibility by the Prime Minister or the Foreign Secretary in the debate or in the Attorney General's statement. In theory, but not in practice, a second vote could have been held when it became clear that the UK was an occupying power in Iraq.

103 Hague Convention IV, 1907, Annex to the Convention: Regulations Respecting the Laws and Customs of War on Land (hereafter, Hague Regulations 1907). See the oral evidence to the Iraq Inquiry of Ms C Short, MP, 2 February 2010.

104 The effect of UN Security Resolution 1483 (2003) was that there was no distinction made between separate parts of Iraq and those States in occupation (which were not named specifically) as occupying powers over the whole of Iraq. For comment on this see oral evidence to the Iraq Inquiry of Clare Short, MP, 2 February 2010, [100]–[101]. The letter addressed to the President of the UN Security Council by the permanent representatives of the UK and the USA, S/2003/538, dated 8 May 2003, to which reference was made in a preambular paragraph in Resolution 1483, did not use the term 'occupation' and referred in a general way to their 'obligations under international law'. For the significance of the reference to the letter see the evidence of Lord Goldsmith, QC, the Attorney General at the time, in his evidence to the Iraq Inquiry, 27 January 2010, [230].

105 Evidence to the Iraq Inquiry, 2 February 2003, 95.

as 'Blair's War' or the 'New Labour Government's War', rather than a war voted on by a majority of the House of Commons. Ironically, the same result would have occurred if the former constitutional practice of going to war on the basis of the royal prerogative had been adopted instead.

Parliamentary select committees can, and often do, consider how the government has conducted military operations. There have been a number of such reports since 2000, some of which have been highly critical.[106] It is likely to be the case that in most democracies the idea of holding the executive to account through some form of parliamentary machinery will be supported by the vast majority of the population. There is, of course, a degree of accountability in the sense that the government will have to accept that a parliamentary body can, and should, question its actions in detail, but how effective this accountability really is in the defence field is a matter upon which judgments will differ.[107] Where, for instance, military operations have been carried over from one government to another, such as in Afghanistan, the possibility of an incumbent government denying responsibility for the acts of its predecessor is always present. A government can, of course, always challenge any criticism contained within the recommendations of a particular select committee and there is unlikely to be any serious follow-up.

ix The role of the Attorney General

An important similarity between all of the motions to take military action was that at least a summary of the Attorney General's legal advice was available for MPs to read.[108] It might be asked why MPs should not see the advice itself, rather than merely a summary of it? The government's view is that 'the confidentiality of the advice is worth upholding and that legal professional privilege remains an essential component of our legal system'.[109] English law recognises

106 See, for example, the House of Commons Select Committee on Defence, *Operations in Afghanistan*, 4th Report, 2010–12, HC 554 (6 July 2011). See, in particular [28], [36], [41], [55], [67]; Defence Committee, 7th Report, session 2014–15, *The Situation in Iraq and Syria and the Response to Al-Dawla al-Islamiya fi al-Iraq al-Sham (DAESH)*, HC 690, 2015, [86]. See further discussion in Chapter 3.

107 In Government Response to 15th Report, Session 2005–06, *Waging War: Parliament's Role and Responsibility*, HL paper 236-I, Cm 6923, November 2006, [6] the government commented that 'The Secretary of State for Defence made two statements on the deployment [to Afghanistan] in 2006, there have been 168 Parliamentary Questions and there have been four debates.'

108 For the role of the Prime Minister in setting out the legal grounds for the air strike on Syria in 2015, see above. *Quaere* whether the recent practice of publishing the legal position of the government prior to a vote to take military action is that of the Attorney General since it is not attributed to him, Defence Select Committee, 14th Report, session 2013–14, *Intervention, Why, When and How?* HC 952, [50]. See discussion of the apparent willingness of the Prime Minister to take on the role of conveying the legal grounds for proposed military action, discussed above, p 79.

109 *Operations in Libya: Government Response to the [Defence] Committee's Ninth Report of Session 2010–12.* HC 1952, 30 April 2012, [4]. See also s 35 Freedom of Information Act

that legal professional privilege can be waived by a client (in this case, the Prime Minister). There is even a modern precedent for it when in April 2005 Mr Blair released the Attorney-General's advice of 7 March 2003 concerning the Iraq war.[110] It is one thing to say that the advice of the Attorney General should remain confidential where the decision to go to war is made on the basis of the royal prerogative; much less so where the legal justification for the use of force must be a key issue for MPs who have to decide whether to support a government motion to do so. Compared with the Attorney General's short statement of the legal position given in the House of Lords on 17 March 2003, his advice of 7 March 2003 did show the various nuances of the legal position. A number of MPs might well think that the full advice, if available before the vote, would have been very helpful to them in trying to weigh the strength of the legal case for war.[111] Indeed, a former senior judge has, however, questioned whether the 'old rules of client privilege . . . should apply to a law officer's opinion on the lawfulness of war . . . it is not unrealistic . . . to regard the public . . . rather than the government, as the client'.[112] Even though a summary is made available to MPs there might, in practice, be little time to read and, if necessary, consider the issues raised in it.[113]

It is also surprising, in principle, that the Attorney General (or other law officer, where the Attorney is a member of the House of Lords) does not speak in the armed conflict debates for the purpose of clarifying for individual MPs any points of detail relating to his legal opinion.[114] Since the legitimacy in international (as opposed to national) law of the proposed action is a matter on which few MPs could be expected to have any detailed knowledge, it might be expected that any queries arising in their minds could be answered by the government's chief legal adviser before they walk in to the voting lobbies. The present position can

2000, which provides that advice by any of the Law Officers is protected from disclosure under the Act; the Ministerial Code 2010 and 2015, [2.13].

110 'Attorney General's Advice on the Iraq War. Iraq: Resolution 1441' (2005) 54 ICLQ 767.

111 The Armed Forces (Parliamentary Approval for Participation in Armed Conflict) Bill 2005 proposed merely that the Prime Minister's report show, *inter alia*, 'the legal authority for the participation', cl 2. For the current practice of non-disclosure, see Ministerial Code 2010 and 2015, [2.13]; HC Debs 29 August 2013, vol 566, col 1426 and the response of the Prime Minister, col 1427.

112 Lord Bingham, 'The Rule of Law', Sixth Sir David Williams Lecture, 16 November 2006, see p 9, note 44.

113 Lord Goldsmith QC, Attorney General at the time of vote to engage in military action in Iraq in 2003 commented that his statement to the House of Lords concerning the proposed action, see HL Debs 17 March 2003, vol 646, cols WA 2–3, 'did not purport to be a summary of my confidential legal advice to the Government', HL Debs 28 February 2005, vol 670, col WA1. During the debate on the proposed action to undertake an air campaign against ISIL over Iraq the Prime Minister stated that 'a summary of his [the Attorney General's] is being placed in the House of Commons Library', HC Debs 26 September 2014, vol 585, col 1263.

114 It appears also that the shadow Attorney General does not speak in the debate.

lead to MPs having to vote without any further legal input or clarification, even if there appears to be a need for it.[115] It is difficult to imagine any other public or private body making a decision as serious as the one to commit British armed forces to war without a legal adviser being present to respond to any queries raised during the discussion prior to a vote. Were the procedure to be changed so as to require the Attorney General to speak to his legal advice it would also enable him or her to give some idea to MPs as to how firm the legal position espoused actually is in international law, or whether there are serious disagreements amongst other states as to the existence of a claimed justification for the use of force. No one could seriously doubt the view of the then Foreign Secretary (Mr Straw, MP) who told MPs in 2005 that, 'there are often disagreements about legal positions and legal advice. There are disagreements in respect of matters of domestic law, on which the law is always more certain; still more are those disagreements in respect of matters of international law.'[116] He went on to say that these 'disagreements were well known in advance of the debate on 18 March 2003 and the House's decision to take military action'.[117] That may have been so, but on the face of the Attorney General's summary of 17 March 2003 there was no reference to any such disagreements.[118] Nor was there any equivocation as to the claimed right of humanitarian intervention in the Attorney General's note of the advice for the Syria debate in 2013, despite the view of the House of Commons Foreign Affairs Select Committee's Fourth Report (2000) on Kosovo concerning its conclusion that 'the doctrine of humanitarian intervention has a tenuous basis in current customary international law'.[119] Although one MP did

115 See, for example, discussion above relating to Iraq. In the debate on 18 March 2003 the Leader of the Liberal Democrats queried whether Resolution 1441 gave states or the UN Security Council the right to make a decision as to whether it had been breached and quoted the British and American ambassadors who had 'secured . . . unanimity' of that resolution in the UN Security Council, HC Debs 18 March 2003, vol 401, col 787. Had one of the law officers been able to speak he or she could have been expected to answer that point. In the Syria debate Mr Arbuthnot, MP, commented, 'that is why I question the Attorney-General's advice, with temerity and diffidence', HC Debs 29 August 2013, vol 566, col 1463. The Leader of the Opposition (Mr Miliband) stated 'Kosovo in 1999 is the precedent cited . . . in the Attorney-General's legal advice', *ibid*, col 1443, but it is not actually to be found there. For limited discussion by the Attorney General of the legal issue concerning possible air strikes over Syria, see HC Debs 26 November 2015, vol 602, cols 1467–8, discussed above.

116 HC Debs 24 March 2005, vol 432, col 1006.

117 *Ibid*. What is unlikely to have been known by MPs was the disagreement between the Foreign Secretary and his legal advisers as to the legality of the war without a specific UN Security Council resolution, see, 'Note from Foreign Secretary J Straw to Michael Wood (FCO Legal Adviser) re Iraq: legal basis for use of force', 29 January 2003, Iraq Inquiry, Declassified Documents; written statements respectively of Sir Michael Wood, 15 January 2010, and of Ms Elizabeth Wilmshurst, 18 January 2010, Iraq Inquiry.

118 Compare the legal risks foreseen by the Attorney General in his advice to the Prime Minister on 7 March 2003, 'Attorney General's Advice on the Iraq War. Iraq: Resolution 1441' (2005) 54 ICLQ 767.

119 HC 28-I, [132]; House of Commons Foreign Affairs Committee, 2nd Report, 2015–16, *The Extension of Offensive Military Operations to Syria*, session 2015-16, HC 457, [17].

quote this paragraph from the Select Committee in 2000 in her speech, she also argued that 'those who want to rest the argument for a Syrian war on the Kosovo conflict need to read their law again'.[120] It would, of course, be unreasonable to expect them to do so but, had the Attorney General been able to speak, he could have given further guidance on his view as to whether the Select Committee was correct in its conclusion in 2000 and, even if it had been, whether the position in international law had changed in the intervening years. As with the advice given by the Attorney General in 2003, the issue for MPs may not be the same as it is in Cabinet discussion.[121] Whilst some Cabinet members may merely want to know whether the Attorney General has come down on the side of the legality of any proposed military action,[122] some MPs may want to assess the *strength* of that legal position.[123]

To illustrate the point, consider the military action taken by British armed forces on 31 October 1956 in the Suez Canal area. In the House of Lords the following day the Lord Chancellor attempted to give what he called a 'clear

120 HC Debs 29 August 2013, vol 566, col 1516, Ms Abbott, MP. Almost ten years previously Mr Hogg, MP stated in the debate on the Iraq war, 'if we go to war we affront . . . the principles of legality, which I think are in doubt', HC Debs 18 March 2003, vol 401, col 797. He also commented that 'I have read what the Attorney-General said . . . many distinguished lawyers-as distinguished as the Attorney-General-will take a contrary view', *ibid*, col 796.

121 For the Cabinet discussion of the Attorney-General's opinion on the eve of the vote in the House of Commons on Iraq see Lord Goldsmith QC's evidence to the Iraq Inquiry, 27 January 2010, 212–4. It had not been general practice for the Attorney to attend Cabinet meetings but he was present on 17 March 2003 although he had not been when he had 'advised that the Afghanistan conflict [2001] was lawful', *ibid*, [199]; A Campbell, *The Burden of Power: Countdown to Iraq*, 507. For the problems which may occur if the Attorney General is not present at the Cabinet meeting which discussed armed intervention, see G Marston, 'Armed Intervention in the 1956 Suez Canal Crisis: The Legal Advice Tendered to the British Government' (1988) 37 ICLQ 773, 805, 810.

122 See, for example, an account of the short discussion of the issue of the legality of taking military action in Iraq at the Cabinet meeting of 17 March 2003 at which the Attorney General was present, evidence to the Iraq Inquiry by Lord Goldsmith, 27 January 2010, 214. Cabinet members had in front of them the Attorney's parliamentary written answer of 17 March and not his advice of 7 March to the Prime Minister, *ibid*. Lord Goldsmith stated that 'I do remember telling Cabinet, "well, there is another point of view, but this is the conclusion that I have reached," and then the discussion on the legality simply stopped', *ibid*. On the issue of whether Cabinet members had 'sufficient evidence to understand and challenge' decisions on which they would take responsibility see the interchange between the chairman and Mr Blair, Iraq Inquiry, 20 January 2010, 227. See also the obligation of the Attorney General to bring to the attention of the Cabinet 'the possibility of actions being taken by a legally competent interested country in an international court, [over the proposed military action against Syria in 2013]', HL Debs 10 July 2014, vol 755, col 334 (Lord Morris, a former Attorney General).

123 The Defence Select Committee, 14th Report, 2013–14, *Intervention: Why, When, How?*, HC 952, 28 April 2014 questioned 'whether the Government's position [relating to humanitarian intervention] is generally accepted by the international community or the British public', [49]. The government maintained its position that humanitarian intervention 'is permitted under international law to take exceptional measures in order to avert

exposition of the legal position'.[124] He went into considerable length in his speech analysing how he had based his conclusion that the UK had the right to take the action it did by way of self-defence under Article 51 of the UN Charter. He was vigorously questioned by other peers on this interpretation and, although they did not have a vote directly to support the military action, they did have an opportunity to clarify in their minds any concerns they may have had about the position under international law.

There is, however, precedent for an Attorney General being asked by backbench MPs to advise them on a legal point relevant to a particular debate. During a backbench debate on voting by prisoners the Attorney gave as his reason for speaking in the debate 'to try to provide some assistance to the House in explaining the legal considerations relating to the complex, difficult and extremely controversial issue . . . I look forward to taking on board and considering all the points raised.'[125] It is likely that this intervention would have improved not only the quality of the debate, but also the understanding of the relevant issues by MPs before they voted. It is not difficult to see that a similar intervention by the Attorney could assist MPs in the same way when they are asked to debate and vote on a motion to engage in armed conflict.

In any vote for military action a substantial majority of MPs will not be ministers, to whom the Ministerial Code will apply, but the significance of what they are called upon to vote upon can hardly be downplayed. It is difficult to accept that MPs who are not ministers are not, at least in decisions of this type, under an 'overarching duty . . . to comply with the law including international law and treaty obligations'.[126] It seems particularly appropriate that the Attorney could be given a role to assist the House in this way.

An alternative way of dealing with such a situation, or where a sufficient number of MPs felt that the Attorney General's advice was in their view inadequate, would

a humanitarian catastrophe', subject to three conditions, Government Response to the 14th Report, Fifth Special Report of the House of Commons Defence Select Committee, 11 June 2014, Annex A. See also HC Briefing Paper 7404, 'Legal Basis for UK Military Action in Syria', 1 December 2015, [21].

124 HL Debs 1 November 1956, vol 199, col 1347, Viscount Kilmuir. This was on the same day that the House of Commons voted to 'approve of the prompt action taken by Her Majesty's Government . . . to safeguard vital international and national interests', HC Debs 1 November 1956, vol 558, col 1743. It appears that the Attorney General was not consulted until after the ultimatum to Egypt had been delivered, see G Marston, 'Armed Intervention in the 1956 Suez Canal Crisis: The Legal Advice Tendered to the British Government' (1988) 37 ICLQ 773, [804]. The Attorney General at the time also pointed out that the Lord Chancellor (unlike him, a member of the Cabinet) 'did not constitutionally have an advisory role similar to the Law officers', [810]. See also discussion of these incidents by Lord Bingham, 'The Rule of Law', the Sixth Sir David Williams Lecture, 16 November 2006, 31–3.

125 HC Debs 10 February 2011, vol 523, cols 510. The Attorney did not vote. See also his intervention (as a former Attorney General) in HC Debs 26 September 2014, vol 585, col 1319 (Mr Grieve, QC, MP).

126 The Ministerial Code 2010, [1.2]. Compare the Ministerial Code 2015, [1.2], which omits any reference to 'international law'.

be for the House to commission its own legal advice.[127] This would, however, be likely to prove to be an unworkable solution, given the need frequently for speed of decision-making and the difficulties, due to security issues, of placing the same facts (particularly relating to intelligence issues) before an independent counsel as had been placed before the Attorney General. A variation on this would be for the Cabinet to receive legal advice from the Foreign and Commonwealth Office lawyers.[128]

There is a further procedural problem shown in all the debates for military action in the House of Commons. This is that the opportunity for MPs to follow up a point raised by a fellow member is often lost since the structure of the debate is that members rise to speak when called by the Speaker, who will not know in advance what points each intends to make. Those speaking on the floor do often, of course, give way to other members who wish to question them, but this is not under the direction of the Speaker. Had the Attorney General been requested to answer queries when made on the floor of the chamber, the Speaker could have called upon him to do so before moving on to the next member who had indicated a wish to speak.

From a position of legal famine, we seem to have arrived at one displaying a feast of legal views, as to the lawfulness of proposed military action. In the Syria vote on 2 December 2015, MPs were faced with the view of the Attorney General, statements made by the Prime Minister as to the lawfulness of the proposed action on 26 November, along with a briefing paper on the legal basis of military action in Syria, produced by the House of Commons Library. For some MPs at least, a legal justification for intervention was provided by UN Security Council Resolution 2449, adopted on 20 November 2015. Where they differed in their legal analysis, which of these should be considered to be authoritative?[129]

127 This possibility is discussed in, but did not form part of the conclusions of, the 15th Report, Session 2005–06, *Waging War: Parliament's Role and Responsibility*, HL paper 236-I, [73]. For the view of the Attorney-General at the time, see Lord Goldsmith's evidence to this Select Committee at HL Paper 236-II, Q 252. Sir Michael Wood, the Legal Adviser, Foreign and Commonwealth Office, considered that the proper office holder to give advice to the Prime Minister should remain as the Attorney General, as a 'colleague of other ministers . . . that is the way to ensure that the law is taken seriously and that they get advice-that they follow', evidence to the Iraq Inquiry, 26 January 2010. Compare Political and Constitutional Reform Select Committee, 12th Report, session 2013–14, *Parliament's Role in Conflict Decisions: a Way Forward*, HC 892, 27 March 2014, [47]. Shortly before the House of Commons was due to vote on whether to support air strikes in Syria the House of Commons Library published its 'Legal Basis for UK Military Action in Syria', HC Briefing Paper 7404, 1 December 2015. This provided legal analysis of the key issues, independently of the view of the Attorney General.

128 This was a suggestion made by Clare Short, MP when giving oral evidence to the Iraq Inquiry, 2 February 2010, 118. The courts will not provide a legal interpretation of international law, *Campaign for Nuclear Disarmament v The Prime Minister, Secretary of State for Foreign and Commonwealth Affairs, Secretary of State for Defence* [2002] EWHC 2777, [44]–[47], Simon Brown, LJ, a case which dealt with an application for an advisory declaration as to the interpretation of UN Security Council Resolution 1441 (2002).

129 The Attorney General's view is at HC Debs 26 November 2015, vol 602, col 1468, whilst the Prime Minister's view is at col 1532. See also 'Legal Basis for UK Military Action in Syria' HC Library Briefing Paper 7404, 1 December 2015. The latter was referred to by one MP during the debate, see HC Debs 2 December 2015, vol 603, col 465.

x Do the reasons given in Parliament for engaging in an armed conflict match the legal justifications given by the Attorney General or the Prime Minister?

The wording of the various motions placed before the House of Commons to go to war gave their own justifications for doing so, based upon a summary of the legal opinion of the Attorney General or the Prime Minister. The legal justification for using military force must, however, limit not only the grounds for doing so but also the action that follows. This legal justification, as bounded by the motion itself with its political aims, should open a door to a narrow corridor of military action rather than to a wide room. So, the motion concerning Iraq in 2003 was involved with disarming Iraq's WMD and not with some form of humanitarian intervention to protect civilians who had been 'groaning under years of dictatorship'.[130] In 2011 it was limited by the terms of Resolution 1973, in 2014 to the request for specific forms of military assistance made by Iraq. At present there would appear to be no parliamentary mechanism to keep a Prime Minister, proposing a motion, within the grounds of the legal justification provided by the Attorney General, nor to keep MPs, who speak in the debate, doing the same.[131]

xi Importance to the British armed forces of a vote in Parliament

It has been argued that a vote by Parliament to support the government's decision to go to war 'may help improve the morale of service personnel, particularly if Parliament expresses its view by a large majority'.[132] Whilst this may be true, it is important also to consider if either there is no such vote in Parliament or, if there is, where it is not carried by a large majority. The military operations in Afghanistan from 2006 did not involve any vote in Parliament, and the Iraq war vote led to some 36% of those MPs who voted, voting against the motion to go to war.[133] There is no evidence that either of these facts led to any weakening of the morale amongst those members of the armed forces engaged in Afghanistan

130 HC Debs 18 March 2003, vol 401, col 773, although Mr Blair had stated that he 'had never put the justification for action as regime change', *ibid*, col 772.

131 See the comments made by Phillippe Sands, QC to the Political and Constitutional Reform Select Committee, 12th Report, session 2013–14, *Parliament's role in conflict decisions: a way forward*, HC 892, 27 March 2014, written evidence. See also the legal grounds advanced by the Prime Minister, HC Debs 7 September 2015, vol 599, col 26 (individual self-defence) and compare the letter of 7 September 2015 from the British Permanent Representative to the President of the UN Security Council, which included 'collective self-defence'.

132 House of Lords Constitution Committee, *Constitutional Arrangements for the Use of Armed Force*, Session 2013–14, HL Paper 46, 17 July 2013, [40]. The Committee drew upon the evidence of two very senior retired Army officers, Lord Guthrie and General Sir Mike Jackson.

133 The voting figures were 412 in favour and 149 against. The vote for participation in Libya in 2011 was 557 against 13, a majority of some 98% of MPs voting and for the vote on the air campaign against Iraq in 2014 the majority in favour was some 92% (524:43).

or in Iraq.[134] The support of the general population within the UK is likely to be a much more significant factor. No one involved in any of the armed conflicts could have failed to have noticed the overwhelming support for the armed forces back home, expressed through a variety of ways, such as public attendance at Wootton Bassett when soldiers killed in these campaigns were repatriated, and from 2007, through nearby RAF Lyneham, Help for Heroes, home-coming parades, Armed Forces Day, the Invictus Games in 2014, and the like.

The legal grounds on which military action overseas is proposed are important not only for MPs or for lawyers to discuss; they are important also to members of the armed forces and to the public at large. Some of the grounds, such as a UN Security Council resolution or the request of a particular state, are not difficult to understand, but the same cannot be said for the idea of a humanitarian intervention. It would seem to be good advice to 'provide the public with greater information on, and understanding of, the government's position . . . rather than waiting to the heat of the debate immediately prior to a potential deployment'.[135]

xii Reform of the constitutional arrangements

It was, perhaps understandable, that a government minister who voted for the motion to go to war in 2003 but who resigned later should, in 2005, propose legislation to give the House of Commons (and the House of Lords) a right to vote on whether to go to war or not.[136] Although the Bill never became law it did lead to serious discussion as to the most appropriate way in a modern parliament to decide the issue of whether to commit British armed forces to military action. A year later the House of Lords Select Committee on the Constitution concluded that the 'Royal prerogative by the Government to deploy armed force overseas is outdated and should not be allowed to continue as the basis for legitimate war-making in our twenty-first century democracy'.[137] It was unwilling to support the legislation option but it did propose a parliamentary convention 'determining the role Parliament should play in making decisions to deploy force or forces outside the United Kingdom to war, intervention in an existing conflict or to environments where there is a risk that the forces will be engaged in conflict'.[138]

134 For discussion of claims of conscientious objection to serving in Iraq or in Afghanistan, see Chapter 8.

135 Defence Select Committee, 14th Report, session 2013–14, *Intervention, Why, When and How?* HC 952, [49]. See the Government's response, HC 581 (2014), [9], which referred to its Annex A.

136 HC Debs 21 October 2005, vol 437, col 1085, Ms Short, MP, first reading of the Armed Forces (Parliamentary Approval for Participation in Armed Conflict) Bill. See also the Armed Forces Deployment (Royal Prerogative) Bill, HL Bill 34, 2014–15.

137 15th Report, Session 2005–06, *Waging War: Parliament's Role and Responsibility*, HL paper 236-I, [103].

138 *Ibid*, [108]. See also House of Lords Constitution Committee, *Constitutional Arrangements for the Use of Armed Force*, 2nd Report of session 2013–14, HL Paper 46, 24 March 2013, [61].

Almost from the date of the 2003 Iraq vote, discussion had taken place to give Parliament a formal role in the decision to go to war. By 2005–2006 the leaders of the two largest parties in the House of Commons appeared to agree that the royal prerogative was no longer the way forward,[139] but no agreement seemed to be forthcoming as to what alternative arrangements should be adopted.[140]

It was the prospect of a no-fly zone being established in Libyan airspace that prompted a significant statement on the part of the government concerning the opportunity for MPs to vote on possible British military action. A 'convention has developed', stated the Leader of the House, 'that before troops are committed, the House would have an opportunity to debate the matter'. He went on to say that, 'we propose to observe that convention except when there is an emergency and such action would not be appropriate'.[141] It may be that this statement of the convention was considered to be an accurate reflection of it at the time, but two years later the Leader of the House described it as applicable if 'UK troops are committed to conflict',[142] thereby emphasising that it applies, in effect, to combat troops and not merely to the deployment of British soldiers abroad, although his statement in 2011 was in response to a question concerning a debate about the possible establishment of a no-fly zone over Libya. The present formulations of the convention seem to be unclear as to whether it applies where the government proposes a motion relating only to an air campaign, as was the case in Libya (2011), Iraq (2014) and Syria (2015), although in each case a substantive vote was held.[143]

Although a parliamentary convention may not be legally binding it is considered to be politically binding on all parties[144] and the convention under discussion has been described as a 'good convention.'[145] Attempts continue in Parliament

139 See note 137, [98].

140 For a summary of the current position see House of Commons Library, *Parliamentary Approval for Deploying the Armed Forces: an Update*, SN05908, 13 October 2014.

141 HC Debs 10 March 2011, vol 524, col 1066, Sir George Young, MP. See also the Cabinet Manual 2011, [5.38]. *Quaere* whether the 'and' after 'emergency' makes this caveat conjunctive or disjunctive. *Quaere* also whether any invocation of the NATO Treaty 1949, Art 5 would also be exempt from the convention, since the obligation to use armed force is a treaty obligation.

142 HC Debs 31 January 2013, vol 557, cols 1059–60. See also HC Debs 20 July 2015, vol 598, cols 75–6WS. The Iraq vote in 2014 concerned an air campaign but not the use of combat troops.

143 For the difficulties of defining a parliamentary convention see A Blicke, 'The Cabinet Manual and the Codification of Conventions' (2014) 67 Parliamentary Affairs 191. There was no reference to the parliamentary convention during the government motion for military action against Syria in 2013.

144 House of Lords Constitution Committee, *Constitutional Arrangements for the Use of Armed Force*, Session 2013–14, HL Paper 46, 17 July 2013, footnote 51. Compare S Payne, 'War Powers: The War Prerogative and Constitutional Change' Vol 153 (2008) RUSI Jo, 28, who commented that, 'conventions do not satisfy some people because they have no legal form at all and depend upon the internalised weight of obligation'.

145 HC Debs 26 September 2014, vol 585, col 1265 (the Prime Minister).

to set out its precise role and, somehow, to 'enshrine' this in law.[146] It is, by no means clear that an attempt to do this will be successful for a number of reasons. First, there is a real fear that any statutory enactment could lead to applications for judicial review,[147] particularly if the government did not put a particular military involvement to a vote. Secondly, problems of defining various terms in any legislation are likely to prove to be considerable, certainly if the government maintains its parliamentary convention line whereby no vote will be required in an 'emergency' or where it would 'not be appropriate' to do so, or if the term 'before troops are committed' is replaced with 'intervention' or something similar. Would a decision by the government to arm the Syrian opposition require, under this convention a vote in Parliament?[148] Finally, it should not be forgotten that difficulties will arise over the precise form in which the Attorney General's advice should be presented to MPs prior to, and even during the debate, and whether MPs will demand a greater amount of security information to be given to them before they are called upon to vote for military action.[149]

The relationship between the royal prerogative, held by the Prime Minister,[150] to commit the UK to playing a part in an armed conflict, and the parliamentary convention discussed above is by no means clear, particularly in the light of the result of the Syria vote in 2013.[151] The issue revolves round whether the convention is additional to, or a replacement for, the royal prerogative. It cannot be the latter. The decision of the Prime Minister in 2013 is merely evidence of a *political* decision made by him rather than a recognition that the legal position had changed so as to make this aspect of the prerogative redundant. There must, after all, be some constitutional law principle permitting the Prime Minister to take military action should there be an 'emergency or where it would not be appropriate to [invoke the parliamentary convention]'.

It is also appropriate to look at what the House of Commons is being asked to do when a motion for military action is proposed by the government. If it is to make a *decision* as to whether the proposed action should go ahead there is some strength

146 HC Debs 21 March 2011, vol 525, col 799 (Foreign Secretary). See also House of Commons Select Committee on Political and Constitutional Reform, *Parliament's Role in Conflict Decisions, An Update*, HC 649, 5 September 2013, [9].

147 15th Report, Session 2005–06, *Waging War: Parliament's Role and Responsibility*, HL paper 236-I, [104]; House of Lords Constitution Committee, *Constitutional Arrangements for the Use of Armed Force*, Session 2013–14, HL Paper 46, 17 July 2013, [54].

148 The Foreign Secretary stated that should the government decide to do this 'there would be a vote . . . we would expect it to be before any such decision was put into action', HC Debs 18 June 2013, vol 564, col 746. Providing equipment to non-state armed groups is discussed in Chapter 2.

149 A number of these difficulties are discussed in *The Governance of Britain-Constitutional Renewal*, Cm 7342-1 (2008), [216–222] and Annex A.

150 15th Report, Session 2005–06, *Waging War: Parliament's Role and Responsibility*, HL Paper 236-I, [12]. See also *ibid*, HL Paper 236-II, Q 3.

151 See the arguments set out in House of Commons Library, *Parliamentary Approval for Deploying the Armed Forces: an Update*, SN05908, 13 October 2014, [9]–[10].

in the argument that the convention operates as a replacement of the prerogative. If, as appears to be the case, MPs are being asked to *support*[152] a decision made by the government then they cannot be seen as the possessors of the legal power of decision-making as to whether the UK takes part in an armed conflict or not. Similarly, they have no power to 'authorise' such action. The further one gets towards MPs being actual, or *de facto*, decision-makers the more their role will change from being 'strategic inquisitors'[153] of the government's plans, to a position where the accountability of the government to parliamentary scrutiny may be weakened.

It is not surprising to see different views in Parliament, and outside it, on how this aspect of constitutional practice could be reformed and whether and, if so, how, it could be 'enshrine[d] in law for the future'.[154] Suggestions have ranged from getting rid of the parliamentary convention altogether,[155] retaining it in some form,[156] agreeing a detailed parliamentary resolution,[157] to a statutory requirement that the House of Commons be involved in the process, or not be involved.[158] An integral part of this process must be an agreement in Parliament as to where the constitutional power of decision-making actually lies, either *de jure* or *de facto*. If it is eventually agreed that it should lie with the House of Commons, in the sense that military action cannot proceed in the face of a negative vote, another issue will need to be resolved. This is whether the Attorney General's advice to the Prime Minister should be published in some form.[159]

Irrespective of any change to the relationship between the government and the House of Commons there may be some sympathy with the suggestion, which drew some support from a former Attorney General, that the legal advice of that law officer should be considered in detail by a sub-committee of the

152 See the Defence Secretary, HC Debs 20 July 2015, vol 598, col 1252. The government motions on all occasions, apart from that relating to Syria in 2013, called for the House of Commons to 'support' it.

153 Defence Select Committee, 14th Report, 2013–14, *Intervention: Why, When, How?*, HC 952, 28 April 2014, [65]. See also HC Debs 26 September 2014, vol 585, col 1351 (Mr Norman, MP). See also Mr Gray, MP, HC Debs 2 December 2015, vol 603, col 409.

154 HC Debs 21 March 2011, vol 525, col 799 (Foreign Secretary).

155 See for example, HC Debs 26 September 2014, vol 585, col 1351 (Mr Norman, MP); *The Times*, 24 September 2014 (leader column); Alistair Burt, MP, *The Guardian*, 31 December 2013.

156 Report, Session 2005–06, *Waging War: Parliament's Role and Responsibility*, HL paper 236-I, [108]. Strictly, this Report recommended establishing a convention since it appeared before such a convention had been recognised by the government in 2011, which is in HC Debs 10 March 2011, vol 524, col 1066, Sir George Young, MP. Compare the view of G Phillipson, http://ukconstitutionallaw.org/2013/11/29/gavin-phillipson-historic-commons-syria-vote-the-constitutional-significance-part-ii-the-way-forward/.

157 See Political and Constitutional Reform Select Committee, 12th Report, session 2013–14, *Parliament's Role in Conflict Decisions: a Way Forward*, HC 892, 27 March 2014. A draft resolution is set out in the Annex.

158 J Gray, MP and M Lomas, QC, *Who Takes Britain to War?* (History Press, 2014), 85. Mr Gray, MP, HC Debs 2 December 2015, vol 603, col 409.

159 See also the Defence Select Committee, 14th Report, 2013–14, *Intervention: Why, When, How?*, HC 952, 28 April 2014, [65] and the Government's Response, Defence Committee,

Cabinet, to ensure that it is fully scrutinised before it is brought to the full Cabinet for decision.[160] Many will find it alarming if procedures are not in place to enable a full discussion of the strengths and weaknesses of the legal position in the Cabinet before a decision to take part in an armed conflict is made. As we have seen above, such a discussion cannot take place at present in the House of Commons since the Attorney General does not participate in the debate. Moreover, MPs will not have received the same security briefings as Cabinet members or be provided with adequate background information on the facts, such as the relationships between different groups in the territory concerned.[161] Members of Parliament could, however, be assisted if a fuller report prepared by the government, as recommended by the Foreign Affairs Committee in 2015, of the strategic plan, were to be made available to them before any vote.[162]

xiii Judicial review of a decision to go to war made by the House of Commons

Over a long period of time the courts have established a principle that that the royal prerogative concerning a decision to take part in an armed conflict is not susceptible to judicial review in the courts. It is considered to be a non-justiciable issue and, in reality, a political decision.[163] The point was forcefully made by a High Court judge who said, 'it is unthinkable that the national courts would entertain a challenge to a Government decision to declare war or to authorise the use of armed force against a third country'.[164]

Fourth Special Report, HC 581, 20 July 2014, [10] and discussion above. Following the attack on 21 August 2015 by an RAF remotely piloted aircraft over Syria, the Prime Minister stated, 'we do not publish the Attorney General's advice but I am happy to discuss the content of the advice and describe what it was about, HC Debs 7 September 2015, vol 599, col 30; HC Debs 17 November 2015, vol 602, col 543, referring to the air strike on Mohammed Emwazi in Syria on 12 November. See also the Prime Minister's response of 26 November 2015, 16–17, to the House of Commons Foreign Affairs Committee, 2nd report, session 2015–16, *The Extension of Offensive Military Operations in Syria*, session 2015–16, HC 457.

160 Lord Goldsmith, QC, evidence to the Iraq Inquiry, 27 January 2010, 234, commented that this proposal had 'huge merit'. This followed his description of the relative lack of discussion of the legal position at the Cabinet meeting on 17 March 2003, on the eve of the Iraq vote, 214.

161 For the briefing of the leader of the official opposition prior to the Syria debate (2013) see HC Debs 29 August 2013, vol 566, col 1446 and for the lack of knowledge of the facts on the ground see HC Debs 13 June 2013 vol 564, col 547 (Mr R Steward, MP). The National Security Council (since 2010) may be able to provide further information to its members.

162 House of Commons Foreign Affairs Committee, 2nd Report, 2015–16, *The Extension of Offensive Military Operations to Syria*, session 2015–16, HC 457, [35–36].

163 See discussion in Chapter 5.

164 In *Campaign for Nuclear Disarmament v The Prime Minister, Secretary of State for Foreign and Commonwealth Affairs, Secretary of State for Defence* [2002] EWHC 277, Richards J, [69].

Experienced lawyers will have known that this position taken by the courts is virtually unassailable and so attempts have been made to try and bring similar issues before the courts in different ways. An application was brought to obtain a court judgment declaring 'that the UK Government would be acting in breach of international law were it to take military action against Iraq without a further Resolution [following Resolution 1441]'. The court would have none of this.[165] Nor would it sanction an attempt to challenge, through an interpretation of the Human Rights Act 1998, the Attorney General's advice concerning the Iraq war and 'how the Government came to go to war on the basis of the wrong advice'.[166]

It is difficult to see how a court could consider an application for judicial review of a decision made through a vote in the House of Commons even if it was taken in breach of the parliamentary convention discussed above. Should the final position end up that Parliament passes a statute to govern decisions relating to going to war, it is likely that any possibility of judicial review would only occur whether there is a breach of the statute. An application for judicial review must be approved by a judge before any hearing of the substantive issue and so any unmeritorious claim could be dismissed fairly quickly.[167]

165 *Ibid*, Simon Brown LJ, [2].

166 *R (Gentle and another) v The Prime Minister and others*, [2008] UKHL 20, Lord Rodger, [35].

167 A possible claim will normally need to follow the procedure set out in the Pre-Action Protocol for Judicial Review. An example is given in HC Briefing Paper 7404, 'Legal Basis for UK Military Action in Syria', 1 December 2015, [22]. See also, *Campaign for Nuclear Disarmament v The Prime Minister, Secretary of State for Foreign and Commonwealth Affairs, Secretary of State for Defence* [2002] EWHC 277. This action concerned an application for an 'advisory declaration as to the true meaning of Resolution 1441', [2]. Resolution 1441 was passed by the UN Security Council on 8 November 2002 and the hearing took place on 17 December 2002. It failed on the preliminary issues.

5 The relationship between the English courts and the government

The importance of the independence of the judiciary from the government of the day takes on a heightened significance during times of armed conflict, due largely to the link between the issues raised in court and the national interest pursued by the government. In the armed conflicts relating to Iraq and Afghanistan, in particular, the judges were faced with a significant number of applications for judicial review and civil claims brought by citizens of those countries, along with those brought on behalf of British nationals, all of which related, in one way or another, to the armed conflicts.[1]

At first sight it seems strange to see those who, in former times, would be classed as 'enemy aliens', having access to the courts in England whilst the armed conflict in which they may have been involved is ongoing. Lord Reading CJ explained that 'by the existing law of the country the mere fact of war operates *ipso facto* to suspend any rights of action . . . during the war.'[2] That these civil actions should be capable of being brought before the courts in England, since 2000, is not due to any change in the law to enable enemy aliens to do so, but is a reflection of the fact that the various military actions in which the UK has been involved since 2000 have been classified as armed conflicts rather than as 'wars'.[3] As a result, Lawrence Collins J concluded that 'the disability of alien enemies is part of the rules of English law relating to the traditional laws of war, and that there is no warrant for extending it to modern armed conflict not involving war in the technical sense'.[4]

1 'The courts have a particular responsibility to uphold the rule of law as it applies to the conduct of Her Majesty's armed forces in situations of armed conflict', *Hussein v Secretary of State for Defence* [2014] EWCA Civ 1087, [84].

2 *Porter v Freudenberg* [1915] 1KB 857, 877, 880. Lord Reading CJ rejected the argument that the Hague Regulations 1907 prohibited such a position since the inability of an enemy alien to sue in the courts in England was an 'existing law of the country' and that the UK had not declared 'abolished, suspended, or inadmissible in a court of law the rights and actions of the nationals of the hostile party' (Art 23(h)). The application for permission to apply for judicial review in *Al-Skeini v Secretary of State for Defence* [2004] EWHC 2911, [5] was brought by an Iraqi national on 11 May 2004 when the UK was an occupying power in Iraq.

3 *Amin v Brown* [2005] EWHC 1670 (CH). For further discussion of the nature of 'war' see Chapter 1.

4 *Amin v Brown* [2005] EWHC 1670 (CH), [46].

i English firms of solicitors acting for Iraqi or Afghan civilians

As a result of this legal environment, it should be no surprise to find firms of solicitors based in England acting for soldiers, their families, and even for citizens of states, in which British soldiers were fighting, to bring civil actions before the High Court in London against the Ministry of Defence or particular government ministers, for judicial review, claims in tort or under the Human Rights Act 1998.[5] The result of them doing so has meant that decisions made during military operations and affecting each different group of claimants, have been subjected to intense legal and judicial scrutiny. In turn, the decisions of the courts, from the High Court to the Supreme Court, have interpreted the law in at least two significant ways since 2003. The Human Rights Act 1998 has been held to apply extra-territorially and, thus, to bring Iraqi and Afghan civilians within its scope in limited, but important, circumstances, and the whole basis of treatment of these civilians detained by British armed forces has also been clarified.[6]

A strong belief by the UK in the rule of law must lead to its courts being open to all who can bring a valid claim, based upon an alleged breach of English law, by the government or its agents. A number of Iraqi and Afghan citizens did so, largely as a result of legal aid being available to support their claims[7] and the presence in the local area, or nearby, of representatives who could make contact, in the first instance, with an English law firm.[8] Indeed, the Court of Appeal considered that one of the firms of solicitors (involved in a particular case) had performed 'a valuable public service in bringing forward their clients' claims and prosecuting them with such conspicuous skill and vigour'.[9]

It is, perhaps, fair to say that the government took a less benign view, particularly of the large number of claims being brought against it relating to the alleged actions of some members of its armed forces in Iraq and Afghanistan or decisions made in the Ministry of Defence. The availability of legal aid funds to support claimants who were not resident in the UK has led ministers to seek reform 'on access to legal aid, particularly in cases brought by overseas claimants'.[10] The case

5 No issue has arisen of the inability to sue in the English courts by 'enemy aliens'.

6 For the extra-territorial application of the Human Rights Act 1998 see Chapter 7 and for discussion of the legitimacy of detention and the treatment of Iraqi or Afghan detainees by British armed forces, see Chapter 9.

7 A minister confirmed that one of the firms 'receives legal aid funding from the Legal Services Commission', HL Debs 17 November 2010, vol 722, col 213W.

8 See *Hassan v United Kingdom*, Application No 29750/09, Grand Chamber Judgment, 16 September 2014, [30] (representative in Syria); *Ismail v Secretary of State for Defence* [2013] EWHC 3032, [17] (representative in Afghanistan and follow up by lawyers).

9 *R (Al-Skeini and Others) v Secretary of State for Defence* [2005] EWCA Civ 1609, Brooke LJ [142]; Sedley LJ, [209]. See also *R (Al-Sweady and others) v Secretary of State for Defence* [2009] EWHC 2387, [67]; *R (Ali Zaki Mousa and others) v Secretary of State for Defence No 2* [2013] EWHC 2941, [63], which related to the claimants' legal team.

10 Select Committee on Defence, 12th Report, 2013–14, *UK Armed Forces Personnel and the Legal Framework of Future Operations*, HC 931 (2014), Written Evidence from the Ministry of Defence [18],

for some change appeared to ministers to be stronger with the publication in 2014 of the Report of the Al-Sweady Inquiry and the withdrawal of the allegation at a very late stage that 'live Iraqis captured during the course of the battle on 14 May 2004 died, or were killed at [the UK detention facility]'.[11]

The attempt by the government to restrict legal aid to UK residents was held to be lawful, despite challenge in the courts.[12] Whilst this may appear to be a technical matter, the significance of its effects on the accountability of the government to the law should not be underestimated. In the Divisional Court Moses LJ thought it 'worth drawing attention to the fact that the residence test will exclude from access to legal aid individuals resident abroad who have been subject to serious abuses at the hands of UK forces'.[13] Had the residence test been in existence in July 2004, when the Al-Skeini litigation was heard for the first time in the High Court, it is unlikely that that case and others, raising important public law issues, could have been brought, and the legal environment would have been quite different.

ii The courts, foreign policy, the act of state doctrine and other instances of judicial restraint

The relationship between the courts and the UK government over issues of foreign policy has been put to the test, largely as a result of the armed conflicts to which the UK has been a party since 2000. The democratic value of governance through the rule of law would suggest that decisions made by government ministers in the field of foreign affairs should be subject to judicial review, or other action in the courts, in the same way as decisions they make in other areas of government. If this were to be the case one aspect of the complex mix of politics, diplomacy and law[14] would be separated with the ultimate decision being made, on the legal issues, perhaps some time later, in the courts and not by government ministers responsible to Parliament.

The relationship between the courts and the government, particularly in relation to foreign policy can be seen as a matter of constitutional principle. Cranston J certainly thought so when he stated that the 'basal principle of our system of representative democracy is that the people of the United Kingdom entrust the conduct of the country's foreign policy to their elected representatives, not to the courts'.[15] This may sound attractive but it does not, by itself, provide a litmus

11 Report of the Al-Sweady Inquiry (2014), vol 1, 48, [2.6]–[2.7]; HC Debs 17 December 2014, vol 589, col 1408.

12 *R (Public Law Project) v Lord Chancellor* [2015] EWCA Civ 1193. See, however, the exceptions in [8].

13 *R (Public Law Project) v Lord Chancellor* [2014] EWHC 2365, [31]. Moses LJ referred specifically to the claims brought by Mr Al-Skeini and others.

14 The phrase is to be found in *R (Noor Khan) v Secretary of State for Foreign and Commonwealth Affairs* [2014] EWCA Civ 24, Laws MR, quoting a witness statement at [22]. See also *Campaign for Nuclear Disarmament v Prime Minister of the United Kingdom and others* [2002] EWHC 2777 (Admin), Richards LJ, [59].

15 *R (Al-Haq) v Secretary of State for Foreign and Commonwealth Affairs* [2009] EWHC 1910 (Admin), [59]. See also Pill LJ, [46].

test to determine which issues of foreign policy should or should not be heard in the courts, since, if the term 'foreign policy' is replaced by 'domestic policy', there is an equal entrusting of these matters to elected representatives, and so the reasoning is the same but domestic policies can, of course, become the proper subject of judicial action.

The experience of the armed conflicts, particularly in Iraq and in Afghanistan, has shown that the appropriate relationship between the courts in England and Parliament is not solely a matter for these courts. In applying the ECHR, the ECtHR has shown that it does not generally apply a 'degree of deference to the autonomy of the executive which characterises recent English law'.[16] Some aspects of the 'conduct of foreign affairs' will be justiciable and, in trying to draw a line between those that are the proper subjects of judicial scrutiny and those that are not, in the areas covered by this book, the following distinct issues should be separated, not as legally separate categories, but for analytical reasons only.

The first is where decisions are made by the Crown (the executive government) that form part of the royal prerogative or, such as the decision to take military action overseas, have become the subject of a vote in the House of Commons. The second is where decisions of the government have an effect on someone outside the UK. The third concerns the decisions of foreign governments. Terminology has not been applied uniformly over the years which, in turn, has caused confusion over the meaning of 'acts of state' or 'Crown acts of state' or 'non-justiciability,' but, it is argued that, 'act of state' should be reserved for the second and third categories. The term, non-justiciability needs to be applied with some caution since it could encompass one or both of the following issues, certainly in relation to act of state. These are whether a court could determine the facts of a claim and form a conclusion based on law to them, and whether any claim based on those facts is defeated by 'compelling considerations of public policy which should prevent reliance [on a claim in tort].'[17]

The first of these categories, in so far as it relates to the royal prerogative, is the most settled and is the product of a reasonably long line of decisions, such as those relating to the armament and disposition of the armed forces and the right of the government to authorise military action against another state,[18] and which, if challenged, have been done so only indirectly. These decisions of the courts generally favour treating the 'high policy' issues raised as being non-justiciable, since they are 'beyond the constitutional competence assigned to the courts

16 Lord Sumption, 'Foreign Affairs in the English Courts Since 9/11', Lecture at the Department of Government, London School of Economics, 12 May 2012 https://www.supremecourt.uk/docs/speech_120514.pdf; *A v Secretary of State for the Home Department* [2004] UKHL 56, [29].

17 *Mohammed v Secretary of State for Defence* [2015] EWCA Civ 843, [364]. See discussion below.

18 *Chandler v DPP* [1964] AC 763, Lord Reid, 791, Lord Pearce, 813; *R (Gentle) and Another v Prime Minister and Others* [2008] UKHL, [62], Lord Carswell; *R v Secretary of State for Defence, ex parte Thring* (2000, unrep., see https://www.ICRC.org) (National

under our conception of the separation of powers'.[19] An alternative way of looking at this is to say that on such matters the courts are just not equipped with the necessary political and diplomatic skills to make such decisions.[20] The conclusion that the issue is non-justiciable does not operate by way of a defence to a claim brought but it actually means that 'no legal right of the citizen is engaged'.[21]

A gloss on the prerogative right of the government to take military action has been, since April 2003, a form of parliamentary convention by which members of the House of Commons have been able to vote on a substantive motion to do so, the details of which are discussed in Chapter 4.

The second is where a decision of the government, particularly during an armed conflict, has an effect on an individual abroad who, in consequence, seeks to sue the British government before a court in England.[22] It is certainly a principle with a long history, stretching back at least to *Buron v Denman* in 1848.[23] The parameters of this aspect of act of state are not easy to define[24] and, even if it was held to apply, it has not been clear whether it shows itself as a rule of non-justiciability, or as a mechanism to deny a claim for damages brought by an individual affected,

Implementation) a case involving a challenge to the RAF enforcing no-fly zones over Iraq in which Pill LJ stated that 'it is not appropriate for the court to intervene upon judicial review in the deployment of the armed forces abroad'; *Campaign for Nuclear Disarmament v Prime Minister of the United Kingdom and others* [2002] EWHC 2777 (Admin), 'to declare war or to authorise the use of armed force against a third country', Richards LJ, [59]. See also *R (Al-Haq) v Secretary of State for Foreign and Commonwealth Affairs* [2009] EWHC 1910, [46], Pill LJ, [59], Cranston J; *R (Abassi) v Secretary of State for Foreign and Commonwealth Affairs* [2002] EWCA Civ 1598, as to whether the Foreign Secretary could be ordered to make representations about a British citizen held at Guantanamo Bay.

19 *Shergill v Khaira* [2014] UKSC 33, [42]. This lack of competence does not derive merely from the fact that the powers are exercised under the royal prerogative. Had they been derived from the prerogative and reviewable, the fact that a decision was made by ministers on the ground of national security would show that it was not reviewable, *Council of Civil Service Unions v Minister for the Civil Service* [1985] AC 374, [403].

20 *R v Secretary of State for Defence ex parte Thring* (2000, unrep., see https://www.ICRC.org), where Bennett J commented, 'I do not rest my decision on prerogative powers. [This application] would involve considerations of the policy and the nature of operations of the armed forces abroad, and particularly of the Royal Air Force. In my judgment these are not matters which can be the subject of judicial review, because the courts are not equipped to do so.'

21 *Shergill v Khaira* [2014] UKSC 33, [43].

22 In *Mohammed v Secretary of State for Defence* [2015] EWCA Civ 843 the claim of SM was brought, partially, in tort on the basis of Afghan law, by virtue of the Private International Law (Miscellaneous Provisions) Act 1995, s 11, see [305]. See also *Bici v Ministry of Defence* [2004] EWHC 786, discussed below.

23 154 ER 450 (1848) which has been the subject of more than one interpretation, reviewed in *Mohammed v Secretary of State for Defence* [2015] EWCA Civ 843, [333], [335]–[336]. There were, however, two clear features of that case: the act of the RN ship's commander was ratified expressly by the Crown and the fact that the claimant (who was a foreign national) brought his action before a court in England under the law of trespass.

24 In *Al-Jedda v Secretary of State for Defence* [2010] EWCA Civ 758, Sir John Dyson JSC, made the point that 'the act of state doctrine raises points of very considerable difficulty', [127].

or both,[25] or indeed, whether it was a rule sitting within private international law concerned with the conflict of laws.[26]

What then is an act of state in this context? Underhill J in *Al-Jedda v Secretary of State for Defence* (2009)[27] explained that the term did not encompass 'every act of policy done by the Crown abroad . . . the rule is confined to acts of a character such that it would be wrong in principle for the court to seek to adjudicate on them', and he went on to say that 'acts done by the Crown abroad in the conduct of foreign relations are of their nature not cognisable in the English courts'.[28] The nature of the act of state was also characterised by Leggatt J in *Serdar Mohammed v Secretary of State for Defence* (2014) in a similar way when he described it as 'Executive acts done abroad pursuant to deliberate UK foreign policy.'[29]

If these principles are accepted, it then becomes necessary to determine what acts could be acts of state. The mere fact that acts are carried out abroad by agents of the state, such as by British soldiers, will not, of itself, be sufficient to establish an act of state. The decision on the part of the British government to establish internment in Iraq following UN Security Council Resolution 1546 (2004) would come within the doctrine[30] as would 'the decision to contribute British forces to the MNF [Multi-National Force (in Iraq)]'[31] and the detention of Afghan nationals in Afghanistan beyond 96 hours[32] but not the occupation of the hotel in Cyprus by British soldiers,[33] nor the ill-treatment of detainees by British soldiers in Iraq.[34]

The effect of a finding that the acts, of which a complainant seeks damages against the UK government, are properly classified as an act of state will lead to the conclusion that the claim is not justiciable and that will be the end of it.[35] If this analysis is correct it would appear illogical to call it a 'defence' as such since there would be nothing to defend.[36] The reason for the principle is said to be that it is for the executive through its activities abroad 'to protect the interests of the state . . . the courts ought not to undermine that executive action by questioning further its legality'.[37]

25 *Mohammed v Secretary of State for Defence* [2015] EWCA Civ 843, [339] treated act of state as bearing both concepts, but compare *Shergill v Khaira* [2014] UKSC 33, [42].
26 *Mohammed v Secretary of State for Defence* [2015] EWCA Civ 843, [359].
27 [2009] EWHC 397 (QB), [75].
28 *Ibid*, [80].
29 [2014] EWHC 1369 (QB), [397], approved on appeal, *Mohammed v Secretary of State for Defence* [2015] EWCA Civ 843, [352], [372].
30 *Al-Jedda v Secretary of State for Defence* [2010] EWCA Civ 758, Arden LJ, [108]. Compare the view of Elias LJ, [215].
31 *Al-Jedda v Secretary of State for Defence* [2009] EWHC 397 (QB), Underhill J, [76].
32 *Serdar Mohammed v Ministry of Defence* [2014] EWHC 1369.
33 *Mohammed v Secretary of State for Defence* [2015] EWCA Civ 843, [319], referring to *Attorney-General v Nissan* [1970] AC 179.
34 *Mohammed v Secretary of State for Defence* [2015] EWCA Civ 843, [309]; *Al-Jedda v Secretary of State for Defence* [2009] EWHC 397 (QB), [87].
35 *Al-Jedda v Secretary of State for Defence* [2009] EWHC 397 (QB), Underhill J, [74].
36 *Ibid.* Compare *Mohammed v Secretary of State for Defence* [2015] EWCA Civ 843, [376].
37 *Al-Jedda v Secretary of State for Defence* [2010] EWCA Civ 758, Elias LJ, [212].

It may seem strange that a foreign national could bring an action in tort before an English court where the damage is suffered abroad and caused by acts of agents of the British government, such as members of the armed forces, and where the applicable law is of that foreign state. The problem that a claimant in this situation would face is that he or she may not be able to commence proceedings against the UK in the state concerned because of the principle of sovereign immunity (discussed below), in this case, of the UK. If an action could not be brought in England the potential claimant would be left without a remedy. There is some judicial support for the position that, in these circumstances, a claim could be brought before a court in England,[38] but it may be defeated by the court holding that the acts of the defendant amounted to an act of state.[39]

There has been no decision of the courts directly on the issue of whether the act of state principle applies to British as well as foreign nationals, although judicial opinion seems to be in favour of its applicability to both.[40] If this is the case it would apply equally to British soldiers, or their families, suing the British government for negligence where the damage occurred abroad during the course of military operations. Although the Ministry of Defence may have considered it insensitive to raise act of state against such claimants, particularly as it has not reactivated the Crown Proceedings Act 1947,[41] it has used a similar concept, that of combat immunity, by way of defence.[42] If it is for the sole discretion of the

38 See Brooke LJ, *Al-Jedda v Secretary of State for Defence* [2006] EWCA Civ 327, [108], with whom Underhill J, *Al-Jedda v Secretary of State for Defence* [2009] EWHC 397, [66], agreed. The applicable law was that of Iraq.

39 This was the result in *Al-Jedda v Secretary of State for Defence* [2009] EWHC 397 and before the Court of Appeal [2010] EWCA Civ 758; *Serdar Mohammed v Ministry of Defence* [2014] EWHC 1369 (QB), Leggatt J, [395]–[396]. Compare *Mohammed v Secretary of State for Defence* [2015] EWCA Civ 843, [364], [376(i)].

40 There was a difference of opinion on this point by Lord Reid on the one hand and the other members of the Board in *Attorney-General v Nissan* [1970] AC 179 but in *Al-Jedda v Secretary of State for Defence* [2009] EWHC 397 (QB), Underhill J, [80], *Al-Jedda v Secretary of State for Defence* [2010] EWCA Civ 758, Arden LJ, [109], *Serdar Mohammed v Ministry of Defence* [2014] EWHC 1369 (QB), Leggatt J, [397] all thought there should be no difference. See also, *Smith v Ministry of Defence* [2014] AC 52, where act of state is not mentioned. In *Al-Jedda v Secretary of State for Defence* [2010] EWCA Civ 758 (*Al-Jedda No 2*, which concerned a claim for damages for unlawful imprisonment) Arden LJ in the Court of Appeal indicated that 'the fact that Mr Al-Jedda is a British national is not, in my judgment, a bar to raising the defence of act of state', [109]; Sir John Dyson JSC concluded that 'the act of state doctrine raises some points of very considerable difficulty [and it was not] necessary . . . to express a view', [127], whereas Elias LJ discussed the issue in detail but concluded that it was 'doubtful whether the issue of the act of state should be raised at this stage of the proceedings', [226]. All other forms of act of state, discussed in this chapter, make no differentiation between British and foreign nationals.

41 The power granted to the Secretary of State by the Crown Proceedings (Armed Forces) Act 1987, s 2, to revive the effect of s 10 of the Crown Proceedings Act 1947 has not been invoked.

42 It did so in *Smith v Ministry of Defence* [2014] AC 5, discussed in Chapter 7. The term, 'act of state' is not to be found in any of the judgments of the Supreme Court in this case. Combat immunity is discussed below.

government to decide whether to raise act of state or not,[43] this would suggest that it could still be used against foreign national complainants or even against British civilian contractors killed or injured abroad during military operations.

Even if logic draws us to the conclusion that act of state is applicable to British soldiers, in the way described above, the result would appear to be harsh and probably unacceptable to most people. Apart from a legislative intervention, or a judicial decision to ensure that it did not apply to British nationals, a narrow interpretation of what actually is an act of state would seem to provide a solution. As an alternative, an individual, whether of British or of foreign nationality, could eschew a claim under common law in favour of one brought under the Human Rights Act 1998, providing he came within the jurisdiction of the UK, when the acts of which he complains occurred.[44] Following the decision of *Mohammed v Secretary of State for Defence* (2015)[45] it is now likely that the sting has been taken out of the second category of act of state, since a foreign national affected by British armed forces abroad, and who might have been defeated by this principle, will probably be able to bring himself within the jurisdiction of the UK under the Human Rights Act and be able to claim a breach of a right owed to him under Articles 2, 3 or 5 of the ECHR.

Before going on to discuss the third category it is worth making two further points should the courts determine that a particular issue is a justiciable one. First, there is an accepted practice of seeking relevant facts on well accepted, but limited areas, by way of a Foreign Office certificate, which will then be treated as binding on the court.[46] Secondly, the courts will generally recognise that it is the government and not themselves, who are best placed to determine national security interests. The views of the government on this issue will be normally be

43 *Bici v Ministry of Defence* [2004] EWHC 786 (QB) where Elias J stated, 'in this case the defendants have expressly disavowed any reliance upon [the act of state] doctrine', [89]. In *Al-Jedda v Secretary of State for Defence* [2009] EWHC 397 (QB) Underhill J stated that 'the basis of the concession is not clearly stated', note 12 at conclusion of his judgment.

44 See Chapter 7. For a successful action based on the Human Rights Act 1998, where an Afghan national claimed that he had been unlawfully detained by British armed forces in Afghanistan, *Mohammed v Secretary of State for Defence* [2015] EWCA Civ 843.

45 [2015] EWCA Civ 843.

46 *R (HRH Sultan of Pahang) v Secretary of State for the Home Department* [2011] EWCA Civ 616, Maurice Kay LJ, [36]; *British Arab Commercial Bank plc v The National Transitional Council of the State of Libya* [2011] EWHC 2274 (Comm), [25]. The reason for the principle is that they will contain facts 'which the court accepts, not so much because they are within the exclusive knowledge of the UK Government, but because they represent matters which are exclusively for decision by the Government and not for the courts', *Khurts Bat v Government of Mongolia, Secretary of State for Foreign and Commonwealth Affairs* [2011] EWHC 2029 (Admin), Moses LJ, [34]. The Court of Appeal in *R v Mohammed Gul* [2012] EWCA Crim 280, [22], considered it unnecessary to determine whether the statements contained in Foreign Office certificates in that case were questions of fact for the jury or whether they were conclusive, although their view was that the certificate was conclusive. See also *Amin v Brown* [2005] EWHC 1670 (Ch), [31]. See generally, E Wilmshurst, 'Executive Certificates in Foreign Affairs: the United Kingdom' (1986) 35 ICLQ 157, 162.

given great weight,[47] but it can no longer be said that the courts 'should speak with the same voice' as the government on matters relating to foreign policy.[48]

The third category concerns an act of state, which, like the other versions of the principle, may well be recognisable, if pleaded, but whose substance and boundaries are not easy to define.[49] One aspect of it is that a court in England will not decide a claim based on an allegedly unlawful act,[50] if to do so would be at the heart of, or would of necessity,[51] 'call into question the activity of a foreign state on its own territory'.[52] Although this so-called doctrine is based, to some extent, on the principle of the equality of states under international law, the avoidance of 'disruption of international relations (or what is also described as the rule of comity)',[53] and on the notion that a state can only act through its officials, the technical side of it can be blinding as to its effect. It could have meant, for instance, that a court in England was not able to proceed with a claim that some UK authorities were alleged to be implicated in the unlawful extra-ordinary rendition of individuals by US officials acting outside the USA, until the Court of Appeal took a different view from the trial judge.[54]

The courts have, however, recognised an exception on grounds of 'public policy where there is a violation of international law or a grave infringement of fundamental human rights'.[55] There is little doubt that a court would determine that torture amounted to a grave infringement of fundamental human rights and it is likely that arbitrary detention would also fall within this category. This would seem to cover the type of case, subject to the facts being established, where an individual is subjected to unlawful rendition by a foreign state. In *Belhaj v Straw (and others)*

47 *Campaign for Nuclear Disarmament v Prime Minister of the United Kingdom and others* [2002] EWHC 2777 (Admin) and see Simon Brown, LJ, [42], quoting Lord Steyn in *Secretary of State for the Home Department v Rehman* [2001] UKHL 47, [31]. Cf *The Zamora* [1916] 2 AC 77, Lord Waddington, 107.

48 *Mohammed v Secretary of State for Defence* [2015] EWCA Civ 843, [354].

49 *Abdul-Hakim Belhaj, Fatima Boudchar v Rt. Hon. Jack Straw MP (and six other Defendants)* [2013] EWHC 4111 (QB), Simon J, [36] and his footnote 3. See also discussion of public interest immunity certificates below.

50 In *Yukos Capital v OJSC Rosneft Oil* [2012] EWCA Civ 855, [60], Rix LJ commented that 'the various formulations of the paradigm principle are apparently wide, and prevent adjudication on the validity, legality, lawfulness, acceptability or motives of state actors'.

51 See *Yukos Capital v OJSC Rosneft Oil* [2012] EWCA Civ 855, [109] where Rix LJ distinguished a situation where the acts of a foreign State were relevant merely as an 'ancillary or collateral aspersion'.

52 *Belhaj v Straw* [2014] EWCA Civ 1394, [133]. See also *Rahmatullah v Secretary of State for Foreign and Commonwealth Affairs* [2012] UKSC 48, [53], which distinguished the act of state doctrine since that case did not require a decision on whether the US authorities had been in breach of the Geneva Conventions.

53 *Yukos Capital v OJSC Rosneft Oil* [2012] EWCA Civ 855, para 65, Rix LJ.

54 *Abdul-Hakim Belhaj, Fatima Boudchar v Rt. Hon. Jack Straw MP (and six other Defendants)* [2013] EWHC 4111 (QB), Simon J was overruled on this point by the Court of Appeal, [2014] EWCA Civ 1394.

55 *Belhaj v Straw* [2014] EWCA Civ 1394, [81]; *Yukos Capital v OJSC Rosneft Oil* [2012] EWCA Civ 855, para 69.

(2013) a claimant alleged false imprisonment (and other torts) before the High Court in London, on the basis that he had been delivered to Libya, by way of an unlawful rendition. The defendants relied upon the act of state doctrine, which succeeded at first instance but which was rejected by the Court of Appeal on the grounds that the limitation to the doctrine concerning a grave infringement of fundamental human rights applied.[56] It was argued for the defendants that to uphold the act of state doctrine in the case would avoid any potential for the embarrassment of the government, or for the disruption of international relations between the UK and the other states concerned, but the Court of Appeal decided that although the doctrine was engaged it would not, for the reasons above, apply.[57] The Court summed up the consequences of upholding the act of state doctrine in this case by drawing attention to the 'stark reality . . . that unless English courts are able to exercise jurisdiction in this case, these very grave allegations against the executive will never be subject to judicial investigation'.[58] Even then the difficulties of proving what were alleged facts in this case cannot be overestimated.[59]

This same lack of accountability could also follow where the courts do not even refer to the act of state doctrine but where the underlying basis of a claim for judicial review or for damages raises the same issue of 'judicial restraint or abstention';[60] whether this is based upon discretion or a lack of jurisdiction the result is the same. It becomes a non-justiciable issue.[61] Thus, the Court of Appeal refused to permit claimants to challenge an alleged decision of the Foreign Secretary 'to provide intelligence to the US authorities for use in drone strikes in Pakistan' on the broad ground that 'however the claims are presented they involve serious criticisms of the acts of a foreign state'.[62]

56 *Belhaj v Straw* [2014] EWCA Civ 1394. For the view of the ECtHR on a particular application based on rendition see *Al Nashiri v Poland* (2015) 60 EHRR 16.

57 A Diplomatic Service witness had commented on, for example, adverse effects on intelligence sharing between the UK and the US authorities, [103]. The Court of Appeal concluded that, 'considerations of embarrassment of the executive . . . in our view, would not be a proper basis for declining jurisdiction', [111].

58 *Belhaj v Straw* [2014] EWCA Civ 1394, [119].

59 *Ibid*, [76]–[77], [89]. In many cases there may be difficulty in determining the facts, a matter to which Lord Wilberforce in *Buttes Gas and Oil Co Hammer (No 3)* [1982] AC 888, 938, drew attention when he referred to 'no judicial or manageable standards by which to judge [the] issues'. Cf *Kuwait Airways Corporation v Iraqi Airways Co (Nos 4 & 5)* [2002] 2 AC 883 in which UN Resolutions 662 (1990) and 664 (1990) declared the annexation of Kuwait by Iraq as null and void. The purported law passed by the Iraqi government was not in doubt; its effect was the issue involved, as had been the situation of the Nazi law in *Oppenheimer v Cattermole* [1976] AC 429.

60 *Buttes Gas and Oil Co Hammer (No 3)* [1982] AC 888, Lord Wilberforce, 931, although see *Yukos Capital v OJSC Rosneft Oil* [2012] EWCA Civ 855, [66], Rix LJ.

61 *Campaign for Nuclear Disarmament) v Prime Minister and Others* [2002] EWHC 2777 (Admin), Simon Brown LJ, [47] referred to by Laws MR, [29] in *R (Khan) v Secretary of State for Foreign and Commonwealth Affairs* [2014] EWCA Civ 24.

62 *R (Khan) v Secretary of State for Foreign and Commonwealth Affairs* [2014] EWCA Civ 24, [4] and [53] respectively. Laws LJ referred to Lord Wilberforce (note 60 above), see [26]. For discussion of 'drones' see Chapter 9.

Similar consequences flow from the related concepts of sovereign immunity and combat immunity. The former is governed by the Sovereign Immunity Act 1978,[63] which was applied in *Jones v Ministry of the Interior of the Kingdom of Saudi Arabia*[64] to provide a jurisdictional bar to proceedings brought by claimants who alleged that they had been tortured in Saudi Arabia by state officials. It also explains the immunity before the courts in England of current heads of state, and 'any whose conduct in the exercise of the authority of the state is afterwards called into question, whether he acted as head of government, government minister, military commander . . . or subordinate public official . . . it is immunity from the civil or criminal jurisdiction of foreign national courts but only in respect of governmental or official acts.'[65] This produces quite a marked difference between a foreign government minister or public official who cannot, and a British one who can, be made a party to a civil or criminal action in an English court, as *Belhaj v Straw*[66] illustrates.

The combined effect of these principles is that it is difficult to challenge in a civil court in England the activities of a state acting as an ally with the UK during an armed conflict, even though some link with British officials can be established. When it is considered that, in the major armed conflicts discussed in this book, the UK has been acting as part of a coalition with other states, the potential for this lack of legal accountability can be greater than if it was acting alone. It is likely that similar principles of act of state and sovereign immunity will also apply in the allied states thereby preventing legal accountability in the courts of those states.[67] Political accountability may, or may not, take place in the British Parliament, but the effectiveness of this may depend more on the willingness of a foreign government to supply information than on the thoroughness of any British political investigations.

63 Although formulated now in an Act of Parliament, it derives its principles from international law while the source of the act of state doctrine is English law, *R v Bow Street Stipendiary Magistrate, ex parte Pinochet Ugarte (No 3)* [2000] 1 AC 147, 269, Lord Millett.

64 [2007] 1 AC 270. See also *R (Al-Haq) v Secretary of State for Foreign and Commonwealth Affairs* [2009] EWHC 1910 (Admin), Cranston J, [52], relating to the position of Israel concerning Operation Cast Lead in Gaza in 2008. In *Jones v United Kingdom* (2014) 59 EHRR 1, the ECtHR held that 'the application [of the Sovereign Immunity Act 1978] cannot . . . be said to have amounted to an unjustified restriction on the applicant's access to a court [under Article 6(1) [of the ECHR]', [198]. The same conclusion was drawn in respect of the state officials, [215].

65 *R v Bow Street Stipendiary Magistrate, ex parte Pinochet Ugarte (No 3)* [2000] 1 AC 147, 269, Lord Millett; *Harb v Prince Fadh Bin Abdul Aziz* [2014] EWHC 1807 (Ch). Compare the liability of a state official before a court established under international law. For further discussion, see Chapter 6 and generally, J Foakes, *The Position of Heads of State and Senior Officials in International Law* (OUP, 2014).

66 *Belhaj v Straw* [2014] EWCA Civ 1394, [50]. None of the states concerned, nor their servants or agents were made parties to the case and thus state immunity could not apply.

67 It does apply, in some form, in the US courts, see *Yukos Capital v OJSC Rosneft Oil* [2012] EWCA Civ 855, [41], Rix LJ, who describes it as 'a long-standing doctrine of Anglo-American jurisprudence' and quotes, with approval, Chief Justice Fuller in *Underhill v Hernandez* 168 US 250 (1897), 274.

iii Combat immunity

Unlike the much more wide-ranging act of state doctrine, combat immunity appears to be, as its name suggests, limited to providing immunity from civil claims derived from acts or omissions of members of the armed forces during combat.[68] The effect of its application is to deny what might otherwise be a successful claim for damages and, as such 'it should be narrowly construed'.[69] It was applied in *Mulcahy v Ministry of Defence* (1996)[70] to defeat a claim for alleged negligence by one soldier who was injured by another during the course of firing artillery rounds into Iraq in 1991, on the basis that the soldiers concerned were 'engaging the enemy in battle conditions in the course of hostilities'. This was clearly an application of the principle to actual combat but other cases have sown the seeds of doubt as to whether it is so limited. In *Bici v Ministry of Defence* (2004) it was said to apply to 'actual or imminent armed conflict'[71] and in *Smith v Ministry of Defence* (2013) the Supreme Court decided that it could not apply to alleged failures at an earlier stage.[72]

In the circumstances in which it might be relied upon by the Ministry of Defence there is also some uncertainty as to its relationship to the claim itself. It has been said not to amount to a defence to the claim but that it will make the issue non-justiciable.[73] Alternatively, it has been approached from the standpoint that, if it applies, it will prevent a duty of care in negligence from arising.[74] The formulation of the combat immunity principle in terms of duty of care is likely to increase, and not to decrease, the uncertainty as to when the principle can be relied upon by the Ministry of Defence to defeat a claim by, or on behalf of, a member of the UK armed forces. What is 'fair, just and reasonable' are concepts open to subjective interpretation and could involve considerable judicial discussion of a range of cases concerned with the general duty of care in negligence, totally unconnected with the facts of combat immunity.[75] Moreover, since the duty of care applies in the tort of negligence there may be some uncertainty as to whether a forging of the principle on the anvil of this concept will cover other torts, such as trespass to the person.[76] The much more straightforward basis for

68 Compare combatant immunity, which is discussed in Chapter 6.

69 *Smith v Ministry of Defence* [2013] UKSC 41, Lord Hope, delivering the judgment of the majority, [92].

70 [1996] QB 732.

71 [2004] EWHC 786 (QB), [90].

72 [2013] UKSC 41, Lord Hope, [92]. Compare the different positions of the Challenger tank claimants and those involving the Snatch Land Rover, [95]–[96]. The claims in this case which were based on the Human Rights Act 1998 are discussed in Chapter 7 and the effect of the case is discussed in Chapter 10.

73 *Bici v Ministry of Defence* [2004] EWHC 786 (QB), [84].

74 *Mulcahy v Ministry of Defence* [1996] QB 732; *Smith v Ministry of Defence* [2013] UKSC 41, Lord Hope, [95], Lord Mance, [114]; *R (Long) v Secretary of State for Defence* [2014] EWHC 2391 (Admin), [77].

75 See, for instance, discussion by Lord Mance in *Smith v Ministry of Defence*, [114]–[122].

76 There was a claim for trespass to the person in *Bici v Ministry of Defence* [2004] EWHC 786 (QB).

the principle of combat immunity as establishing non-justiciability of a claim does at least supply the merit of relative simplicity.

Despite suggestions from various quarters[77] that the effect of the majority judgment of the Supreme Court in *Smith v Ministry of Defence* (2013) has been to abolish the principle of combat immunity it does, in fact, live on to defeat what would otherwise be a successful claim for damages where the events, of which complaint has been made, have occurred during actual or imminent armed conflict. In an unusual step, Lord Hope, who wrote the majority decision in *Smith*, explained during a debate in the House of Lords, that 'we did not say that doctrine of combat immunity no longer exists: it does remain part of our law'.[78] This immunity would not apply, however, to 'things done or admitted to be done at that preliminary stage' such as those contained within the allegations concerning the training and equipment supplied to the Challenger tank, where clear findings of fact would have to be made by a subsequent court.

It might be thought harsh for the government to rely on combat immunity when sued by members of its own armed forces or their families but the Ministry of Defence has expressed the intention to continue to rely on the principle. It has drawn attention to the Armed Forces Compensation Scheme,[79] which it believes is 'preferable to the stress and uncertainty involved in litigation.'[80] It has also indicated that it might introduce legislation, although 'not in the immediate future . . . to clarify and bound the law on combat immunity'.[81]

iv Crown immunity

Many of the tragic events discussed under combat immunity above would not have seen the light of day had the Crown Proceedings Act 1947, s 10 remained in force at the time. This prevented any claims in tort being brought for death or personal injury caused by one member of the armed forces to another member of the armed forces whilst both were on duty, or where a member of the armed forces suffered death or personal injury in consequence of the condition of any Crown land, premises, ship, aircraft or vehicle. Where the secretary of state had certified that the member of the armed forces suffered death, injury or disease that was

77 See, for example, House of Commons Defence Select Committee, 12th Report of session 2013–14, *United Kingdom Armed Forces Personnel and the Legal Framework of Future Operations*, HC 931, [130] and further discussion in Chapter 10.

78 HL Debs 7 November 2013, vol 749, col 398. Lord Hope also explained that the Snatch Land Rover cases were based on a claim under the ECHR, Art 2 (as to which see the Human Rights Act 1998), whereas the Challenger tank cases were based on claims at common law, to which combat immunity could be relevant.

79 For details see https://www.gov.uk/government/publications/armed-forces-compensation/armed-forces-compensation.

80 Written evidence from the Ministry of Defence to the House of Commons Defence Select Committee, 12th Report of session 2013–14, *United Kingdom Armed Forces Personnel and the Legal Framework of Future Operations*, HC 931 (2014), [25].

81 *Ibid*, [26].

attributable to service he would, instead, be entitled to a service pension.[82] Section 10 of the 1947 Act was repealed by the Crown Proceedings (Armed Forces) Act 1987, although it can be revived by the secretary of state where it appeared 'necessary or expedient to do so' for the purposes of 'any warlike operations in any part of the world'.[83] To some extent, the principle of combat immunity made it unnecessary to do so, although, given its limitation to actual or imminent armed conflict, it is much more limited in its scope as a form of crown immunity than would be a revived s 10 of the 1947 Act. Whether a government would actually revive s 10 of the 1947 Act might appear to be 'political death [in respect of] the unpopular wars of choice in Iraq and Afghanistan',[84] but this may not necessarily be so. If the revival of s 10 would actually 'facilitate the grant of a pension . . . by obviating the need to prove that their injury was attributable to service',[85] a claim for damages with all its uncertainty of result (including whether combat immunity would or would not apply to it) would be avoided. Against this conclusion would need to be cast the loss of obtaining a lump sum by way of damages and an opportunity to hold individuals to account before a court.[86]

v Public interest immunity certificates

A certificate signed by a minister claiming public interest immunity (PII) from disclosing evidence has been a feature in some of the cases relating to Britain's wars since 2000 that have come before the courts. It is, perhaps, not surprising that they have appeared, given the nature of armed conflict, which was still ongoing, but too ready an acceptance of them would be likely to defeat, or prejudice seriously, an otherwise justifiable claim. With ministers having the responsibility to protect national security interests it might appear that their certificate, if challenged, would prevail, given that its disclosure could affect the UK's relationship with another state, or give information useful to those who would jeopardise that

82 This was explained in *Roche v United Kingdom* (2006) 42 EHRR 30, [123]. The ECtHR came to the same conclusion on the compatibility of s 10 of the 1947 Act with Art 6 of the ECHR as the House of Lords in *Matthew v Ministry of Defence* [2003] UKHL 4. Both cases discuss the earlier case law relating to s 10.

83 Section 2. Any revival of s 10 is to be made by statutory instrument, subject to annulment by either House of Parliament. No revival order has actually been made, see Written evidence from the Ministry of Defence to the House of Commons Defence Select Committee, 12th Report of session 2013–14, *United Kingdom Armed Forces Personnel and the Legal Framework of Future Operations*, [20]. By the International Criminal Court Act 2001, s 78, neither the Crown nor 'any person in the public service of the Crown' is immune from proceedings under the Act.

84 Lord Thomas, HL Deb 7 November 2013, vol 749, col 395.

85 *Roche v United Kingdom* (2006) 42 EHRR 30, [123].

86 The holding of an individual serviceman or woman to account may occur in ways other than by a High Court action. *R (Connor & Allbutt) v Ministry of Defence* [2009] EWHC 3351 (Admin) shows that an army officer was criticised by the coroner for his involvement in the 'friendly-fire' incident involving a Challenger tank in 2003 and that the army had considered disciplinary action against him.

security. The courts, however, have to balance the requirement of open justice against the national security interests claimed, and they have shown themselves willing to apply independent judgment, whist recognising that the minister is in the best position to assess the potential impact on national security should the information be disclosed.[87] The courts are more likely to order disclosure, in the face of a PII certificate, where the information, upon which it is based, has already entered into the public domain.[88]

Following its experience in *R (Al-Sweady) v Secretary of State for Defence* (2009) the courts have, in effect, been put on notice to 'approach the content of any Ministerial Certificate and Schedule from it with very considerable caution'.[89] The effect is likely to be that the Ministry of Defence, in particular, will have to assess very carefully whether it needs to rely on public interest immunity and be prepared to persuade the court that it does. It may be that the courts will now have to think more carefully whether they should give such claims 'substantial weight and utmost respect',[90] in the absence of strong evidence on behalf of the minister.

vi Undertakings to protect against self-incrimination

Each of the public inquiries into specific events in Iraq or Afghanistan has felt the need to try and ensure that the soldiers who were involved are not deterred from coming forward to give evidence by the risk that their evidence could subsequently be used against them. It has done this by obtaining undertakings from the appropriate law officer or prosecutor that any statements that witnesses make to the inquiry will not be used in any possible prosecution or other action, of the individual concerned.[91] This has included a possible prosecution before the ICC and a similar undertaking was given by the prosecutor of that court.[92] On occasions, the inquiry has also been prepared to take steps to protect the identity of particular witnesses. In any particular case the need, on the part of the inquiry, to obtain information from those involved in the events which it is investigating, has been judged to outweigh the accountability to the criminal law or service law, based on the evidence, of the witness concerned.

87 See *R (Mohamed) v Secretary of State for Foreign and Commonwealth Affairs* [2011] QB 218, [44], [46].

88 See, for example, *R (Mohamed) v Secretary of State for Foreign and Commonwealth Affairs* [2011] QB 218 (published by a court in the USA); *R (Al-Sweady) v Secretary of State for Defence* [2009] EWHC 1687 (published in the Payne court-martial proceedings).

89 [2009] EWHC 1687, [49].

90 *R (Mohamed) v Secretary of State for Foreign and Commonwealth Affairs* [2011] QB 218, [46], [147].

91 See The Report of the Baha Mousa Inquiry, HC 1452–1, vol I, 47–8, [2.2], [2.3]; Report of the Al Sweady Inquiry, HC 818–1, 2014, vol I, 31, [1.144–148]; *The Iraq Fatality Investigations: Inspector Sir George Newman, Consolidated Report into the Death of Nadheem Abdullah and the Death of Hassan Abbas Said*, Cm 9023, March 2015, Appendix 10. A similar power is given to the Director of Service Prosecutions in the Armed Forces Bill 2015–16, cl 8.

92 *The Iraq Fatality Investigations: Inspector Sir George Newman, Consolidated Report into the Death of Nadheem Abdullah and the Death of Hassan Abbas Said*, Cm 9023, March 2015, Appendix 7.

vii International law in English courts

One of the effects of the involvement of the UK in armed conflicts since 2000 has been a sharp rise in the number of cases being heard in the High Court in which international law, in one form or another, has been relevant to the issues to be decided. Reference has been made to English statutes that are based on the UK's treaty obligations,[93] customary international law[94] and to the decisions of international courts and tribunals. Principles derived from international law have no greater effect on English law than those found wholly within that law and the doctrine of *stare decisis* applies in the same way. Thus, a decision of the House of Lords or the Supreme Court will have the same binding effect on lower courts even if an international court has subsequently taken a different view on the interpretation of the point of law in issue. This is more likely to occur where the ECtHR has come to a conclusion on the law different from that made by an earlier decision of the House of Lords or the Supreme Court. Subsequent cases before the High Court in London raising the same legal issue will therefore be required to follow the earlier binding English decision.[95]

Another aspect of this principle is that an English court will not decide upon the meaning of a word or phrase in an international treaty, not because this is a matter for the Foreign and Commonwealth Office, but because the view of a court in one state could not be binding on any other state or an international court and the role of the courts in England is to interpret English law. An application to the High Court for an advisory declaration that the proper interpretation of UN Security Council Resolution 1441 (2002) required there to be a further resolution of the UN Security Council, prior to military action being taken against Iraq, was held not to be justiciable.[96]

viii The role of the coroner

It was common practice up to, and including, the Falklands War in 1982 to bury those who had been killed during military operations at the place where they fell. By 2000 a policy of repatriation of those who had been killed led to the involvement of the coroner, for the area where the body was brought into the UK, to

93 See also discussion in Chapter 6. Of particular significance in the Iraq and Afghanistan armed conflicts is the fact that Common Art 3 to the Geneva Conventions, 1949 is a part of English law through the International Criminal Court Act 2001, ss 50(1) and 51(1), by way of a specific offence.

94 See, for example *R (Al-Jedda) v Secretary of State for Defence* [2007] UKHL 58, [32].

95 For examples, see *Al-Waheed v Ministry of Defence* [2014] EWHC 2714, which relates to the difference in interpretation of the relationship between a UN Security Council resolution and the ECHR in *R (Al-Jedda) v Secretary of State for Defence* [2007] UKHL 58 and *Al-Jedda v United Kingdom* (2011) 53EHRR 23.

96 *Campaign for Nuclear Disarmament v Prime Minister and others* [2002] EWHC 2777 (Admin). The reasoning for the decision on this point is made by Simon Brown LJ, [36], [37].

investigate the cause of death of service personnel who died on, or in preparation for, active service.[97] Since most of these repatriation flights landed at RAF Lyneham in Wiltshire and subsequently at RAF Brize Norton in Oxfordshire, it was the relevant county coroner who took on this role.[98] Those who thought that this would be a mere technical exercise were shown to be mistaken. The various coroners involved with service repatriation inquests have been assiduous in their investigations of the deaths of the individual soldiers concerned, rather than merely adopting the view that the serviceman or woman died while on duty in the course of an armed conflict.[99] The scale of the task has been sobering and gives an insight into the human cost of these wars. By July 2014 there had been 610 inquests in respect of those servicemen and women killed in Iraq or Afghanistan, or who suffered injuries there and who subsequently died in the UK as a result of their injuries.[100]

The individual cases before coroners have, broadly, thrown up three main issues. First, coroners have frequently made a determination that the soldier was 'unlawfully killed'.[101] Secondly, their investigations have often involved hearing evidence as to the actual circumstances of the death, a matter that has attracted media interest, particularly when the coroner's narrative verdict has involved criticism of the Ministry of Defence. The third issue has been the perceived problem of commanders having to explain their actions 'on the battlefield' to a civilian coroner.

The determination by a coroner that a soldier has been unlawfully killed appears to be one that few would dispute, although assessing which body of law provides the framework by which the 'unlawfully' can act as an adverb to 'killed' may be of some interest.[102] The law concerned cannot be English law since that law does not apply to the person who killed the soldier.[103] Although there are a very few offences against English law that would apply to a person abroad who is neither a national of, nor a resident of, the UK, the acts of the insurgent are unlikely to come within the reach of any of them.[104]

Coroners might be referring to IHL but this does not, however, actually prohibit a person during a non-international armed conflict from killing a member of

97 The term, 'active service' is defined in the Coroners and Justice Act 2009, s 48, and 'enemy' is defined in the Armed Forces Act 2006, s 374. The previous legislation was the Coroners Act 1988.

98 Repatriations were made at RAF Lyneham from 1 April 2007 to 31 August 2011 and at RAF Brize Norton from 1 September 2011, HC Debs 14 May 2013, vol 563, col 35W.

99 The effect of the application of the Human Rights Act 1998 to British soldiers killed in Iraq or Afghanistan on the nature of the inquest is discussed below.

100 Ministerial statement, HL Debs 17 July 2014, vol 755, col WS85.

101 For an example see *R (Long) v Secretary of State for Defence* [2015] EWCA Civ 770, [38].

102 I have benefited from discussion with His Honour Judge Risius on this point.

103 The fact that the killing occurred abroad is not, by itself, a limitation on the jurisdiction of a coroner, *R (O'Connor) v Avon Coroner (Visser Intervening)* [2009] EWHC 854.

104 The relevant offences are the Criminal Justice Act 1988, s 134 (torture), the Taking of Hostages Act 1982, s 1, the Geneva Conventions Act 1957 (as amended and which deals with grave breaches of the 1949 Conventions and Additional Protocols I and III) as to which see below and Chapter 6.

the armed forces.[105] It is likely, however that it will be the law of Afghanistan or of Iraq that can provide the necessary basis to show that the killing was unlawful.[106]

Secondly, coroners have not shown themselves to be reticent about drawing to the attention of the Ministry of Defence, under rule 43 of the Coroners Rules 1984,[107] any issues that they think should be considered in order to prevent further deaths in similar circumstances but they can, and have, led to a number of systemic improvements that are likely to have saved the lives of other servicemen and women over the years.[108]

Finally, the giving of evidence by soldiers to a coroner's inquest is nothing new. Soldiers have given evidence concerning the deaths of suspected terrorists in the Northern Ireland campaign,[109] but in relation to deaths in the Iraq or Afghanistan operations those giving evidence will have been either the commander, or colleagues, of the deceased soldier. One of the reasons for this has been the gradual acceptance by the courts of the application of the Human Rights Act 1998 to British soldiers serving abroad.[110] When faced with an inquest in respect of a British soldier who has died abroad, coroners have been required to carry out an Article 2 (of the ECHR) inquest, which includes the issue of the duty of the state to protect life to the 'greatest extent reasonably practicable',[111] even though the actual cause of the death was the act of an unnamed insurgent. Where there is an arguable breach of Article 2 by the UK, coroners are required to conduct an investigation that will comply with the necessary requirements

105 Neither does it permit it. A crime against Common Art 3 of the Geneva Conventions 1949 will be committed only where the 'victim [is not] taking an active part in the hostilities at the time the crimes were committed', *Prosecutor v Haradinaj*, IT-04–84*bis*-T, 29 November 2012, [393]. The British soldier killed by an insurgent is taking an active part in hostilities.

106 In *R (Long) v Secretary of State for Defence* [2014] EWHC 2391 (Admin), following the deaths of six RMP soldiers in Iraq in June 2003 a number of Iraqi suspects were charged before the Iraqi courts but no convictions were secured, [15]. Presumably a so-called jihadi fighter of British nationality killed when fighting for ISIL, and whose body has been returned to the UK, would not have been 'unlawfully killed' if killed by the Iraqi armed forces, but would have been if killed by a member of a rival group fighting in the area. A British national fighting *against* ISIL who is killed during the conflict would also be unlawfully killed, since his status, compared with a British soldier, would be irrelevant.

107 1984/52, as amended, with the additions of Rules 43A, 43B. See also the Coroners (Inquest) Rules 2013/1616.

108 A regular summary of reports and responses under Rule 43 is compiled by the Ministry of Justice. For an example, see *R (Long) v Secretary of State for Defence* [2014] EWHC 2391, [51]. An extract of the Secretary of State's response is at [52]. See also the Report on the death of Sergeant Horton and others, who drowned when their Ridgeback vehicle fell into a canal in Afghanistan, Report of the Coroner, 28 April 2015. These reports are now styled as Prevention of Future Death Reports (previously known as Rule 43 Reports) following implementation of powers under the Coroners and Justice Act 2009 in July 2013.

109 See, for example, *McCann v United Kingdom* (1996) 21 EHRR 97, [103].

110 *R (Smith) v Ministry of Defence* [2014] AC 52. For further discussion, see Chapter 7.

111 *R (Middleton) v West Somerset Coroner* [2004] UKHL 10, Lord Bingham, [2]; *R (Long) v Secretary of State for Defence* [2014] EWHC 2391, [35].

set out for such an investigation by the ECtHR and summarised in various cases before the English courts.[112]

On the face of it, the potential in a coroner's court for a clash between the needs of the armed forces to fight insurgents effectively and the obligations of the state to protect the lives, in this case of its soldiers, is considerable. Legal developments, since at least 2000, have shown that this possible competition between these two goals arises most significantly in the coroner's court and not in the High Court, simply because all soldiers who have died abroad will have been the subject of a coroner's inquest, while only a relatively small number of Iraqi or Afghan civilians have brought claims on specific issues before the High Court.

Some senior military figures have argued that coroners should not be involved at all when a soldier is killed in action abroad on the broad grounds that such procedures impede military action[113] and could cause a greater number of British casualties.[114] Others have argued that the procedure threatens the 'no-blame culture', previously understood as applying to lower ranking soldiers who have tried their best but who have made, what later turn out to have been, a mistake in the heat of battle, and that 'we have coroners making tactical judgments about the case on the battlefield'.[115] Indeed, the House of Lords Select Committee on The Constitution (2013) shared 'the concerns expressed to us about the negative effect on the morale and operational independence of the courts scrutinising operational decisions'.[116]

It is not entirely clear that, in relation to coroners' courts, the problem perceived by the House of Lords Select Committee on The Constitution (2013) of the negative effects on morale and operational independence of the armed forces as a result of the proceedings of coroners' courts is a real one. A coroner is not

112 These were summed up in *R (Middleton) v West Somerset Coroner* [2004] UKHL 10, Lord Bingham, [2]–[3]; *R (Long) v Secretary of State for Defence* [2014] EWHC 2391, [38], [59]. In the Report on Capt Sawyer and Corporal Winters of 16 March 2015, the coroner stated that 'a Coronial Inquest where especially Article 2 is engaged . . . is an area which overlaps between my Coronial function and that of a Service Inquiry', [5]. See also the formal requirement now in the Coroners and Justice Act 2009, s 5(2), to ascertain the circumstances by which the deceased came by his or her death where it is necessary to avoid a breach of Convention rights.

113 '[I]f you are so worried about having a lawyer, or an international lawyer, following you around the battlefield, you will do nothing', Lord Guthrie (a former chief of the defence staff), House of Lords Select Committee on the Constitution, *Inquiry into the Constitutional Arrangements for the use of the Armed Forces*, 2013–14, HL Paper 46 (2013), oral evidence, [21]; Jack Straw, MP, *ibid*, [Q 40].

114 *Ibid*, Lord Stirrup (a former chief of the defence staff). See also General Sir Mike Jackson, *ibid*, 23.

115 *Ibid*, Professor Michael Clarke (Director-General, Royal United Services Institute), 6. For an account of this principle see *R (Long) v Secretary of State for Defence* [2014] EWHC 2391, [19]. It is known as 'mission command', *ibid*.

116 See note 113, [55]. The Government's Response (25 October 2013) to this Report also shared this concern.

permitted to frame a verdict so as to determine any question of criminal or civil liability against an individual.[117] Nor has a service inquiry (formerly a board of inquiry) any power to 'attribute blame or to recommend disciplinary action',[118] although in the light of its report, criminal, disciplinary or administrative action could be brought against one or more individuals by the appropriate service mechanism.[119] It is difficult to square the view of The Constitution Select Committee with what happened following the sad deaths of six members of the RMP killed in Iraq in June 2003, and their inability to communicate with their battle group operations room. Army investigations preceded a board of inquiry, which heard evidence from over 100 witnesses and made recommendations for changes to try and prevent similar incidents.[120] The documentation from the board of inquiry was placed before the coroner and, given the limited role of the coroner, it is likely that any robust questioning of those who gave evidence, if this was felt necessary, was much more likely to take place before a board of inquiry than before the coroner.[121] Indeed, whatever the view of an individual coroner, a civil claim by the family of the deceased soldier could be brought against the Ministry of Defence in appropriate circumstances.[122]

ix Immigration tribunals and former members of, or those who have had links with, insurgent groups

Along with other factors, the armed conflicts, to which the UK has been a party since 2000, have led to instability in the regions concerned, and to some individuals seeking refugee status in the UK. A number of cases have been concerned with former members of insurgent groups in Iraq and Afghanistan, with the result that the Home Office has been required to make decisions on asylum, or on applications for naturalisation, concerning individuals who had been seen as part of 'enemy'[123] organisations, with appeals being brought to tribunals.[124]

117 Rules 42 and 36 of the Coroners Rules 1984 (which remain in force); Coroners and Justice Act 2009, s 10(2).
118 *R (Long) v Secretary of State for Defence* [2014] EWHC 2391, [17]; Armed Forces (Service Inquiries) Regulations 2008/1651, reg 7.
119 The Service Prosecution Authority or, in relation to administrative action, the chain of command.
120 *R (Long) v Secretary of State for Defence* (2015) EWCA Civ 770, [38].
121 *Ibid*, [19]–[20].
122 *Ibid*, [29].
123 'Enemy' is defined in the Armed Forces Act 2006, s 374 as 'all persons engaged in armed operations against any of Her Majesty's forces', and is sufficiently wide to cover all those who participate in some way in insurgent organisations against UK armed forces in Iraq or Afghanistan.
124 The First-tier Tribunals and Upper-tier Tribunal, Immigration and Asylum Chamber. See generally, S Singh Juss, 'Terrorism and the Exclusion of Refugee Status in the UK' (2012) 17 Jo C & SL 465.

The Geneva Convention Relating to the Status of Refugees 1951 and its Protocol of 1967[125] provides a framework for an individual to claim refugee status but he can be disqualified if it is shown that there are serious reasons to believe that he has committed a war crime or a crime against humanity, a serious non-political offence, or is guilty of acts contrary to the purposes and principles of the UN.[126] In coming to a decision as to whether there was a real risk of persecution, tribunals appear to have taken a realistic view of the risks a former member of an insurgent organisation would face if he had to return to Afghanistan, particularly as many applicants will be likely to admit to only low-level engagement with the organisation. In considering a case of this type the Court of Appeal concluded, in relation to a particular applicant, that 'the Taliban would not be interested in devoting part of its limited resources to tracking him down in Kabul in order to assassinate him'.[127]

A further hurdle exists if a person granted refugee status wishes to acquire British nationality. In these circumstances, his past life can be relevant to determine whether he is 'of good character' for the purposes of the British Nationality Act 1981.[128] A claimant who was a member of the Taliban religious police between 1996 and 2001 and who was 'involved in crimes against humanity, or supporting the commission of such crimes' would be unlikely to be able to show that he was of good character for the purposes of obtaining a naturalisation certificate.[129]

Even if granted asylum, humanitarian protection or discretionary leave to remain in the UK, a former member of an insurgent organisation could find himself on

125 This has been implemented into English law by the Refugee or Persons in Need of International Protection (Qualification) Regulations 2005/2525 and see the EU Directive, 2011/95/EU.

126 The Geneva Convention Relating to the Status of Refugees 1951, Art 1F(a), (b) and (c) and for an exception to non-refoulement, see Art 33(2); Refugee or Persons in Need of International Protection (Qualification) Regulations 2005/2525, reg 7(1); EU Directive, 2011/95/EU, particularly on the grounds of exclusion from refugee status, Art 12. See *JS (Sri Lanka)* [2010] UKSC 15, [8]; *Al-Sirri (FC) v Secretary of State for the Home Department, DD (Afghanistan) (FC) v Secretary of State for the Home Department* [2012] UKSC 54, [68] (attacking ISAF could amount to acts contrary to the purposes and principles of the UN Charter). Of some concern by the courts has been the issue of those who were under 18 at the time they played some part in an insurgent organisation who subsequently claim refugee status. There is evidence of such involvement in anti-government armed groups (although not in a claim for asylum in the UK) from the Human Rights Council Report of the Independent International Commission of Inquiry on the Syrian Arab Republic, A/HRC/27/60, 13 August 2014, [90]–[91] and in Yemen, see UN Security Council Resolution 2140 (2014), [7].

127 *DT (Afghanistan) v Secretary of State for the Home Department* [2014] EWCA Civ 259, [18].

128 Section 6 and Sched 1 of the Act.

129 *R (Amiri) v Secretary of State for the Home Department* [2014] EWHC 4418, [33]. The judgment does not spell out how the acts of the claimant in that case came within the definition of crimes against humanity in, for instance, the Rome Statute of the International Criminal Court, 1998, Art 7, although it does use vol 2 of Nationality Guidance, [26]. In any event the court's task was not to determine whether the claimant actually committed a crime against humanity.

trial in England for acts committed whilst he was in his own country, providing the courts in England had jurisdiction over the offence committed abroad. These offences include torture, a grave breach of the Geneva Conventions 1949 or of Additional Protocols I or III and the taking of hostages.[130] The courts in England will also have jurisdiction over the crimes of genocide, crimes against humanity or war crimes if the alleged perpetrator was a British national, a British resident or a person subject to UK service law.[131] In an application of extra-territorial jurisdiction Faryadi Zardad was convicted by a London jury of conspiracy to torture and to taking hostages while in Afghanistan and was sentenced to 20 years' imprisonment.[132]

In being denied their wish to acquire asylum status or British nationality through the courts or tribunals in England, former members of insurgent groups could be said to having been held accountable for their past actions.[133]

130 The Criminal Justice Act 1988, s 134, the Geneva Conventions Act 1957 (as amended), s 1, and the Taking of Hostages Act 1982, respectively.

131 The International Criminal Court Act 2001, s 1. The Genocide Act 1969 was repealed by the 2001 Act.

132 http://news.bbc.co.uk/1/hi/uk/4695353.stm. A ministerial statement about the case is at HC Debs 28 February 2011, vol 524, col 16W. The minister stated that this was the only case within 'the last 10 years.' The Attorney General at the time, who had authorised the prosecution (under the Criminal Justice Act 1988, s 135 and the Taking of Hostages Act 1982, s 2), referred briefly to the case and indicated that he had led for the prosecution, HL Debs 16 June 2011, vol 728, col 1017.

133 In much the same way as the army medical officer was erased from the list of medical practitioners by the General Medical Council on the basis of his actions and omissions relating to the death of Baha Mousa in Iraq in 2003, discussed in Chapter 8. For the attempt to deprive Mr Al-Jedda of his British citizenship, see *Secretary of State for the Home Department v Al-Jedda* [2013] UKSC 62.

6 The United Kingdom's obligations under international humanitarian law

i The relationship between international humanitarian law and human rights law

International humanitarian law and human rights law are discussed in separate chapters to reflect the different origins and procedures inherent in each.[1] There is, however, a great deal in common between these distinct branches of international law and, in many ways, they complement each other. Parts of both are also to be found in English law, principally through the Geneva Conventions Act 1957, the International Criminal Court Act 2001 and the Human Rights Act 1998. The principles derived from these bodies of international law also find their ways into training materials, operating procedures, standing orders and other forms of service practice and, as a result, become alive to the individual soldier on the ground, who is unlikely to be concerned with whether the source is IHL or human rights law.

It has to be said, however, that these two areas of law have, for some, now become treated as virtually interchangeable or are placed together as if there were no significant differences between them. The UN Security Council in various resolutions has tended to adopt this practice.[2] It is also seen in the media where war crimes are often referred to as 'breaches of human rights'. They may well be, but there are good reasons for at least seeing the significant differences between these two areas of international law, despite the fact that the boundaries between them are by no means watertight. The basic structural differences between them should not be overlooked; 'human rights law establishes lists of protected rights whereas international criminal law [based on IHL] establishes lists of offences'.[3]

International humanitarian law (IHL) is firmly rooted in the Geneva Conventions 1949 and their two Protocols of 1977, although it will also encompass other treaties.[4] It imposes obligations on states and some will also be placed on the

1 'The precise relationship between the ECHR and IHL in relation to extra-territorial military operations is a matter of great complexity and uncertainty', *Mohammed v Secretary of State for Defence* [2015] EWCA Civ 843, 96.

2 See for example, UN Security Council Resolutions 1338 (2001), [2]; 1746 (2007), [25] (Afghanistan).

3 *Prosecutor v Kunarac and others*, ICTY, IT-96-23-T, 22 February 2001, [470].

4 See Chapter 1.

shoulders of members of its armed forces.[5] Most importantly, it also applies to non-state actors, however these are described, and in this sense the armed forces and their non-state enemy are compelled to apply the same, at least, basic legal principles to their operations.[6] These principles would be recognisable in any human rights treaty and include prohibitions on murder, torture, inhuman or degrading treatment.[7]

As with international human rights law, IHL also imposes obligations on states to investigate certain breaches of their treaty obligations.[8] Many of the most serious norms of IHL can be enforced directly by a state, such as the UK, which has implemented into English law the crimes set out in the Rome Statute 1998 of the International Criminal Court 2001. In addition, British soldiers will remain liable for crimes, such as the various forms of assault or for torture, under the ordinary English criminal law wherever they are serving. It is not difficult to teach soldiers this basic principle and that a breach could lead to trial by court-martial, as has occurred in a few instances during the course of Britain's wars from 2000.[9]

By way of contrast, human rights law has had its most visible impact since 2000 on claims by British soldiers or their families and Iraqi or Afghan nationals brought under the Human Rights Act 1998 before the High Court in London.[10] It has also been important in driving through changes to the way in which detainees held by the UK armed forces are to be treated during their detention or following their transfer.

5 The state is also responsible for the acts of its armed forces, Hague Convention IV, 1907, Art 3; Additional Protocol I, 1977, Art 91.

6 Common Art 3 to the Geneva Conventions 1949; customary international law, as to which see J-M Henckaerts and L Doswald-Beck, *Customary International Humanitarian Law: Volume 1: Rules* (Cambridge University Press, 2005). A major difference is that only members of the armed forces of a state (along with a few other categories) are entitled to be treated as prisoners of war under Geneva Convention III, 1949. Others cannot be considered to be 'combatants' (see discussion below).

7 Common Art 3 to the Geneva Conventions 1949; Additional Protocol II, 1977, Art 4; the Rome Statute 1998, Art 8(2)(c) and (e) impose obligations on all those who take part in a non-international armed conflict. The term 'murder' would encompass the killing of a person who is not taking an active part in hostilities, see the Elements of Crimes of the International Criminal Court, Art 8(2)(c)(i). During an international armed conflict, murder (styled as 'wilful killing') involves the killing of a person protected by the Geneva Conventions 1949, Elements of Crimes, Art 8(2)(a)(i).

8 See for example, the grave breaches set out in each of the four Geneva Conventions, 1949 and in Additional Protocol I, 1977; J-M Henckaerts and L Doswald-Beck, *Customary International Humanitarian Law: Volume 1: Rules* (Cambridge University Press, 2005), Rule 158. See generally, *Israel's Mechanisms for Examining and Investigating Complaints of Violations of the Laws of Armed Conflict According to International Law* (The Turkel Commission, Second Report, 2013), pp 73–82 and comment on it in 'Report of the Special Rapporteur on the Promotion and Protection of Human Rights and Fundamental Freedoms While Countering Terrorism', A/68/389, 18 September 2013, [41]–[45].

9 Discussed below and in Chapter 8.

10 The Human Rights Act 1998 has also been significant in the form of inquests held by coroners and fatality investigations, conducted by an inspector, see discussion in Chapter 5.

The application of both IHL to human rights law cases and human rights law to criminal prosecutions of individuals for breaches of IHL has now become well-established, although each judicial body, being specialist in its own field, has tended to be cautious about adopting standards from the other branch of international law. This can be seen from the approach of the ECtHR on the one hand and the ICTY or the ICC on the other.

When British armed forces are engaged in an armed conflict abroad serious issues have been raised as to whether only IHL should apply, to the exclusion of human rights law,[11] whether both should continue to form the legal backdrop of military operations in their various forms, or whether IHL should take primacy over human rights law.[12] The courts in England have taken the view that both branches of international law can apply.[13]

ii The nature of international humanitarian law

Large-scale wars have led to a tendency, particularly since the middle of the nineteenth century, to build layers of additional international law to try and lessen the horrors for those taking part, or who are caught up, in them. The individual Geneva Conventions of 1949 remain the primary sources of IHL during an international armed conflict and to which all states in the world are parties. In very recent times the key concerns have been addressed by prohibitions by treaty on the use of certain types of weapons that cannot discriminate between combatants and civilians, such as anti-personnel land mines[14] and cluster munitions,[15] and the difficult question of non-international armed conflicts.[16] International humanitarian law has tended to draw clear distinctions between an international armed conflict, on the one hand, and a non-international armed conflict, on the other. This classification does have a profound effect on the law that applies and

11 The government response to the House of Commons Foreign Affairs Committee 6th Report, session 2014–15, *The FCO's Human Rights Work in 2013*, Cm 8975 (2015), [21], 'in an armed conflict international humanitarian law governs military activity. Outside armed conflict, any action must be in accordance with applicable international human rights law.'

12 See House of Commons Defence Select Committee, 12th Report of 2013–14, *UK Armed Forces Personnel and the Legal Framework of Future Operations*, HC 931, [128], which concluded that 'the Government should work to ensure that IHL is the body of law regulating the conduct of armed conflict with primacy over human rights law'. See also M Meyer, written evidence, [10].

13 See, for example, *Mohammed v Secretary of State for Defence* [2015] EWCA Civ 843, [107] and its discussion, [116], of *Hassan v United Kingdom*, Application No 29750/09, Grand Chamber Judgment, 16 September 2014; *Al-Saadoon v Secretary of State for Defence* [2015] EWHC 715.

14 Ottawa Convention on the Prohibition of the Use, Stockpiling, Production and Transfer of Anti-Personnel Mines and on their Destruction, 1997. It was implemented into English law by the Landmines Act 1998.

15 The Convention on Cluster Munitions 2008. It was implemented into English law by the Cluster Munitions Prohibitions Act 2010.

16 Additional Protocol II, 1977.

it can be clearly seen in the wars discussed in this book. In Iraq and Afghanistan, each war started off as international when the conflict was between a coalition of states on the one side, and Iraq or Afghanistan on the other, and then became a non-international armed conflict when governments in these countries came into existence. During the course of the air campaign against Libya in 2011 the conflict was an international one, to be converted into a non-international armed conflict, in which the UK was not a party, once the air strikes had come to an end. The involvement of British armed forces in Sierra Leone in 2000 and in Iraq in 2014 can only be seen as non-international armed conflicts.[17]

iii The principal treaties relevant to Britain's wars from 2000

The four Geneva Conventions, all of which came into existence in 1949, deal with the wounded and sick on land, the wounded, sick and shipwrecked at sea, prisoners of war and the protection of civilians.[18] Of these, the most significant during Britain's wars from 2000, during the international armed conflict stages, have been Geneva Convention IV, dealing with the protection of civilians as protected persons, particularly under the occupation in Iraq from 2003 to 2004[19] and Geneva Convention I, concerned with the wounded and sick, particularly the obligation to treat those individuals purely on their medical needs, without discrimination. This has meant that a British soldier being treated by British medical personnel as a result of wounds caused during a battle may find himself in a field hospital next to a wounded insurgent.[20] Since Geneva Convention III, is activated only during an international armed conflict, including a period of occupation of territory, it had limited application in Iraq and Afghanistan, although the conditions of detention that it lays down would be able to provide a guideline for the treatment of those detained by UK armed forces but who would not be entitled to prisoner of war status.[21] The UK position was stated by a minister in

17 The 2014 action has been carried out following the invitation and with the consent of the government of Iraq. Neither the armed forces of the UK, nor of Iraqi, are engaged in an armed conflict with another state, since ISIL is not a state in international law.

18 These are generally referred to as Geneva Convention I-IV, 1949.

19 Compare Afghanistan after the Bonn Agreement 2001 where Geneva Convention IV, 1949 did not apply since the armed conflict was not of an international character. For an example, see *R (Haidar Hussein) v Secretary of State for Defence* [2014] EWCA Civ 1087, [35]. Common Art 3 to the 1949 Conventions did, however, apply in these circumstances.

20 The obligations contained in Geneva Convention I apply during an international armed conflict but would do so also, through Common Art 3(2) and customary international law, during a non-international armed conflict, as the conflicts in Iraq and Afghanistan would have been classified for most of the time in which British soldiers were involved. For the customary international law position see Rules 109, 110, J-M Henckaerts and L Doswald-Beck, *Customary International Humanitarian Law: Volume 1: Rules* (Cambridge University Press, 2005).

21 For those entitled to prisoner of war status see the discussion of 'combatant' below.

Parliament in 2005 when he confirmed that 'the UK does not hold any prisoners of war in Iraq'.[22]

In 1977 two additional protocols to the Geneva Conventions 1949 were agreed by states to provide extra legal protection in international and non-international armed conflicts respectively. Other treaties that bear directly upon the issues involved in Britain's wars since 2000 are Hague Convention IV, 1907 and its Regulations, which have been relevant to the occupation of Iraq from 2003 to 2004, and the Ottawa Convention 1997 relating to anti-personnel mines. There was no question of the UK using anti-personnel mines during any of the armed conflicts under discussion since it was a party to the Convention. It did, however, face the fact that members of its armed forces were at serious risk of death or injury through the deployment of IEDs by insurgents in Iraq, but particularly in Afghanistan. A very large number of the deaths and injuries caused to British servicemen and women in Afghanistan can be traced back directly to the use of these devices. The Ottawa Convention is open for signature only by states but since peaceful civilians and NATO soldiers were equally at risk from IEDs, non-state armed groups would be bound by customary IHL which prohibits indiscriminate attacks.[23] Some groups have pledged themselves not to use anti-personnel land mines in the various armed conflicts in Syria.[24]

Although the Geneva Conventions of 1949 have gained universal acceptance the same cannot be said of their two additional protocols of 1977. The USA, Israel and Syria are not parties to either protocol. The UK is a party to both, as is Afghanistan,[25] but Iraq only became a party to Protocol I on 1 April 2010.[26] This does not mean, however, that in Iraq or in Afghanistan the UK was bound to apply the IHL contained in the 1977 Protocols whilst its principal ally, the USA, was not. International law has, over the years, developed another form of itself, customary international humanitarian law, which is binding on all states and which has become very significant in the period covered by this book.

22 HC Debs 30 June 2005, vol 435, col 1690W. It would have held prisoners of war during the international armed conflict phase. There was no international armed conflict involving the UK in Afghanistan after the Bonn Agreement of December 2001 and so Geneva Convention III, 1949 would not have applied.

23 Rules 11 and 12. See J-M Henckaerts and L Doswald-Beck, *Customary International Humanitarian Law, Vol 1: Rules* (ICRC, Cambridge University Press, 2005). Any legal accountability of insurgents for their actions in using IEDs is likely to arise only under Afghan law. The Landmines Act 1998 can apply to acts taking place outside the UK, s 3, although see s 3(3), (5).

24 Geneva Call, a Switzerland based NGO, reported in 2014 that 'the Hazzm Movement, a major brigade of the Free Syria Army had signed Geneva Call's Deed of Commitment banning anti-personnel mines'. Geneva Call also reported that the Syrian–Kurdish armed forces had done so.

25 It became a party to both on 10 November 2009.

26 See www.icrc.org.

iv Customary international humanitarian law

Customary international law is based upon the actual practice of states and it requires states to believe that in engaging in a particular practice they are acting in a way that international law requires of them.[27] In IHL treaty law as well as under customary international law the obligation on individuals is often not to do something, for example, not to target civilian objects, or kill POWs or those not taking an active part in hostilities. The USA is not a party to the Additional Protocol I, 1977 yet it considers that those provisions contained in it relating to the limits of targeting military objectives are customary international law, and therefore apply to it as such, and not as treaty law.[28] There will, however, be other parts of the Protocol on which there is doubt as to whether they actually do reflect customary international law, in the absence of a court declaring them to be so, or a state accepting that it considers that it does so.

All the armed conflicts considered in this book have thrown up the issue of the extent of customary international law during a non-international armed conflict. The reason for this is that, unlike international armed conflicts, the treaty provisions dealing with this type of conflict are sparse. It is not difficult to see why. Over the years it has been common for states to think that civil wars were their concern only and that they had plenty of national law in place to cover virtually all the illegal activities of rebels. The UK is no different and in the criminal law there are offences relating to the carrying of weapons, possession of ammunition and, indeed, all the modern terrorist legislation adds a multitude of new offences to reflect the realities of the different forms of terrorism encountered since the

27 See, for example, *Mohammed v Secretary of State for Defence* [2015] EWCA Civ 843, [220]–[221]. 'A study of customary international law has to look at the combined effect of what states say and what they actually do', J-M Henchaerts, '*Customary International Humanitarian Law*: a Response to US Comments' (2007) 89 IRRC 473, 477. In the field of IHL what states say is largely to be found in their military manuals, and what they do is to be derived from their actions during an armed conflict. The significance of *The Manual of the Law of Armed Conflict* (Joint Service Manual) (UK Ministry of Defence, OUP, 2004) as a source of customary international law appears to be strengthened by *Rahmatullah v Secretary of State for Defence and Secretary of State for Foreign and Commonwealth Affairs* [2012] UKSC 48, where Lord Kerr, [34] concluded that it was not open to the government to take a position contrary to that expressed in the *Joint Service Manual* (although Lord Kerr also referred to a statement reflecting the view of the UK government). This principle must be qualified by a subsequent change in the law as expressed in any amendment to the *Joint Service Manual.*

28 J-M Henckaerts and L Doswald-Beck, *Customary International Humanitarian Law: Volume 1: Rules* (Cambridge University Press, 2005), Vol II, [98]–[99]. For the position of the USA as to the customary international law status of certain Articles of Additional Protocols I and II, see *Israel's Mechanisms for Examining and Investigating Complaints of Violations of the Laws of Armed Conflict According to International Law* (The Turkel Commission, Second Report, 2013), 487, n 7. Compare the US view on causing environmental damage (J-M Henckaerts and L Doswald-Beck, *ibid*, Rule 45, Vol I), J Bellinger III and W Haynes II, 'A US Government Response to the International Committee of the Red Cross Study *Customary International Humanitarian Law* (2007) 89 IRRC 443, 455.

mid-1960s. The development of international human rights after World War II has shown at least one thing: that what a state does to people within its own territory is of concern to the international community, and this applies equally during a non-international armed conflict. Whilst a number of weapons treaties, which have come into existence since 1977, have included non-international armed conflicts within them,[29] there is no wide-ranging treaty law to cover the detail set out in those treaties that are concerned with international armed conflicts. The scope to narrow this gap has been taken up enthusiastically by customary international law, championed by the study carried out by the ICRC.[30] Although there have been powerful argument against this approach[31] there is gradual acceptance by many international lawyers that this can be the only way forward in the short term.

v Armed conflict

The Geneva Conventions of 1949[32] set the starting point for the application of IHL as being the existence of an international armed conflict, which will occur 'whenever there is a resort to armed force between States or protracted armed violence between government authorities and organised armed groups within a State'.[33] For a non-international armed conflict two criteria must be met, namely the intensity of the conflict and the organisation of the parties to the conflict.[34]

Whether an armed conflict is taking place is a purely factual question and is not dependent, in the case of an international armed conflict, upon a declaration of war or, indeed, any state recognising that it is at war.[35] Formal declarations of war[36] seem to be of historical interest only and in the armed conflicts considered in this book none has been made. Although the current factual test avoids the

29 See, for example, Amended Protocol on Prohibitions or Restrictions on the Use of Mines, Booby-Traps and other Devices (1996 amendment to the Convention on Prohibitions, or Restrictions on the use of Certain Conventional Weapons, 1980), Art 1(4).

30 J-M Henckaerts and L Doswald-Beck, *Customary International Humanitarian Law: Volume 1: Rules* (Cambridge University Press, 2005).

31 Largely on the grounds of its methodology and its under-emphasis of operational practice during armed conflicts, J Bellinger III and W Haynes II, 'A US Government Response to the International Committee of the Red Cross Study Customary International Humanitarian Law' (2007) 89 IRRC 443 and compare J-M Henckaerts, 'Customary International Humanitarian Law: a Response to US Comments' (2007) 89 IRRC 473.

32 Common Art 2 to the Geneva Conventions, 1949; Common Art 3 or/and APII for a non-international armed conflict.

33 *Prosecutor v Tadic*, Decision on the Defence Motion for Interlocutory Appeal on Jurisdiction, IT-94–1, 2 October 1995, [70]; *Prosecutor v Boskoski* IT-04–82-A, 19 May 2010, [21]. See generally, International Law Association, *Final Report on the Meaning of Armed Conflict in International Law* (Hague Conference, 2010).

34 *Prosecutor v Tadic, Ibid,* and see *Prosecutor v Haradinaj*, IT-04–84*bis*-A, 29 November 2012, [392–394].

35 C Greenwood, 'The Concept of War in Modern International Law' (1987) 36 ICLQ 283.

36 Although it is recognised in Common Art 2 of the Geneva Conventions 1949 as an alternative means of bringing the Conventions into force.

uncertainty caused whilst waiting to see if a declaration of war would be made it has, nevertheless, its own definitional problem. This is in knowing whether tension between two or more states has gone beyond political rhetoric and has actually become an armed conflict.[37] An obvious sign would be an engagement of opposing armed forces whatever the numbers involved, or the occupation of territory.[38] But the line would also be crossed if, say, armed military aircraft of one state flew over the territory of the other without the latter state's consent with an intent to use force if necessary. Some examples will illustrate the point. The separate attacks by coalition forces on Afghanistan beginning in October 2001, and on Iraq on 20 March 2003, clearly started the armed conflicts between the coalition states on the one hand and Afghanistan and Iraq respectively on the other,[39] whilst the overflight of Libya by armed military aircraft of the UK, France and the USA to enforce UN Security Council Resolution 1973 (2011) led to that action becoming an armed conflict to which IHL applied.

What appears to be a fairly well-settled system of dealing with the different categories of individuals caught up in international armed conflicts came under serious challenge following the events of 11 September 2001 ('9/11') in New York and Washington. The attacks on buildings within those cities by individuals were carried out by those who were not members of the armed forces of another state, and who, it was alleged, had trained and planned their attacks in another country, Afghanistan. Did IHL apply in these circumstances? It is certainly not obvious that it did, since it could not be described as an armed conflict involving two states, Afghanistan and the USA, in the absence of the attack being carried out by the armed forces, or at least under the direction, of Afghanistan. If the events did not fit the classic IHL mould how should they be classified? One answer was to describe it as terrorism but this, in itself does not assist since there is no definition of 'terrorism' under international law, although there will be individual definitions of it in the national law of most states.[40] The UN adopted a number of resolutions immediately after 9/11 and ultimately set up a sanctions system.[41] Without a separate regime established by international law for events of this nature, the USA faced two simple choices, following the subsequent attack on Afghanistan. One was to treat any captured 'terrorists' under its own national law and use its law enforcement mechanisms to determine whether a suspected individual outside the USA could be targeted, or adapt the IHL model, which it

37 International Law Association, *Final Report on the Meaning of Armed Conflict in International Law* (Hague Conference, 2010), 2, which referred also to the existence of organised armed groups who were engaged in fighting of some intensity.

38 For further discussion of the occupation of territory see below.

39 See generally, F Hampson, 'Afghanistan 2001–2010' in E Wilmshurst (ed), *International Law and the Classification of Conflicts* (OUP, 2012), 251; M Schmitt, 'Iraq (2003 onwards)' *ibid*, 360.

40 For the UK see the Terrorism Act 2000, s 1 and Sched 2 for proscribed organisations. See also Chapter 1 above.

41 See UN Security Council Resolutions 1368, 1373, 1377, 1378, 1383 (all of 2001). See also Chapter 2.

preferred to style as 'the laws of war.' It chose the latter option calling its adapted model 'the war on terror' and argued that the Geneva Conventions were written for the form of wars that existed in 1949 and that the Conventions were unable to accommodate this new form of warfare.

The trouble with this approach is that it lacks precision and, as a result, individuals captured or otherwise affected could be argued to be in a 'legal black hole'.[42] If captured it is claimed by the USA that they are 'unlawful combatants'[43] captured on the 'battlefield'.[44]

vi Occupation of territory

Major combat operations in Iraq were declared to be concluded on 1 May 2003.[45] Territory is considered to be occupied when it is 'placed under the authority of the hostile army',[46] but the precise moment UK armed forces actually became occupiers in Iraq is not entirely clear. Was it on 1 May[47] or on a date earlier, or on a date later than this? On 22 May 2003 the UN Security Council adopted Resolution 1483 calling 'upon all concerned to comply fully with their obligations under the Geneva Conventions of 1949 and the Hague Regulations of 1907', which, in effect, recognised that by then Iraq was occupied territory.[48] Yet the ECtHR felt able to conclude that 'by 5 April 2003 British forces had captured Basrah . . . after the British Army entered into occupation of Basrah, they started arresting high ranking members of the Ba'ath Party. . . . [Hassan] was arrested on 23 April 2003',[49] which suggests that the British occupation of Basra was being exercised at least by that date, even though US forces had by then not secured

42 Discussed in Chapter 1.
43 Discussed below.
44 The meaning of the term 'battlefield' is discussed in Chapter 1.
45 HC Debs 15 July 2003, vol 409, col 194W.
46 Hague Regulations 1907, Art 42(1). The authority over the territory must be capable of being exercised, Art 42(2).
47 In a number of judgments this was considered to be the date of the start of the occupation, see *Al-Skeini v United Kingdom* [2011] 53 EHRR 18, [8]; *Jaloud v the Netherlands* (2015) 60 EHRR 29, [56], *Smith v Ministry of Defence* [2013] UKSC 41, where Lord Hope [1], stated that 'the second phase began on 1 May 2003 when major combat operations ceased and were replaced by a period of military occupation'.
48 In UN Security Council Resolution 1472, adopted on 28 March 2003, the first Security Council resolution after the attack on Iraq had begun, a preambular paragraph referred to Art 55 of Geneva Convention IV, 1949, which deals with occupied territories and was subsequently included in an operative paragraph in Resolution 1483, adopted on 22 May 2003. The President of the UN Security Council had been informed by letter on 8 May that the UK, the USA and coalition states had created the Coalition Provisional Authority, see S/2003/538.
49 *Hassan v United Kingdom*, Application No 29750/09, Judgment, 16 September 2014, [9]–[12]. See also Leggatt J in *Al- Saadoon v Secretary of State for Defence* [2015] EWHC 715 (Admin), [75], who in referring to *Jaloud v Netherlands* (2015) 60 EHRR 29, concluded that the occupation by UK forces was in place on 21 April 2003.

their authority over the Baghdad area.[50] It is, perhaps, understandable that the UN should conclude that occupation of the state of Iraq would only occur when the two occupying powers had separately established their own authority over their respective parts of it, which appears to be the case by 22 May 2003, when UN Security Council Resolution 1483 was adopted.

It is not inconsistent with the establishment of occupation that hostilities should continue thereafter, nor that the occupying state finds itself unable to exercise its 'control' over the whole area. Resistance to an occupying force is clearly a foreseeable consequence of occupation itself and is recognised in Geneva Convention IV, 1949.[51] The concept of occupation in IHL and that of 'jurisdiction' under the ECHR are not identical, so whilst a state may be in occupation of territory it may not, at least for part of that time, be able to exercise effective control so as to exercise that form of jurisdiction under the ECHR, Article 1.[52]

The actual date by which the UK, as compared with the USA, became an occupying power is important for one main reason, apart from the beginning of the IHL obligations[53] it owed to those under its occupation. This concerns the interpretation of the ECHR specifically to those individuals within occupied territory where the date of the commencement of occupation could be, although is not necessarily, a critical fact. The issue is, in other words, whether jurisdiction under the ECHR follows automatically from an occupation. In *Hassan v United Kingdom*,[54] the ECtHR seemed to think this was the effect of its earlier decision

50 The Prime Minister told the House of Commons on 14 April 2003 that 'the south of Iraq is now largely under British control . . . in Baghdad itself, the Americans are in control of most of the city but not yet all of it', HC 14 April 2003, vol 403, col 615. The date when the combat phases ended in Maysan Province and the occupation began there 'defies a clear conclusion', *The Iraq Fatality Investigations: Inspector Sir George Newman, Consolidated Report into the Death of Nadheem Abdullah and the Death of Hassan Abbas Said*, Cm 9023, March 2015, [4.19].

51 Article 5(2). See generally, Y Dinstein, *The International Law of Belligerent Occupation* (Cambridge University Press, 2009), 94–95 and as to the theoretical basis of any duty to comply with the obligations imposed by an occupying state see R Baxter, 'The Duty of Obedience to the Belligerent Occupant' (1950) 27 BYBIL 235, 243.

52 See *Hassan v United Kingdom*, Application No 29750/09, Grand Chamber Judgment, 16 September 2014, [75]. In *Al-Skeini v Secretary of State for Defence* [2007] UKHL 26 [83], [129] the House of Lords concluded that the Basra area was not under the effective control of British forces at the time, whilst the ECtHR decided in *Al-Skeini v United Kingdom* (2011) 53 EHRR 18 that the UK had established its jurisdiction for the purposes of the ECHR, Art 1, by 4 August 2003, the earliest date of the various events that formed the substance of that case.

53 Principally these were the Hague Regulations 1907, Geneva Convention IV, 1949, Protocol to the Convention for the Protection of Cultural Property in the Event of Armed Conflict 1954, (as customary law). See also the Iraq (United Nations Sanctions) Order 2003/1519, art 8 of which deals with illegally removed Iraqi cultural property. British armed forces also had responsibilities in safeguarding cultural property, HC Debs 7 February 2005, vol 430, col 1249W.

54 Application No 29750/09, Grand Chamber Judgment, 16 September 2014, [75] in which it accepted that the occupation of Iraq began on 1 May 2003 but 'the United Kingdom was far from being in effective control of the . . . area it occupied'.

in *Al-Skeini v United Kingdom* (2011).[55] The issue in that case was not, however, whether jurisdiction was established by the date of the occupation (taken to be 1 May 2003) but whether it existed at the date when the first of the claims arose, 4 August 2003. On the actual date of the commencement of the occupation of Iraq, different courts have come to different conclusions, although no court has had to make a decision on the actual date of the start of the occupation of Iraq under IHL.

The occupation of territory does not involve a transfer of sovereignty to the occupying state but it does impose responsibility and duties upon that state to 'ensure, as far as possible, public order and safety'[56] simply because no other state entity is available to do so. A breakdown of law and order within the state itself can be just as dangerous to innocent civilians as actual fighting would be, and so it is not difficult to see the importance of this principle, particularly in an urban environment. When the UK became an occupying power in Basra and, at least parts of, the surrounding territory, it fell to them to carry out those tasks which would normally have been undertaken by an Iraqi government, ranging from preventing attacks by insurgents, to protecting cultural property, to tackling ordinary crime and keeping the lights on.[57] They had to steer a course between achieving political and military objectives and not exceeding the limitations placed on an occupying state by IHL.[58]

By 30 June 2004, when the occupation was declared by UN Security Council Resolution 1546 (2004) to have come to an end, the Interim government of Iraq had full sovereignty and, with it, the legal power to invite the UK and other states

55 (2011) 53 EHRR 18.

56 The Hague Regulations 1907, Art 43. UN Security Resolution 1546 (2004), [2], referred to the end of the occupation by 30 June 2004 by which time 'Iraq will *reassert* its fully sovereignty' (emphasis supplied).

57 The detention of civilians in occupied Iraq and after the occupation had come to an end is dealt with in Chapter 9.

58 See, for example, the issue raised by the UK Treasury concerning the 'lack of supply' of the Iraqi currency, Lord Goldsmith, the Attorney General at the time, Evidence to Iraq Inquiry, 27 January 2010, p 227. In a letter, dated 8 May 2003, to the President of the UN Security Council, S/2003/538, the permanent representatives of the USA and of the UK indicated that they had established the Coalition Provisional Authority 'to exercise powers of government temporarily and, as necessary [for the purposes set out, including action to] allow the delivery of humanitarian aid'. This letter was noted in preambular [13] of UN Security Council Resolution 1483 (2003), 22 May 2003. On this basis, Lord Goldsmith concluded that the letter 'effectively got the approval of the Security Council', Evidence to Iraq Inquiry, 27 January 2010, 230. It would, however, be difficult to argue that, by noting the letter of 8 May 2003, the Security Council had *authorised* the USA and the UK to act in occupied Iraq on the basis of it, or even that one or both occupying states had not exceeded the limits of action of an occupying state under IHL. See A Roberts, 'Transformative Military Occupation: Applying the Laws of War and Human Rights' (2006) 100 AJIL 580, who discusses the influences of action by the UN and human rights principles as a means of achieving 'transformative goals' by an occupying state. Compare V Lowe, 'The Iraq Crisis: What Now?' (2003) 52 ICLQ 859, 869.

to assist it in defeating the insurgents.[59] There was no occupation by the UK of Afghanistan at any time since 2001.[60]

vii Who is a combatant?

In an international armed conflict the term, 'combatant' is subject to legal definition in Additional Protocol I, 1977; it refers to a person who is a member of the armed forces, other than medical personnel and chaplains, of a state taking part in the conflict.[61] Although some members of the British armed forces, outside this small group, may be thought of as carrying out a non-combatant role, such as service lawyers, IHL refers to this simple classification based, as it is, on individuals merely belonging to the armed forces. All combatants have a right to take part in the conflict and will, if captured, be entitled to be treated as POWs. Not only that but they will not be liable for any offences against the national law (such as murder, damage to property and so on) of the state in which they are fighting.[62] They would, of course, be liable for trial should they commit any crimes contrary to international law, a matter discussed below.

It is clear then that the term 'combatant' is not a descriptive noun applicable to anyone who happens to take up arms, and there is no need for any of the adjectives, such as 'unlawful' or 'unpriviliged' to be employed.[63] One of the great distinctions in IHL is that between members of the armed forces and everyone else, who are classified as 'civilians'.[64] So, members of the armed forces can

59 The occupation ended on 28 June 2004, *Secretary of State for Foreign and Commonwealth Affairs v Rahmatullah* [2012] UKSC 48, [16]. The Interim government was to be replaced by the Transitional government of Iraq following elections, UN Security Council Resolution 1546 (2004). See also the letter annexed to UN Security Council Resolution 1637 (2005) by the US Secretary of State. For discussion of the legal issues involved following 28 June 2004, see A Roberts, 'The End of Occupation: Iraq 2004' (2005) 54 ICLQ 27; M Sassoli, 'Legislation and Maintenance of Public Order and Civil Life by Occupying Powers' (2005) 16 EJIL 661, 683.

60 This was the view of Lord Goldsmith, Evidence to Iraq Inquiry, 27 January 2010, 225, in his subsequent correction to his evidence. *Quaere* the status of Afghanistan after the government had collapsed and before the implementation of the Bonn Agreement in 2001.

61 Article 43(2).

62 *Public Prosecutor v Oie Hee Koi* [1968] AC 829, 860–1 (JCPC).

63 J Bellinger III, 'Reflections on Transatlantic Approaches to International Law' (2006–07) 17 Duke Journal of Comparative and International Law 513, 521 argues that 'the United States did not invent the concept of "unlawful combatants" to put people in a legal black hole . . . the distinction between lawful and unlawful combatants has deep roots in international humanitarian law'. Compare R Baxter, 'So-Called "Unprivileged Belligerency": Spies, Guerrillas and Saboteurs' (1951) 28 BYBIL 323, 330 on his view of *Ex parte Quirin* (1942) 317 US 1, 30–1; Foreign Affairs Select Committee, 2nd Report, session 2006–07, *Visit to Guantanamo Bay*, HC 44, [77]–[83] in discussing the US usage of the term 'unlawful combatant'; HL Debs 15 January 2004, vol 656, col 682 where a minister stated 'I do not wish to get into this difficult question, which has not been resolved, about the definition of what we mean by "unlawful combatant".' It was also rejected as a term in *Public Committee Against Torture in Israel v The Government of Israel* (2005) HCJ Israel, 769/02, [28].

64 Additional Protocol I, 1977, Art 50(1).

attack members of opposing armed forces but not civilians and this distinction forms the basis of the targeting provisions in the law.[65] It is an undoubted fact, however, that some civilians do take a direct part in hostilities,[66] and when they do they will lose the protection from attack that is granted by IHL to civilians. By so doing they do not become 'combatants' in the legal sense, since they are not members of the armed forces of a state.[67] The experience of fighting in Iraq and Afghanistan, when these conflicts became of a non-international character, has shown the extent of, and the difficulties caused by, civilians who have taken a direct part in the hostilities. In neither of these conflicts did the civilians, who took a direct part in hostilities, form a single homogenous group. The major groupings were al-Qaeda and the Taliban but there were many others, so much so that in Afghanistan they were styled as 'anti-government elements' (AGEs).[68] A civilian who attacked a British soldier could, of course, be attacked in turn but, particularly in relation to drone strikes, it was necessary for the UK to determine 'which armed groups constituted legitimate targets,'[69] for the purposes of the RoE. The issue of a civilian taking a direct part in hostilities is discussed further in Chapter 9.

There can be no doubt that during an international armed conflict a British soldier will be a combatant within the meaning ascribed to the term in IHL.[70] He can therefore kill other combatants during the course of the armed conflict, but he is also subject to English criminal law including when he is serving abroad.[71] The question then arises as to why this is not murder. There is no specific defence

65 See Additional Protocol I, 1977, Art 51. The issue of targeting is discussed in Chapter 9.

66 This phrase is one of legal significance, see Additional Protocol I, 1977, Art 51(3).

67 Although an organised armed group may come within the term, 'armed forces' in Common Art 3 to the Geneva Conventions 1949 and Additional Protocol II refer to 'dissident armed forces', Art 1. Compare the statement of the Minister for the Armed Forces who, in referring to the definition of a 'civilian in use in respect of UK operations in Afghanistan' appears to have used the term 'combatant' to refer to 'those who take part in fighting' and who distinguishes it from 'non-combatants, who do not [take part in fighting] and must be protected as far as possible from its effects', HC Debs 5 November 2012, vol 552, col 437W. This use of the term 'combatant' would seem to include insurgents within it and, as such, it is contrary to the arguments presented above. For discussion of the effect of civilians taking a direct part in hostilities see Chapter 9. Those civilians who work in GCHQ and who may pass on intelligence information to US armed forces could not be considered to be combatants and consequently could not be entitled to 'combatant immunity' despite the equivocation expressed in *R (Khan) v Secretary of State for Foreign and Commonwealth Affairs* [2014] EWCA Civ 24, [19].

68 UN Security Council Resolution 1776 (2007) refers to 'the Taliban, Al-Qaida, illegally armed groups and those involved in the narcotics trade', preambular [8]. In *Report of the Secretary-General on Children in Armed Conflict in Afghanistan*, S/2008/695, 4, AGEs include the Taliban, 'allegedly the most organised', Haqqani Network, Hezb-i-Islami, Jamat Sunat al-Dawa Salafia, other illegally armed groups.

69 HL Debs 19 June 2006, vol 683, col WA 54.

70 Additional Protocol I, 1977, Art 43(2).

71 Both as a British national under the Offences Against the Person Act 1861, s 9, and as a serviceman under the Armed Forces Act 2006, s 42.

to the crime of murder given to a soldier during an international armed conflict and various attempts to reconcile these two positions have been suggested.[72] The better view is that compliance with IHL prevails over English law when they are in opposition to each other, a proposition that can be tested through two examples. In the first, a British soldier kills an enemy combatant during the course of an international armed conflict, and in the second he kills an enemy combatant who has surrendered. In the first example this is permitted[73] by IHL and there could be no charge of murder against him. In the second, it clearly is not and so the soldier would be guilty of murder under English law in these circumstances.[74] A possible approach is to accept that, in the first example, the principle of combatant immunity applies in English law and thereby avoids a charge of murder.[75]

Although the British soldier would commit an offence under English criminal law in the circumstances envisaged by the second example above, he would not be liable to the criminal law of the territory, such as Afghanistan or Iraq during the international armed conflict stage of military operations, in which his acts took place, by virtue of the principle under IHL of combatant immunity.[76]

The more difficult issue is whether this combatant immunity applies during a non-international armed conflict, the situation that prevailed from December 2001 in Afghanistan and from the end of the occupation period in Iraq in 2004. The short answer would seem to be that IHL does not recognise combatant immunity during a non-international armed conflict, and a number of reasons in principle can be advanced for this position.[77] First, the term 'combatant' is linked to entitlement as a member of the armed forces of a state to be a prisoner of war if captured, a situation that can occur only during an international armed conflict.[78] During this type of armed conflict those who are not members of the armed

72 See P Rowe, 'The Criminal Liability of a British Soldier Merely for Participating in the Iraq War 2003: a Response to Chilcot Evidence' [2010] Crim LR 752.

73 *Quaere* whether IHL *permits* this or whether its effect is not to treat it as a breach of that law.

74 As an example, see *R v Blackman* [2014] EWCA Crim 1029. The act is also a war crime under IHL, a crime which could be tried under the Rome Statute 1998 of the International Criminal Court Art 8(2)(a)(i) and, as such, could be tried by an English court or by the court martial as a crime under the International Criminal Court Act 2001, ss 50(1), 51.

75 *Public Prosecutor v Oie Hee Koi* [1968] AC 829, 860–1 (JCPC) was concerned solely with liability of members of regular forces to the national law of the foreign territory on which they are actually fighting and in which the term, 'combatant immunity' is not used.

76 Since the situation referred to involves an international armed conflict there could be no status of forces agreement or memorandum of understanding concerning the exclusive criminal jurisdiction of the UK. Compare when the respective armed conflicts became of a non-international character. In *Hassan v United Kingdom*, Application No 29750/09, 16 September 2014, the ECtHR referred to combatant privilege that allows those who become entitled to be treated as prisoners of war, to 'participate in hostilities without criminal sanctions [and] it would not be appropriate for the Court to hold that this form of detention falls within the scope of Art 5(1)(c) [of the ECHR]', [97].

77 *R v Gul* [2013] UKSC 64, [50].

78 The link between a combatant, as defined in Art 43(2) Additional Protocol I, 1977, and a prisoner of war is one of general principle only since not every prisoner of war, as defined by

forces of a state, such as insurgents, cannot bring themselves within either of the terms 'combatant' or 'prisoner of war'. It would be illogical then to accord them the status of combatant and prisoner of war during a non-international armed conflict, particularly in the light also of the status of members of the armed forces of a state who will not strictly be combatants under IHL.[79] A British soldier who had taken part in the non-international armed conflicts in Iraq or Afghanistan was not entitled under IHL to be treated as a prisoner of war if captured by insurgents,[80] but both he, and the insurgents, will have been bound to comply with Common Article 3 to the Geneva Conventions, 1949[81] and he, alone, with English criminal law. In a non-international armed conflict it is always likely to be the case that the UK, if invited to participate, will enter into a status of forces agreement or a memorandum of understanding to grant exclusive criminal jurisdiction over British soldiers to the UK.[82] Strictly, this would not be necessary if a British soldier was entitled to combatant immunity in this type of armed conflict. The issue before a British coroner's court of whether a British soldier had been 'unlawfully killed' by Iraqi or Afghan insurgents is discussed in Chapter 5.

Geneva Convention III, 1949, Art 4, would have been entitled to be a combatant. Moreover, a combatant could forfeit his prisoner of war status should he be shown to have engaged in espionage while not wearing uniform or if he had disguised himself as a civilian to carry out an attack, *Ali v Public Prosecutor* [1969] 1 AC 430. Nor will a member of the armed forces of a state be entitled to the status of a prisoner of war if he is of the same nationality or he owes allegiance to the detaining power, *Public Prosecutor v Oie Hee Koi* [1968] AC 829. An example would be a British national who fought as a member of the Afghan armed forces and who was subsequently captured by British armed forces while the armed conflict in that state was of an international character. Where the British national fights on behalf of ISIL, the Kurdish forces against ISIL, or the Free Syrian Army he would be neither a 'combatant' or, if captured, a prisoner of war either because he is not a member of the armed forces of a state (or a defined national liberation movement under Additional Protocol I, 1977, Art 1(4)), or because the armed conflict is not of an international character.

79 The Court did not express a view as to whether members of the UK armed forces were entitled to combatant immunity during a non-international armed conflict, *R v Gul (Mohammed)* [2013] UKSC 64, [31]. Compare the passage in *Keyu v Secretary of State for Defence* [2012] EWHC 2445 (Admin), [120] that the 'British Army . . . may well have had combatant immunity under customary international law', during what was essentially a non-international armed conflict in the (then) Federation of Malaya in 1948. Although the principle of distinction between combatants and civilians would suggest that in a non-international armed conflict some distinction must be drawn between members of the armed forces of a state and others in order to protect civilians, See Rule 3, J-M Henckaerts: Volume 1: Rules and L Doswald-Beck, *Customary International Humanitarian Law* (ICRC, Cambridge University Press, 2005), 12.

80 Since neither Geneva Convention III, 1949 nor Additional Protocol I, 1977 applied, given that the conflicts were not of an international character.

81 This article forms part of the definition of war crimes applicable during a non-international armed conflict, the International Criminal Court Act 2001, ss 50(1), 51. The UK is bound also by Additional Protocol I, 1977, as was Afghanistan from 10 November 2009. Iraq is not a party to Additional Protocol II.

82 This has taken place with both Iraq and Afghanistan. In Iraq, the Coalition Provisional Authority Order 17 followed by a new version approved by the Iraqi government, HC Debs

viii The role of the International Committee of the Red Cross/Red Crescent

In the nineteenth century those killed or injured in a battle involving two or more states would, predominantly, be those who had taken part in it. After the fighting very large numbers of men would lie where they fell suffering from wounds. Just such events occurred after the battle of Solferino in Italy in 1859. Henri Dunant, a Swiss citizen, saw what had happened, published his *A Memory of Solferino* in 1862 and ultimately led others into establishing the International Committee of the Red Cross (ICRC), based in Geneva.[83] The most effective way of getting states to agree to search for and treat the wounded and sick, whether they were enemy soldiers or their own forces, was by a treaty. In 1864 the first Geneva Convention came into existence for this purpose. As a tribute to this Swiss initiative the emblem to be used to indicate the medical services of an army became the red cross on a white background, the reverse of the colour arrangements of the national flag of Switzerland.[84] The red crescent on a white background was also adopted for the same purpose and both, along with a new one, the red crystal on a white background adopted in 2005, are in use today.[85] The Geneva Conventions 1949 themselves place particular responsibilities on the ICRC[86] and, in this regard, it is clearly the pre-eminent humanitarian organisation, particularly during the course of an armed conflict.

8 July 2004, vol 423, col 827W; HC Debs 4 October 2004, vol 424, col 1878W. For the problems involved after 28 June 2004 see A Roberts, 'The End of Occupation: Iraq 2004' (2005) 54 ICLQ 27, 44. Following the withdrawal of UK armed forces from Iraq and their replacement by UK armed forces training teams no new status of forces agreement has come into operation. Instead, members of the UK armed forces will be accredited to the British embassy in Baghdad, HC Debs 18 December 2014, vol 589, col 129WS. Following the withdrawal of UK armed forces from Afghanistan, those who remain for training purposes are covered by the 'NATO Bilateral Security Agreement and NATO Status of Forces Agreement', HC Debs 29 January 2015, vol 591, col 32 WS. The Status of Forces Agreement referred to was signed on 30 September 2014 and it grants exclusive jurisdiction over 'criminal or civil offences committed in the territory of Afghanistan' to the UK (as all other NATO Force components), Art 11, http://www.nato.int/cps/en/natohq/official_texts_116072.htm?selectedLocale=en.

83 For general reading see C Moorehead, *Dunant's Dream: War, Switzerland and the History of the Red Cross* (Harper Collins, 1998).

84 The first reference to a red cross on a white background is contained in the Geneva Convention for the Amelioration of the Condition of the Wounded in Armies in the Field 1864, Art 7. See now Geneva Convention I, 1949, Art 38.

85 Protocol Additional to the Geneva Conventions, 1949 and Relating to the Adoption of an Additional Distinctive Emblem (Protocol III), 8 December 2005. The UK became a party in 2009. Neither Afghanistan nor Iraq is a party.

86 See, for example, Geneva Convention IV, 1949, Art 143; Common Art 3(2); the role played by the ICRC where no protecting power has been appointed, Additional Protocol I, Art 5(4).

The ICRC has performed a number of significant functions during Britain's earlier wars. Its delegates in the field have had exclusive[87] access to those detained by British forces in Iraq and Afghanistan in order to assess whether their conditions match the requirements of the Geneva Conventions 1949. They also have access to detainees transferred by the UK to the Afghan and Iraqi authorities[88] and who are imprisoned there, along with access to those transferred by the UK to the US armed forces. The ICRC visited British detainees in Iraq at the end of March 2003, to inspect the way in which they are being treated and to make reports, if necessary to the relevant British authorities.[89] Those detained during an armed conflict can also communicate directly with the ICRC about their conditions of detention.[90] Of equal importance is the report the ICRC sent to the British government concerning any issues that needed to be addressed following these visits.[91] The practice of the ICRC over very many years, and wherever it is involved, is to treat these reports as confidential to the government concerned.[92] Whilst this policy does, no doubt, encourage governments to permit access to

87 Unlike the ICRC, other international organisations, such as Amnesty International, have no right of access to detainees under the Geneva Conventions 1949. A minister confirmed that Amnesty International had not been granted access, HC Debs 13 May 2004, vol 421, col 514. In Afghanistan the UK has granted access also to the Afghan Independent Human Rights Commission, HC Debs 18 May 2009, vol 492, col 1166W.

88 HL Debs 11 February 2009, vol 707, col 185W (relating to Afghanistan) and HL 26 February 2009, vol 708, col 352.

89 The report of February 2004, relating to this visit, was 'leaked and thus, uncommonly, was in the public domain before the instigation of this Inquiry, *Report of the Baha Mousa Inquiry*, HC 1452, 2011, vol III, 1343, [381].

90 This is the case where there is no protecting power appointed, as occurred during the occupation of Iraq between 2003 and 2004, Geneva Convention IV, 1949, Art 101; HC Debs 30 June 2005, vol 435, col 1690W. In a non-international armed conflict, the ICRC can offer its service to the parties, Common Art 3, which could include insurgent groups.

91 In relation to the ICRC report in February 2004, see the ministerial statements, HC Debs 13 May 2004, vol 421, col 514; HL Debs 7 July 2004, vol 663, col 89W; HC Debs 11 December 2008, vol 485, col 5MC. It also produces confidential working papers which raise issues more suitable to be dealt with at the local level, see HC Debs 7 September 2004, vol 424, col 1186W. The treatment of detainees by British armed forces is discussed in Chapter 9.

92 See, however, the statement by an MP, HC Debs 11 May 2004, vol 421, col 147. The Director of Operations at the ICRC gave a press conference on 8 May 2004 on 'the leaked report' in which he stated that 'excerpts of the [2004] report were made public without the consent of the ICRC', https://www.icrc.org/eng/resources/documents/interview/audio_conf_iraq_070504.htm. The issue of the confidentiality of ICRC reports following visits to detainees is set out in 'Action by the International Committee of the Red Cross in the event of Violations of International Humanitarian Law or of other Fundamental Rules Protecting Persons in Situations of violence' (2005) 87 IRRC 393. This document also deals with the situation where the ICRC decides to make public its concerns through a public declaration where 'it hopes that this will prompt a party to a conflict to improve the substance of its dialogue with the ICRC and take account of its recommendations', 397. The document was referred to in a ministerial statement, HC Debs 6 March 2007, vol 457, col 434WH.

the ICRC,[93] it does have the effect also of making it more difficult to hold the government accountable for the treatment of those it detains, an issue discussed in Chapter 1.

The policy of using armed force by air strikes alone, as the UK has adopted in Libya (2011) and Iraq (2014), can result in unintentional injury to civilians to whom British armed forces medical forces will have no access in order to provide treatment. It is in this situation that the ICRC, as a non-governmental organisation, can perform a valuable role. In order to assist it to do so the UK government funded the ICRC to 'provide medical teams to treat and provide medical supplies to 3,000 people in Libya affected by ongoing fighting'.[94]

There is, no doubt, a fine line between being an independent and impartial organisation as the ICRC endeavours to be, and co-operating in a limited way with one of the parties to an armed conflict. The ICRC is, however, a practical organisation, which could hardly achieve its goal of providing some form of protection to those considered by the Geneva Conventions to be victims of an armed conflict – civilians, the wounded and sick and those detained by a party to the conflict – by remaining in Geneva and shouting from afar. Certainly at a policy level, the aims of the UK in regard to those protected by the Geneva Conventions 1949 have been similar to those of the ICRC and it is natural, in these circumstances, to see some measure of co-operation between civil and military officials to achieve them. Access to detainees held by the UK armed forces, and the confidential reports produced by the ICRC following their visits, have been discussed above. Other forms of co-operation have included British forces assisting ICRC workers to gain access to a water plant near Basra airport,[95] providing security information to enable them to meet up with beneficiaries of the 'restoring family links' programme[96] and reporting to them of civilians killed, or allegedly killed, by British forces in Iraq, to enable the ICRC to inform their relatives.[97] The ICRC can, and does, remind parties to an armed conflict of their obligations under IHL, particularly in relation to the treatment of detainees.[98] In this regard the government has stated that the training of those dealing specifically with

93 The Iraqi government refused access to the ICRC during the Gulf war 1990–1991, M Meyer 'The Role of the International Red Cross and Red Crescent Movement: Problems Encountered' in P Rowe (ed), *The Gulf War 1990–91 in International and English Law* (Routledge, Sweet & Maxwell, 1993), 228 who discusses the possible reasons for the refusal of access by Iraq. One result of this was that ICRC delegates were unable to visit the RAF aircrew taken prisoner of war by Iraq.

94 HC Debs 5 April 2011, vol 526, col 862W. Other funds for specific purposes in Iraq and Afghanistan have been provided, usually through the Department for International Development. See, for example, HC Debs 23 April 2007, vol 459, col 886W; HL Debs 21 April 2008, vol 700, col 252W.

95 HC Debs 10 April 2003, vol 403, col 350W.

96 HC Debs 3 June 2003, vol 406, col 247W.

97 HC Debs 12 January 2004, vol 416, col 536W. Similarly, with those detained by UK armed forces, HL Debs 9 March 2006, vol 679, col 149W.

98 HC Debs 26 May 2004, vol 421, col 1634W. This collaboration occurred in 2003 when 'it was clear that there was a possibility of UK troops being involved in Iraq'.

detainees has been 'subject to ICRC and British Red Cross observations . . . and [the government has] engaged both organisations to ensure United Kingdom planning and treatment of detainees is appropriate'.[99] Whether it has achieved this aim, in all respects, is discussed further in Chapter 9.

ix International humanitarian law as part of English law

It is not only IHL that will be of significance during armed conflict but, as Chapter 5 shows, English law will play its part also, often in a manner closely linked to the UK's international law obligations. The UK had, over the years, developed a practice in which the government, by way of the royal prerogative and not through a vote in Parliament, decided whether to ratify a treaty, which has now been reformed by statute.[100] If it is minded to do so it may be necessary to pass legislation to give effect to some of the provisions of the treaty that, for instance, require the creation of criminal offences. Good examples are the Geneva Conventions 1949, which the government of the day wished to ratify, but it was recognised that a very small number of its provisions needed to become part of English law. This was achieved by the Geneva Conventions Act 1957, in which the grave breaches of the Conventions and the use, without authorisation, of the protected emblems (the red cross and the red crescent on white backgrounds) became criminal offences and paved the way for the government to ratify the treaty, which it did in the same year.[101] The fact that it took between 1949 and 1957 for the government to put the necessary draft legislation to Parliament shows the often lengthy time that this process takes and also that a treaty will only be part of English law if it is actually made so by legislation, or a source of it if it reflects customary international law.[102] The vast majority of all the provisions in the Geneva Convention of 1949 and of its Additional Protocols of 1977 are

99 HC Debs 24 October 2006, vol 450, col 1737W. See also the Government Response, 3rd Special Report, HC 548 (2014) to the House of Commons Defence Select Committee, session 2013–14, *UK Armed Forces Personnel and the Legal Framework of Future Operations*, HC 931 (2014), [1].

100 The Ponsonby Rule (re-stated in HC Debs 6 August 1924, vol 176, col 3012), and now by the Constitutional Reform and Governance Act 2010, ss 20–25.

101 The Geneva Conventions Act 1957 was further amended to incorporate a number of the obligations contained in Additional Protocol I, the Geneva Conventions (Amendment) Act 1995. It was amended further by the International Criminal Court Act 2001 and the Geneva Conventions and United Nations Personnel (Protocols) Act 2009. For the limitations on a private person seeking an arrest warrant in relation to the 1957 Act, s 1 (grave breaches), see Police Reform and Social Responsibility Act 2011, s 153.

102 That customary international law is a source, rather than a part, of English law see Lord Bingham, *R v Jones (Margaret)* [2006] UKHL 16, [11]. Proof that a particular principle reflects customary international law cannot, by itself, create criminal offences under English law, *R v Jones (Margaret)* [2006] UKHL 16. In the same way, it is unlikely to be able to provide a defence to a charge drawn under English law. Thus, although customary international law might have provided a defence of superior orders in 1914, *Manual of Military Law* (1914), [443] (which was relied on by the German Supreme Court in Leipzig in 1921

not therefore part of English law, as such, but will be binding on the UK because they are contained in a treaty to which it is a party. A further example is the Rome Statute 1998 of the International Criminal Court. Legislation was clearly necessary to make the crimes set out in the Rome Statute part of English law in order to ensure that British courts would have jurisdiction to try members of its own armed forces (and UK nationals or residents) for these alleged crimes wherever in the world they may be committed.[103] This was carried out by the International Criminal Court Act 2001. Subsequently, a British soldier pleaded guilty to an offence under that Act when charged before a British court-martial,[104] which is discussed in Chapter 8.

It is an established principle that once the UK government has ratified a treaty it will consider itself 'bound by its terms . . . the ministerial code [also] says that this is the case'.[105] This statement needs to be approached with caution since, by itself, it cannot make terms in a treaty a part of English law and whilst ministers may, as a general principle, feel bound to observe the obligations contained in a treaty, they will not be bound by English law to do so, unless a particular term has been implemented through a statute[106] into that law, or if it reflects customary international law.[107] The same can be said also for the statement that members of the armed forces must comply with IHL during an armed conflict.[108] Any

in the Judgment in the *Case of Commander Karl Neumann, Hospital Ship 'Dover Castle'*, Report of Proceedings Before the German Supreme Court in Leipzig, Cmd 1450, 1921, 44), a British soldier tried by a British court-martial at the time would not have been able to rely on it as it was not consistent with English law. The issue remains a live one since the International Criminal Court Act 2001 does not incorporate Art 33 of the Rome Statute (superior orders), with the consequence that English law will be the sole basis of criminal responsibility should a British soldier claim before the court martial that he was ordered to commit what is charged against him as a war crime.

103 The practical effect of trials before a national court is that, in most cases, the ICC will not have jurisdiction to try those individuals, Rome Statute of the International Criminal Court, 1998, Art 17. See discussion below.

104 See *R v Payne and others*, court-martial 2006–07, see http://www.internationalcrimesdatabase.org/Case/811.

105 Mr Dominic Grieve, MP, Attorney General, HC Debs 10 February 2011, vol 523, col 510. See also Earl Granville, oral ministerial statement, HL Debs 8 August 1870, vol 203, col 1672, who refers to the honour of this country concerning its treaty obligations of 1839. The Ministerial Code (Cabinet Office, 2010), stipulated that it should be read 'alongside the . . . background of the overarching duty of Ministers to comply with the law including international law and treaty obligations, [1.2]. The 2015 edition removed reference to 'international law and treaty obligations'.

106 It is the statute which is part of English law, not the treaty, *Campaign for Nuclear Disarmament v Prime Minister and others* [2002] EWHC 2777, [27].

107 Customary international law will become a part of English law, providing it is not in conflict with an Act of Parliament, *Mutua v Foreign and Commonwealth Office* [2011] EWHC 1913, [82]. By itself, it cannot create an offence under English law, *R v Jones (Margaret)* [2006] UKHL 16.

108 See Chapter 8. In referring to prosecution policy in relation to British soldiers the Solicitor General commented that 'if we demand that other countries comply with international law and basic standards, we must show that we do to [*sic*]', HC Debs 27 April 2006, vol 445, col 734.

failure on the part of a soldier to do so could result only in a prosecution before an English court if he or she had committed a crime under English law, whether styled as a war crime under the 2001 Act,[109] or an offence under the ordinary English criminal law.

x War crimes, the International Criminal Court and the court-martial

The International Military Tribunal at Nuremberg (IMT) in 1946[110] recognised that 'crimes against international law are committed by men, not by abstract entities, and only by punishing individuals who commit such crimes can the provisions of international law be enforced'.[111] It had been argued before the IMT, with what one might be considered to be a degree of logic, that since international law governed the relationship between or among states, a breach of the law by the organs of the state, its armed forces, could make only the state liable. That approach was rejected[112] and the IMT convicted a number of high-ranking officials, and some civilians, of crimes against the peace, crimes against humanity and war crimes. The state could itself be liable[113] but concentration then and since has been on the trial of individuals. Apart from the IMT and its Far East version held in Tokyo[114] a number of states held war crimes trials under their own

109 The crimes that could be charged under the 2001 Act match those that could be tried by the International Criminal Court and include genocide and crimes against humanity. A point of difference between the two relates to the defences which are set out in the Rome Statute 1998, Arts 31–33, but which have not been implemented by the 2001 Act and thus the normal defences to a crime under English law, such as superior orders, duress and drunkenness, will continue to apply to a British soldier on trial before an English court.

110 The trials after World War I were conducted by a German court under German law, see *German War Trials: Report of the Proceedings before the Supreme Court in Leipzig*, Cmd 1450 (1921), although an international court to do so had been proposed in 1919 by the Commission on the Responsibility of the Authors of the War and on Enforcement of Penalties (1920) 14 AJIL 95, which was recognised, to a limited extent, by the Versailles Treaty 1919, Art 229.

111 Judgment: The Law of the Charter, http://avalon.law.yale.edu/imt/judlawch.asp.

112 As it had been by the German Supreme Court in Leipzig, which had tried a number of individuals for crimes committed, while serving in the German armed forces, during World War I. The parallel is not exact since at Leipzig the defendants were tried under German law, whilst at Nuremberg the charges were framed under international law, although the IMT did refer to the Versailles Treaty 1919, Art 228 as an authority for the principle that individuals could be liable for a breach of international law.

113 See The Hague Convention IV, 1907, Art 3, Additional Protocol I, Art 91. See also Additional Protocol I, Art 91; F Kalshoven, 'State Responsibility for Warlike Acts of the Armed Forces' (1991) 40 ICLQ 827, 858, comments that 'States that send their armed forces into war will have to count more seriously . . . the possibility that they will be held effectively liable for all violations of the law of armed conflict committed by these forces in the course of their operations.' *Quaere* how, in practice, such a claim could be made against the UK in the absence of a concurrent breach by it of the ECHR.

114 See N Boister and R Cryer, *Documents on the Tokyo International Military Tribunal, Charter, Indictments and Judgments* (OUP, 2008).

law. The USA established military commissions, a form of which would reappear some nearly 60 years later to try individuals at Guantanamo Bay, whilst the UK set up a military court in that part of the former Germany that it occupied to try those charged with war crimes. These war crimes were 'a violation of the laws and usages of war'[115] and it can be seen that no jurisdiction was given to the British military court to try crimes against the peace or crimes against humanity.[116] The court was established through the royal prerogative and not by statute and it has never formally been revoked, although it is never likely to see the light of day again in the form in which it appeared then. Another feature of it, which was unusual, was that it was a British military court that sat in occupied territory and, although modern IHL permits this, the practice was not repeated in Iraq when parts of that country were occupied by British armed forces in 2003–2004.

The trial of war crimes before a court set up under international law, as the IMT had been, did not occur again until 1993 and 1994 respectively when the UN Security Council established two international criminal tribunals, one for crimes committed in the former Yugoslavia (ICTY) and the other for crimes committed in Rwanda (ICTR).[117] The ICTY was given power to try genocide (which had been called crimes against humanity at the IMT Nuremberg), crimes against humanity, grave breaches of the Geneva Conventions 1949 and war crimes. Since the events in Rwanda in 1994 occurred during a non-international armed conflict, a specific crime was included, along with genocide and crimes against humanity, namely, crimes contrary to Common Article 3 to the Geneva Conventions of 1949. Following the incorporation of the crimes that can be tried by the ICC by the International Criminal Court Act 2001, an English court or the court martial[118] can now try war crimes allegedly committed during a non-international armed conflict.

The ICTY, which continues to sit in The Hague, has indicted 161 individuals,[119] and although a number of British lawyers were involved as counsel, a few as judges, and convicted defendants might serve their prison sentence in a British prison,[120] it might be thought there has been little to attract the interest of the UK, since the war was fought amongst different parts of the former Yugoslavia.

115 Royal Warrant: Regulations for the Trial of War Criminals, 14 June 1945, reg 1.

116 There had been disagreement in 1919 as to whether crimes against humanity existed in international law as a basis for the trial of members of the German armed forces. Compare the view of the majority in the Commission on the Responsibility of the Authors of the War and on Enforcement of Penalties (1920) 14 AJIL 95 with the partially dissenting view of the US delegation. No charges were laid as crimes against humanity in the Leipzig trials of 1921, *Report of Proceedings before the Supreme Court in Leipzig*, Cmd 1450 (1921).

117 United Nations Security Resolutions 808 (1993) and 955 (1994).

118 The legal basis and powers of the court martial are set out in the Armed Forces Act 2006.

119 For the ICTY statistics see http://www.icty.org/sid/24. This figure can be compared with the numbers tried by the IMTs at Nuremberg and Tokyo, which were 22 and 25 respectively.

120 Former General Krstic, convicted by the ICTY, is serving his sentence in a British prison, see HC Debs 29 June 2006, vol 448, col 662W.

Although UK armed forces operated through NATO, no indictments were brought against any British personnel. The judgments given by the ICTY have, however, done much to clarify IHL in its application to an armed conflict.

When Saddam Hussein was captured by US soldiers in Iraq in 2003 it was clear that he would have to stand trial.[121] The former government, which he led, had collapsed, as had most of the structures of the state including the legal system. There were a number of options available for a suitable trial process. The pattern of the ICTY and the ICTR could have been followed, with his trial being conducted by an international criminal tribunal established for Iraq and which would sit outside that country. There were certainly a number of advantages in conducting proceedings in this way. The trial judges would have no connection with the ethnic divide in Iraq, and would be free from any suggestion of a lack of impartiality or independence. The trial could be conducted in conditions of relative security for witnesses, the accused individuals and their lawyers. A further option would have been to have adopted the hybrid model as in Sierra-Leone, where Iraqi judges would sit alongside international judges. Finally, the trial could be held in Iraq under its national criminal law with Iraqi judges. It may be unduly cynical to reflect on the fact that if the establishment of the tribunal had involved the UN directly it would have insisted, as it had made clear in its earlier involvement in the establishment of criminal tribunals, that the death penalty could not be a sentencing option.

Iraq decided to try Saddam Hussein and the other defendants under its own law according to its own criminal law processes, although with some principles drawn from international law.[122] No international judges took part in the trials and security breaches did occur but the result was that Saddam Hussein was convicted and sentenced to death, as were a number of the other defendants. Even if the conduct of his trial followed all the procedures set down in Iraqi law the result of it could hardly have been in doubt. It illustrates a number of difficulties that war crimes, as contrasted with ordinary criminal trials, face. These include balancing the need to ensure a fair trial for defendants with creating an opportunity

121 *Quaere* whether he was entitled to be treated as a prisoner of war under Geneva Convention III, 1949 if he actually was at that time a member of the armed forces of Iraq. See discussion by A Roberts, 'The End of Occupation: Iraq 2004' (2005) 54 ICLQ 27, 45. It is not clear whether Saddam Hussein was merely granted the protection of a prisoner of war compared with accepting that he was entitled to this status, see D Orentlicher, 'Venues for Prosecuting Saddam Hussein: The Legal Framework', American Society of International Law Insights, Vol 8, Issue 30, 30 December 2003, note 22. The ICRC took the view that he was entitled to this status whilst held by US armed forces, 'Iraq: What Does Prisoner of War Status Mean for Saddam Hussein?' https://www.icrc.org/eng/resources/documents/faq/5v7kdz.htm. He was visited by the ICRC, but since he was not detained by UK armed forces any confidential reports prepared by the ICRC would not have been made available to the UK, see HC Debs 8 February 2005, vol 430, col 1464W.

122 See K Heller, 'Comparing the Trial to International Standards of Due Process', in M Scharf and G McNeal, *Saddam on Trial: Understanding and Debating the Iraqi High Tribunal* (Carolina Academic Press, 2006), [155].

to provide justice to the many victims of a defendant's long-term actions. UN established criminal tribunals could hardly be seen to be satisfied with anything less than a fair trial system that matches the human rights standards of its own treaties, but this may, or may not, be the case for other tribunals. Where, like Saddam Hussein, a defendant is tried for a smaller number of war crimes than it is alleged he has committed, there are likely to be victims who protest that the defendant will not be held legally accountable for the crimes committed against them or members of their families. To meet this possible objection, some war crimes tribunals have tended to charge defendants with a large numbers of separate counts of the same crime. The result of this is that trials can take a long time to conclude as each count must be proved by the prosecutor. Perhaps the best example of this was the trial before the ICTY of Slobodan Milosevic, which began on 12 February 2002 and ended with his death on 11 March 2006. To be fair, it should be added that Milosevic insisted, as some other defendants have done at the ICTY, in representing himself.[123] When this occurs the speed of any trial process will slow down, often become acrimonious between the defendant and witnesses, and cause the judges to be on their guard against the production of irrelevant evidence or the making of political speeches.

Some commentators have argued that the decision to try Saddam Hussein before Iraqi judges alone was a mistake since it has fuelled controversy over the fairness of the proceedings, which has not been alleged seriously against those criminal tribunals with international judges on the bench.[124]

A war crimes trial held before national judges alone under national law, as was the trial of Saddam Hussein, is certainly not a new development. It happened in Leipzig in 1921 where a small number of Germans were tried by a German court for offences committed in World War I,[125] and it was the form in which the trial took place of Adolph Eichmann, who was tried and convicted, by an Israeli

123 See generally, C Harvey, 'The "right to conduct one's own defence in person" and a "fair and expeditious trial" Before the ICTY: An Impossible Balancing Act?' in C Harvey, J Summers and N White (eds), *Contemporary Challenges to the Laws of War* (Cambridge University Press, 2014), 337.

124 M Schraf and G MacNeal, *Saddam on Trial: Understanding and Debating the Iraqi High Tribunal* (Caroline Academic Press, 2006), 233; M Newton, 'The Iraqi High Criminal Court: Controversy and Contributions' (2006) 88 IRRC 399, 424–5.

125 This was not the procedure envisaged by the Treaty of Versailles, 1919, which in Art 228 had envisaged trials of German individuals before the military courts of the Allies. Problems of extraditing these individuals foreseen by the German government led to a proposal by it, which was accepted by the Allies, that the trials be held before the Supreme Court in Leipzig, see Protocols and Correspondence between the Supreme Council and the Conference of Ambassadors and the German Government and the Peace Delegation between 10 January 1920 and 17 July 1920, Respecting the Execution of the Treaty of Versailles of 28 June 1919, Cmd 1325 (1921), Document 20. Although there had been many allegations of German 'outrages' during the war and immediately after it, see for example, the Report of the Committee on Alleged German Outrages Appointed by Her Majesty's Government, chaired by Viscount Bryce, Cd 7894 (1915) and the Commission on the Responsibility of the Authors of the War and on Enforcement of Penalties (1920) 14 AJIL 95, only 12 trials took place.

court in 1961[126] for 'crimes against the Jewish people' in World War II. In 1999 Sawoniuk was convicted at the Central Criminal Court of a violation of the laws and customs of war committed in Eastern Europe in 1942.[127] His trial was made possible by the passing of the War Crimes Act 1991, which gave jurisdiction to the English courts to try a person for what were clearly breaches of the laws of war, between 1939 and 1945 in territory occupied by Nazi Germany.

Until 1998 the jurisdiction of all international criminal tribunals was limited geographically to the area in which the alleged war crimes had taken place, but it had been suggested in 1919 that a universal court should be established to try war crimes wherever they were alleged to have taken place. Negotiations in Rome in 1998 led to the Statute of the International Criminal Court of that year. Despite use of the word 'statute' this was, in fact, a treaty, open for signature and ratification by all states in the world. It was clearly important that the Rome Statute should have as wide an acceptance by states as possible so the establishment of the Court would 'put an end to impunity for the perpetrators of these crimes and thus [it would] . . . contribute to the prevention of such crimes'.[128] The treaty would only therefore come into force once 60 states had become a party to it, a milestone that was passed in 2000. Whilst virtually every political leader is likely to agree with the proposition that 'war criminals should have no hiding place in the world' (which is, perhaps, better than the less-than-catchy mantra of 'end impunity for war criminals') he or she could easily foresee difficulties of a political nature at home. A government needs to maintain the morale of its armed forces and handing individuals over for trial could clearly be foreseen to undermine it.

Unlike the UN Security Council criminal tribunals, which could demand that a state hand over to it an indicted individual, the Rome Statute provided that the ICC would only be able to try a case where the state party, to which the offender belongs is unwilling or unable to try him.[129] This means that, in the majority of cases, a defendant can be tried before his own courts and the ICC will not be able to do so. In 2006 a British soldier entered a guilty plea at his court-martial to the crime of inhuman treatment, one of the war crimes set out in the Rome Statute, which involved the ill treatment and subsequent death of Baha Mousa, an Iraqi civilian, who had been detained by British soldiers.[130] States could feel fairly secure, therefore, that if they had a proper trial procedure, whether military or civilian, to which members of their armed forces or civilians would be subject, should it be alleged that they have committed any of the crimes set out in the Rome Statute, they would be tried at home and not before the ICC.[131]

126 *Attorney-General of the Government of Israel v Eichmann* (1961) 36 ILR 5.

127 On appeal, see *R v Sawoniuk* [2000] 2 Cr App R 220.

128 Rome Statute 1998, Preamble.

129 The Rome Statute 1998, Art 17. The ICC is 'complementary to national jurisdictions', Art 1.

130 *R v Payne* http://www.internationalcrimesdatabase.org/Case/811.

131 Compare, however, the perceived concern amongst service personnel about the risks of sending British soldiers to be tried before the ICC at the Hague, discussed in Chapter 10.

It is, however, possible that if information is submitted to the Prosecutor of the ICC that a state appears to be unwilling or unable to investigate or to try someone within its jurisdiction for a crime under the Rome Statute, a preliminary examination under Article 53 of the Rome Statute 1998 may be carried out. In May 2014 the Prosecutor decided to re-open a preliminary examination into alleged 'systematic detainee abuse in Iraq from 2003 until 2008 . . . [which was] attributed to the armed forces of the United Kingdom deployed in Iraq between 2003 and 2008'.[132] The UK Attorney General rejected the allegations.[133] It falls to the Iraq Historic Allegations Team (IHAT) to 'provide relevant information to allow the UK Government to draft a response to the dossier submitted to the Office of the Prosecutor of the International Criminal Court'. As part of this process it is continuing investigations into 'approximately 800 additional cases provided by [two firms of solicitors] since July 2014'.[134]

The UK played a major part in encouraging states to become parties to the Rome State and, although there are now some 123 states parties, there are some militarily significant states that have decided not to join, at least at the present time. These include the USA, Russia, China and Israel. Neither Iraq nor Syria is a party, with the result that the ICC may find itself unable to try those responsible for alleged crimes committed on behalf of ISIL on the territory of either of those states.[135] It would be open to the UK to try any of its nationals should evidence be forthcoming that a British citizen or a British resident was involved.[136]

States that are not parties to the Rome Statute will remain bound by the pre-existing customary international law relating to war crimes. It has been reported in April 2013, for instance, that Syria used a chemical weapon against rebel held

132 Statement by the Prosecutor, 'Prosecutor of the International Criminal Court, Mrs Fatou Bensouda, re-opens the preliminary examination of the situation in Iraq', 13 May 2014, see http://www.icc-cpi.int/en_menus/icc/structure%20of%20the%20court/office%20of%20the%20prosecutor/reports%20and%20statements/statement/Pages/otp-statement-iraq-13-05-2014.aspx.

133 Statement on ICC Preliminary Examination into Iraq Allegations, 13 May 2014, https://www.gov.uk/government/news/statement-on-icc-preliminary-examination-into-iraq-allegations.

134 Iraq Historic Allegations Team (IHAT) Quarterly Update-October to December 2014, https://www.gov.uk/government/news/statement-on-icc-preliminary-examination-into-iraq-allegations.

135 The ICC will have jurisdiction (broadly) where the crime is alleged to have been committed on the territory, or where an accused is a national, of a state party or of a state that has accepted the jurisdiction of the court, or where the situation is referred to the Prosecutor by the UN Security Council, Rome Statute, 1998, Arts 12 and 13.

136 International Criminal Court Act 2001, s 51(2)(b). That a British resident could be charged with an offence is wider that the Rome Statute, 1998, Art 12, which referred to a 'national'. For an account of the activities of ISIL in Iraq and Syria see Defence Committee 7th Report, 2014–15, *The Situation in Iraq and Syria and the Response to al-Dawla al-Islamiya fi al-Iraq al-Sham (DAESH)*, HC 690 (2015), [13]–[17] and on the role of the ICC in relation to such alleged crimes, see the statement of the Prosecutor of the ICC, 8 April 2015, http://www.icc-cpi.int/en_menus/icc/Pages/default.aspx.

positions and that individuals were killed or injured as a result.[137] Syria is not a party to the Rome Statute of the ICC, nor at the time was it a party to the Chemical Weapons Convention 1993,[138] but it had become a party in 1968 to the 1925 Geneva Gas Protocol, which prohibits the 'use in war of asphyxiating, poisonous or other gases and of all analogous liquids, materials or devices gases'. It is generally accepted that 'war' includes civil war and, even if it did not, customary international law points to the conclusion that the use of such material would be contrary to IHL and therefore a war crime.[139] The Review Conference of the ICC in 2010 adopted an amendment to Article 8 of the Rome Statute to make the employment of asphyxiating, poisonous, or other gases a war crime if committed during a non-international armed conflict.[140]

The further away a military leader appears from the commission of the crime itself the higher one looks in the military chain of command, or the comparable chain amongst organised armed groups, for evidence of culpability. Any liability for war crimes that he has is likely to be based, not on his ordering or encouraging the crime, but for his failure to prevent it. This has become known as command responsibility and it applies to anyone who has effective control over other soldiers or of insurgents. The commander could be a corporal or a general or be the leader of a small group of fighters.[141] The military leader is not liable simply because his subordinates have committed war crimes but because he was in a position to prevent a crime of which he was, or should have been, aware was likely to occur and he has failed to take steps available to him to prevent it, or to report the incidents with the object of having them investigated. The principle applies also to those political leaders who are in a comparable position.[142] The idea behind command responsibility is that it should encourage military leaders to ensure that their subordinates do not commit war crimes, since liability will attach to the perpetrators as well as to themselves. General Strugar was sentenced by the ICTY to a term of seven and a half years' imprisonment for failing to prevent his men from shelling Dubrovnic in 1991[143] and General Galic received a life sentence for his own activities and on the basis of his command responsibility for those under his command, who engaged in sniping and the shelling of the market place in Sarajevo.[144] The ICC had issued an indictment against Saif Al-Islam

137 See the Syria debate in the House of Commons on 29 August 2013, discussed in Chapter 4.

138 It became a party on 14 September 2013.

139 *Prosecutor v Tadic,* Decision on the Defence Motion for Interlocutory Appeal on Jurisdiction, IT-94–1, 2 October 1995, [121].

140 Amendment to Art 8(2)(e), by adding (xiii) and (xiv), Resolution RC/Res.5, Annex I.

141 *Situation in the Central African Republic, Prosecutor v Bemba Gombo,* ICC-01/05–01/08, 15 June 2009, [414]; *Prosecutor v Hadzihasanovic,* IT-01–47-T, 15 March 2006, [80].

142 This principle, derived from the Rome Statute 1998, Art 28, was implemented into English law by the International Criminal Court Act 2001, s 65, as amended by the Coroners and Justice Act 2009, s 70(7), (8).

143 *Prosecutor v Strugar,* IT-01–42-A, 17 July 2008.

144 *Prosecutor v Galic,* IT-98–29-A, 30 November 2006.

Gadaffi and, although the government of Libya challenged the admissibility of this case before the Court, the challenge was dismissed by the Appeals Chamber on 21 May 2014.[145]

There are likely to be difficult questions of fact where command responsibility is invoked by a prosecutor. These will include whether the military or political leader knew or should have known of the commission of the ICC crime. It will not be sufficient to assume that he must have known. In practice direct evidence of such an engagement with the details by political leaders may be difficult to obtain but proper inferences could be drawn about this by a court or tribunal.[146]

Although the details of command responsibility are set out clearly in the Rome Statute of the ICC, any argument by a military or political leader that his state is not a party to the ICC would cut no ice since the principle can fairly be said to exist under customary international law. The first modern case involving it was the trial and subsequent conviction of General Yamashita before a US military commission held in Tokyo in 1946,[147] where the prosecution was able to show that the General ought to have known that his subordinates were committing war crimes against the local people in the Philippines during World War II and that he had failed to prevent them.

It has now become something of a mantra to say that superior orders will not amount to a defence to war crimes. Certainly, this has been the case since the Charter of the IMT at Nuremberg expressly said so.[148] All subsequent war crimes tribunals have refused to accept that the order of a superior could amount to a defence. An identical approach has been taken against the claim that a defendant is immune from liability for war crimes either because he or she is the head of state or because of holding some other high office. There have been examples in recent times of former and even current heads of state being placed on trial or indicted for war crimes.[149] Mr Milosevic was tried before the ICTY, but died before his trial was completed, whilst the President of Kenya was indicted by the ICC, as was Omar Hassan Ahmad Al Bashir, the President of the Republic of Sudan, but he remains at large.

Concentration on war crimes trials held by international tribunals alone runs the risk that the military courts of states concerned in the war will be overlooked. It is noticeable that a number of British and US soldiers have been tried by their own military courts for acts, which may, or may not, be described as war crimes, but which have involved breaches of a soldier's military law or his obligations to comply with the criminal law of his own country. A report compiled by

145 *The Prosecutor v Saif Al-Islam Gaddafi and Senussi*, ICC 01/11–01/11.

146 The modes of participation of a crime are set out in the Rome Statute 1998, Art 25.

147 *In re Yamashita* (1946) 327 US 1.

148 Charter of the International Military Tribunal 1945 (Nuremberg), Art 8. It had, however, been recognised as a defence before the German Supreme Court at Leipzig, 1921, in the case of Lt Commander Karl Neumann, see note 102.

149 See generally, J Foakes, *The Position of Heads of State and Senior Officials in International Law* (OUP, 2014).

Brigadier Aitken[150] lays bare the details of investigations and court-martial trials of a number of British soldiers for their activities in Iraq. In *R v Payne and others* (2007), which involved the death of Baha Mousa, a number of soldiers and their commanding officer appeared as defendants before a court-martial. Apart from the charges against the individual soldiers, the case illustrated the possibility of bringing charges against the men's commanding officer, in this case for neglect of his duty.[151] This is not the same as command responsibility discussed above since, if found responsible, the commanding officer would have committed a quite separate service, rather than a criminal, offence. He was acquitted by the court-martial. The possibility of telling soldiers that they might face charges of neglecting a duty if, for instance, they fail to report having witnessed what might be a war crime (or any offence against English service law) to commanders, offers those commanders an effective means of enforcing military discipline, and avoiding the predictable consequences once the facts come to light. It is surprising how often they do come to light in modern armed conflicts, largely because virtually every soldier now possesses a mobile phone and, unless prevented from taking it on operations, is able to take pictures that can be easily sent in a text message to any recipient.

Events, particularly in Iraq, have shown that civilians who have been affected by the actions of British soldiers have wanted something more than merely knowing that the actions of one or more soldiers would be investigated by the British military authorities. It has to be said that most investigations of these incidents do not lead to prosecutions, not because of any bad faith on the part of British officials but largely due to a combination of factors. It is, for instance, difficult, although certainly not impossible, to conduct criminal investigations where deaths have occurred during combat overseas. It is, of course, easy to interview the soldiers concerned but problems may arise at a practical level in interviewing civilian witnesses, or where an autopsy cannot be carried out where local custom or religious practice is to bury a body within a very short period after death. Nevertheless, a demand to know why, for instance, a relative has been killed by British soldiers is not an unreasonable one which has been met, to some extent, by British solicitors taking cases, based mainly on the Human Rights Act 1998, before the High Court in London on behalf of their Iraqi clients. The role played by British lawyers and the impact of the Human Rights Act is discussed in Chapter 5.

150 *An Investigation into Cases of Deliberate Abuse and Unlawful Killing in Iraq in 2003 and 2004* (Ministry of Defence, UK, 2008).

151 An offence, at the time, under the Army Act 1955, s 29A(2). See now Armed Forces Act 2006, s 15(1)(c), (2).

7 The influence of human rights law on the UK armed forces

Some may find it hard to accept the idea that human rights can apply during an armed conflict, when killing the enemy will often be necessary and where soldiers run the obvious risk of being killed themselves. The very idea appears to be counter-intuitive but, like many simple propositions, the reality is that it is much more nuanced. We need, however, to look briefly, at what is meant by the term 'human rights law', and how it has developed over the period since 2000 so as to have a profound effect on Britain's wars since then.

Although the Universal Declaration of Human Rights, adopted by the new UN General Assembly in 1948, sets out what would be seen today as the fundamental freedoms possessed by everyone, it was, at the time, declared not to be binding on states. In 1950 the ECHR was opened for signature by states which were members of the Council of Europe. The Universal Declaration can easily be identified as an important influence on the form the ECHR took but it provided a number of important additional features. First, and foremost, it was a treaty, binding on those states that ratified it, creating direct obligations on them towards those who within its jurisdiction, and other state parties. Secondly, it established a court, rather than an advisory body, to make decisions as to whether a breach had been committed by a state party to it and it required those states to carry out the decisions of the ECtHR.[1] Of equal importance was the opportunity for individuals to claim that their rights under the Convention had been breached by the public authorities of the state. Individual states would have to agree for themselves whether to give such a right to individuals within their jurisdiction. The UK agreed to do this in 1966,[2] and, by so doing, it set in motion an important means by which individuals could make a claim to the European

1 Article 46(1).

2 The Prime Minister (Mr Wilson) made the announcement in the House of Commons on 7 December 1965, HC Debs 7 December 1965, vol 722, col 235. It was to last for an initial period of three years and was to come into effect as soon as the Government had notified the Council of Europe. The right of individual petition to the Human Rights Committee under the International Covenant on Civil and Political Rights 1966 (ICCPR) has not yet been accepted by the UK. Where, however, any part of the ICCPR reflects customary international law it may become a part of English law. Even if it is not customary international law a policy decision to act on the basis of it could lead to a breach of the policy in an individual

Commission (and subsequently to the Court) of Human Rights (ECtHR) in Strasbourg that their rights under the Convention had been breached by a public authority, which the UK would have to defend before the Court. The first case to reach the ECtHR from the UK was one that involved a prisoner who had been denied the opportunity to consult a solicitor.[3] Between 1 January 2010 and September 2011 there were 18 cases in which the European Court of Human Rights (ECtHR) found the UK to be in violation of the ECHR, of which three related to Britain's overseas military operations, all of which originated in individual petitions.[4]

An important state against state case was decided in 1978. This was the case brought by the Republic of Ireland against the UK, which related to various techniques used against some of those whom the British army detained whilst conducting military operations in Northern Ireland.[5] These had involved wall-standing, hooding, subjection to noise, deprivation of sleep and deprivation of food (or reduced diet) of suspected terrorists.[6] The Court had been asked by Ireland to rule that these techniques amounted to torture, inhuman or degrading treatment, contrary to Article 3 of the Convention. The background to this claim needs to be considered since it involved a long campaign by various groups in Northern Ireland which, on the UK's figures, showed that by '1975 over 1,100 people had been killed and over 11,500 injured',[7] and where pressure on the part of the security forces to gain information to prevent future attacks was intense. The ECtHR decided by a majority that the interrogation techniques did not amount to torture but that they were inhuman and degrading, in itself, a breach of Article 3. When the allegations of all-treatment by British soldiers had come to light in 1971 and following a report of an inquiry into them, the Prime Minister at the time, Mr Heath, made a statement to the House of Commons on 3 March 1972 that these prohibited techniques would no longer be used as 'an aid to interrogation'.[8] The meaning of Mr Heath's statement to the

case becoming 'unlawful in public law terms', *R (Haider Ali Hussein) v Secretary of State for Defence* [2013] EWHC 95, Collins J [20].

3 *Golder v United Kingdom*, Application No 4451/70, Judgment, 21 February 1975.

4 Ministerial Statement, HL Deb 12 September 2011, vol 532, col 44W. The three cases involving British military operations were *Al Saadoon and Mufdhi v United Kingdom* (2010) 51 EHRR 9; *Al-Skeini v United Kingdom* (2011) 53 EHRR 18; *Al-Jedda v United Kingdom* (2011) 53 EHRR 23. See also *Hassan v United Kingdom*, Application No 29750/09, judgment, 16 September 2014. A number of individual petitions will have been declared inadmissible by the ECtHR and will have proceeded no further.

5 *Ireland v United Kingdom* (1979–80) 2 EHRR 25. For the possibility that the ECtHR may be requested to re-consider this case see F de Londras, 'Revisiting the Five Techniques in the European Court of Human Rights' (12 December 2014) EJIL: Talk! http://www.ejiltalk.org/revisiting-the-five-techniques-in-the-european-court-of-human-rights/.

6 The ECtHR noted in its judgment that hooding, subjection to noise, deprivation of sleep and deprivation of food and drink all occurred 'pending interrogation'.

7 *Ireland v United Kingdom*, Judgment, [12].

8 HC Debs 2 March 1972, vol 832, col 744. At the hearing before the ECtHR the Attorney General had given an 'unqualified undertaking that the 'five techniques' will not in any circumstances be reintroduced as an aid to interrogation', *Ireland v United Kingdom*, [102].

House, was to become significant nearly 30 years later during the Baha Mousa public inquiry.[9]

The Ireland case was the first one to involve a complaint before the ECtHR involving Britain's armed forces[10] but a number of other cases followed in relation to the policy of internment in Northern Ireland. In 1995 the ECtHR dealt with a complaint brought by family members of three alleged IRA suspects who had been shot and killed by British soldiers in Gibraltar.[11] The soldiers claimed that they had opened fire on the three when they suspected that they were about to detonate remotely a bomb placed in a car, which they had parked near a military parade to be held in the centre of Gibraltar. The ECtHR decided that the UK had deprived the three individuals of their right to life. But it was to the action of those who had planned the military operation that had done so to which it directed its attention, holding that those more senior officers could have arranged for the three suspects to be arrested when they passed from Spain to Gibraltar, or later on, rather than merely being left with the option to do nothing, or to shoot them. Although this case involved military operations, which did not amount to fighting in an armed conflict, it has had a significant effect in setting the standards for the right to life in Article 2 of the Convention. It has been applied by that Court in a number of subsequent cases involving, for example, the killing of civilians in Chechnya by Russian armed forces, of alleged terrorists by the Turkish armed forces, as well as the killing of suspects by civilian police.[12]

The consequences of passing the Human Rights Act 1998[13] and its effects during Britain's wars were to become clear when proceedings were brought before the High Court in London by a number of Iraqi citizens, whose family members had either been shot dead, or who had been detained by British soldiers.

9 See however, the Report of the Baha Mousa Inquiry, HC 1452–1, 2011, and its interpretation of the Heath Statement in the House of Commons in 1972 relating to the five prohibited techniques. It concluded that the Statement, which included the words 'as an aid to interrogation', were such as 'to limit the effect of the ban', Vol II, 434, [4.85], vol III, 1324, [253] *et seq*.

10 In *de Ibanez v United Kingdom*, Application No 58692/00, 19 July 2000, the ECtHR dismissed an application concerning the sinking of the Argentine Navy warship, *General Belgrano* by the Royal Navy during the Falklands conflict in 1982, on the broad ground that the application was out of time.

11 *McCann v United Kingdom* (1996) 21 EHRR 97.

12 See, for example, *Isayeva v Russia* (2005) 41 EHRR 38; *Ergi v Turkey* (2001) 32 EHRR 18; *Makaratzis v Greece* (2005) 41 EHRR 49.

13 The Human Rights Act 1998 applies also to Northern Ireland, s 22(6). Scotland passed its own Act. See V Bogdanor, *The New British Constitution* (Hart Publishing, 2009), 60, referring to the fact that Art 13 of the ECHR has not found a place in the 1998 Act. In *R v Lyons (No 3)* [2002] UKHL 44, Lord Hoffmann concluded that 'the metaphor of incorporation may be misleading. It is not the treaty but the statute which forms part of English law', [27]. See also *Campaign for Nuclear Disarmament v Prime Minister and others* [2002] EWHC 2777, [27].

i The extra-territorial application of the ECHR

That government ministers could have contemplated proceedings on the basis that the UK had denied Iraqi civilians their Convention rights would probably have been thought unthinkable on the eve of the Iraq war in 2003. Article 1 of the ECHR declares that a state owes the Convention rights to all those 'within its jurisdiction'.[14] Article 1 does not refer to 'territory' and so the issue became whether a state owed obligations to those outside its territory, but who were affected by the acts of its organs, in this case its armed forces. A case had been brought to the ECtHR in 2001, following the attack, in 1999, by NATO aircraft on a broadcasting station in Belgrade, in which it was argued that since NATO aircraft had exclusive control over the airspace it could exercise its jurisdiction over the inhabitants on the ground. The Court did not accept this argument, although it indicated that, in certain circumstances, a state could exercise its jurisdiction in the territory of another state.[15]

The law is replete with examples of where, what may be considered to be ordinary events, lead eventually to landmark rulings by a court, where the individuals involved in those events achieve the long-lasting legacy of contributing their names to the ruling. Two such individuals were Mr Al-Skeini and Mr Al-Jedda, although the name of Mr Baha Mousa, who was one of the applicants, along with Mr Al-Skeini, has become much better known as an individual whose treatment by British soldiers led, first to a court-martial of a number of soldiers, and then to the Baha Mousa public inquiry held in London.[16] The case of *Al-Skeini and Others v United Kingdom* was decided by the ECtHR in 2011[17] having made a long journey through the English courts, starting in 2004, on the issue of whether all, or any, of the applicants came within the jurisdiction of the UK when the actions of which they complained had occurred in Iraq in 2003. During the various court proceedings in London, a concession had been made by the Secretary of State for Defence that Baha Mousa, an Iraqi citizen, who had been detained in a British

14 This article was not included in the Human Rights Act 1998. The ICCPR 1966 is not discussed since it has not figured to any great extent in Britain's wars 2000–2014 and the UK had not yet accepted the right of individuals to petition the Human Rights Committee, see note 2. The Joint Committee on Human Rights, *UN Convention Against Torture*, 19th Report, session 2005–06, HC 701, 26 May 2006 recommended that the government should accept 'the application of all the rights and duties under [UNCAT] to territory controlled by UK armed forces abroad', [73]. The government, in its response to this Report, did not accept the recommendation, arguing that it was not 'able to implement the provisions of Art 2 of UNCAT in Iraq or Afghanistan in relation to the public officials or citizens of those countries', HL 276/HC 701, 13 November 2006. This treaty does not give rights enforceable in English law, *Al-Saadoon v Secretary of State for Defence* [2015] EWHC 715.

15 *Bankovic v Belgium (and other NATO States)* Application (2007) 44 EHRR SE 5. The attack by a UK remotely piloted aircraft on two British nationals in the territory of Syria on 21 August 2015 is discussed in Chapter 4.

16 Report of the Baha Mousa Inquiry, HC 1452 (2011).

17 (2011) 53 EHRR 18.

detention unit in Iraq, came within the jurisdiction of the UK and was therefore owed Convention rights.[18] The House of Lords decided that he did, but that this was the limit of the scope of extra-territorial jurisdiction and that the other five applicants, whose relatives had been shot, or were otherwise killed by British soldiers in the streets in Iraq, were not and, as a result, they could not exercise any Convention rights in UK courts. The Convention right that they all wished to exercise was that an independent investigation, as a procedural obligation under Article 2, should be conducted into the circumstances of their respective deaths.

When the case, now styled as *Al-Skeini v United Kingdom*, came before the Grand Chamber of the ECtHR in 2011, the UK argued that the House of Lords had reached the right result on the basis of the earlier jurisprudence of the Court, and that only Baha Mousa, who died whilst in the custody of the British army, came within the jurisdiction of the UK. An independent investigation would be conducted into the circumstances surrounding his death,[19] but that the other five claimants did not come within jurisdiction and were owed no duty on the part of the UK authorities to investigate their deaths in the manner required under the Convention. A further argument advanced by the UK was that if the Convention did apply to all those in the territory of Iraq occupied by British armed forces, this would mean that the UK had obligations to protect family life, freedom of assembly, freedom of expression and all the other rights contained in the Convention. It clearly could not do this at a practical level and it took the view that if any Convention rights were owed then all of them were.[20]

In its ruling in 2011 the Grand Chamber concluded that all of the applicants in the case came within the jurisdiction of the UK, simply because the UK had carried out 'some of the public powers normally to be exercised by a sovereign government [by assuming] authority and responsibility for the maintenance of security in South East Iraq [and it had] exercised authority and control over individuals killed in the course of its security operations'.[21] The Court did not

18 In *R (Al-Skeini and Others) v Secretary of State for Defence* [2005] EWCA Civ 1609, [185]. The term 'military prison' covered the detention facility in which Mr Mousa was held since it was 'a United Kingdom enclave within the territory of another state', *ibid.*

19 The investigation took the form of a public Inquiry under the Inquiries Act 2005. See Report of the Baha Mousa Inquiry, HC 1452 (2011).

20 *Bankovic v Belgium (and other NATO States)* (2007) 44 EHRR SE 5, [75].

21 *Al-Skeini and Others v United Kingdom* (2011) 53 EHRR 18, [149]. The ECtHR seems to have gone further than its previous decisions, which had linked the exercise of public powers to situations where the territorial state had consented, invited or acquiesced in such powers being used by another state in its territory, [135]. The UK could not fall within these requirements since it was in actual occupation (with the USA) of the territory of Iraq at the time. For the interpretation by the Supreme Court of the basis of the decision in *Al-Skeini* see *Smith v Secretary of State for Defence* [2013] UKSC 41, Lord Hope (majority decision) at [46], draws the conclusion that in [137] of *Al-Skeini*, the ECtHR indicates 'the extent to which the principle relating to state agent *authority* [emphasis supplied] and control is to be regarded as one of general application'. His Lordship does, however, omit the phrase used in [137], 'over an individual.'

expressly declare that the UK had exercised effective control of an area, which it had discussed earlier in its judgment as a ground for establishing extra-territorial jurisdiction.[22] This was despite the fact that the incidents raised on behalf of all the applicants had occurred after the start of the occupation of Iraq by the UK (with the USA) at least by 1 May 2003.

It may well be the case that the ECtHR had assumed that a state that was in occupation of territory could, by that very fact, 'exercise authority and control over individuals' for the purposes of establishing the necessary jurisdictional link. By 22 May 2003, when the UN Security Council adopted Resolution 1483, which recognised, without expressly saying so, that the UK and the USA were in occupation of Iraq, the status of these countries as being occupiers was not based solely on the actual fact of control over the territory but, no doubt, on wider political and other matters.[23] At that date it would have been Panglossian to believe that the Basra area of Iraq had been 'actually placed under the authority of the [British army]' as the Hague Convention 1907 required[24] or that the UK had effective control over the territory. Indeed, even by November 2003 when the last death, which formed the subject matter of the *Al-Skeini* case, occurred, the House of Lords considered that the UK did not in fact have effective control over the area.[25] Indeed, it may be that this ground for the assumption of jurisdiction will now be purely of historical interest, since the Court of Appeal in *Mohammed v Secretary of State for Defence* (2015) concluded that the *Al-Skeini* decision had rendered the exercise of power and control over an individual as the most likely ground and that 'effective control over territory is made largely redundant'.[26]

The ECtHR also decided that a state's obligations to those within its jurisdiction in these circumstances could be tailored to fit the situation.[27] So, there was

22 At [138].

23 See, for example, the view of the (then) Attorney General, evidence to the Iraq Inquiry, 27 January 2010, 227.

24 The Hague Regulations, 1907, Art 42. The authority over the territory must be able to be exercised, *ibid*.

25 *Al-Skeini v Secretary of State for Defence* [2007] UKHL 26, [83], [97]. For the extent of the military presence to establish effective control over territory see *Issa v Turkey*, Application No 31821/96, Judgment, 16 November 2004 (and the cases referred to therein); *Catan v Moldova and Russia*, Application No 43370/04, Judgment, 19 October 2012, [117]–[119].The Grand Chamber in *Hassan v United Kingdom* Application No 29750/09, Grand Chamber Judgment, 16 September 2014, also took the view that the 'United Kingdom was far from being in effective control of the south eastern area [of Iraq] which it occupied [*sic*]', [75].

26 [2015] EWCA Civ 843, [93]. See, however, discussion below of possible differences between these two alternative bases of jurisdiction.

27 Although the Grand Chamber in *Al-Skeini v United Kingdom* stated that Convention rights could be 'divided and tailored' when it referred to state agents who exercise control and authority over an individual, [137] the absence of this phrase from its discussion, at [138], on the separate issue of where a state exercises effective control over territory, appears to be significant. The Court did not refer specifically to the 'effective control over territory' ground in its conclusion at [149].

no question of the UK having to protect the right to family life and so on in Iraq, but only to protect those rights that it could directly affect, such as the right to life, including the holding of an independent investigation where an Iraqi civilian was killed by a British soldier, the right to detain and not to be subjected to torture, inhuman or degrading treatment whilst held in British military custody. The Baha Mousa public inquiry, which reported in 2011, satisfied the requirements for an independent investigation but, as a result of the ruling, an independent investigation was also required into the other five deaths.[28]

In a similar case, the ECtHR decided in November 2014 that an Iraqi civilian shot and killed by a Dutch army unit at a vehicle check point when the vehicle in which he was travelling did not stop, came within the jurisdiction of the Netherlands. Like the case of the five applicants in the *Al-Skeini* case, the events occurred during the period when Iraq was occupied by the USA and the UK. In holding that the Netherlands had exercised its jurisdiction 'for the purpose of asserting authority and control over persons passing through the checkpoint' it also asserted that 'the status of "occupying power" within the meaning of Article 42 of the Hague Regulations [1907], or lack of it, is not *per se* determinative'.[29]

Both the *Al-Skeini* and the *Jaloud* cases involved the deaths of civilians by foreign armed forces in Iraq during the period of occupation. In *Al-Skeini* the UK was an occupying power but in *Jaloud v Netherlands*, the Netherlands was not, although it had 'accepted the operational control of the commander of the MDN (SE) [Multinational Division Central South], a United Kingdom officer'.[30]

What does seem clear is that if an ECHR state holds foreign nationals in its custody, it will exercise its jurisdiction over them for these purposes, whether this occurs during a period of occupation or not.[31] *Al-Jedda v United Kingdom*, a judgment of the Grand Chamber of the ECtHR given on the same day as the *Al-Skeini* case, involved an individual who held both British and Iraqi citizenship and who was arrested by the British military authorities in Iraq and interned by them from 2004 until 2007. His internment had begun after the occupation itself had come to an end[32] and the UK claimed that his internment was necessary for imperative reasons of security. There was little doubt before the ECtHR that he came within the jurisdiction of the UK by dint of the fact

28 See ministerial statement, HC Debs 26 March 2012, vol 542, col 87WS. There is an account of at least one of the other investigations in *R (Ali Zaki Mousa) v Secretary of State for Defence* [2013] EWHC 1412, [158].

29 *Jaloud v Netherlands* (2015) 60 EHRR 29, [152], [142], respectively.

30 *Ibid*, [143]. The multinational force was established by UN Security Council Resolution 1511 (2003), [13]–[14]. For discussion of the role of the UK as a coalition partner see below.

31 The ECtHR drew upon its earlier jurisprudence to illustrate that a foreign state could exercise its jurisdiction in the absence of occupation, see *Jaloud v Netherlands*, [142].

32 He was detained from 10 October 2004 until 30 December 2007, [10]. The occupation of Iraq was declared to be ended on 30 June 2004, UN Security Council Resolution 1546 (2004), [2].

that he had been detained by the British army and he was therefore owed rights under the ECHR.[33]

In 2014 the ECtHR was faced with an application on behalf of an Iraqi citizen who had been arrested by British armed forces on 23 April 2003, and therefore prior to the formal declaration on 1 May 2003 that combat operations had been concluded.[34] Mr Hassan had been transferred almost immediately to Camp Bucca, a US-run detention facility, which caused the English courts to decide that he had ceased to be within the jurisdiction of the UK.[35] The ECtHR came to a different conclusion on the facts and decided that the 'United Kingdom retained authority and control over all aspects of the detention . . . [and Mr Hassan] fell within the jurisdiction of the United Kingdom from the moment of his capture by United Kingdom troops until his release from the bus[36] that took him from Camp Bucca . . . most probably on 2 May 2003'.[37]

33 *Al-Jedda v United Kingdom* (2011) 53 EHRR 23, [86]. The British government conceded during the proceedings in the Divisional Court and the Court of Appeal that Mr Al-Jedda fell within the jurisdiction of the UK, but in the House of Lords it argued that the acts of the UK armed forces in respect of Mr Al-Jedda should be attributed to the UN and that, therefore, the ECHR was not relevant as far as the UK was concerned. It took the same stance before the ECtHR, which rejected it, see [75], [83]. The government had made a similar concession in *R (Al-Skeini and Others) v Secretary of State for Defence* [2005] EWCA Civ 1609, [185], which it maintained in the House of Lords.

34 *Hassan v United Kingdom*, Application No 29750/09, Grand Chamber Judgment, 16 September 2014. For discussion as to the date on which the occupation began, see Chapter 6. In *Al-Saadoon v Secretary of State for Defence* [2015] EWHC 217, Leggatt J concluded, [75], that the occupation was in existence on 21 April 2003.

35 *R (Hassan) v Secretary of State for Defence* [2009] EWHC 309 (Admin). The UK 'took over the running of Camp Bucca from the US on 25 September 2003', ministerial statement, HC Deb 21 May 2004, vol 421, col 1252W. This statement also confirmed that allegations made by the ICRC concerning the treatment of two detainees 'occurred while the facility was run by the US [and that] these are matters for the US'. It is not stated whether these two individuals were UK detainees, as was Mr Hassan.

36 Even though he had left Camp Bucca he remained within the jurisdiction of the UK for the whole of the journey by bus, since there were 'armed guards on board and armed military escort vehicles to the front and rear', *Hassan v United Kingdom*, Application No 29750/09, Grand Chamber Judgment, 16 September 2014, [27]

37 *Ibid*, [78], [80]. The memorandum of understanding, which, in this case referred to the detaining state (the UK) and the accepting state (USA) is set out in the judgment of Walker J, in *R (Hassan) v Secretary of State for Defence* [2009] EWHC 309 (Admin), [9]. This provides that UK officers at the US run Camp Bucca were there 'in order to facilitate the implementation of the Agreement' [8] which would suggest that the UK personnel were at the Camp purely for this purpose. Moreover, 'primary jurisdiction over breaches of disciplinary regulations [at Camp Bucca] . . . will rest with the Accepting Power [the USA]', [12]. The power to discipline detainees is a key factor in showing power, authority and control over them, which in this case would be held by the US and not the UK authorities. For discussion of the effect of Art 5, ECHR, on Mr Hassan's detention see below. For the numbers of transferees between the UK and the US relating to Camp Bucca, see HC Debs 26 February 2009, vol 488, col 394. Compare the application to the ECtHR of Saddam Hussein, who was arrested and detained by US forces was held not to be within the jurisdiction of a ECHR state, none of which had 'any responsibility for, or any involvement in, his arrest and subsequent detention, *Hussein v Albania (and other States)*, Application No 23276/04, Admissibility Decision, 14 March 2006.

The position is less clear where civilians are killed by members of the armed forces of an ECHR state acting in the course of their duty. The ECtHR was prepared to accept that in both *Al-Skeini* and *Jaloud*, coalition forces in Iraq had, as a result of 'asserting authority and control over individuals' brought the applicants within their respective jurisdictions during the course of the occupation of Iraq. Although the Court stated in *Jaloud* that the fact of occupation was 'not *per se* determinative',[38] it is clearly a relevant factor.

In the course of war fighting during an international armed conflict (where there is no occupation of territory) it is difficult to accept that the killing of a member of the opposing armed forces, or a civilian who is taking a direct part in hostilities, during the course of a battle would bring that individual within the jurisdiction of an ECHR state. He would not be in the custody of the state, nor is he under its authority, power or control in circumstances where the state does not possess effective control over an area of the territorial state. The threshold of Article 1 has not been met and no rights under the ECHR (as opposed to IHL) can be owed to such a person. If, on the other hand, he is captured or is in need of medical attention and is brought into the custody of the ECHR state he will then be owed rights under the ECHR and under IHL.[39] Can it be said then that a person is under the power and control of foreign armed forces if he is shot in the street during the course of an international armed conflict? In *Al Skeini* and in *Jaloud* the ECtHR thought so, but in both cases the events occurred during the occupation of Iraq. In *Issa v Turkey* there had been no occupation by Turkish forces of northern Iraq, but the victims were under the actual control of Turkish soldiers because they were rounded up and taken to a cave where they were then shot. Although in *Smith v Ministry of Defence* the Supreme Court applied *Al-Skeini v United Kingdom*, and thereby established a binding precedent for lower courts in England to follow, it is important, in future cases, to analyse exactly what Al-Skeini actually decided and, in turn, what the Supreme

38 At [142]. In *Hassan v United Kingdom*, Application No 29750/09, Grand Chamber Judgment, 16 September 2014, the ECtHR seems to have considered that occupation was a central feature in the *Al-Skeini v United Kingdom* case, see [75]. There was no use of the word 'authority' in *Al-Saddoon and Mufdhi v The United Kingdom* (2010) 51 EHRR 9, [88], or in *Medvedyev v France* (2010) 51 EHRR 9, [67]. In both cases the ECtHR referred solely to the 'control' over individuals. See also *Hassan v United Kingdom*, Application No 29750/09, Grand Chamber, 16 September 2014, [75], [78]. The ECtHR seems willing to equate the ability to control individuals with actual control over them. This reasoning is also seen in the judgment of Leggatt J in *Al-Saadoon v Secretary of State for Defence* [2015] EWHC 715, [95].

39 See, for example, *Al-Saadoon v Secretary of State for Defence* [2015] EWHC 715; *Hassan v United Kingdom*, Application No 29750/09, Grand Chamber Judgment, 16 September 2014, [104]. *Legal Consequences of the Construction of a Wall in the Occupied Palestinian Territory* (2004) ICJ Rep 136, [106]. In *Case Concerning Armed Activities on the Territory of the Congo (Democratic Republic of Congo v Uganda)* (2005) ICJ Rep 168. In quoting from the *Wall* case the ICJ decided that international human rights law applied alongside IHL, '*particularly in occupied territories*', [216], [italics supplied].

Court accepted from it as the legal norm binding on lower courts. Al-Skeini, for instance, used the term 'public powers' but subsequent decisions of the Grand Chamber, in *Hassan* and in *Jaloud*, did not.

Where the armed forces of a state are operating abroad during a non-international armed conflict, with the consent of the territorial state (as in Iraq, after the occupation came to an end on 28 June 2004, and in Afghanistan, following the Bonn Agreement of December 2001), there could be no exercise of public powers or authority possessed by foreign armed forces unless it was 'through the consent, invitation or acquiescence of the Government of that territory',[40] or granted by a UN Security Council resolution. If such authority can be established, the extra-territorial reach can extend to executive or judicial acts carried out by the foreign state.[41] It is not unusual to find that in peacetime a territorial state has consented to foreign armed forces being stationed or being present in its territory. It is standard practice for the sending and receiving states to agree a status of forces agreement (or a memorandum of understanding) in which the sending state is permitted to carry out its disciplinary procedures over its own armed forces by way of a military court or otherwise.[42] There can be no doubt that the sending state, if a party to the ECHR, will be responsible for the conduct of its military court in the same way as it would in its own territory. There can also be no doubt that the sending state has sufficient 'authority and control' over members of its own armed forces for the purpose of establishing jurisdiction over them. It would seem to follow that if the territorial state has invited another state to assist it in conducting military operations during a non-international armed conflict on its territory, it could authorise that state to carry out executive acts 'normally to be exercised by that Government'[43] such as, for instance, the arrest and detention of its citizens.[44]

That the ECtHR had left uncertainty in the wake of its earlier decisions[45] on the limits of extra-territorial jurisdiction can really be seen by the approach of the UK in all the litigation deriving from the six cases brought together under the name of the lead applicant, Mr Al-Skeini and in subsequent cases. The UK had expressed the view in 2004 that 'our best judgment is that the ECHR does not apply [in Iraq]'.[46] It appears therefore that the UK government had taken the

40 *Al-Skeini v United Kingdom* (2011) 53 EHRR 18, [135].

41 *Ibid.* Complying with the executive orders of another foreign state 'is not in itself sufficient to relieve a Contracting State of the obligations which it has taken upon itself under the Convention', *Jaloud v Netherlands*, [143].

42 See, for example, Agreement Between the Parties of the North Atlantic Treaty Regarding the Status of Forces, 1951 and related treaties.

43 *Al-Skeini v United Kingdom*, [135].

44 See *Mohammed v Secretary of State for Defence* [2015] EWCA Civ 843, [41] referring to the memorandum of understanding, UK and Afghanistan.

45 *Al-Skeini v United Kingdom*, as set out in [130]–[142]; *Mohammed v Secretary of State for Defence* [2015] EWCA Civ 843, [93(iii)–(iv)]. See further discussion below.

46 Ministerial statement, HC Debs 4 May 2004, vol 420, col 1214. A similar view was expressed about its application in Afghanistan, see below and HL Debs 7 November 2013, vol 749, cols 416–17.

view early on during the Al-Skeini case before the High Court, that the ECtHR had limited the reach of extra-territorial jurisdiction to those cases where a person was actually within the custody of organs of the state, in this case, its armed forces.

The criticism made by Judge Bonello, in his separate judgment in *Al-Skeini v United Kingdom*, in which he characterised the UK as wanting members of its armed forces to be 'gentlemen at home, hoodlums elsewhere',[47] can hardly be a true reflection of the UK's attitude to its responsibilities in Iraq. All its soldiers carried English criminal law with them when they were operating abroad and there have been a number of prosecutions brought against individuals for their alleged ill-treatment of Iraqi civilians, including one case where the army had decided not to prosecute a particular soldier but where the Attorney General subsequently authorised a prosecution before a civilian court in London.[48]

The UK had defended the claims made in *Al-Skeini* and the *Al-Jedda* cases vigorously before the English courts as well as the ECtHR and it was to be expected that the government would take some time to consider how it would react to the judgments. As part of the practice of ensuring that the government takes into account fully the decisions of the ECtHR, the Parliamentary Joint Committee on Human Rights monitors its response to each judgment and how it plans to make any necessary changes to the law or to policy as a result. The Government's response[49] to these cases indicates that, in its view, each judgment relates to the particular circumstances of 'the UK's past operations in Iraq and it has no implications for its current operations elsewhere including in Afghanistan, where the legal basis for UK operations is materially different from that which pertained in Iraq'.[50] It did, however, seem unduly optimistic to discount these decisions as applicable only to the circumstances pertaining to Iraq in the period covered by each case.

The acceptance by the Supreme Court in *Smith v Ministry of Defence*[51] of the judgment of the ECtHR in *Al-Skeini v United Kingdom* has led the courts in England to apply these decisions to detention by British forces in Afghanistan[52] and the shooting dead of an Iraqi citizen.[53] In the absence of the UK having had effective control of the territory of Iraq or Afghanistan, the test of when a foreign national came within its jurisdiction still lacks precision. Does, for instance, the

47 Concurring Opinion of Judge Bonello, [18].

48 For details see Chapter 8. By the date of *Al-Skeini v UK* (2011) 53 EHRR 18, the UK had also established two public inquiries, the Baha Mousa Inquiry and the Al-Sweady Inquiry both of which were concerned with allegations of ill-treatment of Iraqi detainees.

49 See Ministry of Justice, *Responding to Human Rights Judgments. Report to the Joint Committee on Human Rights on the Government Response to Human Rights Judgments 2011–12*, Cm 8432 (2012).

50 At 29, *Al Skeini* judgment and for the position in respect of *Al Jedda v United Kingdom*, 27.

51 [2013] UKSC 41.

52 *Mohammed v Secretary of State for Defence* [2015] EWCA Civ 843.

53 *Al-Saadoon v Secretary of State for Defence* [2015] EWHC 715.

UK need to be exercising some form of 'public powers', however this may be construed,[54] and does it require 'authority and control' or 'physical power and control'[55] for an individual to come within UK jurisdiction?

The doctrine of precedent requires English courts to follow the decisions of its highest courts, even if they are at variance with subsequent decisions of the ECtHR.[56] Certainty of the legal position, particularly over a relatively short period of time, is likely to be more valuable to a state than the ECtHR's principle of treating the ECHR as a 'living instrument'.

ii Attribution to the UN, another international organisation, or to another state

It is a well-understood principle of international law that an international organisation may be responsible when action on its behalf is carried out by a state, but where it is the organisation itself that has 'effective control over that conduct'.[57] In *Al-Jedda v United Kingdom*, the UK had argued, before both the House of Lords and the ECtHR, that its action of interning Mr Al-Jedda in Iraq should be attributed to the UN, the legal effect of which would have been that the actions of the British armed forces would not be attributable to the UK and, thus, it could not owe any obligations under the ECHR to Mr Al-Jedda. There was a precedent for this in relation to Kosovo, which the ECtHR had accepted,[58] but the House of Lords distinguished the situation in Iraq, principally on the wording and effect of the different UN Security Council resolutions.[59] The acts of the UK could not therefore be attributed to the UN and, although the issue of jurisdiction within the ECHR is not identical with attribution to an international

54 This seems to be required in *Al-Skeini v United Kingdom* [135], [149], although not relevant to the decisions in *Hassan v United Kingdom* or in *Jaloud v Netherlands*. It was required in *Al-Saadoon v Secretary of State for Defence* [2015] EWHC 715, [86]. *Quaere* whether a requirement for foreign armed forces to be exercising public powers is helpful in determining jurisdiction, outside a period of occupation of territory. It should be sufficient to show that soldiers were acting in that capacity.

55 *Al-Skeini v United Kingdom* itself used the terms loosely, see [136], [149]. In *Al-Saadoon v Secretary of State for Defence* [2015] EWHC 715, Leggatt J applied the phrase, 'physical power and control', which avoids the need to decide on the meaning of 'authority' where there is no occupation of territory.

56 In the English courts *Smith v Ministry of Defence* [2013] UKSC 41 will bind lower courts on its interpretation of *Al-Skeini v United Kingdom*. For an example of this principle, see *Al-Saadoon v Secretary of State for Defence* [2015] EWHC 715, 116; *Al-Waheed v Ministry of Defence* [2014] EWHC 2714 [2].

57 Article 5 of the Draft Articles on The Responsibility of International Organisations, International Law Commission, 2004, set out in *Al-Jedda v United Kingdom* [56]. See now Draft Articles on the Responsibility of International Organisations, 2011, Art 7.

58 *Behrami v France; Seramati v France, Germany and Norway* (2007) 45 EHRR SE 10, particularly relating to the detention of Mr Seramati.

59 *Al-Jedda v United Kingdom*, [75]–[86], where the ECtHR agreed with the House of Lords in *Al-Jedda v Secretary of State for Defence* [2007] UKHL 26.

organisation, it seemed clear that Mr Al-Jedda, held by UK armed forces, came within the jurisdiction of the UK for the purposes of the ECHR.

Two further issues would seem to arise. First, could the acts of one state, acting in coalition with another during a military operation overseas, cause its acts to be attributed to the state whose armed forces are taking the lead?[60] An example would be where that other state is in occupation of territory and is assisted by other members of the coalition to maintain order in the part of the territory it occupies. This was the position in *Jaloud v Netherlands* when its armed forces had 'accepted the operational control of the commander [of part of the multinational force] a United Kingdom officer'.[61] The ECtHR held that since the Dutch armed forces unit retained 'full command over its military personnel' the Netherlands could not attribute its act of killing of Mr Jaloud to the UK.[62]

Secondly, could the state with operational control, in this case the UK, bring the killing of Mr Jaloud within the jurisdiction of the UK, in addition to the Netherlands? As a result of the ECtHR decision in relation to the Netherlands it became unnecessary for it to determine whether the UK could also have exercised its jurisdiction concurrently with the Netherlands.[63] It is perhaps just as well that the Court did not feel the need to do so since it would then have been faced with problems concerning whether both states were, or only one state was, required to carry out the necessary investigation into the killing of Mr Jaloud and, in the latter case, what responsibility towards the investigation was to be borne by the other state?

Despite the fact that the ECtHR in 2011 did not accept the argument of the UK government that its internment of Mr Al-Jedda should be attributed to the UN, the UK has taken a similar view in relation to the application of the ECHR to its military activities in Afghanistan.[64] As late as November 2013 the government argued that its armed forces operate in Afghanistan 'through ISAF, a multinational force under the ultimate authority and control of the United Nations Security Council. Consequently, we contend that the United Kingdom's acts and omissions are, for Convention purposes, attributable to ISAF and hence to the United Nations.'[65] It would seem difficult to establish, except in the most unusual circumstances, that the UN could have 'effective control' over the conduct of armed forces in a situation such as those of UK military operations in Afghanistan, given the often intense nature of the combat

60 See generally, Art 8 of the Articles on the Responsibility of States for Internationally Wrongful Acts, 2001, International Law Commission, UN General Assembly A/RES/56/83.

61 *Jaloud v Netherlands* (2015) 60 EHRR 29, [143].

62 For the importance of the rules of engagement in showing command over armed forces see Chapter 8.

63 *Jaloud v Netherlands*, [153].

64 House of Commons Defence Select Committee, 12th Report session 2013–14, *United Kingdom Armed Forces Personnel and the Legal Framework of Future Military Operations*, Evidence submitted by the Ministry of Defence, [10].

65 Ministerial statement, HL Debs 7 November 2013, vol 749, cols 416–17.

there and the extent of the casualties, let alone the fact that the discipline of the members of its armed forces is governed by the UK rules of engagement[66] and its own disciplinary systems.

Just as the nature of the UN Security Council resolutions were different between the Kosovo situation and those applicable to Iraq, so they will need to be interpreted on the issue of attribution in relation to Afghanistan. The fact, however, that the killing of Mr Jaloud came within the jurisdiction of the Netherlands despite that state not being in occupation in Iraq and of it coming under the operational control of a UK armed forces officer, would suggest that the scope for a state to claim that its acts and omissions can be attributed to the UN seems, except in the most unusual circumstances, to be most unlikely. Yet, that is exactly what the Court of Appeal decided in 2015, although it went on to hold that, on the facts, ISAF had not authorised the detention of SM and, thus, the UK was responsible was for this.[67]

iii Independent investigations

The obligation to conduct, and the procedure involved in, an independent investigation have proved to have been one of the most practical consequences of the application of the ECHR to UK military action abroad since 2000. The ECtHR has shown, in a long line of cases,[68] that an investigation is required following the death of an individual through the use of force by an agent of the state, or where there is a credible assertion that a person has been subject to torture, inhuman or degrading treatment.[69] These investigations must be independent of the organ of the state whose activities are under investigation.[70] In the case of the armed forces, the investigation must not only be, but be perceived to be, independent of the chain of command. It must be initiated by the state as soon

66 The existence of Dutch rules of engagement in *Jaloud v Netherlands* was sufficient to show that that state was not ' "under the exclusive direction or control" of any other State', [151]. For the same reason it could not be under the effective control of the UN.

67 *Mohammed v Secretary of State for Defence* [2015] EWCA Civ 843, [65], where the Court of Appeal concluded that 'the actions of ISAF are attributable to the United Nations'. The Court of Appeal, [63], distinguished *Sirri v Secretary of State for the Home Department* [2012] UKSC 54, [58], on the basis that that case was 'not concerned with the question of attribution now under consideration'. *Jaloud v Netherlands* was not referred to in the judgment of the Court of Appeal.

68 The ECtHR set out the principles of an investigation, citing many of its earlier decisions, in *Al-Skeini v United Kingdom* (2011) 53 EHRR 18, [163]–[167], which was itself quoted in *Jaloud v Netherlands* (2015) 60 EHRR 29, [44].

69 *Hassan v United Kingdom*, Application No 29750/09, Grand Chamber Judgment, 16 September 2014, [62].

70 Compare, however, *Stoyanovi v Bulgaria*, Application No 42980/04, Judgment, 9 November 2010, where, according to *R (Long) v Secretary of State for Defence* [2015] EWCA Civ 770, [58] 'the fact that the investigation [in that case] was not conducted by an institutionally independent body seems to have counted for little'.

as events that give rise to it come to its attention, and thus the investigation must be conducted speedily, and to be effective it must be of a type that could lead to the identification and punishment of those responsible, and be subject to public scrutiny. It is therefore a means of holding state agents accountable before the law for their acts or omissions. By investigating promptly, a state can show other soldiers that, what may turn out to be an unlawful act, will not be tolerated and that individuals could be held legally accountable for their actions within the service disciplinary system. Finally, the next of kin are also to be involved in the process.

The large number of allegations made by Iraq citizens who had been detained in British army facilities about physical assaults and other serious allegations led to the requirement to investigate each one. No investigation could be independent if it was perceived as being conducted by the army into its own conduct unless, for example, the service police were shown to be sufficiently independent of the chain of command. The Court of Appeal concluded that the Iraq Historic Allegations Team (IHAT) was not sufficiently independent of the armed forces that it was investigating[71] but, in the form in which it appeared in May 2013, it won the blessing of the High Court as being sufficiently independent to satisfy the procedural safeguards of Article 2 (the right to life) and Article 3 (torture, inhuman and degrading treatment) of the ECHR.[72]

The ECtHR has recognised that it is likely there will be considerable practical problems in carrying out an investigation in a 'foreign and hostile area [but the obligation to do so] must be applied realistically, to take account of specific problems faced by investigators'.[73] These can include the 'shortages of local pathologists and facilities for autopsies [and] the scope for linguistic and cultural misunderstandings between the occupiers and the local population'.[74] Investigations for these purposes have been carried out in England by courts-martial, two

71 *R (Mousa) v Secretary of State for Defence* [2011] EWCA Civ 1334, [38]. For an example of an ineffective investigation see *R (Al-Sweady) and others v Secretary of State for Defence* [2009] EWHC 2387 (Admin), [54].

72 *R (Ali Zaki Mousa) v Secretary of State for Defence* [2013] EWHC 1412, [109]–[119]. The Court saw no objection to service police in, say, the army investigating soldiers providing that on the facts they were sufficiently independent from the chain of command. It is always possible for one force to investigate another, eg the RAF police investigating the conduct of soldiers. The Court also considered that IHAT had not always fulfilled the duty on the part of the UK to investigate, see [178]–[196] ; its caseload had also become very large, particularly from 2014, see *Al-Saadoon, v Secretary of State for Defence* [2015] EWHC 1769, discussed below. For the progress and significance of IHAT in relation to the preliminary examination being conducted by the Prosecutor of the ICC into allegations against British soldiers in Iraq see Chapter 6. The Special Investigations Branch of the Royal Military Police did not lack independence, *R (AB) v Secretary of State for Defence* [2013] EWHC 3908, [60].

73 *Isayeva v Russia* (2005) 41 EHRR 38, [224]; *Khashiyev v Russia*, Application No 57942/00, [16]; *Bazorkina v Russia*, Application No 69481/01, [13], [125]; *Al-Skeini v United Kingdom* (2011) 53 EHRR 18, [168]; *Jaloud v Netherlands* (2015) 60 EHRR 29, [226].

74 *Al-Skeini v United Kingdom* (2011) 53 EHRR 18, [168].

public inquiries (Baha Mousa[75]; Al-Sweady[76]), coroners and fatality investigations,[77] along with investigations carried out by the service police abroad. Each of these separate forms of investigation has been faced with considerable difficulties in attempting to satisfy the obligation placed on the UK by the ECHR. When a British soldier has died in Iraq or in Afghanistan these Article 2 investigations have been conducted by the coroner's court.[78] Where civilians have died in the custody of British armed forces in Iraq the Divisional Court called for a similar inquisitorial process to be conducted.[79] This has now been activated, subject to any decisions being made about prosecutions of British soldiers in relation to the death concerned.[80]

It has been very common for the ECtHR to make a finding that a number of states had failed to comply with the procedural obligations in Articles 2 and 3 of the ECHR. The development of formal procedures such as 'serious incident reports',[81] to be compiled when weapons are fired, will provide a means to alert the service police that an investigation may be required. In practice, the RoE will also provide an important, although rough, yardstick by which an individual's conduct can be assessed during the investigation process.[82] Although the ECtHR has stressed that the next of kin of the victim should be involved in

75 This inquiry represented the investigation into one of the applicants in *Al-Skeini v United Kingdom*. The other five cases were to be investigated by IHAT, ministerial statement, HC Deb 26 March 2012, vol 542, col 87WS.

76 Report of the Al Sweady Inquiry, HC 818 (2014), discussed in Chapter 9, where the allegations made by Iraqi civilians were withdrawn at a late stage of the Inquiry. The Report found that the various allegations against the UK armed forces were not credible.

77 These are 'Inquisitorial investigations modelled on coronial inquests', and follow IHAT investigations, where prosecutions of British service personnel relating to the incidents concerned have led to acquittals or where no prosecutions have been brought. For further discussion, see below.

78 See also Chapter 5.

79 *R (Ali Zaki Mousa) v Secretary of State for Defence* [2013] EWHC 1412, [214]; [2013] EWHC 2941, [9]; *Al-Saadoon v Secretary of State for Defence* [2015] EWHC 1769.

80 Evidence provided by the Ministry of Defence to the House of Commons Select Committee, session 2003–04, HC 931, 2 April 2014, *United Kingdom Armed Forces Personnel and the Legal Framework of Future Operations*. See also the Government's response to this report, HC 548, 11 July 2014 in which it describes the process as Fatality Investigations. The first two (of 11) such investigations were chaired by a retired High Court judge, Sir George Newman, following the earlier acquittal of two British soldiers on charges related to the deaths of Mr Abdullah and Mr Said in 2003, ministerial statement, HC Debs 27 March 2014, vol 578, col 29WS. The report is *The Iraq Fatality Investigations: Inspector Sir George Newman, Consolidated Report into the Death of Nadheem Abdullah and the Death of Hassan Abbas Said*, Cm 9023, March 2015. For the investigation into the death of Mr Muhammed Salim see the Public Statement of the Inspector, Sir George Newman, 7 August 2015, http://www.iraq-judicial-investigations.org/linkedfiles/latest/publicstatement7august2015.pdf. For a review of progress on the work of IHAT, possible prosecutions and resulting inquiries under ECHR Arts 2 or 3, see *Al-Saadoon v Secretary of State for Defence* [2015] EWHC 1769.

81 See Report of the Al-Sweady Inquiry, HC 818 (2014), Vol II, 932, [5.13], 959, [5.142], 959, [5.139]. A similar procedure is required for incidents relating to detainees held in custody.

82 The significance of the rules of engagement, including their status in the law, is discussed in Chapter 8.

the investigation process, he or she will not usually be able to gain sight of the relevant RoE and thus be able to scrutinise fully the investigation process.[83] The difficulties faced by an applicant who is unable to have sight of a document of this nature was explained by the ECtHR. It considered that 'the absence of any realistic possibility for the applicant to challenge the conclusions of the report and, ultimately, those of the investigation, cannot be said to be in conformity with the principles . . . concerning whether force used was justified in the circumstances'.[84] The specific issue as to whether the rules of engagement, in the form given to soldiers, should be disclosed to an applicant has not, so far, been addressed by the ECtHR but it is quite foreseeable that an applicant will, at some time, challenge the effectiveness of an investigation on this ground.

iv Detention abroad and the ECHR

The House of Lords in the *Al-Skeini* case had accepted that a foreign national detained by UK armed forces on a military base abroad would come within the jurisdiction of the UK (the situation of Baha Mousa), but the ECtHR, in the same case, appeared to widen this ground to cover all cases where a state agent (in this case, the armed forces) exercised 'physical power and control over the person in question'.[85] Once this has occurred the individual is owed those Convention rights most appropriate to his case.[86] Clearly, this will involve the right to liberty in Article 5. When it is considered that this form of extra-territorial jurisdiction can come into existence quite irrespective of whether the state concerned is an occupying power, or has effective control of an area outside its national territory, it can be seen how significant this is in the conduct of military operations where the detention of individuals may arise from vehicle check points, or from the search of houses for weapons.

In considering whether there would be a breach of the right to liberty in these circumstances, two separate issues require exploration. First, do their acts amount to a deprivation of liberty? Secondly, if they do, is the deprivation 'lawful' and what procedures should be followed by a state to keep itself within the confines of Article 5?

An individual detained abroad on a British military bases is clearly within the jurisdiction of the UK for the purposes of the ECHR. Suppose, instead, a civilian is detained by British soldiers at a vehicle check point, or is on a British stretcher or field hospital. At that moment, it would seem clear that he would also be

83 See, for example, the request to do so, which was refused, in *Jaloud v Netherlands* (2015) 60 EHRR 29, [41]–[42]. See also P Rowe, 'The Rules of Engagement in Occupied territory: Should they be Published?' (2007) 8 MJIL 327.

84 *Isayeva v Russia* (2005) 41 EHRR 38, [223].

85 *Al-Skeini v United Kingdom*, [136] and see discussion above on the extra-territorial application of the ECHR.

86 Compare if the state concerned has effective control over the territory, *ibid*, [138].

within the jurisdiction of the UK, because of the physical power and the degree of control exercised over him by British soldiers.[87] If he tried to get away from them it is foreseeable that he could be shot at since it would be too dangerous for the soldiers to chase after him.[88] This degree of control over him will also show that he will have been deprived of his liberty, rather than merely having restrictions placed on his liberty.[89] Since the grounds set out in Article 5, which would justify a deprivation of liberty, could not be met from the moment of his coming into the hands of British soldiers, or for any period thereafter, a finding that Article 5 had been breached would seem to be inevitable, unless he was being arrested for the purpose of bringing him before a judge or a court.

It is a fundamental requirement of Article 5 that any deprivation of liberty should be 'lawful'. The UK government had argued before the ECtHR in *Hassan* that only IHL applied,[90] the effect of which would have been be to 'disapply' its obligations to him under Article 5 of the ECHR. The ECtHR held, however, that, since the ICJ had accepted that human rights law could also apply during an armed conflict, Article 5 could apply even during an international armed conflict, although its obligations would need to be 'interpreted against the background of the provisions of international humanitarian law'.[91] This would mean that the permitted grounds for detention, set out in Article 5 (1)(a)–(f), must be 'accommodated, as far as possible, with the taking of prisoners of war and the detention of civilians who pose a risk to security within the Third and Fourth Geneva Conventions'.[92] International humanitarian law provides only very limited grounds for a deprivation of liberty during the course of a non-international armed conflict[93] where attention has to be given specifically to Article 5, ECHR, to justify detention for short or longer periods.

87 *Al-Saadoon v Secretary of State for Defence* [2015] EWHC 715 (Admin), [121]. See also *Medvedyev v France*, Application No 3394/03, Judgment, 29 March 2010, [74]; *Hirsi Jamaa v Italy*, Application No 27765/09, judgment, 23 February 2012, [81]; *Al-Saadoon v Secretary of State for Defence* [2015] EWHC 715.

88 See, for example, the death of a crew member who refused to obey the commands of French forces on board a Cambodian ship, *Medvedyev v France* (note 87), [13].

89 *HM v Switzerland*, Application No 39187/98, Judgment, 26 February 2002, [42]. Although crew members of a ship captured at sea were allowed to move about the ship they were under the supervision of French armed forces and were therefore deprived of their liberty, *Medvedyev v France* (note 87) [15]. It is likely that the son of the fifth applicant in the *Al-Skeini* case who had been 'arrested by British soldiers . . . beaten up and forced into the waters of the Shatt Al-Arab' [56] would have been deprived of his liberty under Art 5. The substance of his case was brought under Art 2 and not under Art 5.

90 Geneva Convention, IV, 1949, Arts 42, 78, give power to an occupying power to subject protected civilians to assigned residence or internment for 'imperative reasons of security'. For the position in IHL, see generally (2005) 857, IRRC, *Detention*; ICRC, 'Internment in Armed Conflict: Basis Rules and Challenges, Opinion paper, November 2014.

91 At [104].

92 *Ibid.* Considerable difficulty might be experienced in doing so in relation to the detention of prisoners of war under Geneva Convention III, 1949.

93 See *Al-Jedda v United Kingdom* (2011) 53 EHRR 23. The issue is discussed in *Mohammed v Secretary of State for Defence* [2015] EWCA Civ 843, [217].

The lawfulness of any detention could be sought in English law (as it had been in the Northern Ireland campaign),[94] but this would now have to be consistent with the Human Rights Act 1998, and hence, in this case, with Article 5. To comply with that article any detention must not only be lawful, but its lawfulness must be capable of being determined by a court.[95] In *Hassan* the ECtHR drew attention to the requirement for a periodical review of assigned residence or an internment decision in Geneva Convention IV, 1949,[96] and concluded that Article 5, ECHR would be satisfied if 'a competent body [could] provide sufficient guarantees of impartiality and fair procedures to protect against arbitrariness'.[97] The same principles must apply also for any deprivation of liberty imposed by armed forces during the course of a non-international armed conflict, certainly where that period exceeds 96 hours.[98]

The consequence of these decisions of the ECtHR is likely to be that, should armed conflicts similar to Iraq and Afghanistan, arise again the UK could find itself between a rock and a hard place.[99] One option would be for British soldiers to arrest and detain civilians in order solely to bring them before the local courts on the basis of the local criminal law, acting within the local and English law as agents of the local law enforcement body. This is a possibility more theoretical than real where the local state is not a party to the ECHR, since it could not then be assumed to have procedures in place which would conform to Article 5 standards or indeed those of Article 3 (preventing torture, inhuman or degrading treatment). No judicial procedures conforming to Article 5 were introduced by the UK in Iraq or Afghanistan and it is not easily foreseeable that anything would be different in any future wars. By acting as agents of the local law enforcement body British soldiers would be unable to question detainees about general security concerns, unless the local law permitted this for a period of up to 96 hours. The alternative course of action would be for the UK to derogate from Article 5, the effect of which would be to deny civilians arrested or detained by British soldiers any of the rights of that Article. Through adopting the derogation option the UK could find itself introducing internment or, where it could do so, detaining civilians for a period before handing them over to the local authorities.[100]

94 The Northern Ireland (Emergency Provisions) Act 1973, s 12 gave a limited power to members of the armed forces to arrest civilians for a very short period.

95 Article 5(4).

96 Articles 43, 78. Strictly, these two articles did not apply to the case of Mr Hassan since he was not an 'alien in the territory of a party to the conflict' (Art 43); nor was his internment (except for his last two days) in occupied territory (Art 78). Neither would Geneva Convention IV, 1949, Art 5(1) apply since this relates to removing 'rights and privileges' from a person by the territorial state.

97 *Hassan v United Kingdom*, Application No 29750/09, Grand Chamber Judgment, 16 September 2014, [106].

98 See discussion in Chapter 9.

99 See also *Al-Saadoon v Secretary of State for Defence* [2015] EWHC 715, [106]–[107].

100 The UK has been faced with the difficulties of handing detainees over to Iraqi and the Afghan local authorities where there is a real risk of serious mistreatment that the individuals could be

Neither course of action is attractive. The first is unlikely to work in practice, whilst if it results in British military authorities not being able to transfer detainees to the local law enforcement body it is likely to create the same difficulties as if internment was introduced. The effort needed to retain the detainees, both in terms of manpower and financial resources, can hardly be over-estimated.[101] Whether detainees could, however, consent to a transfer to their own state from British custody and thereby waive their rights under Article 5, with or without legal advice, is currently being determined by a court in England.[102] This apparent solution will not work in all cases, since the courts in England have had to deal with a number of detainees who have sought an injunction to prevent their transfer, certainly to some, prisons in Afghanistan.

The practical problems encountered by the UK in Iraq and in Afghanistan over the detention of civilians, along with a need to prepare for any future military operations abroad, has caused some to reflect on whether the UK should choose the less worse option and derogate from Article 5.

v Derogation from Article 5 ECHR

A state is permitted to issue a notice to the Council of Europe to the effect that it wishes to derogate from Article 5 on the grounds, permitted under the ECHR, of 'war or other public emergency threatening the life of the nation'.[103] Although this ground was accepted by the ECtHR when it was invoked by the UK for a short period to cover internment in Northern Ireland in the early 1970s,[104] it is not at all clear that the same view would be taken where the claimed need to arrest civilians is in a foreign country. Certainly, Lord Hope in *Smith v Secretary of State for Defence* was of the view that 'the circumstances in which that power can properly be exercised are far removed from those where operations are undertaken overseas with a view to eliminating or controlling threats to the nation's security'.[105] No such notice was issued over the internment of civilians in Iraq,

subjected to the death penalty or to torture, inhuman or degrading treatment which would be a breach of Art 3. See, for instance *R (on the Application of Maya Evans) v Secretary of State for Defence* [2010] EWHC 1445 (Admin) where transfers could be made to some Afghan prisons but not to others; *Serdar Mohammed v Secretary of State for Defence* [2012] EWHC 3282 and [2012] EWHC 3946; *Al-Saadoon and Mufti v United Kingdom* (2010) 51 EHRR 9 (where the detainees were actually handed over to the Iraqi authorities); *Ismail v secretary of State for Defence* [2013] EWHC 3032, [28]. For further discussion, see Chapter 9.

101 See *Serdar Mohammed v Secretary of State for Defence* (note 100) [16].

102 *Ismail v Secretary of State for Defence* [2013] EWHC 3032.

103 Article 15, a proviso to which is that 'such measures [taken following a derogation] are not inconsistent with [the state's] other obligations under international law'.

104 *Brannigan and McBride v United Kingdom* (1994) 17 EHRR 539, [74].

105 [2013] UKSC 41, [60]; *R (Al-Jedda) v Secretary of State for Defence* [2008] UKHL 58, Lord Bingham, [38]. The courts have taken a different view where there is a threat within the UK itself, see *A and others v Secretary of State for the Home Department* [2004] UKHL 56, where the majority held that the derogation made by the UK, following the events of 9 September 2001, was a valid derogation. Lord Hoffmann dissented on this point, [96].

presumably because the UK government took the view at the time that Geneva Convention IV, 1949, and then UN Security Council Resolution 1546 (2004) gave legal cover for internment. Nor was one issued in relation to Afghanistan probably because internment was not envisaged there and the intention was to pass individuals over to the local Afghan authorities within 96 hours under the policy adopted by NATO.[106] In *Al-Jedda*, the ECtHR referred to the fact that the UK had not derogated from the obligations under Article 5 but it did not offer any guidance on whether, if it had, such a derogation notice would have complied with the Convention.[107] In *Hassan v United Kingdom* the ECtHR drew attention to the fact that no state engaged in an international armed conflict had issued a derogation notice under the ECHR.[108]

Why this should be so is not at all obvious. It could be that states had taken the view that to have done do so would have been to admit that their extra-territorial jurisdiction applied when conducting military operations abroad, a claim that the UK had denied. It is, perhaps, more likely that they considered derogation inapplicable to the circumstances of these operations. It may therefore be too sanguine a view to predict that the ECtHR will take the view that the actual practice of states involved in military operations overseas, in not derogating, is such as to establish a valid re-interpretation of Article 15, having the effect that a derogation made in any future military operations will not be valid.[109]

Derogation does raise a difficult political dilemma for the government. In arguing for it the government would be seeking to do something abroad (to detain civilians outside the parameters of Article 5), which it could find difficult to do within the UK,[110] even assuming that the ECtHR would accept that derogation could ever be invoked by one state to protect its troops and other civilians in a foreign state. Notice to derogate from Article 5 of the ECHR could, of course, be given to the Council of Europe but, prior to doing so, the UK government would have to involve Parliament, since to do so would have the effect of altering temporarily the Human Rights Act 1998.[111]

106 See *Mohammed v Secretary of State for Defence* [2015] EWCA Civ 843 and for further discussion see Chapter 9.

107 *Al-Jedda v United Kingdom* (2011) 53 EHRR 23, [99].

108 At [40] and for the position in relation to the ICCPR and the ECHR, see [42].

109 Although compare *R (Al-Jedda) v Secretary of State for Defence* [2007] UKHL 58, Lord Bingham, [38] who argued that 'since subsequent practice [through non-derogation in these types of situation] in the application of a treaty may (under article 31(3)(b) of the Vienna Convention [on the Law of Treaties 1969]) be taken into account in interpreting the treaty it seems proper to regard article 15 as inapplicable'.

110 *A and others v Secretary of State for the Home Department* [2004] UKHL 56, where the Human Rights Act 1998 (Designated Derogation) Order 2001 was quashed. See note 111 below.

111 The only attempt made by the UK to derogate from any of the articles from which such action can be taken after the Human Rights Act 1998 was by way of the Human Rights Act 1998 (Designated Derogation) Order 2001/3644, which paved the way for the UK formally to issue a derogation notice in respect of Art 5 of the ECHR to the Council of Europe, as envisaged by Art 15. This Order was quashed by the House of Lords in *A v Secretary of State for the Home Department* [2004] UKHL 56 on the grounds that it was discriminatory, taking into account Arts 5 and 14 of the ECHR.

Governmental thinking on the matter, derived from *Al-Jedda v United Kingdom*, can be seen from a ministerial statement made in November 2013. The minister stated that 'the legal and political questions which derogation would raise would be difficult ones, and we would need to be very clear that the benefits outweighed the disadvantages before proceeding with this option'.[112] Such a decision may be even more difficult to achieve if the UK government has to rely on the support of one or more smaller parties.[113]

vi Coalition forces

The UK has played its part, during the armed conflicts in Iraq and in Afghanistan, as a member of coalitions of other states, some of which were parties to the ECHR but where the USA, Canada and Australia were not. Although all the coalition states were parties to the ICCPR, it has been the dynamic effect of the decisions of the ECtHR that has resulted in different obligations being owed by states working together, principally over issues of the killing, or the detention, of civilians. The fact that the obligations of states and of the individual members of armed forces working together on military operations will differ is nothing new. The national law and the RoE of each state are likely to be tailored specifically for that state and some NATO states have issued caveats to their own participation. All these differences will be known by the senior commanders and they can be taken into account in military planning.

At least since the Gulf war in 1991 it has become common practice to transfer detainees from the custody of one member of the coalition to another, depending on which state is designated to take the lead role in prisoner of war or civilian detainee handling in a particular area. The fact that a non-ECHR state is the assigned detaining state will not necessarily relieve an ECHR state of its obligations under that Convention when it transfers an individual to the custody of that non-ECHR state, as *Hassan v United Kingdom* shows. Nor will it do so if the killing of a civilian is caused by the armed forces of one ECHR state even if another ECHR state exercises operational control over its actions, as in *Jaloud v Netherlands.*

vii Human rights of British soldiers

So far we have been looking at the obligations that the UK owes during the conduct of armed conflict (as well as in time of peace) to those who are affected by the activities of members of its armed forces on duty. Is there a similar duty owed to its own soldiers? In other words, must we say that soldiers have human rights, including the right to life, while fighting during an armed conflict?

112 HL Debs 7 November 2013, vol 749, col 417.

113 The minister, *ibid*, concluded his statement by drawing attention to the fact that 'the coalition agreement is also clear that no such changes would be contemplated at present.' *Quaere* whether the coalition agreement of 2010 was 'clear' on this point.

Once it is accepted that, within the context of an armed conflict, human rights obligations are owed by the state to those affected by the actions of its armed forces, such as enemy soldiers and civilians, it appears illogical to say that those same obligations are not owed to a state's own soldiers. If there is a right to life given to all those within the jurisdiction of a state under the ECHR, then it cannot be denied to some whilst accepted for others. British soldiers must therefore have the right to life during military operations.

The key question is what does this right to life mean? There is, of course, no suggestion that the UK would kill its own soldiers. The direct cause of any deprivation of life during an international armed conflict will be the acts of the enemy who, in accordance with IHL, are permitted to kill enemy combatants and to target military objectives, such as the vehicles in which they are moving, their bases, other military installations and so on. In a small number of cases and, since the carrying out of military operations during an armed conflict is such a dangerous business, soldiers may also die as a result of accidents on the battlefield.

The ECtHR has, however, developed over time another aspect to this right to life. It involves an obligation on the state to protect life by taking reasonable steps to guard against a real and immediate risk to the life of an identified individual or individuals.[114] A clear example would be that a state must take reasonable steps to protect a prisoner, who has shown an intention to take his own life, from actually committing suicide and, if there is a death it must be fully investigated.[115] The risk to life during combat can, of course, be substantial and be foreseen by military commanders in the planning stage, although they cannot predict how any engagement with the enemy will turn out.[116] They cannot protect the lives of all their soldiers but the law does not actually require them to do so. It requires them to take reasonable steps to do so and what is reasonable will vary according to the circumstances. So, it would be reasonable to check up on a potentially suicidal prisoner every so often during the night to ensure that he does not kill himself, but it would not be reasonable to expect military commanders to plan for military operations in which not a single solder could be killed. One must also take into account that British soldiers are all volunteers; they can be expected to know that being a soldier could result in them being killed during an armed conflict. Once the battle begins it will take its own, largely unpredictable, course and whether a particular soldier lives or dies will depend largely on factors outside the control of any military planner.

What is clear is that the right to life, in Article 2 of the ECHR and embedded into English law by the Human Rights Act 1998, will continue to apply

114 *Osman v United Kingdom* (2000) 29 EHRR 245, [116]; *Tagayeva v Russia (Admissibility)*, Application No 26562/07, 9 June 2015, [517].

115 *Shevchenko v Ukraine*, Application No 32478/02, Judgment, 4 April 2006, [75]–[76].

116 Brigadier Butler is reported as saying 'this what we intend to do, but the enemy gets a vote', quoted by Lord Browne, House of Commons Select Committee on Defence, 4th Report, session 2010–12, *Operations in Afghanistan*, HC 554, Q 586.

during armed conflict. The difficulty arises when we try to analyse what it actually requires the state (acting through the Ministry of Defence and military commanders) to do. To argue that in armed conflict it does not apply at all is to deny its existence or to rob it of any value to British soldiers. It might be suggested that, in an international armed conflict, the right to life has to give way to IHL as the *lex specialis*, which says quite clearly that combatants do not breach IHL if they kill enemy combatants, providing they do not do so by one of the prohibited means, or kill those who are protected persons. No one could seriously doubt that this rule of IHL does apply but it cannot provide a complete answer to the other side of the coin, the right of combatants to life itself.

The ECHR does recognise that a state can derogate from the right to life only in respect of individuals killed as a result of 'lawful acts of war' but only if a formal derogation notice to the Council of Europe is given.[117] In the absence of such a derogation from Article 2 (the right to life), it would appear that the UK owes the right to life to all those, including individuals, who take part in the conflict and who come within its jurisdiction abroad. It is, however, interesting to note that it was not claimed on behalf of those applicants, in the *Al-Skeini* case, who were shot and killed by British soldiers in Iraq, that they had been denied the right to life, but that the procedural obligation within Article 2 of the ECHR, which required that there be an investigation into their deaths, had not been applied. Between the dates of the initial attack on Iraq in March 2003 and the beginning of the occupation, it is unlikely that any enemy fighters, whether members of the Iraqi army or others, would have come within the jurisdiction of the UK, unless they were taken into British custody, and so there could be no question of owing the right to life under the ECHR to any of them.

As we have seen, the ECtHR in the *Al-Skeini* case did decide that, certainly during the period of occupation, those who were shot and killed by British soldiers in the street did come within the jurisdiction of the UK and each was owed the right to life. Neither in this case, nor in any other, has the ECtHR had to decide whether a state owes this duty to protect the lives of its own soldiers while they are taking part in military operations during an armed conflict. It would indeed be strange if a state owed obligations under the ECHR to foreign nationals abroad who came within its jurisdiction and not to its own soldiers, given the degree of control that an army can exercise over them. In the absence of any ruling from the ECtHR the English courts have had to decide whether the ECHR does apply to British soldiers during armed conflict and, if so, the limits of this right to life.[118]

These issues came ultimately before the Supreme Court in *Smith v Ministry of Defence* (2013),[119] in which a number of separate actions were consolidated. These included claims brought on behalf of individual British soldiers who were

117 Article 15. *Quaere* whether 'war' includes a non-international armed conflict.

118 *Pritchard v United Kingdom*, Application No 1573/11, 18 March 2014, which involved the death of a British soldier in Iraq, was the subject of a friendly settlement.

119 [2013] UKSC 41.

killed in Iraq when their Snatch Land Rovers ran over IEDs, and another group who were killed or injured when their Challenger tank was fired upon by another British Challenger tank in a so-called 'friendly fire' incident. Once the Court had analysed the effect of *Al-Skeini v United Kingdom* and had decided that all the soldiers were within the jurisdiction of the UK[120] it was faced with having to decide whether the individual claims for damages could be brought under Article 2 of the ECHR (as enshrined in the Human Rights Act 1998) and on the basis of common law negligence. The Snatch Land Rover claims were based on the allegation that, in lacking the necessary armour and electronic counter-measures systems, they could not withstand an IED explosion. The basis of this set of claims was that these vehicles should not have been deployed in the circumstances[121] since, by doing so, the UK was unable to comply with the positive duty on a state to protect the life of those within its jurisdiction under Article 2 ECHR,[122] along with common law negligence. The Challenger tank incident raised issues only at common law, mainly in negligence, which concerned the claim that no equipment or recognition training was provided to protect against one British tank firing by mistake at another.[123]

The Supreme Court started from the proposition that the duty to protect life under Article 2 must have some meaning for every individual within a state's jurisdiction, although the circumstances of participation in an armed conflict on behalf of that state would clearly be relevant. It was not willing to accept that the duty to protect life under Article 2 had no application to a state's soldiers killed during an armed conflict in the absence of a ruling by the ECtHR to this effect.[124]

In assessing whether a state has taken reasonable precautions to protect life, a soldier taking part in an armed conflict is clearly not in the same position as a

120 See Lord Hope on behalf of the majority, *ibid*, [46]. In doing so it departed from its earlier decision in *R (Smith) v Oxfordshire Assistant Deputy Coroner* [2010] UKSC 29, as a result of the later ruling of the ECtHR in *Al-Skeini v United Kingdom* (2011) 53 EHRR 18. The link between 'full command over its military personnel' and jurisdiction over others is seen in reverse in *Jaloud v Netherlands* (2015) 60 EHRR 29, [143].

121 The Snatch Land Rover incidents occurred in 2005 and 2006, after the period of occupation in Iraq had come to an end and when the armed conflict taking place there was of a non-international character. The Challenger tank incident occurred on 25 March 2003, during the international armed conflict in Iraq.

122 This is well established in principle and is discussed by Lord Hope in *Smith v Ministry of Defence* [2013] UKSC 41, [72]. It is set out in *Stoyanovi v Bulgaria*, Application No 42980/04, Judgment, 9 November 2010, [58]–[61] and it is not breached 'through the negligent conduct of an individual', *ibid*, [61]. Compare *R (Long) v Secretary of State for Defence* [2015] EWCA Civ 770 where the failure to comply with an order to carry an iridium phone on patrol was evidence of a 'systemic insufficiency of control and not mere negligence', [28].

123 For discussion of the issue of combat immunity in its application to the claims at common law, see Chapter 5.

124 [2013] UKSC 41, [58], [69]. The opposite conclusion could also be drawn, as it was by Lord Mance, [141], [143].

civilian at work, although the similarity will be much closer where the soldier is killed whilst in barracks or even during some types of training exercises. In other activities, such as training as a parachutist or as a fast jet pilot the risks to life and limb are much greater.[125] The context is, however, crucial but where the dividing line lies between those circumstances, where a claim for damages brought on behalf of a soldier killed in combat could proceed and where it could not, was a difficult issue for the Supreme Court.

The view of the majority was that English law did not automatically deny a claim under the Human Rights Act 1998 by representatives of members of the armed forces killed during an armed conflict. It was less difficult for the Supreme Court to say when such a claim would not be possible than when it might, which would itself be so dependent on the actual facts. So, executive decisions could not form the basis of a claim if they related to 'training, procurement or the conduct of operations . . . made at a high level of command and closely linked to the exercise of political judgment and issues of policy . . . [or those which] . . . relate to things done or not done when those who might be thought responsible for avoiding the risk of death or injury to others were actively engaged in direct contact with the enemy'.[126] It was left for a further hearing to determine the facts in each of the separate Snatch Land Rover cases and in the Challenger tank case to determine whether either set of claims fell within the middle ground[127] outside these two areas. Merely because the facts of a particular claim fall within the middle ground does not mean that there will be an 'arguable case that there has been a breach of Article 2'.[128]

The Supreme Court also stressed that the obligations on a state in this context must not be 'unrealistic or disproportionate', that 'the widest measure of appreciation to commanders on the ground' should be given and that 'a court should be very slow indeed to question operational decisions made on the ground by commanders, whatever their rank or level of seniority'.[129] These considerations were also relevant to the claims at common law.[130]

125 For an example of a soldier killed whilst undertaking a parachute jump see *Stoyanovi v Bulgaria*, Application No 42980/04, where the ECtHR stated, 'parachute training was inherently dangerous but an ordinary part of military duties', [61].

126 *Smith v Ministry of Defence* [2013] UKSC 41, [76].

127 Lord Hope, [76], who added that even if a claim does fall within this middle ground 'the wide margin of appreciation which must be given to the authorities or to those actively engaged in armed conflict [must be] fully recognised without depriving the article [2] of its content'. Its content is limited to 'where it would be reasonable to expect the individual to be afforded the protection of the article', *ibid.*

128 *R (Long) v Secretary of State for Defence* [2015] EWCA Civ 770, [25], a case that did fall within this middle ground. See discussion below.

129 [2013] UKSC 41, [76], [71], [64] respectively. See also [99]. Lord Hope also concluded that 'it is far from clear that [the claimants in the new hearings] will be able to show that the implied positive obligation under article 2.1 of the Convention to take preventative operational measures was breached in either case', [81].

130 *Ibid*, [99]. The majority appeared to have linked the issue of the duty of care in negligence with the applicability, or otherwise, of combat immunity, see [95].

The Ministry of Defence had argued that all the cases should be struck out on the ground of combat immunity, an established principle that created an absolute bar to a claim in negligence.[131] The difficulty in the Challenger tank case was that the allegations of negligence did not relate to the actions of the crew of the tank who fired the shell with such devastating results but to the decisions made much earlier, when there was time to plan the type of equipment to be fitted to the tanks and to give recognition training to the crews in order to prevent a 'friendly-fire' incident. None of the previous cases on combat immunity had envisaged decisions at such an early stage of possible combat action. By its judgment the Supreme Court had left open the possibility that combat immunity in some instances, depending on the facts, would not apply (and so claims based on alleged negligence might be successful).

The majority judgment also drew considerable criticism, particularly when it was contrasted with the dissenting opinion of Lord Mance.[132] In an unusual development, Lord Hope, who drafted the judgment of the majority, 'appreciated that the decision has given rise to concern' and explained during the course of a debate in the House of Lords that 'we did not say that the doctrine of combat immunity no longer exists . . . there is nothing here which deprives commanders, and those serving under them in that situation, of that protection while they are engaged in combat'.[133]

The judgment in *Smith* has been applied in subsequent cases, including one that involved the death of a corporal in the RMP who, with five other colleagues, was killed by a mob in Iraq during the period of the occupation.[134] His death was allegedly contributed to by the failure of other members of the armed forces to enforce a senior commander's order that a satellite phone should be taken with the men on patrol. The alleged failure was not the result of a decision made at a high level of command based on issues of policy, nor was it made while actively engaged in direct contact with the enemy and so, according to the *Smith* judgment, the facts could be considered to determine whether there had been a breach of Article 2.[135]

131 Combat immunity as a complete bar to an action in negligence is discussed in Chapter 5.

132 Lord Mance, with whom Lord Wilson agreed, considered that there was no duty of care in negligence, relying, *inter alia*, on *Mulcahy v Ministry of Defence* [1996] QB 732 and that it would be unlikely that the ECtHR would decide that Art 2 was applicable to issues that were essentially political. Their conclusion was that all the claims should be struck out. For discussion of whether the majority decision could lead to an impairment of the effectiveness of the armed forces see Chapter 10.

133 HL Debs 7 November 2013, vol 749, col 396. Lord Hope might also have drawn attention to the fact that the government had previously stated that 'the safety of our personnel is a prime concern', Response of the Government to the Defence Select Committee, HC 1525 (2011), *Operations in Afghanistan*, response to recommendation 20.

134 *R (Long) v Secretary of State for Defence* [2015] EWCA Civ 770. See also *Durrheim v Ministry of Defence* [2014] EWHC 1960 (QB) concerned with noise induced hearing loss.

135 [2015] EWCA Civ 770, where the Court of Appeal considered that the failure to comply with the order that a satellite phone should be carried on patrol, was 'a system failure by the military authorities to permit soldiers to routinely disregard the order', *R (Long) v Secretary of State for Defence* [2015] EWCA Civ 770, [28].

One effect of the majority decision in *Smith v Ministry of Defence* is that decisions relating to procurement and equipment might, or might not, be relevant to the UK's obligation to protect the lives of its soldiers, depending on the level of the decision makers. Whether to purchase better armoured vehicle or more helicopters would seem to be outwith the obligation in Article 2. In advising the Prime Minister about the practicalities of any possible military action it should be for the service chiefs (through the chief of the defence staff) to weigh up all these factors in the light of both the known facts and of those that could be predicted as following any military action.[136]

Experience in the Iraq and Afghanistan armed conflicts shows that this relatively straight-forward arrangement may not match the actual realities on the ground in the Ministry of Defence, where service chiefs may not be able to agree on short-term procurement decisions. These particular armed conflicts raised problems relating to the Snatch Land Rover, the subject of one of the actions in *Smith v Ministry of Defence*, the scarcity of support helicopters and, according to the minister responsible for procurement, showed that 'there was a lack of single point accountability'.[137]

viii The ECHR and service justice systems

An essential tenet of the Geneva Conventions 1949 is that it is for the state to discipline members of its own armed forces for acts committed during armed conflict. Many states will take the view, and certainly the UK does, that the military discipline system should work in the same way during armed conflict as it would in peacetime.

A number of cases concerning court-martial and the service disciplinary system applying in the UK reached the ECtHR, which were significant in showing that the disciplinary systems of the armed forces were not beyond the competence of the ECtHR.[138] When France ratified the Convention in 1974, it entered a reservation to the effect that disciplinary matters within the French armed forces were not included within the obligations under Articles 5 and 6 of the ECHR.[139] The opportunity to make a reservation can only be taken advantage of at the stage in which a state becomes party to a treaty, and not later.[140] So, although some in the

136 For discussion of the deployment to Helmand Province in 2006, see Chapter 3.

137 See Lord Drayson, Minister for Defence Procurement and Defence Equipment and Support 2005–2007, who informed the Iraq Inquiry that 'problems mainly arose around vehicles and helicopters. In both these cases the military found it very difficult to reach agreement upon what was required . . . in the case of helicopters, the lack of a single service responsibility for helicopters mean that they were not championed properly during tough negotiating rounds over resources', Iraq Inquiry, written statement, 18 January 2011.

138 *Findlay v United Kingdom* (1997) 24 EHRR 221; *Grieves v United Kingdom* (2004) 39 EHRR 2; *Cooper v United Kingdom* (2004) 39 EHRR 8.

139 A number of other states have made similar reservations or have done so in respect of Art 5 alone, see the reservations made by Azerbaijan, Armenia, Czech Republic, Moldova, Portugal, Russia, Slovakia, Spain, Ukraine.

140 ECHR, Art 57.

late 1990s argued that the same rule should apply to the British armed forces, the UK had not made a similar reservation and could not do so subsequently.

ix Obligation on the UK to ensure compliance by other states and by non-state actors

Both Iraq and Afghanistan are parties to the ICCPR, the Geneva Conventions 1949, Additional Protocol I, 1977 and to the UN Convention Against Torture 1984. Afghanistan became a party to Additional Protocol II, 1977 in November 2009, whilst Iraq is not a party to this instrument.

Although UK policy in Iraq and in Afghanistan had, at the later stages, been that the armed forces of those states should take the primary role in security matters it seems clear that any involvement by British armed forces along with their Iraqi or Afghan allies would not thereby exclude the UK from exercising its jurisdiction under the ECHR, in suitable circumstances.[141] Whether there was any obligation on the UK to ensure that its allies complied with their human rights obligations[142] there was certainly an obligation to do so in relation to the Geneva Conventions 1949 and their additional protocols.[143] These treaties, supported by customary international humanitarian law, do impose many obligations on a state, and on non-state actors,[144] which any human rights treaty would recognise.

141 *Jaloud v Netherlands* (2015) 60 EHRR 29.

142 In *Case Concerning Armed Activities on the Territory of the Congo (Democratic Republic of Congo v Uganda)* (2005) ICJ Rep 168 the ICJ was prepared to hold an occupying state responsible 'for acts of its own military that violated its international obligations and for any lack of vigilance in preventing violations of human rights and international humanitarian law by other actors present in the occupied territory, including rebel groups acting on their own account', [79]. Compare the situation where a state is not in occupation, as in Iraq after 28 June 2004 and in Afghanistan, and also where there is no lack of vigilance on the part of a state, in which case human rights obligations will not apply to non-state actors, *Prosecutor v Kunarac and others*, ICTY, IT-96–23-T, Judgment, 22 February 2001, [470]. This can become an issue for a state, such as the UK, which is supporting a group to overthrow a government and where it is alleged that the 'liberated people have turned on their oppressors', HC Debs 14 November 2001, vol 374, col 861 (Prime Minister). Compare where a state exercises effective control over a non-state group, *Catan v Republic of Moldova and Russia* (2013) 57 EHRR 4, where the acts of a non-state group in Moldova came within the jurisdiction of Russia through Russia's 'effective control and decisive influence over' it, [122]. UN Security Council resolutions often draw attention to the obligation of all parties to a conflict to comply with IHL and human rights law. See, for example, Resolutions 1378 (2001), [2]; 1746 (2007), [25].

143 Common Art 1 to the Geneva Conventions 1949, which refers to the obligation on a state 'to respect and to ensure respect 'of the Conventions; Additional Protocol I, Art 1(i); Additional Protocol II, Art 1 (by supplementing common Art 3 to the Geneva Conventions, 1949).

144 The wording of Common Art 3 to the Geneva Conventions 1949 makes it clear that it applies to 'each Party to the conflict'. Insurgent or other groups would qualify as parties

It has become a feature of both these armed conflicts that individuals from Iraq and Afghanistan have sought refugee status in the UK. In this event, the UK does have an opportunity to prosecute, in the UK, an individual for acts of torture committed abroad and to deny refugee status, or British nationality, to someone who is alleged to have committed war crimes.[145]

to the conflict if their organisation was of such a nature that had they alone taken up arms against the government the resultant activity would be such as to qualify it as a non-international armed conflict. On this issue see Chapter 6. For the accountability of a state for the acts of non-state actors see, L Zegveld, *The Accountability of Armed Opposition Groups in International Law* (Cambridge University Press, 2002), chap 5.

145 For the prosecution in England of an Afghan 'warlord' see *R v Faryadi Sarwar Zardad* [2007] EWCA Crim 279, discussed in Chapter 6 and for denial of refugee status, see Chapter 5.

8 The individual British serviceman or woman

This chapter discusses a number of issues that affect members of the armed forces and that arise when the UK takes part in an armed conflict, although they can be relevant in peacetime also. There is, for instance, no sharp legal divide between these two situations in relation to service discipline and, indeed, much training time of the armed forces is spent in preparing for armed conflict itself. It is in the nature of an armed conflict, however, that certain issues will rise to the foreground, a number of which are discussed below. For convenience the term 'soldier' will be used to encompass any member of the British armed forces, whether male or female.

i The principle of personal accountability of the serviceman or woman

Few would doubt the proposition that the armed forces, like all parts of the government, must act within the law, but it is when it comes to armed conflict that this principle is tested most sharply, since conduct that is prohibited in peacetime becomes, in certain circumstances, lawful during an armed conflict. The fact that during armed conflict members of the armed forces act on behalf of a state, and not for any personal motive, gives them one great advantage over those who take up arms without being part of the armed forces of a state. This is that, what would otherwise amount in the national law of virtually all states, to serious crimes, such as murder, assaults and destruction of property will not lead to personal accountability under international or national law if the acts concerned are not prohibited by IHL. This is often referred to as 'combatants' immunity' and is discussed in Chapter 6. It follows that if combatants attack civilians, who are known not to be taking an active part in the hostilities, or civilian objects, crimes against international law, and English law, will have been committed and it will be the actual soldier who could find himself charged with an offence, along with his commander if he had ordered the crimes to take place, or was aware that they were taking place and did not do what he could have done to prevent them, or has performed any duty negligently.[1]

1 See *Price v R* [2014] EWCA Crim 229 for the *mens rea* of the military offence of 'performing a duty negligently', the Armed Forces Act 2006, s 15. The predecessor of this Act was the Army Act 1955, which made it an offence to neglect to perform a duty, s 29A. For discussion of the effect of civilians taking an active part in hostilities, see Chapter 9.

For IHL to work effectively the armed forces involved must be disciplined so that the prevention of illegal conduct during armed conflict becomes an essential ingredient of the way in which they conduct themselves. An undisciplined force has little chance of achieving this. A government that operates within the rule of law, and a military chain of command that gives effect to it, makes it acceptable for international law to refuse to accept superior orders as a defence. If the government and the military chain of command both work through the rule of law the orders given to a soldier should not be illegal. One of the responsibilities that a government has in protecting its own soldiers when they carry out its orders, is to ensure that they are never required to do anything that would be illegal under international law or under English criminal law. A soldier therefore needs his government and his military superiors to uphold a strong belief in the rule of law if he is able to concentrate on the risks of war and not those of trial. Neither should they be left in a position of uncertainty as to the legality of particular actions during an armed conflict. It is more likely that, if British soldiers break the law, they will do so not because they have been ordered to do so, but because they are uncertain during an armed conflict as to where a particular boundary of illegality lies.[2]

ii Training in the law of armed conflict: Preventing legal uncertainty

The armed conflicts in Iraq and Afghanistan have given rise to a number of reported incidents where it has been alleged that some British soldiers have fallen below the standards expected of them and, in some cases, have committed criminal acts (under IHL and/or English criminal law). There have been trials by court-martial, cases brought before the High Court in London, public inquiries (Baha Mousa; Al-Sweady), the Aitken Report, and even a reference to the International Criminal Court.[3] Apart from the court-martial cases, investigations have been concerned with the acts of individual soldiers, but also the role of the chain of command in some form or other.

It seems obvious that soldiers will need to be trained to perform the roles set out for them by their military superiors in the chain of command, subject to any ministerial direction.[4] Apart from their normal military tasks, soldiers will need to know the basic principles of the legal regime applying to them at any one time. They will, for instance, have to feel assured that the armed conflict in which they are to take part has a legal underpinning,[5] know when they may open fire or attack property and how they should treat detainees. If those in the military

2 See, for example, discussion of the treatment by British soldiers of detainees, in Chapter 9.

3 See Chapter 6.

4 An account of the training offered to British soldiers on LOAC is given in the Baha Mousa Inquiry Report, vol II, 509, [6.4]. For the role of government ministers in determining targeting policy and the appropriate rules of engagement see Chapter 3 and below.

5 See the discussion of the assurance requested of the Attorney General by the chief of the defence staff prior to the Iraq war in 2003 in Chapter 3.

chain of command, ranging from corporals to generals, are unclear about these issues it is almost certain that their subordinates will be also. Where this happens there will be created a 'fog of knowledge', leading to an even greater risk of illegal conduct by soldiers on the ground.

Those in the military chain of command needed to be clear as to the major issues that they would face during each of Britain's wars from 2000. These included whether particular armed conflicts were of an international or a non-international nature, the legal obligations flowing from being an occupying state and the legal status of those who are believed to be taking part in the hostilities, or who are detained by British armed forces. The law does not recognise the 'battlefield' as an homogenous legal environment. There is, for instance, some difference of legal regime between an international armed conflict and one that is of a non-international character, although the 'battles' might look similar. In a non-international armed conflict, for instance, although the targeting rules may be very similar there is no legal concept of a prisoner of war and the right to detain foreign nationals is extremely limited.[6]

The risks of this 'fog of knowledge' occur not just on the main issues, but also where vague or very limited guidance is given to individual soldiers. An example would be where a commander, recognising that he has a legal duty towards detainees, tells his subordinates to treat a detainee 'humanely', a term used regularly in various parts of IHL. The soldier could be forgiven for asking 'what does this mean? Can I interrogate him harshly[7], blindfold[8] him at any stage, or deprive him of sleep to get the information I need to protect other British soldiers?' It will be of little comfort to him to know that lawyers have sometimes disagreed over the meaning of the term.[9] In addition, there is always a risk that soldiers involved with the detention of a suspected insurgent will draw an irrelevant (although, perhaps, understandable) inference from reciprocity: he did not show humanity towards other British soldiers, so he does not deserve to be treated with humanity now. The inference is irrelevant simply because the rights given to protected persons under IHL do not depend, at the individual level, upon reciprocity of treatment. They can only be qualified if that law actually provides so.[10]

The risks of mistreatment of civilians tend to increase where it is not clear to soldiers what the law, or their commanders, expect of them and, particularly, where they are acting as a group. In virtually all the cases where it has been alleged that US or British soldiers have mistreated civilians whom they have

6 See Chapter 9.
7 See *R (Hussein) v Secretary of State for Defence* [2014] EWCA Civ 1087.
8 See Chapter 9.
9 Baha Mousa Inquiry Vol III, 1331, [302]. See also *R (Hussein) v Secretary of State for Defence* [2014] EWCA Crim 1087, [40].
10 An example is provided by Geneva Convention IV, 1949, Art 5. Certainly, protected persons cannot renounce their rights under the Geneva Conventions, 1949.

detained for short or longer periods, these factors have been present.[11] Mistreatment will not occur in all cases; far from it. But there are danger signals that commanders cannot ignore. Instances of mistreatment, such as occurred in Abu Ghraib prison, Camp Bread Basket[12] or of the detainees of whom Baha Mousa was one, cannot be explained solely on the basis that the soldiers concerned were 'bad apples'. Some, or all, of the individuals involved with these incidents may well have been, but to argue that if the bad apples can be removed at an earlier stage of military service, the problem will be solved is to ignore the group nature of soldiers' actions. This is not surprising since military training, quite properly, actively encourages soldiers to be part of a team able to support each other to achieve the common objective. But it has a downside, where individual soldiers will sometimes try to support their colleagues who face some sort of investigation over their actions during military operations. This can take the form of claiming that they have no memory of the events,[13] or even to providing false statements as to what happened.[14]

Where individuals or groups of soldiers are given specific and detailed orders of how detainees are to be treated it is much more likely that a norm of legality will be instilled in them and in their environment. This is the case in relation to the detention of those who are entitled, during the course of an international armed conflict, to the status of prisoner of war, where Geneva Convention III, 1949 provides a very detailed set of regulations covering questioning, accommodation, food and the release of prisoners of war. The consequences of this difference in detailed regulation as to the treatment of civilian detainees can be seen where a comparison is drawn between the treatment of a prisoner of war and of a civilian detainee during the presence of UK armed forces in Iraq.[15]

The importance of providing as high a degree of legal certainty as possible is that it can create for the soldiers involved an atmosphere of legal compliance, especially where the life or limb of a soldier is not threatened, such as when he is engaged in guarding or questioning civilian detainees. In this way, an individual soldier should be able to feel confident that, in following specific instructions, he will be able to keep himself within the limits of the law. This is, after all, one of the main functions of the RoE when the soldier is carrying out actual military operations.

11 See the cases discussed in P Rowe, 'Military Misconduct during International Armed Operations: "Bad Apples" or Systemic Failure?' (2008) 13 Jo C&SL 165, 180; *R v Blackman* [2014] EWCA Crim 1029.

12 Ministerial statement, HC Debs 1 March 2005, vol 431, col 77–8WS; the Aitken Report: An Investigation into Cases of Deliberate Abuse and Unlawful Killing in Iraq in 2003 and 2004 (Ministry of Defence, 25 January 2008).

13 See, for an example, Report of the Baha Mousa Inquiry, vol III, 1294, [50].

14 See, for example, *R v Clegg* [1995] 1 AC 482, [490], Lord Lloyd referring to the evidence of Private A.

15 See Chapter 7 for the effect of the ECHR on the detention of individuals and Chapter 9 for discussion of the detention of civilian detainees.

This training will, however, only be of any significance if it is actually effective and soldiers are taught the most relevant parts of IHL that will apply to the roles that they will actually undertake. Instruction of what that law requires when dealing with prisoners of war is not identical with the legal regime when civilians are detained, as in a non-international armed conflict, such as Iraq after 2004 and in Afghanistan. Those soldiers who may be involved with the custody of civilian detainees need to be trained for the specific task – in particular as to what they should, and must not do, and not be confused by some generalised training on prisoner of war handling.[16]

It is difficult to disagree with the view expressed by the court in a war crimes trial that stated that 'it is quite obvious that no sailor and no soldier can carry with him a library of international law, or have immediate access to a professor in that subject'.[17] Nevertheless, the Geneva Conventions of 1949 require that members of the armed forces receive instruction in IHL,[18] and on many occasions government ministers have stated that British soldiers have been trained in the obligations imposed on them by LOAC and human rights law.[19] Most responsible armed forces will wish to do this in any event. It may be reasonably expected that those in command of troops, such as commissioned officers, will receive more detailed instruction relating to their particular roles than will the private soldier. Senior commanders are more likely to have access to legal advice from the services legal officers and those directing targeting by air delivered weapons will need to be very familiar with the details of what, in the circumstances, could amount to a military objective and the need to avoid unnecessary collateral damage during an air attack.[20]

16 The Report of the Baha Mousa Inquiry found that before September 2003 'training on prisoner handling concentrated on the handling of prisoners of war', vol II, 509, [6.5]. It also considered that commanders were entitled to rely on JWP 1–10, and that the 'MoD [was] corporately responsible for the fact that the guidance in JWP 1–10 was itself inadequate', Report of the Baha Mousa Inquiry, vol III, 1339, [351]. See also its recommendation 48; the Report of the Al-Sweady Inquiry, vol II, 965, [5.167].

17 *Peleus Trial* 1945, cited, Y Dinstein and M Tabory (eds), *War Crimes in International Law* (Nijhoff, 1996), 9.

18 Geneva Convention I, Art 47; II, Art 48, III, 127; IV, Art 144; Additional Protocol I, 1977, Art 87(2). The Joint Select Committee on Human Rights, *The UN Convention Against Torture*, 19th Report of session 2005–06, HL185, HC 701, 26 May 2006, [74], [80] recommended that British soldiers also receive training in the obligations under Art 10 of the UN Convention Against Torture and other Cruel, Inhuman or Degrading Treatment or Punishment, 1984, despite the fact that the government 'has not expressly accepted the application of other rights and duties under UNCAT to territory controlled by UK forces abroad', [73]. The Criminal Justice Act 1988, s 134, makes it a criminal offence to commit torture anywhere in the world. For the 'judgment training' of combat soldiers see F Ledwidge, *Losing Small Wars* (Yale University Press, 2012), 176–9.

19 See, for example, HC Debs 15 July 2004, vol 423, col 1236W; HC Debs 17 June 2013, vol 564, col 494W.

20 See the discussion of the round-the-clock access to legal advice provided to the pilots of remotely piloted aircraft in Chapter 9.

Providing training on IHL for lower ranking soldiers in a meaningful way can be a real challenge if it is not to turn out to be merely a tick-box exercise. A one-hour lecture in a crowded room may or may not leave a lasting impression, but any form of training needs to address the specific issues that the soldiers will actually face.[21] Instruction on what they are permitted to do during an international armed conflict may not be the same where the soldiers become part of an occupation force or are taking part in a non-international armed conflict. On top of all of this there are likely to be practical problems of ensuring all soldiers receive the necessary training. Units will often be moved with little notice, some will have received the training, whilst others may not. Some soldiers will be posted to new units and miss out on the training and so on.[22] Statements by ministers in parliament are only ever likely to paint what is seen as the general picture in relation to training and will not usually be sufficiently detailed to assure MPs of the overall position. The British armed forces are, however, usually very good at producing practical solutions to practical problems and soldiers who have missed out on the formal training may well get some form of training from their immediate military superiors.

Individual soldiers do not live purely in a military bubble. Prior to being sent to Iraq or Afghanistan many will become aware of publicly espoused views on the nature of the armed conflict, particularly where there is no UN Security Council resolution in place to authorise it. The conflict in Iraq can clearly be distinguished from that in Afghanistan after the Bonn Agreement in late 2001 and its approval by UN Security Council Resolution 1383 (2001). In relation to Iraq much of the public debate in the UK in 2003 centred on the issue of whether a UN Security Council resolution could be secured to authorise the proposed attack. When this did not occur some of those who were opposed to it categorised the attack on Iraq as an 'illegal war'. A small number of soldiers, believing they were being required to take part in an illegal war, openly refused to serve and, in consequence, came up against the service disciplinary system.

iii 'Don't want to fight in *this* war'

Members of the British armed forces cannot pick and choose which wars they will take part in. It might look as if those who do not wish to fight are conscientious objectors, but there is one significant difference from those who took this line during World Wars I and II.[23] Whilst this status can be claimed by those conscripted but who refuse to enter military service, it cannot be asserted in the same way by those who are already members of the armed forces when they first raise the issue.

21 See, for example, HC Debs 2 December 2009, vol 501, col 727W; HC Debs 8 September 2010, vol 515, col 539W; Baha Mousa Report, vol III, 1332, [305].

22 See generally, P Rowe, 'Military Misconduct during International Armed Operations: "Bad Apples" or Systemic Failure?' (2008) 13 Jo C&SL 165, 173–4.

23 For the earlier position see *Khan v Royal Air Force Summary Appeal Court* [2004] EWHC 2230 (Admin), [30].

The wars in Iraq and Afghanistan led to a very few members of the British armed forces deciding that they did not wish to serve, either because of a similarity of religious belief with the people of the country concerned or, more frequently, a belief that the war, particularly in Iraq, was illegal.[24] They do, however, have a right to make out a case to their commanding officer that they have a conscientious objection to taking part in a particular military operation and 'since the start of the recent conflict in Iraq, three service personnel have been classified as conscientious objectors and have been discharged from the armed forces through the internal service procedures'.[25] Had their applications been refused, an appeal to the Advisory Committee on Conscientious Objectors could have been brought, but between 2003 and 2006, no such appeals came before the Committee.[26]

In all of the cases that have come before the courts the serviceman has refused to serve in either Iraq or Afghanistan in the belief that the war was illegal.[27] It was, perhaps, a concern of the Chief of the Defence Staff, Admiral Boyce, that the demonstrations in 2003 in various cities in the UK might lead members of the armed forces to think that the war would be illegal, which caused him to seek comfort from the Attorney General that the proposed military action would be in conformity with international and English law.[28] It is unclear whether this declaration of legality was passed directly on to individual members of the armed forces, since it did not cause the issue to go away.[29] Those who refused to serve were charged under the appropriate service discipline Act with being absent without leave or disobeying a lawful command, and all were convicted. It is ironic that three of the four individuals were serving in a medical unit at the time of their refusal.

These cases show that it is a pretty risky business for a serviceman or woman to allege that what he or she has been ordered to do is illegal. If they get it wrong, they could end up in prison.[30] So far no one has got it right and, in reality, it is

24 For the role of service chaplains in advising a serviceman who claims to have a conscientious objection to specific military action see, *R v Lyons* [2012] 1 WLR 2702, [18] and generally, G Zahn, *Chaplains in the RAF* (Manchester University Press, 1969), [127].

25 House of Commons Select Committee on the Armed Forces Bill, session 2005–06, HC 828-II, Ev 198, Ministry of Defence-Conscientious Objectors.

26 *Ibid.* The Committee was not convened at all between 2001 and 2006, HC Debs 23 May 2006, vol 446, col 1606W. It heard one case, which it dismissed, between 2010 and 2011 and none between 2011 and 2012, HC Debs 25 February 2013, vol 559, col 16W. The case it dismissed in 2010 was that of the accused in *R v Lyons* [2012] 1 WLR 2702.

27 *Khan v Royal Air Force Summary Appeal Court* [2004] EWHC 2230 (Admin); *R v Kendall-Smith*, unreported, but discussed in *R (Gentle and another) v Prime Minister and others* [2008] UKHL 20, [50]; *R v Glenton* [2010] EWCA Crim 930; *R v Lyons* [2012] 1 WLR 2702. See also D Gee, 'Informed Choice? Armed Forces Recruitment Practice in the United Kingdom', 72–80, available at http://www.informedchoice.org.uk/informedchoice/informedchoicefull.pdf.

28 This issue is discussed further in Chapter 3.

29 See the oral evidence of Admiral Lord Boyce, the Chief of the Defence Staff in March 2003, Iraq Inquiry, 3 December 2009, 88–9.

30 See the view of Baroness Hale in *R (Gentle and another) v Prime Minister and others* [2008] UKHL 20, [50] in discussing the dilemma faced by such as the accused in *R v Kendall-Smith*, unreported.

very unlikely that they ever would do so where their argument is based on the illegality under international law of the war itself. This is a matter over which specialist lawyers argue, as the Iraq war in 2003 shows.[31] For their argument to succeed the war must actually be illegal and not merely believed by them to be so.[32] The real difficulty is to be able to distinguish the serviceman or woman who objects to a particular military operation on grounds of conscience and religion from one who has, in reality, an objection based on political grounds,[33] or who merely wishes to leave the armed forces.[34] Even if an objection is based on conscience or religion under the ECHR Article 9, a soldier, as a member of a disciplined force, cannot just go absent without leave or refuse to obey an order; he must go through the appropriate procedures, whether at the internal service level, or on appeal to the Advisory Committee on Conscientious Objectors, to enable the claim to be assessed before any refusal to serve.

If, on the other hand, the claim of illegality relates instead to the way in which a soldier is ordered to act during the armed conflict, such as by killing detainees or deliberately targeting civilians, this would be an entirely different matter. In these examples the law is much more clear and most soldiers would recognise that, if they obeyed the orders, they would end up committing war crimes and the fact that a superior gave them the orders would not provide a defence to the crime itself. War is a chaotic business which appears to turn, what in peacetime, is considered to be illegal, on its head. Even then, there are matters on which international lawyers will disagree and it will be just as risky for a soldier to disobey an order on the ground that what he is actually being asked to do would be illegal.[35]

iv Rules of engagement

It is not unreasonable for soldiers to expect that their military superiors, from corporal to colonel, will keep them within the limits of the law when giving them

31 See the vote in the House of Commons to go to war in Iraq on 18 March 2003, Chapter 4 and, generally, Chapter 2.

32 See *R v Lyons* [2012] 1 WLR 2702, [36].

33 In *Khan v Royal Air Force Summary Appeal Court* [2004] EWHC 2230 (Admin), [4] the decision of the RAF Summary Appeal Court, [27] accepted that the accused's objection was based on grounds of religion. Where this is the case a serviceman or woman might now invoke the ECHR, Art 9, see *Bayatyan v Armenia*, Application No 23459/03, Judgment, 7 July 2011, [110]. In *Kendall-Smith* (see note 27) the refusal to return to Iraq occurred after UN Security Council Resolution 1546 (2004) which had restored full sovereignty to Iraq at the end of the period of occupation, and after the authorisation of a MNF by UN Security Council Resolution 1511 (2003), [13].

34 In *R v Glenton* [2010] EWCA Crim 930 the Court-martial Appeal Court quoted [14] from the trial judge advocate who commented that 'absence without leave should not be seen as a means of securing a quick exit from the Service. Absence without leave is a serious offence, particularly given the intensity of operations.'

35 The issue may be heightened for pilots of remotely piloted aircraft, as to which see generally, Chapter 9 and for the specific incident of the air strike in Syria on 21 August 2015, see Chapter 4.

orders or particular tasks to perform. In a democracy it is expected that the state and its agents, such as the armed forces or police, will act in this way. This is what, during military operations, the rules of engagement (RoE)[36] are designed to do, but they cannot cover all eventualities simply because if they were to attempt to do so they would become overlong and defeat the purpose of giving easy-to-understand instructions to the soldier on the ground. The term RoE is used here, in its narrow sense, to mean any form of guidance issued to members of the armed forces to govern the way in which they are to conduct themselves, whether in using weapons or in dealing with civilians. From a practical point of view, the RoE become difficult to change quickly to meet the ever-changing nature of military operations since they have to be printed and distributed to each soldier. Clear examples of where the RoE required alteration include the time when the international armed conflict in Iraq ended, in early May 2003, and a period of occupation began,[37] and when a decision was made at commander level to ban the use of hooding of detainees.[38]

The status of the various forms of RoE is no more than that of guidance issued by higher authority to members of the armed forces in performing their duties

36 Although the rules of engagement may cover aims, objectives and methods to be employed in an armed conflict the term is usually understood to refer to forms of guidance issued to members of the armed forces. The latter is, in effect, 'a sub-set of the other', HL Debs 31 October 2006, vol 686, col 211. They can be in various formats including standing orders, standard operating procedures, cards (or *aides memoire*) issued on, for instance, the use of weapons, the treatment of detainees and arrest procedures. See generally, 'Further Memorandum from the Ministry of Defence', April 2006, to the House of Commons Select Committee on the Armed Forces Bill, session 2005–06, HC 828-II; the Baha Mousa Report, vol III, 951, [11.3].

37 Changes to the RoE in Iraq 'to reflect the transition from war-fighting to military occupation. They took effect on 11 July 2003 and 17 October 2003 and a further change was promulgated in November 2004 in recognition of the challenges UK armed forces face in dealing with counter-insurgency', HC Debs 14 March 2005, vol 432, col 30W. It should be noted that these changes occurred some months after the occupation of Iraq began and also after it ended. If, in using the term, RoE, the minister was referring to the guidance issued to soldiers there would have been a significant period when the guidance would not have reflected the new legal position of the UK. Compare the dates of the relevant RoE in *The Iraq Fatality Investigations: Inspector Sir George Newman, Consolidated Report into the Death of Nadheem Abdullah and the Death of Hassan Abbas Said*, Cm 9023, March 2015, [4.11] where they were stated to be published on 3 March 2003, with fresh RoE being promulgated on 13 July 2003. At [4.31] the Inspector concluded that 'for practical purposes the legal situation remained the same during war fighting and the initial stages of occupation'. The danger of not altering the RoE to reflect the different legal environment between these two phases is that during the initial period of the occupation of Iraq it was 'a commonly held belief by most of the soldiers, on reasonable grounds, that they were still deployed in combat conditions', [11.24]. Difficulties are, however, likely to arise, and did so in Iraq, when commanders and their legal advisers try to ascertain the date at which the occupation by British armed forces had actually begun, an issue discussed in Chapter 6.

38 See the view of Lord Thomas, HL Debs 11 October 2006, vol 685, col 292. As to the change in policy over hooding see Baha Mousa Inquiry Report, vol III, 955–8, [11.7]–[11.16].

during an armed conflict.[39] They are designed to reflect the law applicable to the particular[40] military operations to which they refer and cannot, in themselves, be a source of law.[41] They must, however, reflect legal limitations on the use of force accurately; they cannot replace these limitations.[42] Within the limits of that law they may be further restricted by political or policy considerations so as, for example, to direct that certain military objectives should not be attacked.[43] They need to be carefully drafted not only to ensure that the soldier who complies with them is able to stay within the legal limits imposed by relevant international or English law, but also so that they can be understood by those who use them. The choice by armed forces lawyers of specific terms or phrases when drafting the RoE may be understood by them, but not necessarily by those who have to use them.[44]

That the RoE do not possess the status of law has been seen by some as a drawback to the individual soldier who claims to have followed the procedures set out when using a weapon against a civilian.[45] There was, therefore, an attempt,

39 This book is concerned with armed conflicts, but RoE may be issued in other circumstances. They were issued as the 'yellow card' in Northern Ireland to British soldiers as guidance on when weapons could be used, see *R v Clegg* [1995] 1 AC 482, [491] and as card Alpha in Iraq, *The Iraq Fatality Investigations: Inspector Sir George Newman, Consolidated Report into the Death of Nadheem Abdullah and the Death of Hassan Abbas Said*, Cm 9023, March 2015, [4.27].

40 They will differ as between different military operations, HL Debs 29 November 2000, vol 619, col 133W (Sierra Leone); HC Debs 14 January 2002, vol 378, col 4 (Afghanistan).

41 *R v Clegg* [1995] 1 AC 482, [491], 'it is not suggested that the yellow card has any legal force', Lord Lloyd.

42 See, for example, on the right to life, ECHR, Art 2. The RoE were adjudged to 'reflect . . . the Convention standard' in *McCann v United Kingdom* (1996) 21 EHRR 97, [156]. Compare *Nachova v Bulgaria* (2006) 42 EHRR 43, [99]–[100].

43 Action may remain within the law but a particular level or form of military action may not be desirable from the point of view of the British government, hence the rules of engagement need to be approved by ministers, see HC Debs 11 March 2013, vol 560, col 76W; HC Debs 20 July 2015, vol 598, col 1240. See further discussion in Chapter 9 and for their importance in the use of remotely piloted aircraft (drones). These political or policy considerations cannot be such as to direct that those who comply with the RoE are authorised to act beyond the limits of the law.

44 A term such as 'treat detainees humanely' had given rise to different views when specific issues were tested against it, such as the hooding of detainees. A candidate for the army must reach at least 'Entry Level 2 (numeracy and literacy of an average seven year old)', D Gee, 'Informed Choice? Armed Forces Recruitment Practice in the United Kingdom', [50], available http://www.informedchoice.org.uk/informedchoice/informedchoicefull.pdf.

45 The drawback relates to the lack of certainty for the soldier who may still be prosecuted even though he and his commanding officer believed that the RoE had been complied with. The examples given by a proposer of the amendment were the cases of *R v Clegg* [1995] 1 AC 482 and *R v Fisher and Wright*, NI Unrep Jts, 15 December 1995 (Lexis), HL Debs 11 October 2006, vol 685, col 289 and the conclusion of the Army Board on compliance with their RoE at col 290. For examples of where commanding officers reviewed the actions of soldiers under their command against their RoE see *R (Al-Skeini and others) v Secretary of State for Defence* [2005] EWCA Civ 1609, [22–26]; *Al-Skeini v United Kingdom* (2011) 53 EHRR 18, [51].

during the passage of the Armed Forces Bill in 2005–2006, to enshrine the RoE in law so as to give the soldier the comfort of knowing that he would have an absolute defence to a charge if he had complied with it.[46] The proposed amendment was eventually withdrawn and it did not form part of the Armed Forces Act 2006. It is difficult to resist the conclusion that this proposed amendment, along with questions to the Attorney General about criminal proceedings being brought against individual soldiers,[47] were earlier manifestations of the view, expressed by former chiefs of the defence staff, that there was a 'creeping legal expansion on to the battlefield'.[48]

Current RoE have generally been seen by the British government as classified documents the contents of which will not be disclosed in Parliament,[49] although relevant parts relating to the grounds on which force may be used have been set out occasionally in the judgment of individual cases.[50] The reasons given by ministers for their confidentiality do not distinguish between the different types of RoE and are based on the necessity to protect the lives of members of the British armed forces and to prevent the RoE from being known by the enemy. Whilst this is no doubt true in relation to the wider range of documents encompassed by the term, the disadvantage of this approach, in relation to the guidance offered to soldiers about the use of weapons, is that their contents are also unknown to MPs, or members of the House of Lords, or those civilians in Iraq or in Afghanistan who come into contact with British soldiers at vehicle check points or in their own communities, particularly during a period of occupation, and who will not know the circumstances in which they can be fired upon.[51]

46 Amendment No 61, see HL Debs 11 October 2006, vol 685, col 288. The view of the government minister is set out at col 301.

47 See, for example, HL Debs 27 April 2006, vol 681, col 262; HL Debs 16 February 2006, vol 678, col 1292; *Al-Skeini v United Kingdom* (2011) 53 EHRR 18, [54].

48 Letter to *The Times*, 7 April 2015. See discussion in Chapter 10.

49 See, for example, HL Debs 20 June 2007, vol 693, col 51W; HC Debs 13 May 2008, vol 475, col 1518W; HL Debs 11 July 2011, vol 729, col 472. A proposal by some members of the House of Lords to see 'an out of date set of rules of engagement. In that way . . . Lords would have a much better understanding of what the Minister is saying', HL Debs 11 October 2006, vol 685, col 301. The minister approved the suggestion.

50 *R v Clegg* [1995] 1 AC 482, [491]; *Bici v Ministry of Defence* [2004] EWHC 786, [6]; *R (Al-Skeini and others) v Secretary of State for Defence* [2004] EWHC 2911, [45] referring to 'Card Alpha'. For the ECtHR see *Jaloud v Netherlands* (2015) 60 EHRR 29, [59]; *Al-Skeini v United Kingdom* (2011) 53 EHRR 18, [24]. Compare the '1991 Operation Desert Storm, US Rules of Engagement: Pocket Card', in A Roberts and R Guelff, *Documents on the Laws of War* (OUP, 3rd edn, 2000), 562–3.

51 In *Nachova v Bulgaria* (2006) 42 EHRR 43, [99] the ECtHR was concerned that the relevant regulations, concerning authorisation to open fire, were not published. See generally, P Rowe, 'The Rules of Engagement in Occupied Territory: Should They be Published?' (2007) 8 MJIL 327. For discussion of the confidentiality of ICRC reports and the difficulties in parliament caused as a result see Chapter 6.

A feature of Britain's wars since 2000 has been the involvement of the British armed forces with other states forming part of a coalition, the armed forces from which will normally have their own RoEs, which could contain 'specific caveats or restrictions',[52] although in Afghanistan they were also subject, in general terms, to the NATO RoE.[53] The personal accountability of the British soldier was, however, based on the UK, and not on the NATO RoE. At various times since 2003 a small number of British armed forces personnel, such as RAF pilots engaged in flying remotely piloted aircraft (drones), have been embedded with US forces and the issue has arisen as to whether they would be subject to UK RoE, or to those applicable to US forces.[54] The position reported to Parliament appears to have changed from 2006, where embedded UK personnel were stated to be subject to US RoE,[55] to 2014 where it was stated that 'UK pilots always operate to UK rules of engagement',[56] to 2015 where they were to apply UK RoE where those RoE were more restrictive than those applicable to US aircrew.[57] It is difficult to accept the 2006 position since the embedded personnel will remain subject to UK service law[58] and their legal accountability for their actions can only be based on that body of law.

Whatever view one may hold about the precise meaning of RoE and their relationship with English law it is clear, from a practical point of view, that the cards issued to members of the armed forces, the guidelines for arrest and detention, serious incident reports, the forms that need to be completed about the details of capture and detention and so on, are the essential means of ensuring compliance with the law, whether it is IHL, English law (including the Human Rights Act 1998) or other international obligations. These various procedures can, and should, capture the essence of the legal obligations on members of the armed forces and on the UK itself. It is not surprising therefore to see both the Baha Mousa Inquiry Report[59] and the Al Sweady Inquiry Reports[60] paying particular attention to these administrative processes as a means of compliance with the

52 HL Debs 20 June 2007, vol 693, col 51W. Senior commanders of NATO forces would have to be able to see at least some part of the UK RoE to determine whether there were any limitations imposed on British armed forces.
53 HL Debs 24 November 2008, vol 705, col 1283. See also Chapter 9 for discussion of the 96 hour NATO limit on detention.
54 For discussion of the use by the RAF of remotely piloted aircraft see Chapter 9.
55 HL Debs 19 June 2006, vol 683, col WA 54.
56 HC Debs 10 February 2014, vol 575, col 588.
57 See discussion in Chapter 4.
58 See Lord Garden, HL Debs 11 October 2006, vol 685, col 289. The position of UK personnel would have been, effectively, the same under the 2014 and the 2015 positions taken by ministers.
59 See recommendation 4. The ban on hooding of detainees did not appear on the arrest procedures card, vol III, 954, [11.7]. If it had been there would have been a much greater chance that the hooding, condemned by the Report, would not have occurred.
60 See, for example, recommendations 4 and 5.

law. The training of members of the armed forces in the law applicable to their actions during an armed conflict is, of course, essential, but it is likely to produce only moderate returns towards compliance with legal obligations, compared with robust and very specific administrative processes dealing with, for example, serious incidents affecting the civilian population and the detailed processes of capture and detention.

v Service law and discipline

Whilst it may not always be recognised by soldiers, the law plays a significant role during armed conflict. They will be used to peacetime disciplinary rules, a breach of which could involve punishments being imposed on them. This is because they are subject to English criminal law, even if they belong to a Scottish regiment, and service law, both of which can be enforced through the court martial or by way of a commanding officer dealing with a charge summarily.[61]

The court martial is broadly modelled on a crown court trial in England and is normally presided over by a judge advocate, a civilian holding judicial office.[62] Instead of a jury a panel of commissioned officers[63] decides guilt or innocence and, along with the judge advocate, the sentence to be imposed.[64]

Although a British court martial can be held abroad, it can also be held in the UK for acts committed abroad.[65] Moreover, the ordinary criminal courts do not lose their jurisdiction over members of the armed forces in these circumstances as the case of one soldier, discussed below, illustrates.[66] It is the Attorney General who possesses a supervisory role over the Service Prosecution Authority, and any discussion as to whether a soldier should be tried by the ordinary criminal court, or by the court martial, will ultimately be taken by the Attorney General.[67] It is, however, rare for this possible conflict of jurisdiction to occur, particularly after the coming into force of the Armed Forces Act 2006.

61 Armed Forces Act 2006, which codified the disciplinary systems for all branches of Britain's armed forces. A finding of guilt 'may be recorded on the Police National Computer', ministerial statement, HC Debs 5 March 2014, vol 576, col 843W.

62 See Armed Forces Act 2006, s 362. This can include a High Court judge, an example being the court-martial of Corporal Payne and others, 2006–2007, where the judge advocate was McKinnon J, http://www.internationalcrimesdatabase.org/Case/811.

63 Armed Forces Act 2006, s 156, although warrant officers may also serve as members.

64 *Ibid*, s 160.

65 'A prosecution of [members of UK armed forces for rape or sexual assault] would not be held in theatre, provided the case could be heard in the United Kingdom at a later stage', HC Debs 5 November 2012, vol 552, col 439W.

66 HL Debs 16 February 2006, vol 678, col 1292 (Attorney General).

67 See the statement by Lord Goldsmith, then Attorney General, HL Debs 14 June 2004, vol 662, col 22WS; HL Debs 16 February 2006, vol 678, col 1292. A possible factor to take into account is that only a simple majority is required to convict before a court martial, whereas in the Crown court a majority verdict can only be accepted by the judge if the majority is of a sufficient size, see *R v Blackman* [2014] EWCA Crim 1029, [30].

Unless the stationing of British forces abroad is in peacetime, as it was and continues to be in Germany,[68] the UK (like a number of other states), has always taken the view that it expects to have exclusive jurisdiction over any crimes committed by members of its armed forces. This means that they will be subject only to British investigation and trial of any suspected crimes against English law committed abroad. The usual practice is to agree a status of forces agreement or memorandum of understanding between the UK and the government of the foreign state. Agreements of this type have been made with Iraq and Afghanistan after the emergence of some form of governing authority in those countries. Before this stage had been reached, and where an international armed conflict was taking place, no agreement of this type could be contemplated and so the UK retained full jurisdiction over its armed forces under both UK and international law.

There are the obvious advantages in British soldiers being liable only to British courts for their actions during an armed conflict, or in war-like situations, but it does have the effect that the local populations in Iraq and Afghanistan may not see, or hear, anything about what happened over the alleged crimes committed by British soldiers against their fellow citizens.

In practice, however, trials are only likely to take place if a soldier has not complied with his RoE during the course of military operations or where he has mistreated detainees.[69] During the actual course of combat operations, with its inevitable chaos and fear, mistakes will inevitably be made.[70] Any system of justice in a democracy that did not take into account these factors in judging an individual would be unlikely to be able to live up to its name. Only a very small number of serious criminal charges have been brought against British soldiers for their acts during active military operations, as compared with the alleged ill-treatment of detainees. One case involved a soldier charged with an alleged wrongful shooting of a civilian in Iraq, which came before the Crown Court in London since it was no longer possible to prosecute him before a court-martial.[71] The prosecution case was considered by Hallett J, following which the prosecution decided

68 Agreement Between the Parties to the North Atlantic Treaty Regarding the Status of their Forces 1951, Art VII.

69 Between 2003 and 2006, some 159 cases of shooting incidents, which may have been in breach of the soldier's RoE, were investigated by the service police and during the same period there were seven successful prosecutions, HL Debs 2 November 2006, vol 686, col 47W. See also the Aitken Report: An Investigation into Cases of Deliberate Abuse and Unlawful Killing in Iraq in 2003 and 2004 (Ministry of Defence, 25 January 2008), [2]–[3]. Compare the statement of the Solicitor General that information 'on the prosecution of soldiers for war crimes or serious offences while on operations is not centrally recorded and to retrieve the information would incur disproportionate cost', HC Debs 15 March 2007, vol 458, col 453W.

70 See generally the Report of the Al-Sweady Inquiry and its discussion of the 'battle of Danny Boy', vol I, 69, [2.102].

71 The reason for this was that his commanding officer had dismissed the charge and, under the Army Act 1955 it could not be revived under military jurisdiction. The power of a commanding officer to dismiss a charge such as this has not survived the Armed Forces Act 2006, see ss 114, 116. For the background see HL Debs 16 February 2006, vol 678, col 1292 (Attorney General). Since the charge could not be laid under the Army Act 1955, s 70 (now replaced by

not to proceed further to trial before a civilian jury. Other cases were held at a court-martial.[72]

There is little scope to argue that the chaos of combat, or that an honest mistake has been made, if soldiers are accused of mistreating a person who has been detained by British forces. Most of the alleged serious wrongdoing in Iraq and in Afghanistan has been in these circumstances and it is difficult in principle to draw any distinction between such acts being committed in peacetime or in an armed conflict. The two situations will, of course, differ in that the need to acquire intelligence information from a detainee during an armed conflict could be a matter of life and death, whereas in peacetime this is unlikely to be the case. But, even in time of an armed conflict, there must be a limit as to what a soldier can do and stay within the law.[73]

Very large numbers of UK service personnel served in Britain's wars from 2000, many of whom were in the front line, but the proportion of those whose acts resulted in a serious issue of whether to prosecute was extremely small. Despite the reporting of each death of a serviceman or woman widely in the media and individual tributes being paid by the Prime Minister in the House of Commons, the recruitment, particularly of soldiers to serve in infantry regiments, has continued, although from time to time the harmony rules have been breached.[74]

vi Do British soldiers have to obey international law?

That 'all members of Her Majesty's armed forces must comply with the Law of Armed Conflict'[75] is, without doubt, a treaty obligation on the UK, but does it impose legal obligations on British soldiers during the course of an armed conflict? It clearly does where those obligations arise from English law, such as

the Armed Forces Act 2006, s 42) the jurisdiction to try the soldier before a civilian court was based upon the extra-territorial jurisdiction for the crime of murder set out in the Offences Against the Person Act 1861, s 9.

72 See HC Debs 7 November 2005, vol 439, col 21; the Aitken Report: An Investigation into Cases of Deliberate Abuse and Unlawful Killing in Iraq in 2003 and 2004 (Ministry of Defence, 25 January 2008), [3]; *R v Blackman* [2014] EWCA Crim 1029. He was charged with murder under the Armed Forces Act 2006, s 42 (which makes it an offence to commit a crime against the law of England and Wales). For debate in the House of Commons on this case, see HC Debs 16 September 2015, vol 599, col 339WH.

73 The treatment of detainees is discussed in Chapter 9.

74 The deployment to Afghanistan in 2006 'reduced Joint Helicopter Command's flexibility to reduce time away from home for personnel', Air Chief Marshall Torpy, written statement, Iraq Inquiry [27]. The harmony guidelines are set out in HC Debs 7 January 2013 vol 556, col 32W and breaches of them for the period 2010–2014 are at HC Debs 14 May 2014, vol 580, col 606W. See also N Fear (lead author), 'What are the Consequences of Deployment to Iraq and Afghanistan on the Mental Health of the Armed Forces?' (2010) 375 The Lancet, No 9728, [1783] who conclude that 'our finding of no association between multiple deployments and mental health can be viewed as support for the appropriateness of the UK military's harmony guidelines'.

75 HC Debs 3 September 2007, vol 463, col 1610WA.

through the International Criminal Court Act 2001. Acts that do not fall within English law, but that are contrary to IHL,[76] will also impose personal obligations on the British soldier enforceable only by an international court or tribunal, or even by another state, but the probabilities of any indictment or trial on this basis can properly only be considered to be remote. There are no means of enforcing directly such an obligation under English law, unless specific international law norms are contained in the RoE, or made the subject of service standing orders or other form of order that can be enforced, as such under the Armed Forces Act 2006.[77] It is no argument to say that the main IHL obligations form part of customary international law, which in turn, automatically forms part of English law, since the House of Lords has held that offences under English criminal law can only be created by parliament.[78]

In much the same way, a UN Security Council resolution cannot be part of English law unless any of the obligations on states contained with it form a part of English law. The United Nations Act 1946 gives a power to do so through subordinate legislation, but only in respect of 'measures not involving the use of armed force' under the UN Charter, Article 41.[79] The 1946 Act cannot be invoked to give statutory authority to authorisations by the UN Security Council to 'take all necessary measures'[80] to achieve the aims of the resolution through the use of armed force, or to intern individuals.[81] Lawful authority under English law (as compared with international law) to act on this basis must be derived from some other source.[82]

vii Doctors, lawyers, chaplains and police officers

Doctors, lawyers, chaplains and police officers serving in the armed forces will be subject to service law in the same way as any other member of the British armed

76 There are many IHL obligations which are not reflected in English law.
77 An example is the recommendation in the Report of the Baha Mousa Inquiry (2011), vol III, 1267, Recommendation 2, that the ban on the use of any of the prohibited techniques should be made the subject of a service standing order, a breach of which would be a service offence under the Armed Forces Act 2006, s 13.
78 *R v Jones (Margaret)* [2006] UKHL 16, which confirmed that the crime of aggression exists under international law but not in English law. See generally, P Rowe, 'The Criminal Liability of a British Soldier Merely for Participating in the Iraq War: a Response to Chilcot Evidence' [2010] Crim LR 752. Parliament may not implement the whole of a treaty provision. It did not, for example, incorporate into the International Criminal Court Act 2001, the defences set out in Arts 31–33 of the Rome Statute 1998. See S Wallerstein, 'Why English Law Should Not Incorporate the Defence of Superior Orders' [2010] Crim LR 109.
79 Section 1. For discussion of economic sanctions, see Chapter 2.
80 See, for example, Resolution 1973 (2011) concerning Libya; Resolution 1511 (2003), concerning the multinational force in Iraq.
81 Resolution 1546 (2004).
82 Lawful authority derived from international law may provide a basis for detention under ECHR, Art 5. For an example, see *Mohammed v Secretary of State for Defence* [2015] EWCA Civ 843 and Chapters 7 and 9.

forces.[83] In addition, they can be held accountable to their own professional body and the standards that they impose on their respective practitioners.[84] On this basis a medical or legal officer may face a situation that ought to cause him or her concern in terms of a conflict with relevant professional requirements. A danger, inherent in many organisations, to be guarded against is that the doctor or lawyer will, unwittingly, come to view the circumstances in a way similar to his other military colleagues. Thus, the doctor could be led into accepting that the rough questioning of detainees to obtain intelligence is necessary to save the lives of other British soldiers in combat. The inherent ambiguities of IHL, or even of the applicability (certainly until the decision of the ECtHR in 2011)[85] of English law to a given situation can also give rise to problems for the lawyer in forming advice to commanders upon which he or she can be confident.

The Baha Mousa inquiry showed the pressure that service officers of all three professions can face when their military colleagues act in a way that could give rise to concerns for them in their individual professional capacities. On 15 September 2003 a British army doctor, serving with an infantry unit in Basra from August to November 2003, was summoned to provide medical treatment to a detainee, an Iraqi civilian who had been subjected to tactical questioning by British soldiers.[86] Despite the clinical care provided by him the detainee died shortly afterwards.[87] Some nine years later, and after leaving the army, the doctor was summoned before a fitness to practise panel of the General Medical Council,[88] which found that he had 'failed to safeguard the wellbeing of the civilian detainees then held at [the British detention facility]'.[89] The Panel also did not believe his assertion that he had not seen any injuries on the detainee, apart from 'old dried blood around his nose'.[90] It took into account the lack of his professional experience and that he was 'unexpectedly thrown into a war zone at very short notice' but concluded that his 'failure to check on the detainees left them at risk of harm [since] they did not have the freedom to come and see [him] as and when they wished or needed'.[91] The finding that the statements he made were

83 Medical personnel and chaplains are not permitted by IHL to carry weapons or to use them, except in self-defence of themselves, or of those whom they have a duty to protect, Geneva Conventions I and II, 1949, Arts 35, 36 and 22, 24 respectively. As such, they are not 'combatants', see Chapter 6.

84 The General Medical Council, the Law Society or the Bar Council. In relation to medical practitioners this will include nurses and other allied professions. Chaplains, as members of a religious body will be subject to their respective codes of conduct.

85 On the extent of the extra-territorial applicability of the ECHR, *Al-Skeini v United Kingdom* (2011) 53 EHRR 18, discussed in Chapter 7.

86 This particular individual was Mr Baha Mousa, the subject of the Inquiry.

87 See the *Report of the Baha Mousa Inquiry*, HC 1452 (2011), vol 1, 312, [2.1259].

88 By virtue of the Medical Act 1983, s 35C(2)(a) the task of the Panel was to determine whether a registered medical practitioner's fitness to practise was 'impaired' through 'misconduct'.

89 Fitness to Practise Panel of the Medical Practitioners Tribunal Service, 21 December 2012.

90 *Ibid.*

91 *Ibid.* See also *Report of the Baha Mousa Inquiry*, vol I, 298, [2.1192] which concluded that he had had 'no time to acclimatise to conditions before taking over from [his predecessor

'misleading'[92] led the Panel to conclude that he should be erased from the register of medical practitioners.

Gui lance for medical officers in the armed forces has been provided by the British Medical Association in handling what may involve conflict obligations during armed conflicts.[93]

Service lawyers,[94] who like their medical colleagues, will be commissioned officers retain, even during time of armed conflict, the same obligations under their respective professional codes of conduct established by the Bar Council or the Law Society as they would if they were practising in any part of the UK. Their actions came under close scrutiny by the Baha Mousa inquiry (2011), which concluded that 'the only fair criticism that can be made of the legal officers is that in most cases they did too little to find out what precisely was happening at the [detention facility] before giving advice'.[95]

The Baha Mousa inquiry was, of course, limited by its terms of reference to consider incidents occurring at a particular time. Legal officers have been involved in giving advice to commanders on many other occasions during the armed conflicts between 2000 and 2015, but their duty to comply with their professional standards may impose an obligation to set out in written form to the most senior commander their concern about whether their legal advice is being complied with on the ground.[96]

Chaplains or padres also have obligations imposed by their own religious organisations towards those in need of some form of assistance. Although there may be little to do at the spiritual level for those professing a different faith it could reasonably be expected that they would concern themselves actively with the protection of the vulnerable.[97]

medical officer]' 298, and the 'failure to give him any training or instructions in respect of prisoner handling was an unfortunate omission.' It also considered that he 'ought to have gone back to the TDF [Temporary Detention Facility] after Baha Mousa's death in order to examine all of the detainees [his failure to do so was a serious failing [and he] ought to have reported what I find he knew to . . . a senior officer', vol I, 320, [2.1301].

92 The *Report of the Baha Mousa Inquiry* concluded that he 'must have known following the resuscitation process that Baha Mousa had sustained injuries in the TDF', vol 1, 318, [2.1293].

93 *Ethical Decision-Making for Doctors in the Armed Forces: a Tool-Kit, Guidance from the BMA Medical Ethics Committee and Armed Forces Committee*, 2012.

94 To be distinguished from civilian lawyers working at the Ministry of Defence, some of whom will be involved in advising on matters relating to IHL and operations law, ministerial statement, HC Debs 25 November 2010, vol 519, col 395W.

95 *Report of the Baha Mousa Inquiry*, vol III, 1342, [375]. Favourable comments were, however, made of the actions of some legal officers, see, for example, vol III, 1347, [404]. See also F Ledwidge, *Losing Small Wars*, 180.

96 See, for example, the memorandum sent by a legal officer to General Brims (General Officer Commanding 1 (UK) Division) about the hooding of detainees in Iraq, *Report of the Baha Mousa Inquiry*, vol II, 710, [8.54], 1343, [379].

97 See the comments concerning the actions of the padre in the *Report of the Baha Mousa Inquiry*, vol III, 1303, [112]; vol I, 229, [2.835] and generally, G Zahn, *Chaplains in the RAF* (Manchester University Press, 1969) who commented that 'Only . . . (62.2% of the chaplains interviewed) took the position that the use of torture is intrinsically wrong and may never be permitted', 147.

It can be seen therefore that the service medical or legal officer and the chaplain face similar issues relating to their respective professional obligations. Each may be required to report to higher service authority issues on which they have concerns from their professional point of view. This may not be an easy thing to do and will often require 'moral courage',[98] particularly where they are working in a small unit in a combat zone.

Service police officers have obligations derived from the practices and expectations of any police officer, whether serving in the British armed forces or not. The standards expected of them in relation to the investigation of crime and their obligations to the judicial process, in whatever form, will be similar to their civilian counterparts. It is for this reason, along with the need to establish independence from the service chain of command, that investigations carried out by the service police are subject to periodical review by HM Inspectors of Constabulary.[99] The service police are required, however, to perform a role, particularly when the British armed forces are conducting military operations abroad, which has no real equivalent in civilian policing. This is to conduct investigations, often in active service conditions.[100] Should the conduct of a particular investigation come before the civilian courts, senior service police officers may be called upon to provide statements or to give evidence in court. Any serious failings on their part in giving evidence or in the disclosure of documents to the court can give rise to judicial criticism of the service police officer, in much the same way as would be expected of his civilian counterpart.[101] The need on the part of service commissioned and non-commissioned officers to display the professional standards of a civilian police officer may be as difficult for them as for the doctor, lawyer or chaplain, given the often harsh conditions experienced during military operations abroad and the workload placed upon them, particularly in relation to the substantially increased need to conduct investigations.

viii Service morale

Serious combat operations have been carried out by British forces since the invasion of Afghanistan in 2001. This is a long period of time during which the recruitment of young soldiers on a volunteer basis has had to continue. It might be expected that this would prove to be difficult, especially as the Iraq conflict, in particular, was not popular amongst a large section of the British public, but this has not been the case.[102] The number of those who have refused to

98 The term is to be found in the *Report of the Baha Mousa Inquiry*, vol III, 1243, [16.348], 1316, [203].

99 Armed Forces Act 2011, s 4.

100 For discussion in detail see Chapter 7.

101 See, for example, *R (Al-Sweady and Others) v Secretary of State for Defence* [2009] EWHC 2387 (Admin), [50]–[51], [56], which dealt with the evidence of a senior RMP officer.

102 Neither the initial attack on Afghanistan in 2001, nor the substantial involvement in Helmand Province in 2006, were the subject of a debate in the House of Commons, as the

serve in Iraq or in Afghanistan has been very small and there is no evidence of any significant rise in summary hearings or trials of army personnel before the court-martial that might suggest a weakening of military discipline, even when the total manpower figures are assessed.[103] The importance of service morale is heightened particularly during an armed conflict.[104] Soldiers appear to have accepted with stoicism the tough conditions experienced in Iraq and Afghanistan, along with separation from their families. To some extent all these factors must indicate that the morale of the armed forces has remained high in these difficult circumstances. This can be seen as a real achievement on the part of the armed forces themselves, but the public have played a significant part too. Various charities have been active for a long time in assisting former servicemen and women but one, Help for Heroes, was started only in October 2007. It caught the imagination of the public very quickly, largely because it was able to separate the relatively unpopular conflict to which the soldiers were sent to fight, from the need to help the wounded serviceman or woman return to a normal life.[105] Those who had been killed were repatriated through Wootten Bassett (now with a Royal prefix) where the streets were often lined with the general public paying their respects to those whose who had been killed in Iraq or Afghanistan. These events were often screened during TV news broadcasts and they contributed greatly to the sense that these were individual soldiers and not just a constituent part of the overall casualty numbers.[106] What went largely unseen, however, were the much larger number of soldiers who had suffered severe injuries resulting in loss of limbs. These were serving or former soldiers who could be helped directly on their road to recovery and the donations made

attack on Iraq in 2003 had been. At the conclusion of the vote in 2013 to carry out airstrikes against Syria, the prime minister stated that 'the British Parliament, reflecting the views of the British people, does not want to see British military action', HC Debs 29 August 2013, vol 566, col 1556.

103 For the numbers of trial by the court-martial between 2003 and 2009 see https://www.gov.uk/government/uploads/system/uploads/attachment_data/file/16792/FOI09062010120433002_Court_Martials_20002009.pdf.

104 Armed Forces Continuous Attitude Surveys, ACAS 2010, Ministry of Defence: https://www.gov.uk/government/uploads/system/uploads/attachment_data/file/280711/2010.pdf. This figure, has, however, fluctuated between 60% in 2007 to 45% in 2012, see Armed Forces Continuous Attitude Surveys, 2012 Report: https://www.gov.uk/government/uploads/system/uploads/attachment_data/file/280180/2012.pdf table B2.12.

105 See generally, R Gribble et al, 'Public Awareness of UK Veterans' Charities' (2014) who conclude that, 'despite opposition to these missions [Iraq and Afghanistan], more than 90% of those surveyed support veterans of these campaigns', p 55: available at http://www.kcl.ac.uk/kcmhr/pubdb/.

106 See S Schilman and H Strachan, 'The Town That Weeps: Commemorating Life and Loss in Wootton Bassett' (2010) 155 RUSI Jo 76. A King, 'The Afghan War and "Postmodern" Memory: Commemoration and the Dead of Helmand' (2010) 61 British Journal of Sociology 1, refers to the publication of a picture of the 'smiling images of the dead soldier'. He goes on to conclude that these photographs show that 'they are no longer universal, anonymous soldiers in the service of the state but each is a distinct living personality'.

to Help for Heroes by large numbers of people show widespread support for the wounded in a way totally unrelated to the unpopularity of the armed conflicts in which they fought.

The government also recognised the importance of public support for the armed forces. The effect of the long involvement of the army in Northern Ireland with its attendant terrorist threats had, quite understandably, led soldiers not to wear uniform in public. To many people the armed forces were no longer visible, although there were short periods after the Falklands war in 1982 and the first Gulf war in 1991 when they were lauded for their achievements. With the reduction in risk following the Belfast Agreement in 1998, the armed forces began to be seen around much more. The lead up to the armed conflict in Iraq in early 2003, with thousands marching under a banner of 'Not in my Name' and a sizeable proportion of MPs voting not to support the decision to go to war in Iraq; this was a difficult time although all would have supported the troops. It is worth noting that the amendment to the government motion in the debate in the House of Commons on 18 March 2003, which called for more time before taking military action, nevertheless voiced its support for the armed forces.

In 2007, the Prime Minister set up a committee to report to him on developing a greater understanding and appreciation of the armed forces in British society. The report was produced in May 2008 as a Report of the Inquiry into National Recognition of Our Armed Forces.[107] Among its recommendations were the establishment of an armed forces day, home-coming parades in a public location and the creation of a new offence of discrimination against members of the armed forces.

ix Combat stress[108]

Evidence is also emerging of the effects of post-traumatic stress disorder (PTSD)[109] being suffered after return to the UK, although studies have shown that combat veterans are a resilient group and that 'approximately 7% of combat troops were found to have symptoms of PTSD following deployment to Iraq and

107 Report of an Inquiry into National Recognition of our Armed Forces, 19 May 2008. The Government's Response is at https://www.gov.uk/government/uploads/system/uploads/attachment_data/file/28287/govt_response_recognition_armed_forces.pdf.

108 In *R v Blackman* [2014] EWCA Crim 1029, [36]–[40] reference is made to 'combat stress'. The term 'post-traumatic stress disorder' is described as 'an overused explanation of a wide range of mental health issues experienced by those who have served in the Armed Forces who subsequently find themselves in trouble', Stephen Phillips, QC, MP, *Former Members of the Armed Forces and the Criminal Justice System: A Review on Behalf of the Secretary of State for Justice* (2014) available at https://www.gov.uk/government/uploads/system/uploads/attachment_data/file/389964/former-members-of-the-armed-forces-and-the-criminal-justice-system.pdf.

109 Issues relating to post-traumatic stress disorder and other mental health issues relating to serving and former members of the armed forces is discussed in the House of Commons

Afghanistan'.[110] They also 'experience lower than expected numbers of suicides in comparison with the UK general population'.[111] A proactive approach to the issue would seem a much better policy and it has been reported that soldiers will be tested for potential stress problems prior to their deployment.[112] There is, for instance, a procedure in place to deal with 'trauma management' amongst those pilots who fly remotely piloted aircraft (drones).[113]

x Veterans in prison

Concern has also been expressed about the number of former armed forces personnel in prison and in January 2014 the Justice Secretary announced a review to investigate the broad issue of veterans in the criminal justice system.[114] One of the conclusions of the Review was that 'depression, often fuelled by alcohol misuse, is a much greater problem [than PTSD] and it is on those aspects of mental health that interventions should largely focus'.[115] It has also been suggested that 'deployed personnel in combat roles were at increased risk of subsequent violent offending'.[116] There would seem, however, to be no clear causal link between service in Afghanistan or Iraq and

Defence Committee, *The Armed Forces Covenant in Action?*, Part 1, Military Casualties, Seventh Report of Session 2010–12, HC 762 and the Government's Response, at HC 1855. See, however, http://www.kcl.ac.uk/kcmhr/pubdb/.

110 D MacManus et al, 'The Mental Health of the UK Armed Forces in the 21st Century: Resilience in the Face of Adversity' (2014), www.kcl.ac.uk/kcmhr/pubdb/, 3. In L Goodwin and R Ronan, 'PTSD in the Armed Forces: What Have We Learned From the Recent Cohort Studies of Iraq and Afghanistan?' (2013) the authors conclude that 'deployment is not the main factor related to PTSD, combat is not the only trauma and reservists may have different mental health needs compared to regulars', [398], both available at http://www.kcl.ac.uk/kcmhr/pubdb/ See also N Fear (lead author), What are the Consequences of Deployment to Iraq and Afghanistan on the Mental Health of the Armed Forces?' (2010) 375 The Lancet, No 9728, [1783], who show that 'having a combat role was associated with increased reporting of probable post-traumatic stress disorder . . . [and] alcohol use is more of a problem, both before and after deployment'.

111 D MacManus et al, [4].

112 The *Telegraph*, 15 September 2013, 'Forces to be tested for combat stress'.

113 It is known as TRiM, see House of Commons Select Committee on Defence, Tenth Report of session 2013–14, *Remote Control: Remotely Piloted Air Systems-Current and Future UK Use*, HC 772, [52]. For discussion of 'drones' see Chapter 9. Pre-deployment briefing on Trauma Risk Management is discussed in *R v Blackman* [2014] EWCA Crim 1029, [39].

114 See Stephen Phillips, QC, MP, *Former Members of the Armed Forces and the Criminal Justice System: A Review on Behalf of the Secretary of State for Justice* (2014) available at https://www.gov.uk/government/uploads/system/uploads/attachment_data/file/389964/former-members-of-the-armed-forces-and-the-criminal-justice-system.pdf.

115 *Ibid*, [6]. The Report also deals with a wide range of issues relating to veterans in prison.

116 D MacMahon (lead author), 'Violent Offending by UK Military personnel Deployed to Iraq and Afghanistan: a Date Linkage Cohort Study' (2013) 381 The Lancet No 9870, [907]. See also Ministry of Justice, *The Needs of Ex-Service Personnel in the Criminal Justice System: a Rapid Evidence Assessment,* Analytical Series, 2014 [28] available at https://www.gov.uk/government/uploads/system/uploads/attachment_data/file/389855/

being sentenced to a custodial sentence. The various studies draw attention to a wide range of causes and concentration on just one, PTSD, to the exclusion of others, such as homelessness, substance misuse or unemployment, is likely to be misleading.[117]

the-needs-of-ex-service-personnel-in-the-cjs-rapid-evidence-assessment.pdf. In November 2009 it was estimated that the proportion of ex-regular members of the armed forces serving a prison sentence was 3.5% of the total prison population: *Ministry of Defence, Estimating the Proportion of Prisoners in England and Wales Who are Ex-Armed Forces-Further Analysis* (2010) https://www.gov.uk/government/uploads/system/uploads/attachment_data/file/280048/15-september-2010.pdf [8], [13], [20].

117 Phillips Report, note 114 above.

9 The conduct of British military operations

i Introduction

At the beginning of the new millennium British armed forces had had recent experience of a wide variety of military operations. The UK had completed its involvement (which began in 1969) in aiding the civil power in Northern Ireland; it had taken part in the coalition to drive Iraqi forces from Kuwait and it had been involved in the NATO campaign in Kosovo. Each of these operations called for different tactics and strategy and each raised different legal issues.

After the decision by the UK government to ratify the 1977 Additional Protocols to the Geneva Conventions, which occurred in 1998, the Ministry of Defence published in 2004 its *Manual of the Law of Armed Conflict* which was 'intended to enable all concerned to apply the law of armed conflict when conducting operations and when training or planning for them'.[1] In their foreword to the *Manual* the Chief of the Defence Staff and the Permanent Under Secretary, Ministry of Defence wrote that 'law, both domestic and international, plays an increasingly important part in Defence activities these days'.[2] Prior to 2004, each of the three services had published its own manual dealing with its individual spheres of operations but this new one would apply to all the UK's armed forces. What has become known as 'operations law' was, on the eve of military activities against Iraq in 2003, not new. A separate branch of Army Legal Services was established in April 2003 to deal specifically with operations law in the various spheres in which it would have to be applied.[3]

Some may, no doubt, regret that 'when undertaking operations, commanders must take into account a broad and increasingly complex body of operational

1 OUP (2004), Preface, vii. It is also known as 'the *Joint Service Manual*'. It is not open to the government to take a position contrary to that expressed in the *Joint Service Manual*, *Rahmatullah v Secretary of State for Defence and Secretary of State for Foreign and Commonwealth Affairs* [2012] UKSC 48, Lord Kerr, [34] (although Lord Kerr also referred to a statement reflecting the view of the UK government). This principle must be qualified by a subsequent change in the law as expressed in the *Joint Service Manual*.

2 *Manual of the Law of Armed Conflict*, Foreword.

3 HL Debs 19 February 2008, vol 699, col 31W; A Rogers and G Risius, in *Contemporary Challenges to the Laws of War* (Cambridge University Press, 2014), 43. For the Operational Law Training Directive, see FOI, Ministry of Defence, release 8 December 2014.

law'[4] but this is the reality of modern warfare and the UK would hardly wish that the obligations it had accepted, or those which are binding on it, under international law should be flouted.

The most significant single activity, which became wrapped in a fog of uncertainty as to what the law actually required, was the handling of detainees. In addition, UK armed forces were faced with a change in the interpretation of Article 1, relating to the extent of the extra-territorial jurisdiction of the ECHR by the ECtHR, with its implications for Articles 2, 3 and 5 as from 2011.[5] We have seen that many of the legal issues raised have been before the courts in England and not before international courts.[6]

ii Intelligence gathering

Although the importance of accurate intelligence on the activities of an enemy can hardly be over-stated, the fact that the vast majority of Britain's military operations, between 2000 and 2015, have involved defence against, and attack on, non-state organised armed groups during non-international armed conflicts, has greatly added to the normal confusion to be expected in any armed conflict. Added to this mix has been, in some quarters, an imprecision of language such as the use of 'battlefield', combatant', 'war on terror', 'terrorist', 'lawful target', blurring well-established classifications of individuals and property.[7]

New technology has certainly helped in the quest to be a step ahead of the enemy[8] and, during the course of the various armed conflict since 2000, the use of remotely piloted aircraft and other intelligence-gathering robotic devices, has greatly assisted the British, and other, armed forces where the sharing of such information has taken place. It has, however, been one of the oldest forms of intelligence gathering that has given rise to the greatest legal concern, the questioning of those detained by coalition forces, a form of which is known as 'tactical questioning'. The vast majority of those detained by British armed forces have not been entitled to be classified as prisoners of war and they have, therefore, been classified as civilians of one type or another.[9]

4 *Manual of the Law of Armed Conflict*, Foreword.
5 *Al-Skeini v United Kingdom* (2011) 53 EHRR 18, although it was accepted much earlier by the Ministry of Defence that the ECHR could apply to those in detention in Iraq, such as Baha Mousa. See generally Chapter 7, including discussion of the obligations under the same provisions owed by the UK to its own soldiers.
6 See Chapters 5 and 7.
7 For discussion of these terms see Chapter 1 and below.
8 For the meaning of this term see Chapter 1.
9 In the course of the international armed conflicts in Afghanistan and Iraq those not entitled to be classified as prisoners of war would have been civilians protected under Geneva Convention IV, 1949. See, for example, *Rahmatullah v Secretary of State for Defence and Secretary of State for Foreign and Commonwealth Affairs* [2012] UKSC 48. When these armed conflicts became of a non-international character the same individuals would have to look for their protection under Common Art 3 of the 1949 Conventions and Additional Protocol II, 1977, customary international law and English law (including the Human Rights Act 1998).

iii Targeting

One of the essential functions of IHL is to protect, from the effects of the armed conflict, those who are not taking an active part in hostilities, their property and their means of survival. In doing so it concentrates not only on what cannot be attacked as well as what can be targeted, along with the issue of unintended, but collateral damage. These principles, in turn, guide the type of weapons that may be used lawfully within particular contexts,[10] and it is not surprising to see that service lawyers, and even the Attorneys General on occasions, have been called to advise on the lawfulness or otherwise of a particular planned military operation.[11] The issues raised by the targeting of individuals and of property are not identical and, for convenience, they are discussed separately, whilst the use of 'drones' justifies a distinct analysis.

(a) Civilians taking a direct part in hostilities

The very nature of international armed conflict has always involved attacks by the armed forces of one state against the armed forces of another. Members of the armed forces of a state will be combatants with 'a right to participate directly in hostilities'.[12] It follows that those who are not members of the armed forces must

10 Particularly those that could cause undesired collateral harm to individuals, such as the use of cluster bombs, depleted uranium weapons, anti-personnel land mines or through unexploded ordnance. Cluster bombs 'were used by UK armed forces against dispersed Iraqi military forces in the open and on the periphery of built up areas', HC Debs 11 February 2004, vol 417, col 1459W. It is in the nature of such weapons that their effects may not be discovered, so a minister stated in parliament that 'we have no viable means of ascertaining the numbers of civilians who were killed or injured by cluster bombs during or since the coalition's military action', HL Debs 8 September 2003, vol 652, col WA 40. However, 'since 1 May 2003-when it was declared that major combat operations were over-the United Kingdom has used no cluster bombs', HC Debs 15 July 2003, vol 409, col 194W and 'UK aircraft have not dropped cluster bombs in Afghanistan, HC Debs 30 January 2004, vol 417, col 577W. It has also been stated that 'all UK cluster munitions were withdrawn from service in May 2008', HL Debs 21 December 2010, vol 723, col 277W. The UK became a party to the Convention on Cluster Munitions 2008 on 4 May 2010. As early as 2003 a minister confirmed that there were 'no weapons containing low yield uranium in our inventory', HC Debs 28 April 2003, vol 404, col 152W. The UK became a party to the Convention on the Prohibition of the Use, Stockpiling, Production and Transfer of Anti-Personnel Mines and on their Destruction 1997, on 31 July 1998. To combat the dangers to the civilian population of unexploded ordnance after the war-fighting in Iraq parliament was informed that 'United Kingdom armed forces have launched an awareness programme, aimed at children and young adults in particular, about the dangers of unexploded ordnance of all types', HL Debs 8 July 2003, vol 651, col 31W.

11 HC Debs 7 February 2005, vol 430, col 1249W; HC Debs 2 December 2009, vol 501, col 727W and for the role of ministers, see HC Debs 15 October 2013, vol 568, col 633W. See also the evidence of Lord Goldsmith, Iraq Inquiry, 27 January 2010, [221], in which he stated that, in respect of one proposed target during the Iraq conflict, 'I actually blocked it and said it could not take place with British participation', [223].

12 Additional Protocol I, Art 43(2). The term 'combatant' excludes medical personnel and chaplains. See further discussion in Chapter 6.

be classified differently. They are civilians who, because of their status, do not possess a right to participate, and who may not be attacked unless they take a direct part in hostilities.[13] In non-international armed conflict, such as in Iraq (after the end of the occupation) and in Afghanistan, the British armed forces have been engaged in military operations against organised armed groups,[14] whether they are styled as al-Qaeda, the Taliban, the Mahdi army, insurgents, rebels, terrorists or are known by any other name. In the Al-Sweady Inquiry Report the conclusion is drawn that 'the nine detainees went willingly to the scene of the engagement . . . each did so for the sole purpose of participating in the planned ambush of and armed attack on British troops that day'.[15] Neither these individuals, nor others forming these separate groups, can be considered to be prisoners of war, if captured and detained, for two reasons. First, Geneva Convention III, 1949, relating to prisoners of war applies only during an international armed conflict and, secondly, they are not members of the armed forces of a state party to the conflict.[16] They are civilians who have clearly taken a direct part in hostilities and can therefore be attacked, at any time, since it is likely that each individual will have had a continuous combat function.[17] Although they may not be prisoners of war and have no right (as members of the armed forces of a state do) to take part in the conflict they are, nevertheless, owed some obligations under international law,[18] and under English law. For a British soldier to attack them would not be

13 *Ibid*, Art 51(3).

14 For the requirements before a collection of individuals can be considered to be an organised armed group and thus be a party to a non-international armed conflict, see *Prosecutor v Boskoski*, IT-04–82-A, 19 May 2010, [23]; *Prosecutor v Haradinaj*, IT-84*bis*-T, 12 November 2012, [393]. For the meaning of 'armed conflict' see Chapter 6.

15 Vol 1, [2.140].

16 Geneva Conventions III, 1949, Art 4. See also *Military Prosecutor v Kassem* (1971) 42 ILR 470.

17 Interpretive Guidance on the Notion of Direct Participation in Hostilities under International Humanitarian Law, ICRC, (2008) 90 IRRC 991. This argues that such individuals actually 'cease to be civilians for as long as they remain members [of an organised armed group] by virtue of their continuous combat function', [1036]. C Garraway, 'Direct Participation and the Principle of Distinction: Squaring the Circle' in C Harvey, J Summers and N White (eds), *Contemporary Challenges to the Laws of War* (Cambridge University Press, 2014), 169, 176–7 points out that the Guidance 'created a new category of persons who were neither members of the regular armed forces nor civilians'. The Guidance drew some serious criticism, see N Melzer, 'Keeping the Balance between Military Necessity and Humanity: A Response to Four Critiques of the ICRC's Interpretive Guidance on the Notion of Direct Participation in Hostilities' (2009–10) 42 New York University Journal of International Law and Politics 831. In *Prosecutor v Haradinaj*, IT-84*bis*-T, 12 November 2012, [398] the ICTY described participation in hostilities as 'participating in acts of war that aim by their nature or purpose to cause actual harm to the personnel or equipment of the armed forces of the opponent'.

18 See the ICRC's Interpretive Guidance, section IX, 'Restraints on the use of force in direct attack'. For criticism of this section see H Parks, 'Part IX of the ICRC "Direct Participation in Hostilities" Study: No Mandate, No Expertise, and Legally Incorrect' (2009–10) 42 New York University Journal of International Law and Politics 769 and the reply by N Melzer,

contrary to either set of norms, but to act towards them in breach of IHL could amount to a war crime and a crime under English law. Thus, in *R v Blackman*,[19] a British soldier was convicted by the court martial of murder under English law in killing a wounded insurgent. The treatment of detainees in the custody of British armed forces is discussed below.[20]

A feature of the conflicts in which the UK has been involved in since 2000 is the fact that members of organised armed groups have appeared no different in appearance from the local civilian population, who are not taking a direct part in hostilities. They do not wear a uniform or any form of a fixed distinctive sign recognisable at a distance, which makes it difficult for soldiers to know whether an individual belongs to one group or the other, particularly when faced with threats from IEDs and, from time to time, from suicide bombers. When confronted with this form of conflict the risk for soldiers of getting it wrong and killing an innocent civilian is high, and it is inevitable that mistakes will be made. They were made during the army involvement in Northern Ireland after 1969[21] and probably have been made also in Iraq and Afghanistan.[22] It is no answer for a state wishing to uphold democratic values, which include the rule of law, to argue that the fault for the inevitable mistakes lies with the insurgents who can foresee clearly that, by their wearing of ordinary civilian clothes, they are putting innocent civilians at risk of being killed or injured by state forces. The gradual acceptance by the UK courts of the application of the ECHR to bring within UK jurisdiction certain groups of civilians who have been killed, has led to the need to conduct independent investigations into each death.

The identification of those who may be targeted with lethal force may be relatively straightforward for those British servicemen who were facing armed insurgents on the ground in Iraq and in Afghanistan. The position is likely to have been more difficult for those who were carrying out air attacks, where the risks of making mistakes may be higher, particularly if it is not clear to the pilot whether a person who appears to be a civilian is as he appears, or is a person taking a direct part in hostilities at the time, or is one who has a continuous combat function (and who may therefore be targeted at any time).[23]

note 25 above at 892–912. For the link with the *Targeted Killings* case (below) see D Akande, 'Clearing the Fog of War? The ICRC's Interpretive Guidance on Direct Participation in Hostilities (2010) 59 ICLQ 180, 189.

19 *R v Blackman* [2014] EWCA Crim 1029. It seems clear that the soldier concerned knew that the wounded man was *hors de combat*, see [32]. For further discussion, see Chapter 8.

20 The obligation to provide detained or other insurgents with medical care is to be found in Geneva Convention I, 1949, Art 12 and see Chapter 8.

21 See, for example, *Farrell v Secretary of State for Defence* [1980] 1 All ER 166, [168]; *McCann v United Kingdom* (1996) 21 EHRR 97.

22 See the discussion below concerning the targeting of individuals by way of a 'drone' attack.

23 'There have been no known civilian casualties resulting from RAF weapon releases over Iraq from the RAF's first weapon release on 30 Sept 14 to early May 2015', FOI release, Ministry of Defence, week commencing 3 August 2015. See also FOI release, Ministry of Defence, week commencing 6 July 2015, which comments that 'figures for enemy combatants [*sic*]

The main practical issue is, however, the use, and the degree, of force that may be used lawfully against insurgents, which will depend on all the circumstances. Although it is argued[24] that the two basic paradigms are the conduct of hostilities and that of law enforcement, these terms tend to reflect an academic classification rather than significant boundaries of activities prohibited or permitted by law. It would have been difficult for soldiers of any state, in a situation similar to the occupation of Iraq, to be able to switch, at any one moment, from a conduct of hostilities to a peace-enforcement paradigm.[25] Their replacement by 'other troops more familiar with law enforcement [such as a] gendarmerie or a carabinieri'[26] would, in the circumstances, have not proved to have been a practical solution for the USA or the UK. Although occupying states have a duty to take those 'measures necessary to ensure, as far as possible public order and safety',[27] they were also attempting to defeat insurgent forces, a role suited primarily for combat troops. It is difficult to categorise the role of the occupation forces in Iraq as one requiring predominantly police operations, when 74 British soldiers were killed there in the years 2003–2004[28] and the occupying forces saw their role, certainly since UN Security Council Resolution 1483 (2003), as being one that involved more than maintaining the *status quo*.[29] The occupation of Iraq took place prior to the publication by the ICRC of its Interpretive Guidance and so it was the appropriate RoE, based upon an understanding of the applicable law at the time, to which soldiers and commanders were required to comply.[30] The individual threats posed to occupation forces had to dictate the degree of force used, so an attack by insurgents with rocket-propelled grenades would require a different degree of force in response from that in which a car failed to stop at a vehicle check point.[31]

It is of note that a number of the critics of the ICRC's Interpretive Guidance were those who have served in senior positions as lawyers in the armed forces of the UK, the USA and Canada and, it might be argued, that in combination

killed by RAF airstrikes have not been verified because the UK cannot visit strike sites and conduct detailed investigations on the ground'.

24 M Sassoli, 'Legislation and Maintenance of Public Order and Civil Life by Occupying Powers' (2005) 16 EJIL 661. This was published prior to the ICRC's Interpretive Guidance and the positions taken in it may have to be re-considered in the light of that Guidance.

25 Some of the difficulties are drawn out by *The Iraq Fatality Investigations: Inspector Sir George Newman, Consolidated Report into the Death of Nadheem Abdullah and the Death of Hassan Abbas Said*, Cm 9023, March 2015, [11.24], [17.12].

26 M Sassoli, 'Legislation and Maintenance of Public Order and Civil Life by Occupying Powers' (2005) 16 EJIL 661, 668.

27 Hague Regulations 1907, Art 43.

28 The statistics can be found at https://www.gov.uk/government/uploads/system/uploads/attachment_data/file/369400/20141104_UK_Armed_Forces_Operational_deaths_post_World_War_II_O.pdf.

29 See discussion in Chapter 6.

30 See Chapter 8 for the relationship between the law and the RoE, particularly on the need to change the RoE following the transition from war fighting to military occupation in Iraq.

31 These were two examples given, M Sassoli, 665–6.

they expose a structural weakness and a lack of practicality in the Guidance. This may or may not be so. Whilst lawyers may, and frequently do, argue about the detail of international law, what should not be forgotten is that for the (British) soldier engaging Taliban or other non-state forces in Iraq or in Afghanistan, his guidance will be provided by his RoE and not directly by the ICRC's Interpretive Guidance.[32] Service and government lawyers advising on the RoE will, of course, have to take into account international law, along with English law (including the effect of the Human Rights Act 1998) and they will know that, for instance, the law of murder will, in the circumstances of an armed conflict, have to be interpreted in line with IHL.[33] In addition, the context in which the engagement takes place will be of great significance;[34] one aspect of which was that British forces were operating between 2003 and 2004 while occupying territory in Iraq, which is not identical with the situation at other times in Iraq or in Afghanistan.[35]

(b) Targeting property

In modern times the risks to civilians or their property during armed conflict has increased exponentially as a result of the use of long-range field guns but, more particularly, the involvement of aircraft. After World War II customary international law began to crystallise around the idea that attacks could be made only on military objectives, which would have to be defined in some way. Additional Protocol I of 1977 defines military objectives as 'objects which by their nature, location, purpose or use make an effective contribution to military action and whose total or partial destruction, capture or neutralisation, in the circumstances ruling at the time, offers a definite military advantage'.[36] Anything else is a civilian object and must not be attacked.[37]

During an international armed conflict, a military objective is relatively easy to judge. There will always be a risk that buildings, which were at one time a military objective, will have subsequently been put to purely civilian uses. Recent examples of when mistakes of this type occurred include the bombing of the 'Amiriya

32 This is recognised by Melzer, note 17 above, at 914.
33 See the discussion on this issue in Chapter 6.
34 This is also recognised by Melzer, note 17 above, at 914.
35 See the *Public Committee Against Torture in Israel v The Government of Israel* (2005) HCJ Israel, 769/02, [40] referring to 'belligerent occupation'.
36 Article 52(2). Like the rules of engagement, the Targeting Directive is approved by ministers, ministerial statement, HC Debs 15 October 2013, vol 568, col 633W.
37 There are limitations also on certain objects, such as cultural or religious property, dams and dykes. See API, Arts 53–56, Hague Convention for the Protection of Cultural Property in the Event of Armed Conflict 1954 and its second Protocol 1999 (which the UK has not ratified). A minister stated that 'during the combat phase [in Iraq] legal advisors briefed commanders deploying to theatre about the importance of cultural property', HC Debs 7 February 2005, vol 430, col 1249W. Plans to introduce the necessary legislation to ratify the Convention were announced in HL Debs 2 July 2015, vol 763, WA p 9.

bunker' during the Gulf War in 1991[38] and the bombing of the Chinese Embassy in Belgrade in 1999.[39] In other cases it may not be clear why a particular building was considered to be a military objective. It was the bombing of the broadcasting station in Belgrade in 1999 that caused the House of Commons Foreign Affairs Committee to recommend that the 'Government set out the reasons for the attacks on broadcasting stations in order to make clear the legal justification.'[40] Where attacks are carried out by air-delivered weapons the risk of making a mistake as to the use of a particular building or the type of vehicle seen on a road will, of course, always be present although the use in Iraq and Afghanistan of unmanned aerial vehicles ('drones') with high definition camera equipment can permit close observation of a potential target and so provide the capability of reducing the risk of hitting a civilian object.

Where the armed conflict involves attacks by the armed forces of a state on insurgent vehicles, equipment or buildings that they use, the risks of making a mistake are that much greater. A house used by insurgents as a meeting place to plan their operations can, within hours or even minutes, revert to being a family home. School buildings are commonly used by rebels for their own purposes, during which time they will become a military objective and may be attacked, but those buildings will cease to be so when the rebels leave and the school re-opens.[41]

Whether some form of infrastructure is labelled as a military objective, which can therefore be attacked, will depend on the circumstances at the time. The planners will also have to take into account the risks of, and take precautions against, 'collateral damage'. International humanitarian law requires that an attack on a military objective must not be '*expected* to cause incidental loss of civilian life, damage to civilian objects, or a combination thereof, which would be excessive in relation to the concrete and direct military advantage anticipated'.[42] It involves questions of discrimination and of proportion. On the other hand, it may be less difficult to isolate objects such as 'armed pick-up trucks . . . and heavy weapon positions'[43] in the territory of Iraq controlled by ISIL for attack by coalition aircraft if these are to be found in the open with few, if any, innocent civilians in the area.

38 C Greenwood, 'Customary International Law and the First Geneva Protocol of 1977 in the Gulf Conflict' in P Rowe, (ed) *The Gulf War 1990–91 in International and English Law* (Routledge, Sweet & Maxwell, 1993), 84–5.

39 Final Report to the Prosecutor by the Committee Established to Review the NATO Bombing Campaign Against the Federal Republic of Yugoslavia, http://www.icty.org/sid/10052, [80]; House of Commons Foreign Affairs Select Committee, 4th Report, session 1999–2000, *Kosovo*, HC 28-I, [155].

40 House of Commons Foreign Affairs Select Committee, 4th Report, session 1999–2000, *Kosovo*, HC 28-I, [152].

41 See the presumption in Additional Protocol I, 1977, Art 52(3).

42 Additional Protocol I, 1977, Art 51(5)(b). See generally, W Boothby, *The Law of Targeting* (OUP, 2012), 94.

43 *ISIS: The Military Response in Iraq and Syria*, House of Commons, SN/IA/6995, 8 December 2014, [3.1].

Whilst it is often difficult to weigh in the balance a potential attack on what is believed to be a military objective against the possible loss of civilian life, or the extent of it, 'all feasible precautions' to prevent an imbalance of goals and consequences must be taken, particularly if the military objective is located within an urban area.[44] Whether all feasible measures have been taken must, of course, depend on the circumstances of the particular incident, whether based on accurate, or on genuinely believed, but inaccurate information.[45] The so-called 'fog of war' can be used, and often is, as an excuse for battlefield misbehaviour, but it is also a reality when an individual is trying to assess accurately, often at great speed, the facts of a particular situation. To some extent, the problem of inaccuracy as to the actual facts may be exacerbated by the need to seek permission from a more senior officer to open fire, who may not be on the spot, with all the risks that that involves in relaying accurately what is happening on the ground. A commander at a headquarters building who has the time to consider targeting options, and to assess the likely effect on civilians before an air attack is launched, will be in an entirely different position from one on the ground whose men are being fired on from what appear to be civilian buildings, and who calls in close air support, as in Helmand Province. Nevertheless, it is hard to imagine that any British military commander would authorise an operation in the *expectation* that the loss of life to civilians or destruction of their property would outweigh any military advantage to be gained.[46] It is much more likely that, if such loss or damage is caused, it will be the result of a weapons system malfunctioning or an unforeseen change in the circumstances at the time the weapon is used. Although the same principles apply in all armed conflicts, the risks of faulty intelligence about a military objective or the effect on innocent civilians is likely to be greater in a non-international armed conflict, largely because of the inherent difficulties of separating innocent civilians from those engaged in the fight as members of organised armed groups, or as civilians taking a direct part in the conflict.

44 Additional Protocol I, 1977, Art 57. See also the comment concerning the air campaign in Libya in 2011, 'not a single target was struck if there was any reason to believe that civilians would be injured or killed. NATO has stated that two-thirds of possible targets were not struck for that very reason and other air strikes were aborted at the last moment due to the possibility of a civilian presence . . . [although] . . . without significant resources on the ground we are not in a position to make an assessment of the number of civilian casualties', House of Commons Defence Committee, *Operations in Libya: Government Response to the Committee's Ninth Report of 2010–12*, HC 1952, [8].

45 Indeed, when the UK ratified Additional Protocol I, 1977 it entered a reservation to the effect that it understood the meaning of the term, 'feasible' as 'that which is practicable or practically possible, taking into account all circumstances ruling at the time, including humanitarian and military considerations'.

46 In its response to the House of Commons Defence Select Committee Report, 'Operations in Libya', 8 February 2012, HC 950, the government stated that 'some civilians may have been unintentionally affected by NATO action and we deeply regret any resulting loss of life or injury', 'Operations in Libya: Government Response to the Committee's Ninth Report of Session 2010–12', HC 1952, [8].

When the Afghan and Iraqi government forces were defeated in 2001 and 2003 respectively, the air campaigns had to change also to reflect the fact that the targets would be insurgents and their, often temporary, bases. Most of the fighting remained at ground level with air strikes being called in to assist groups of soldiers, who could often see from where the attacks against them were taking place. The possibility of causing collateral damage cannot be eliminated where the insurgents fire from areas in which innocent civilians live and it soon became clear that the number of their deaths was giving rise to political problems for the temporary governments in both Iraq and Afghanistan. A policy of 'counter-insurgency' operations was initiated, particularly by US armed forces in Afghanistan, in an attempt to reduce considerably the loss of life and damage to property caused by way of collateral death, injury or damage. Whether the term, 'counter-insurgency' adds any light to the existing legal framework of military operations carried out during a non-international armed conflict is discussed elsewhere.[47] The change in policy has certainly resulted in a considerable reduction in the numbers of civilians killed during the course of air strikes by ISAF forces in Afghanistan.[48]

The specific requirement to protect civilians may be the predominant reason for the carrying out of an air campaign, as it was in Libya (2011), where the object was 'to protect civilians and civilian populated areas'[49] and so it is, perhaps, no surprise to learn that 'it was necessary for UK Armed Forces to use costly precision guided weapons on some missions in order to minimise or avoid civilian casualties and collateral damage'.[50] In its response the government stated that 'our policy has been to invest in the acquisition of precision weapons over the less accurate and higher-yield ballistic weapons that previously formed the majority of our weapons inventory. Experience on operations in Iraq, Afghanistan and most recently in Libya has reinforced this decision as adversaries continue to engage friendly forces in the urban environment . . . cost is not a factor in the decision to deploy a weapon'.[51]

International humanitarian law imposes an obligation on states to investigate certain incidents, particularly if there is an indication that a breach of it has

47 See Chapters 1 and 10.

48 In 2008 the number was 552 civilian deaths; in 2009 it was 359. The United Nations Assistance Mission in Afghanistan, *Annual Report on Protection of Civilians in Armed Conflict, 2009* (2010) concludes that this reduction in numbers 'appears to be a result of the 2 July Tactical Directive that authorized the use of aerial attacks under very specific conditions', [17], http://unama.unmissions.org/Portals/UNAMA/human%20rights/Protection%20of%20Civilian%202009%20report%20English.pdf. The UN Security Council recognised 'the robust efforts taken by ISAF and other international forces to minimize the risk of civilian casualties, notably the continuous review of tactics and procedures', Resolution 1806 (2008), [13].

49 UN Security Council Resolution 1973 (2011) op [4], [6].

50 Defence Select Committee, 9th Report, session 2010–12, *Operations in Libya* HC 950, [125].

51 Government Response, HC 1952, 30 April 2012, [25].

occurred.[52] Where there is plausible evidence that an offence might have been committed, the position is relatively straightforward. For the British armed forces there is a specific duty on a commanding officer to report to the service police a Schedule 2 (of the Armed Forces Act 2006) offence, which includes genocide, crimes against humanity and war crimes.[53] Schedule 2 offences also include a wide range of offences under English criminal law, such as murder, manslaughter, wounding with intent, which could all be tried by the court martial. In addition, the service police have an obligation to investigate such offences and, if there is sufficient evidence to charge a person with a Schedule 2 offence, refer the matter to the Director of Service Prosecutions.[54] Where there is no evidence that an offence has taken place but where civilian casualties have occurred the position is less clear. Some states will, as a matter of policy, conduct fact-finding investigations in all cases, others may do so only where unintended civilian casualties have occurred. In a case where the victim(s) are within the jurisdiction of the UK for the purposes of the ECHR, there is a very clear obligation to investigate where there is evidence to suggest a person has been deprived of life or has been the subject of torture, inhuman or degrading treatment.[55] Certainly, the view of various organs of the UN is that, at least where unintended civilian casualties are caused during armed conflict states should conduct an investigation.[56] The nature of the investigation is of crucial importance also. It must be independent of the executive arm of the armed forces, be conducted on the initiative of the state itself, be promptly conducted and involve the victim or next of kin. In addition, it would

52 There is a clear obligation on states to investigate grave breaches of the Geneva Conventions 1949 and of Protocol I, 1977. Aside from grave breaches the obligation appears to be less strident, Geneva Convention III, 1949, Art 129 (para 3); Additional Protocol I, 1977, Arts 86(1), 87; Rome Statute 1998, Art 28(a)(ii) of the International Criminal Court. Some have asserted that the obligation arises only where the breach of IHL amounts to a 'war crime'. See, for example, the *Public Commission to Examine the Maritime Incident of 31 May 2010, Second Report – The Turkel Commission* (2013), [76]. This stand, however, raises the question of how 'war crimes' are defined. If these are to be defined under national law or under international law? If the latter, there may be some ambiguity if a state is not a party to the Rome Statute 1998 of the International Criminal Court.

53 These are offences under the International Criminal Court Act 2001, ss 51, 52. As the armed conflict in Afghanistan is non-international it would be difficult to show that any RAF Reaper pilot would be in breach of Art 8(2)(e) of the Rome Statute 1998 (the basis of the crimes in ss 51, 52 of the 2001 Act, along with its Elements of Crimes Regulations 2004/3239) unless he or she deliberately departed from the RoE. A soldier may also commit an offence if he fails to perform a duty, Armed Forces Act 2006, s 15, providing such a duty is imposed on him, by way of standing orders or otherwise, to report to his military superior any breaches of IHL (or English law) of which he is aware.

54 Armed Forces Act 2006, s 116. See Chapter 8 for discussion of the court-martial of members of the British armed forces.

55 These issues are discussed in Chapter 7.

56 See Report of the Special Rapporteur on the Protection of Human Rights and Fundamental Freedoms while Combating Terrorism (Ben Emmerson), A/HRC/25/59 (11 March 2014), [32]; A/68/389 (18 September 2013), [78]. Both referred to the protection of civilians during armed conflict.

be difficult to uphold the principle that a state should be accountable for its actions if the results of the investigation were not made public, in some form.[57]

iv Drones

Although the term 'drone' is in common usage to refer to armed unmanned aerial vehicles there are a wide range of these vehicles capable of performing different functions.[58] As far as the armed version is concerned the UK has operated the Reaper in Afghanistan, which is controlled by an RAF pilot remotely from the aircraft itself. It is more accurately described as a remotely piloted aircraft (RPA). Other types are unarmed but, like the RPA, have various types of camera on board and can be used for intelligence gathering, surveillance and reconnaissance.[59] Collectively, they can be referred to as unmanned aerial systems (UAS), a term, which, with that of RPA for the potentially armed vehicle, will be used in this discussion. They are not autonomous vehicles and all depend upon a trained pilot to release any munitions or a soldier to interpret the results of their various intelligence-gathering functions.[60]

Unmanned aerial systems are able to carry out the 'dull, dirty, and dangerous jobs [and] do not mind circling the skies of Afghanistan for dozens of hours'.[61] The mere use of an RPA cannot realistically be considered to be contrary to international law,[62] although, like all legitimate weapons systems used during

57 See generally, Chapter 7.

58 For a discussion of the nomenclature see *Remote Control: Remotely Piloted Air Systems-Current and Future UK Use*, Report of the House of Commons Select Committee on Defence, Session 2013–14, HC 772, written evidence from the Ministry of Defence, HC 772-II and Report, [9]–[19], where the various types are explained. See also *The Security Impact of Drones: Challenges and Opportunities for the UK*: Birmingham Policy Commission (University of Birmingham, 2014), p 22, http://www.birmingham.ac.uk/Documents/research/policycommission/remote-warfare/final-report-october-2014.pdf.

59 House of Commons Select Committee on Defence, Session 2013–14, HC 772, [20]. NATO uses the generic term, unmanned aerial vehicle (UAV), see NATO, *Unmanned Aerial Vehicles: Opportunities and Challenges for the Alliance*, Special Report, November 2012, 157 STC 12 E rev. 1 (Pierre Nolin). UNAMA uses the term UCAV (unmanned combat aerial vehicle) or UAV or drone, *Afghanistan Annual Reports* 2012, 2013.

60 The government has stated that 'current UK policy is that the operation of weapons systems will always be under human control', House of Commons Defence Select Committee, *UK Armed Forces and the Legal Framework for Future Operations*, 12th Report of session 2013–14, Government Response, HC 548, [16]. As to autonomous weapons generally, see T Krupiy, 'Of Souls, Spirits and Ghosts: Transposing the Application of the Rules of Targeting to Lethal Autonomous Robots' (2015) 16 MJIL 145.

61 Pierre Nolin Report, note 59 above, [9].

62 M E McConnell, 'The International Law of Drones', Insight, ASocIL, Vol 14, 12 November 2010. Compare Written Evidence from Public Interest lawyers to the House of Commons Select Committee on Defence, 10th report, session 2013–14, HC 772-II. In *R (Khan) v Secretary of State for Foreign and Commonwealth Affairs* [2014] 1 WLR 872, the Court of Appeal refused an application for judicial review, the effect of which would have been to decide whether an attack carried out by a US drone in Pakistan was unlawful. A review was

an armed conflict, the actual way in which they are used may show a breach of that law. The firing of a missile from a Reaper RPA against a military objective (as defined above), during the armed conflict in Afghanistan, can be contrasted with its use against a known group of innocent civilians. Their use during the course of an armed conflict is also to be contrasted with the discharge of weapons from an RPA in other situations, such as in countering terrorism, which are often described as 'extra-judicial killings',[63] or 'targeted killings', an issue discussed below.

The Reaper RPA has been flown over Afghanistan by RAF pilots located in military bases within the UK and in the USA.[64] They have also been deployed over Iraq and Syria following the vote in the House of Commons on 26 September 2014, although they are not authorised by that vote to fire weapons if flying over Syria.[65] Those who operate them have been trained as, and have considerable experience as, pilots of other RAF aircraft.[66] They are subject to the same body of international law, the same English law and the same RoE that apply to all other British armed forces aircrew.[67] Some British personnel were seconded to the US armed forces in connection with the use of their drones, but Parliament was informed that the rules of engagement by which they are bound are those applying to British armed forces members and not those of the US.[68]

carried out by the UK as required by, Additional Protocol I, 1977, Art 36, following which the use of the Reaper and Predator aerial vehicles were 'deemed permissible subject to the existing Laws of Armed Conflict', HC Debs 18 October 2013, vol 568, col 883W.

63 See generally, Report of the Special Rapporteur on Extra-Judicial, Summary or Arbitrary Executions, Philip Alston, A/HRC/14/24/ Add.6, 28 May 2010; Report of the Special Rapporteur on the Protection of Human Rights and Fundamental Freedoms while Countering Terrorism, Ben Emmerson, A/HRC/25/59, 11 March 2014. For the position taken by the EU Parliament, see its resolution 'On the Use of Armed Drones', 2014/2567 (RSP), 17 February 2014.

64 House of Commons Select Committee on Defence, 10th report, session 2013–14, HC 772, [46]–[47].

65 HC Debs 21 October 2014, vol 586, col 63W. Compare the incident of 21 August 2015 when an RAF remotely piloted aircraft attacked British subjects in Syria. For further discussion of this incident, and that of 17 November 2015, see Chapter 4. *Quaere* the legal justification for overflying the territory of another state unless there is some form of consent given to do so by the state concerned. The Secretary of State for Defence stated that the 'legal basis for this authorisation [to do so] is as set out to Parliament in the debate of 26 September [2014]', *ibid*. This legal authorisation referred to can only reflect the position as between the UK government and parliament, as to which see Chapter 4. The legal justification given by the USA for its airstrikes on Syrian territory against ISIL is set out in HC Library, Briefing paper, *ISIS/Daesh: The Military Response in Iraq and Syria* (2015), SN 06995, 20 and the reported cooperation of President Assad, *ibid*, 19, note 52. The first discharge of a weapon by a Reaper RPV in Iraq following the vote in the House of Commons on 26 September 2014, was reported in *The Times*, 11 November 2014.

66 House of Commons Select Committee on Defence, Session 2013–14, HC 772, [48].

67 House of Commons Select Committee on Defence, Session 2013–14, HC 772, [39]–[40].

68 For their secondment to the US, see HC Debs 24 April 2013, vol 561, col 906W and for the RoE, see Chapter 8.

Unmanned aerial systems have become a very prominent tool in the armoury, particularly of the USA, and have been used extensively in Afghanistan and Libya for aerial surveillance and as a platform for the firing of missiles.[69] Since the introduction of the Reaper to the RAF in 2007, some 50,000 hours have been flown on operations and they have fired 418 weapons.[70] There can be little doubt that purely surveillance UAS also have the capacity to save the lives of British soldiers and Afghan civilians, by showing the operator in real time what is happening out of his sight. They can, on occasion, detect the laying of IEDS and 'by creating a safer environment for troops to operate in, drones [*sic*] facilitate ISAF's engagement with the Afghan population, an integral part of the counter-insurgency strategy'.[71]

It is fair to say that the use of armed RPAs (drones) has received considerable unfavourable comment in the media, largely, perhaps, because of its use by the US to attack suspected terrorists in Pakistan,[72] where no international armed conflict is taking place, and the fact that no distinction is normally drawn by commentators between armed and surveillance only unmanned aerial systems, or between RPAs and possible autonomous variants.[73] A further criticism of the use of armed RPAs has been the fact that those who control them, sitting in front of screens in the UK or the USA, are immune from the risks of war themselves. That the operator of the drone is largely immune to the risks of the battlefield is not a breach of IHL by itself where that individual is a member of the armed forces of the state involved in the armed conflict, as they will be in the case of the UK.[74] It would, in practice, be difficult to draw a clear line between a soldier who fires a

69 For their role, particularly in the urban environment in Libya, see NATO (Pierre Nolan) **[n above]** [27].

70 House of Commons Select Committee on Defence, Session 2013–14, HC 772, [44].

71 NATO, *Unmanned Aerial Vehicles. Opportunities and Challenges for the Alliance*, Special Report, November 2012, 157 STC 12 E Rev.1, [24].

72 RAF Reaper attacks have taken place in Afghanistan as part of ISAF but not Pakistan, FOI, June 2014 https://www.gov.uk/government/uploads/system/uploads/attachment_data/file/322359/20140616-FOI-Reaper-Missions-In-Pakistan-2010–2013.pdf. See also HL Debs 20 November 2012, vol 740, col 1713.

73 For a view that the drone is the 'most democratic weapon ever invented', see Lord Ashdown, *The Times*, 14 February 2014, p 29.

74 Although there has been a tendency to transfer some tasks previously performed by UK armed forces personnel to civilian operators, and it would probably be cost effective to replace highly trained RAF pilots with civilians, it is very unlikely that they would be employed to fly armed RPAs during an armed conflict to which the UK was a party. Although they would not be mercenaries, since civilian RPA pilots would be UK nationals, they would, nevertheless, be classed as civilians taking a direct part in hostilities. Although the risk of these pilots being attacked as civilians taking a direct part in hostilities, or being captured, is virtually negligible, the predominant reason for not taking this course is that the UK would hardly want to be seen as a state which employs civilians, who would not be subject to service law whilst within the UK, to fire weapons during an armed conflict. A civilian will be subject fully to service law if he or she belongs to a 'specified organisation' as designated by the Secretary of State, and is located within a 'designated area' for the purposes of work for that organisation, Armed Forces Act 2006, Sched 15, [6]. It is unlikely that such a designation would take place for the purposes discussed.

weapon from a place of relative safety, from one who runs virtually the same risks as the insurgent he is attacking.

In the absence of clear evidence it is difficult to accept at face value the statement of the ICRC that, 'studies have shown that disconnecting a person, especially by means of distance (be it physical or emotional) from a potential adversary makes targeting easier and abuses more likely . . . leading to questions about the operator's ability to fully comply with [IHL]'.[75] Indeed, the House of Commons Select Committee on Defence in 2014 concluded that, being subject to the same rules of engagement as other RAF pilots flying manned aircraft, Reaper pilots 'exhibited a strong sense of connection to the life and death decisions they are sometimes required to make. This was in stark contrast to the image portrayed by some commentators of "drone" pilots as video gaming "warrior geeks".'[76] The key point is that all RAF pilots (and any other member of the armed forces) will be accountable for their actions. Their distance from the target of their attack is, in this sense, irrelevant.

The ability of the armed RPA to show the pilot what is actually happening on the ground before any missile is launched from it gives it the potential to be the ultimate in smart weapons. It may be ironic that the ability of an armed RPA to get closer, both in terms of distance and height, to an individual or a group of insurgents or other military objective, and remain there for much longer than could soldiers on the ground, or even a manned aircraft, may not necessarily result in this smart weapon being able to avoid causing unacceptable collateral damage. So, if the military purpose is to attack one or two leading insurgents, the pilot of the armed RPA may identify the individual(s) correctly, but he or she is unlikely to know how many innocent civilians will be in the house, or in a car, at which he subsequently fires the RPA's missile. If there are, for instance, two others in the car or in the house, it may be questioned whether the operator would have expected, in attacking the house or car, that the loss of those civilian lives would outweigh the military advantage of killing the insurgents.

There is a considerable amount of literature on what has become known as 'targeted killings'.[77] In the context of this book, the term is actually an oxymoron

75 ICRC, *International Humanitarian Law and the Challenges of Contemporary Armed Conflicts* (2012), 39. Whilst many would agree that humans find it easier to target an enemy combatant from a distance (certainly compared with hand-to-hand combat) it is much more difficult to accept that this distance is more likely to lead to 'abuses'. No evidence is given of the nature of the 'studies' or of their conclusions.

76 *Remote Control: Remotely Piloted Air Systems-Current and Future UK Use*, Report of the House of Commons Select Committee on Defence, Session 2013–14, HC 772-I, written evidence from the Ministry of Defence, HC 772-I, [57]. The Ministry of Defence Written Evidence to this Committee argued that the Reaper pilots could exercise their 'judgment in a more measured way, free from the stresses of the combat zone or concerns about survivability . . . [they can] see the aftermath of their attacks, a sobering experience, rarely shared by other pilots or artillerymen', [7.5].

77 See, for example, N Melzer, *Targeted Killing in International Law* (OUP, 2008); A Rogers and D McGoldrick, 'Assassination and Targeted Killing-the Killing of Osama Bin Laden' (2011) 60 ICLQ 778.

as IHL requires all killing during an armed conflict to be 'targeted', since otherwise an attack would be indiscriminate and, as such, unlawful *ab initio.* Neither can the 'targeted' part of the term mean that the object of the attack has to be a named individual. In some cases this might be so, but certainly not in all. Does this mean, therefore, that a civilian taking a direct part in hostilities (whether styled as an insurgent, terrorist or 'combatant') can be targeted by a Reaper pilot merely because of his status? If he could be shot by a British soldier on the ground and his status as a member of an organised armed group is clear, the answer would appear to be in the affirmative.[78] What difference, then, would it make if he is, instead, targeted by the Reaper pilot? Both the soldier and the pilot are subject to the same RoE. Does the UK, as with any other state, have a legal obligation at least to consider whether the insurgent could be arrested and detained before making the decision to fire? Probably all would agree with Supreme Court of Israel President (Emeritus) Barak, who stated that, 'if a terrorist taking a direct part in hostilities can be arrested, interrogated, and tried, those are the means which should be employed . . . Trial is preferable to the use of force.' He went on to consider where arrest is not possible and concluded that, 'at times the possibility does not exist whatsoever; at times it involves a risk so great to the lives of the soldiers, that it is not required . . . However, it is always a possibility which should always be considered.'[79]

Whether this principle is derived from human rights law applicable during an armed conflict, or from the requirement of proportionality under IHL, or whether it does not amount to a separate legal obligation at all, it is, in any event, a prudent basis of action, particularly for a state that prides itself on living by the rule of law.[80] The practical effect of it will, of course, vary in the circumstances. During the period of British occupation in Iraq it was possible at times to mount patrols to arrest suspected insurgents and a number were detained as explored below. In Helmand province the situation was quite different and the opportunity to arrest insurgents was often absent, without placing the lives of British soldiers in great danger. In other cases, the opportunity to arrest suspects is non-existent, as there were no British, or other NATO, combat soldiers on the ground in Libya in 2011 or in Iraq or Syria from 2014.

78 It is assumed that the member is one with a continuous combat function, see the discussion above of the ICRC Interpretive Guidance on a civilian taking a direct part in hostilities.

79 *Public Committee Against Torture in Israel v the Government of Israel*, Israel High Court of Justice, 769/02 (2005), [40]. The President referred to *McCann v United Kingdom* (1996) 21 EHRR 97, but this was a case where no armed conflict was in existence and in which the ECtHR saw the issue as a law enforcement one. See M Lesh, 'The Public Committee Against Torture in Israel v The Government of Israel. The Israeli High Court of Justice Targeted Killing Decision' (2007) 8 MJIL 373, 389, who draws attention to the lack of clarity as to with 'what crimes the accused would be charged'.

80 See A Rogers and D McGoldrick (note 77) footnote 22, who reject the view of Melzer (note 77, at 419) that 'lethal force may be used only if there is no non-lethal alternative'. Following the publication of the ICRC *Interpretive Guidance on the Notion of Direct Participation in Hostilities,* Melzer explained the possibility of a non-lethal alternative, see discussion above, note 17 above.

It may be that armed RPAs fall into a class of weapon system that require a review to be conducted every time one fires a missile, but where unintended civilian casualties occur this falls short of an independent investigation as discussed above. An example is the incident of 25 March 2011, when an RAF Reaper missile caused the deaths of four innocent civilians, resulting in an ISAF investigation to determine whether any lessons could be learned from it.[81] In drawing attention to this incident the House of Commons Defence Select Committee concluded that, 'whilst the public do not need to know every time weapons are released they do need to feel confident that that the rules of engagement are applied and followed consistently'.[82] It did not suggest how the confidence of the public could be secured. In practical terms, this confidence will be difficult to achieve in the absence of independent reports, which could explore the issue of accountability, whether of individuals or by way of systems failings. It was, no doubt, for this reason that a call has been made for the UK 'to declassify and publish the results of the investigation report (and any other report relating to the infliction of civilian casualties through the use of remotely piloted aircraft by the United Kingdom in Afghanistan)'.[83]

There can be no doubt that RPAs and all forms of UAS are not going to disappear from the inventory of those states that possess them, and that they will play an increasingly significant role in future armed conflicts. Although they may enable British forces to reduce civilian deaths and other collateral damage, and they may also protect the lives of soldiers, there is a risk that their widespread use could reduce the barriers to taking military action in the first place.[84] The view of the House of Commons Select Committee on Defence (2014) was that, 'it is important in maintaining the public acceptability of remotely piloted air systems that the perception cannot be allowed to develop that their increased use has in

81 Ministry of Defence in its Written Evidence to *Remote Control: Remotely Piloted Air Systems-Current and Future UK Use*, Report of the House of Commons Select Committee on Defence, Session 2013–14, HC 772, [63] written evidence from the Ministry of Defence, [4.3] referred to the incident of 25 March 2011 where two insurgents and four Afghan innocent civilians had been killed. This incident is also referred to in the Report of the Special Rapporteur on the Promotion and Protection of Human Rights and Fundamental Freedoms while Countering Terrorism, A/HRC/25/59, 11 March 2014, [39], who describes the incident and states that two combatants and four non-combatants had been killed, along with a further two non-combatants who received serious injuries. The different labels adopted by the UK Ministry of Defence and the Special Rapporteur, 'insurgents' and 'civilians' compared with 'combatants' and 'non-combatants' are worthy of note. For further discussion on this issue see Chapter 1.

82 House of Commons Select Committee on Defence, 10th Report, Session 2013–14, 'Remote Control: Remotely Piloted Air Systems-Current and Future UK Use', HC 772, [66].

83 Report of the Special Rapporteur on the Protection of Human Rights and Fundamental Freedoms while Combating Terrorism (Ben Emmerson), A/HRC/25/59 (11 March 2014), [39]. The government has stated that 'we do not publish these reports for reasons of operational security', Government Response to *Remote Control: Remotely Piloted Air Systems-Current and Future UK Use*, HC 772 at HC 611 (2014), [24].

84 This would be an even greater risk if an autonomous version of a UAS is brought into service, which by its very nature, could not be a RPA.

some way reduced the threshold for military intervention'.[85] The Defence Committee was concerned only with what have been called 'discretionary wars' where the UK mainland has not been threatened with, or has not actually become subject to, an armed attack from another state. If that state possessed advanced forms of RPA, its threshold for military intervention may be lowered sufficiently to threaten or to carry out an attack on the British mainland or on a dependent territory or on another NATO state. One response to this possibility would be to engage with disarmament issues for armed RPAs and ban the development, production or use of fully autonomous UAS vehicles.[86] It is more likely that the UK would be attracted to the second of these two possibilities through support for a possible treaty to ban the development, production, transfer or use of fully autonomous armed aerial vehicles.[87]

v Detaining foreign nationals

Whether the detention of civilians in Iraq was consistent with the ECHR has been discussed in Chapter 7, and it is now proposed to consider the difficulties over classification of those detained by UK armed forces, the effect of ministerial approval for detention in Afghanistan beyond a period of 96 hours, and the practical difficulties faced by the armed forces over the legal regime applying to the detention of civilians during the course of an armed conflict.

The term, 'detainee', used during an armed conflict, is not one with a precise legal meaning. It could mean any person physically detained by state authorities or even by non-state actors, irrespective of the circumstances of the detention. Although those entitled to prisoner of war status under Geneva Convention III, 1949[88] and those interned by virtue of Geneva Convention IV, 1949[89] are physically detained, the justifications for, and the treatment to which each group is

85 Session 2013–14, HC 772, [137]. For the Government Response to this Report see HC 611, [17]. The threshold for military intervention is discussed in Chapter 2.

86 See the Resolution of the European Parliament, On the Use of Armed Drones', 2014/2567 (RSP), 17 February 2014, [2(c)] and [2(d)].

87 This could be achieved by a specific treaty or by an additional protocol to the Conventional Weapons Convention 1980. This Convention became the vehicle for the banning of blinding laser weapons (Protocol IV, 1995). These weapons were banned before they had come into use in an armed conflict.

88 The practice of the UK was to register an individual captured in Iraq, whose status was unclear, as a prisoner of war, *Hassan v United Kingdom*, Application No 29750/09, Grand Chamber Judgment, 16 September 2014, [21]. During the war-fighting stage of the armed conflict in Iraq, tribunals envisaged by Geneva Convention III, 1949, Art 5, were established by the UK armed forces to determine whether detained individuals were entitled to the status of prisoner of war, see Report of the Baha Mousa Inquiry, vol II, 716, [8.72] and for the issue of whether the ECHR applied to these tribunals, vol II, 667, [7.96]; N Mercer in C Harvey, J Summers, N White (eds), *Contemporary Challenges to the Laws of War* (CUP, 2014), 149. There was no legal reason why these tribunals could not be relevant during the period of occupation; compare Report of the Baha Mousa Inquiry, vol 1, 21, [1.106].

89 The classification of the two applicants in *Al-Saadoon and Mufdhi v United Kingdom* [2010] 51 EHRR 9, [46] as 'security internees' until May 2006, nearly two years after Geneva

entitled, are different from those detained on some other legal basis. The latter group has been distinguished from the former groups in the eyes of the UK government, which referred to 'detainees' as those who are suspected of committing a crime against the local law of Iraq.[90] In Afghanistan, since the Bonn Agreement of December 2001, there could be no entitlement to prisoners of war status, nor as internees, as that armed conflict has been of a non-international character. This terminology has not been applied uniformly, however, due largely to the fact that the UK armed forces have adopted another, 'captured persons' (CPERS),[91] and the US military authorities yet others, such as 'unlawful enemy combatants',[92] or 'enemy prisoner of war'.[93] It may be that adopting a uniform term where armed forces are acting in coalition will never be easy in relation to those who are, in effect, civilians taking an active part in hostilities.[94] The classification of those who are detained during an armed conflict[95] is not a discretionary matter. It is vitally important that a person receives the appropriate legal classification of his status in order that the correct legal regimes[96] are applied to him or her in terms of the length of the detention, treatment, liability to stand trial and so on. Where there is uncertainty amongst those who run the detention facilities, about the appropriate legal regime to apply to those in their charge, it is more likely that ill-treatment of them will take place. As a general statement, it seems fair to conclude that recent practice, stretching at least back to the Falklands war in 1982, shows that the treatment of those entitled to prisoner of war status under Geneva Convention III, 1949,[97] or as internees under Geneva Convention IV,[98]

Convention IV, 1949 ceased to apply (at the end of the period of occupation), was based on UN Security Council Resolution 1546 (2004), which authorised internment for 'imperative reasons of security', annexed letter from the US Secretary of State, of 5 June 2004.

90 HL Debs 8 June 2004, vol 662, col 26W. Once the occupation of Iraq ended on 28 June 2004 anyone detained by UK armed forces subsequently was required, under Geneva Conventions III or IV, to be classified as someone other than a prisoner of war or internee since there was no longer an international armed conflict taking place.

91 Reference to this term by the armed forces is made in *Hussein v Secretary of State for Defence* [2014] EWCA Civ 1087, [13]–[14] and it was also referred to by the Secretary of State for Defence, HC Debs 12 March 2015, vol 594, col 22WS.

92 Referred to in Foreign Affairs Committee, 2nd Report, session 2006–07, *Visit to Guantanamo Bay*, HC 44, [77].

93 *Hassan v United Kingdom*, Application No 29750/09, Grand Chamber Judgment, 16 September 2014, [19].

94 For civilians taking an active part in hostilities see above.

95 As contrasted with a situation which does not amount to an armed conflict and may be seen as terrorism.

96 In the case of the UK these would include one or more parts of the Geneva Conventions 1949 and other aspects of IHL, the ECHR and English law.

97 The comparison is not, however, an exact one since prisoners of war will not be liable for crimes against the national law of the state concerned, see Chapter 6.

98 During the period of the occupation in Iraq, internees were entitled under Geneva Convention IV, 1949 to make complaints concerning the conditions of their internment as envisaged by Art 101. This could include complaints made directly to the ICRC. It was confirmed that this obligation on the UK had operated in practice towards its 'security internees', HC Debs 30 June 2005, vol 435, col 1690W. For the role of the ICRC see Chapter 6.

with their detailed rules as to treatment, have fared better than those who do not qualify for this status, either because they were 'security internees' in Iraq held by virtue of the authorisation to intern given by UN Security Council Resolution 1546 (2004),[99] or as 'criminal detainees'.

Given the need to arrest and detain individuals suspected of being involved in the attack on British soldiers, or even of ordinary crimes, it became obvious that some legal power to do this would be necessary. The unpalatable alternative would have been to kill suspects or to let them go.[100] Unlike a statutory power given to soldiers to arrest civilians for short periods of time in Northern Ireland,[101] no similar legislative power to arrest and detain was given by the UK Parliament to British soldiers in Iraq or Afghanistan.[102] In relation to Afghanistan, NATO did permit ISAF to arrest and detain an individual for a maximum period of 96 hours.[103] This was, however, consistent with the maximum period of detention that a judge advocate can permit of a British soldier, who had been arrested by the service police,[104] and thus under the ECHR, which applied to anyone arrested by British armed forces. It would appear that detention of civilians by UK armed forces, acting as part of ISAF in Afghanistan, could only be authorised for a longer period than 96 hours by government ministers.[105] Although the power to do was stated as being limited to cases of 'exceptional circumstances or *in extremis*', it was authorised on 845 occasions between November 2009 and December 2014.[106]

It is difficult to see how this arrangement had any objective legal basis. This is not to suggest that military operations in Iraq (after the period of occupation) and

99 With the end of the occupation of Iraq declared by this Resolution, the application of Geneva Convention IV, 1949, specifically those parts relating to internment, would also have come to an end.

100 M Sassoli referred to the risk, in the absence of a policy of detaining suspects, that these individuals could become 'disguised battlefield casualties', 'The International Legal Framework for Stability Operations: When may International Forces Attack or Detain Someone in Afghanistan' (2009) 39 Israeli Year Book on Human Rights 177, 201.

101 The Northern Ireland (Emergency Provisions) Act 1973, s 12 gave a limited power to members of the armed forces to arrest and by s 13 a power to search a dwelling house.

102 Compare the position of US armed forces, *Mohammed v Secretary of State for Defence* [2015] EWCA Civ 843, [10].

103 Ministerial Meeting of North Atlantic Council, NATO, 8 November 2005. Ministers in the UK Parliament referred to this as the 'NATO Guidelines', HC Debs 9 November 2009, vol 499, col 5WS.

104 Armed Forces Act 2006, s 101(4), which is consistent with the ECHR, Art 5(3).

105 HC Debs 9 November 2009, vol 499, col 5WS. The process of authorisation is set out in SOI J3–9, *Stop, Search, Question and Detention Operations in the Operation Herrick JOA* (Ministry of Defence), see J3–9–2–13, [51]; J3–9–2–15. This document was referred to in *Mohammed v Secretary of State for Defence* [2015] EWCA Civ 843 and is available at FOI, Ministry of Defence, release 10 August 2015. The criteria for 'extended detention' were set by the National Security Council, J-3–9–2–13, [51].

106 The limited nature of the power is discussed in *Mohammed v Secretary of State for Defence* [2015] EWCA Civ 843, [153(vii)]. Between 9 November 2009 and 16 December 2014, this 'extended detention' occurred in 845 cases, see FOI Ministry of Defence, release 10 August 2015.

in Afghanistan should have been directed by lawyers, but it is important, as the cases before the High Court in London show, that the British government and its armed forces conduct their activities in accordance with the rule of law, which they clearly seek to do. Those on the ground need to be able to rely upon the lawfulness of the policies they are to apply as directed by their most senior commanders, who are, in turn, guided by relevant government ministers applying sound legal advice. When it comes to detaining insurgents who did not qualify as prisoners of war, the lawfulness (or otherwise) of that detention is clearly a key issue.

There was no equivalent to the NATO decision when British soldiers arrested and detained civilians in Iraq for similar reasons, although UNSCR 1546 (2004) appeared to authorise internment for imperative reasons of security.[107] The difference between Iraq and Afghanistan was summed up by Richards LJ in *R (Maya Evans) v Secretary of State for Defence* (2010) who stated that, 'the Secretary of State takes the view that the UK has no power [in Afghanistan] of indefinite internment'.[108] The following year the ECtHR decided that the power to intern, given by UNSCR 1546 (2004), had to be applied in a way consistent with the UK's obligations under the ECHR, given that it had made no derogation from Article 5 of it.[109]

In *Mohammed v Secretary of State for Defence*,[110] the Court of Appeal decided that, despite ministerial approval, the detention of the claimant, alleged to be a Taliban commander, by British armed forces in Afghanistan beyond the 96 hours NATO detention policy, but with ministerial approval, was unlawful, despite the fact that Afghanistan had requested the UK to retain him due to overcrowding within its criminal justice system.

Could an agreed policy adopted by NATO of holding for a maximum period of 96 hours an individual captured in Afghanistan provide the necessary ground of lawfulness? It is not clear whether this was a policy decision, or one based on an interpretation by the ECtHR of the meaning of 'brought promptly before a judge' in Article 5 of the ECHR.[111] A basis for it could be argued to be one derived from UN Security Council Resolution 1890 (2009), which authorised states, participating in ISAF, to take 'all necessary measures to fulfil its mandate'.[112] Assuming that a power to detain anyone who threatened the security of ISAF forces could be implied from this resolution, which is not an unreasonable interpretation of it, the question then arises whether UNSCR 1890 was an essential pre-requisite for any detention to be lawful or whether it was merely a 'belt

107 Operative [11] and annexed letters.
108 [2010] EWHC 1445 (Admin), [17].
109 *Al-Jedda v United Kingdom* (2011) 53 EHRR 23.
110 [2015] EWCA Civ 843. See discussion in Chapter 7.
111 Parties to ISAF include states, such as Australia and New Zealand, which are not members of NATO.
112 Operative [2]. This was the basis of the decision in *Mohammed v Secretary of State for Defence* [2015] EWCA Civ 843, [138]–[157], which attached the authorisation to ISAF and not to the UK as one of the participating states.

and braces' measure, convenient, but not essential, to have. This is not merely a theoretical question since it is not unforeseeable that UK ground forces could be involved, at some time in the future, in the territory of another state, which has invited the UK to assist it to defeat insurgents, in circumstances where no UN Security Council resolution is in place. It is entirely possible that, in a SOFA or a MoU, the UK and the territorial state could agree a maximum period after which UK armed forces would have to transfer or release its detainees. Of course, if the legal authority to detain is based upon the agreement of the territorial state, there would be another issue that the UK would have to take into account, both as a holding and a transferring state, that of Article 5 of the ECHR, a matter discussed below, and in Chapter 7.

The presence of UK armed forces in Afghanistan was based upon the agreement of the government of that state and not solely on a UN Security Council resolution,[113] and so any legal 'authorisation' of a policy of detention cannot depend for its legality on ISAF, which has derived its authority from UN Security Council resolutions. No doubt the NATO detention policy made sound political sense for those states acting together as part of ISAF, but NATO cannot be said to possess law-making powers affecting the inhabitants of non-NATO States. Even if UN Security Council Resolution 1890 (2009) determined the lawfulness of detention for a maximum period of 96 hours, the further issue arises of whether the resolution had been implemented into the national law of Afghanistan, or of the UK. It had certainly not been implemented into English law so as to create a ground for arrest, let alone detention for up to 96 hours, nor had it been implemented into the law of Afghanistan.[114]

Even if it is accepted that the NATO policy, in some form or other, provided sufficient legal cover for the arrest and detention of civilians in Afghanistan by British soldiers for up to 96 hours, what of the decisions by UK government ministers to authorise detention for a longer period? Could the lawfulness of this action be based upon Resolution 1890 (2009), since it was outwith the NATO agreed policy? In this context the difficulty is that such a policy would appear to be unlawful, as being contrary to the right not to be subject to arbitrary detention, as set out in the Human Rights Act 1998, applicable to the individual held in British military custody, as well as to the government minister sitting in London. It must be the case that a UNSCR could not be interpreted in such a way as to provide legal cover when the effect on an individual would be to infringe a right given to him by the state concerned, in this case, the UK?[115]

113 The establishment of ISAF was authorised by UNSCR 1386 (2001), following the Bonn Agreement, S/2001/1154. The UK offered to act as the lead nation for an initial period, see S/2001/1217.

114 In *Mohammed v Secretary of State for Defence* [2015] EWCA Civ 843, [301] the court concluded that '[in] English law, detaining someone is *prima facie* the tort of imprisonment', see also [130(ii), (iii)].

115 See, for example, the view of the ECtHR in *Al-Jedda v United Kingdom* (2011) 53 EHRR 23 concerning the interpretation of UNSCR 1546 (2004).

The practical problems thrown up by the detention of civilians during any non-international armed conflict are considerable.[116] If British soldiers capture an individual, they will only be able to hold him for 96 hours, and it must be asked whether this process can serve any meaningful purpose, particularly if a hardened insurgent is unlikely to answer the questions asked of him without the soldiers infringing the current interpretations of Article 3 of the ECHR?[117]

What could the UK do to try and ensure that it would not be acting unlawfully in this type of situation? To issue a notice of derogation, even if this were to prove valid under Article 15 of the ECHR, is unlikely to prove a tempting option for government ministers for the reasons discussed in Chapter 7. To create its own 'legal system' in the territory of the state that it is assisting, including a legal power to arrest and to detain, detention facilities, independent judges, courts and so on, would be likely to prove even more unattractive to ministers, and is unlikely to win the support of the territorial state.[118] To bring insurgents within the discipline system, set out in the Armed Forces Act 2006,[119] *as if* they were prisoners of war would, in theory, enable them to be tried for crimes committed prior to capture,[120] but the jurisdictional and practical problems involved would be considerable and would require Parliament to pass primary legislation.[121] There seems to be little alternative but to continue with the process of trying to ensure that the legal system within a host state is such that captured insurgents can be transferred within the limited period permitted under the ECHR and within the terms of the rights granted by that Convention to those who come within the jurisdiction of the UK. The inevitable consequence of the legal system of the host state being of such a standard that the UK is unable to transfer its detainees to it, is that it will have to continue the detention of individuals knowing that such action will be judged to be unlawful and that a claim against it, based upon the Human Rights Act 1998, could be waiting in the wings.

116 See *Al-Saadoon v Secretary of State for Defence* [2015] EWHC 715, [106]–[107].

117 Parliament was informed that 'many insurgents are aware of the 96 hours policy and simply say nothing for that entire period', HC Debs 9 November 2009, vol 499, col 5WS. For the treatment of detainees see below.

118 Even if the territorial state considered this a viable option it would need to agree that the UK be granted the legal powers under its legal system to arrest on the one hand and to detain on the other. Were this to occur the UK could then acquire these powers through its legislative processes and remain liable on an exclusive jurisdictional basis for the acts of British soldiers. In this way the acts of British soldiers would be lawful under English law, a prerequisite for detention under the ECHR, Art 5.

119 See also Armed Forces Act 2011, s 23(1), inserting s 371A into the Armed Forces Act 2006. Such a proposal would, however, raise a sensitive issue, that of the trial of a foreign civilian by a military court.

120 See Geneva Convention III, 1949, Art 85.

121 See, for example, the difficulties faced by the USA in the trial by military commission of those individuals captured in Afghanistan but tried in Guantanamo Bay, *Al Nashiri v Poland* (2015) 60 EHRR 16, [566]. The ECtHR referred to *Hamdan v Rumsfeldt* (2006) 548 US 557, which also decided that the Uniform Code of Military Justice had not been complied with by the procedure established to try non-US nationals by military commission.

vi The transfer of detainees

When a conflict is of a non-international character, as it was for long periods in Iraq and Afghanistan, the UK released those who, in its judgment, would not place the lives of its soldiers, or the local population, in further harm. A small number of detainees were, however, suspected of planting IEDs,[122] or otherwise killing British soldiers,[123] and without any means of placing them on trial itself, it sought to transfer them to the local criminal justice system for eventual trial. In developing a policy on the transfer of such detainees, the UK had to take note of the fact that, as its armed forces were on the territory of Iraq and Afghanistan with the consent of the territorial state concerned, the wishes of those states had to be taken into account,[124] along with its own desire that, following any transfer, those individuals would not be subjected to torture, inhuman or degrading treatment and would receive a fair trial.[125]

To enable the transfer of individuals detained by its armed forces the UK government entered into a separate Memorandum of Understanding (MoU) with Iraq and Afghanistan in 2004 and 2006 respectively.[126] Similarly, arrangements

122 See *Ismail v Secretary of State for Defence* [2013] EWHC 3032 (Admin), [1], or were suspected of possessing information about the production of IEDs, see *Mohammed v Secretary of State for Defence* [2015] EWCA Civ 843, [43(vi)].

123 *Al-Saadoon v United Kingdom* [2010] 51 EHRR 9, in which it was alleged that the applicants had been involved in the deaths of British soldiers, who should have been treated as prisoners of war, during the course of the international armed conflict.

124 See, for example, the information given to the court that 'the inability of the Secretary of State to transfer detainees was causing political difficulties with the Government of Afghanistan', *Ismail v Secretary of State for Defence* [2013] EWHC 3032 (Admin), [11].

125 Although Geneva Convention III, 1949 did not apply to these detainees, Art 12 does illustrate, by way of an analogy, that a state which transfers prisoners of war to another state does have continuing obligations to those transferred. *Quaere*, however, whether there is a continuing *legal* obligation towards transferred civilian detainees. The view of the Ministry of Defence was that there was no such obligation, see Foreign Affairs Committee, Minutes of Evidence: Iraq and Afghanistan, session 2007–08, HC 1145-i, Supplementary Memorandum from the Ministry of Defence, 17 November 2008. There would have been a legal obligation arising from the Memorandum of Understanding signed with Iraq and Afghanistan respectively, see note 126 below. The UK government also took the view that the transfer of detainees from its custody in Iraq or in Afghanistan did not give rise to the application of the Convention Against Torture and other Cruel, Inhuman or Degrading Treatment or Punishment, 1984, Art 3, since there was no transfer to another state, Response by the United Kingdom to the Recommendations by the United Nations Committee Against Torture following its Examination of the United Kingdom's 4th Periodical Report on 17 and 18 November 2004, Written Evidence to the Joint Committee on Human Rights, 19th Report, session 2005–06, *The UN Convention Against Torture (UNCAT)*, HL 185-II, HC 701-II, EV 68, [14]. For the transfer among US, UK and Australian forces, see HC Debs 8 June 2004, vol 422, col 293W.

126 HC Debs 26 February 2009, vol 488, col 394 (Secretary of State for Defence).The Memorandum of Understanding with Iraq in November 2004 was published by the Foreign Affairs Committee, Minutes of Evidence: Iraq and Afghanistan, session 2007–08, HC 1145-i and is set out in http://www.publications.parliament.uk/pa/cm200708/

for the transfer of detainees between the UK and the US and Australia were also agreed.[127] None of these states was, of course, a party to the ECHR but the UK could not avoid its obligations under the ECHR, especially as it had accepted at an early stage[128] that detainees in Iraq did come within the jurisdiction of the UK, certainly for the purpose of Articles 2 and 3 of the ECHR. Where there was a real risk that the transfer of a detainee from UK authorities to those of any other state, despite the assurances[129] of proper treatment set out in the MoU, might result in a breach of one or both of these articles, any transfer would amount to a breach of the ECHR and the Human Rights Act 1998. In the case of a transfer to the Afghan authorities, the UK has adopted the same basic principles, since it has challenged the applicability of the ECHR to its operations in Afghanistan.[130] The principle was tested in *R (Maya Evans) v Secretary of State for Defence* (2010),[131] which prohibited a number of transfers to certain detention facilities in Afghanistan and which led to a moratorium on further transfers.[132] In one case, however, the UK did transfer two Iraqi citizens to the Iraq authorities in breach of an interim measure imposed by the ECtHR, on the ground that it had no legal power to continue their detention after 31 December 2008,[133] when

cmselect/cmfaff/1145/8102807.htm. For the terms of the Memorandum of Understanding with Afghanistan, see *R (Maya Evans) v Secretary of State for Defence* [2010] EWHC 1445, [95]–[98] and for the Exchange of Letters, involving Canada, UK, Netherlands, Australia, Denmark, on the one hand and Afghanistan on the other, see [105]–[108].

127 Memorandum of Understanding, *ibid.* The agreement with the USA also included a provision that 'no person captured with UK assistance will be removed from the territory of Iraq without prior consultation with the United Kingdom.' It is likely that the UK government's main concern would have been if any of these individuals was transferred to Guantanamo Bay.

128 See Chapter 7.

129 The MoU are, in effect, a form of assurance that transferees will be treated in accordance with its terms. As to the propriety of seeking and receiving assurances from a receiving state see *Othman v United Kingdom* [2012] 55 EHRR 1, [187], [193].

130 The applicability of the ECHR to Afghanistan was challenged by the UK in *Serdar Mohammed v Secretary of State for Defence* [2014] EWHC 1369 (Admin), and on appeal in *Mohammed v Secretary of State for Defence* [2015] EWCA Civ 843. The government's long-standing policy is that the ECHR has no applicability to its operations in Afghanistan, Foreign Affairs Committee, 12 Report, *UK Armed Forces Personnel and the Legal Framework of Future Operations*, 2013–14, HC 931 (2014), written evidence submitted by the Ministry of Defence; government Response, 3rd Special Report, 2014–15, HC 548, [1].

131 [2010] EWHC 1445. Subsequently, UK detainees could only be transferred to approved Afghan detention facilities and 'Ministers may impose temporary bans on transfers to facilities if allegations of mistreatment are received from former detainees', SOI J3–9, *Stop, Search, Question and Detention Operations in the Operation Herrick JOA* (Ministry of Defence), J-3–9–2–16.

132 See HC Debs 28 June 2010, vol 512, col 23WS; *Ismail v Secretary of State for Defence* [2013] EWHC 3032 (Admin), [4]–[10]. The difficulties arising from this decision are considered in *Mohammed v Secretary of State for Defence* [2015] EWCA Civ 843, [153].

133 HL Debs 26 January 2009, vol 707, col WA11. The Court of Appeal had found there to be no legitimate reasons to prohibit the UK government transferring the appellants,

the UN mandate relating to the MNF in Iraq came to an end.[134] The ECtHR decided that it was 'not open to a Contracting State to enter into an agreement with another State which conflicts with its obligations under the Convention',[135] and that the UK was in breach of Article 3 of the ECHR since there was a real risk that the applicants would be caused psychological suffering through the risk of being sentenced to the death penalty if convicted by an Iraqi court.[136]

The UK was faced with the problem of wishing to transfer detainees to the Afghan authorities but being unable to do either because of the risks of torture, inhuman or degrading treatment that a detainee might face, or through a request by the Afghan government to continue the detention of a particular individual for logistical reasons.[137] Protection of the first group could be achieved through transfers to particular detention facilities, along with an acceptance by the receiving state that the sending state could subsequently inspect the facilities and interview transferred detainees. Extended detention of the second group, the 'logistical detainees', will cause greater problems to the detaining state. It might feel uncomfortable about transferring them to a coalition partner, not a member state of the ECHR, until the territorial state is able to receive them.

vii The treatment of detainees by UK armed forces

It is always likely to be important for military forces operating during a non-international armed conflict to 'arrest' suspected insurgents, and to detain them for questioning, if only to find out from them the location of arms, ammunition and other war-like equipment. In the case of those detained by UK armed forces, the form in which this questioning occurred, and the treatment of these detainees held on various military bases, has been subjected to considerable judicial analysis.

R (Al-Saadoon and Mufdhi) v Secretary of State for Defence [2009] EWCA Civ 7. On the day following this judgment, 31 December 2008, the government transferred the appellants to the Iraqi High Tribunal. Further leave to appeal to the House of Lords had been refused.

134 See UN Security Council Resolution 1790 (2007). The initial authorisation was given by UN Security Council Resolution 1511 (2003), which was renewed periodically.

135 *Al-Saadoon and Mufdhi v United Kingdom* [2010] 51 EHRR 9, [138]. Compare the view of the Court of Appeal in *R (Al-Saadoon and Mufdhi) v Secretary of State for Defence* [2009] EWCA Civ 7, [51]. This is a significant principle when a Memorandum of Understanding between the UK and the territorial state concerned is thought to be necessary. The Memorandum of Understanding with Iraq in 2004 was published by the Foreign Affairs Committee, Minutes of Evidence: Iraq and Afghanistan, session 2007–08, HC 1145-i and is set out in http://www.publications.parliament.uk/pa/cm200708/cmselect/cmfaff/1145/8102807.htm.

136 *Al-Saadoon and Mufdhi v United Kingdom* [2010] 51 EHRR 9, [144]–[145].

137 It was styled as 'logistical detention' in *Mohammed v Secretary of State for Defence* [2015] EWCA Civ 843, [43(x)]. See also SOI J3-9, *Stop, Search, Question and Detention Operations in the Operation Herrick JOA* (Ministry of Defence), [8].

It is probably fair to say that the actual practice of UK armed forces when questioning suspects[138] has, as a result, altered considerably since the investigations and subsequent proceedings following the death of Baha Mousa on 15 September 2003, while in British custody in Iraq. It would, for instance, be much less likely now for suspects to be hooded, put into stress positions and be subjected to violence, although earlier instances are still working their way through these various accountability mechanisms. The practice of harsh questioning, whereby the questioner deliberately displayed anger, could include the use of indirect threats to instil fear,[139] and it was replaced by 'challenge direct' following the Report of the Baha Mousa Inquiry (2011). This new policy was considered not to infringe the requirement of humane conduct in Common Article 3 to the Geneva Conventions 1949.[140]

The fact that these very significant changes in the way in which the UK armed forces treat in custody those whom they have captured have come about not, generally,[141] from initiatives within the armed forces but, largely as a result of claims brought by Iraqi or Afghan civilians based on the Human Rights Act 1998, or at common law, a significant number of which were heard in the High Court in London. It is interesting to speculate whether the treatment of suspects held in British custody would have been any different had the 1998 Act not been in existence, or if it had been interpreted as applying only to acts of public bodies within the UK.[142] Even if the ECHR had been interpreted, as it subsequently was, to apply extra-territorially to the activities of the UK armed forces in Iraq and in Afghanistan, a claim brought in Strasbourg, would have been unlikely to have had the same immediate effect on the British armed forces as one brought in London. This is not because of any superiority of one system over another but simply as a matter of practical reality, in terms of the number of claims that could be brought covering a wide range of issues, along with the speed of decision making and of the implementation of English court rulings.[143] A few significant

138 Questioning, which occurs soon after capture, should be distinguished from interrogation that is carried out by trained service interrogators in premises approved for that purpose, see ministerial statements, HC Debs 8 September 2011, vol 532, col 580; HC Debs 17 December 2014, vol 589, col 1419.

139 Report of the Baha Mousa Inquiry, vol III, 1334, [317]. The recommendation concerning tactical questioning was not accepted by the government (although it has become 'challenge direct'), HC Debs 8 September 2011, vol 532, col 571; HC Debs 27 March 2014, vol 578, col 32WS.

140 *R (Hussein) v Secretary of State for Defence* [2014] EWCA Civ 1087, [60]. Between 1 August 2011 and 28 February 2014 'challenge direct was authorised for use on 60 occasions and used on 15 occasions', [56].

141 Compare the influence of service lawyers, Report of the Baha Mousa Inquiry, vol III, 1342, [375], 1347, [404] and see Chapter 8.

142 Lord Bingham, *Al-Skeini v Secretary of State for Defence* [2007] UKHL 26, was in the minority in deciding that the Human Rights Act 1998 applied only within the UK, save for Scotland, which has its own Act.

143 As a matter of judicial precedent, the English courts will be bound by the rulings of the English superior courts, even if they are inconsistent with subsequent decisions of

cases did reach the ECtHR,[144] which took a more expansive view on the issues raised within them than had the courts in London and so the corpus of judicial interpretation of the relevant law has been contributed to by both systems.[145]

Those who are detained by UK armed forces abroad can reasonably expect to be informed of the grounds for their detention, to regular reviews by some form of independent objective body to determine whether their continued detention can be justified, and to make their grievances known.[146] The use of torture or inhumane treatment is absolutely prohibited by IHL,[147] let alone by human rights treaties, and torture is a criminal offence under English law wherever it is committed and whoever commits it.[148] What of the employment of any of the five prohibited techniques of wall-standing, hooding, loud noise, sleep deprivation or deprivation of food and drink as a means of trying to secure information from a detainee?[149] The difficulty for a soldier, his superior officers and even those who have been trained in tactical interrogation of detainees, has been to determine at the time which, if any, of these techniques was permitted, and in what circumstances.

The practice of hooding had been used on occasions in Iraq, but whether it was illegal to do so, or only so in certain circumstances, did not seem to be clear at the time.[150] Indeed, the Report of the Baha Mousa Inquiry concluded

the ECtHR, see discussion *Mohammed v Secretary of State for Defence* [2015] EWCA Civ 843, [93], concerning the decision of the Supreme Court in *Smith v Ministry of Defence* [2013] UKSC 41, and its misgivings over the decision of the ECtHR in *Al-Skeini v United Kingdom* (2011) 53 EHRR 18.

144 See Chapter 7.

145 Each system considers the law of the other. The courts in England may also be called upon to interpret IHL, see, for example, *Hussein v Secretary of State for Defence* [2014] EWCA Civ 1087, [37]–[60].

146 See *Mohammed v Secretary of State for Defence* [2015] EWCA Civ 843, [254], which considered 'procedural safeguards'. For regular reviews, see HC Debs 14 March 2005, vol 432, col 89W (in relation to Iraq); *Hassan v United Kingdom*, Application No 29750/09, Grand Chamber Judgment, 16 September 2014, [26]. *Quaere* whether the system of review was able to provide 'sufficient guarantees of independence and fair procedures to protect against arbitrariness', *Hassan v United Kingdom* [106]. For the position relating to Afghanistan, see HC Debs 9 November 2009, vol 499, col 5WS, which referred to 'monitoring by in-theatre military commanders and civilian advisers', although compare *Mohammed v Secretary of State for Defence* [2015] EWCA Civ 843, [285]–[290]. See generally, discussion in Chapter 7.

147 Geneva Conventions 1949, I, Art 12, II, Art 12, III, Arts 13, 87, IV, Arts 27, 32; common Art 3 and APII, Art 4, in the case of a non-international armed conflict. It is prohibited generally by the Convention Against Torture and other Cruel, Inhuman or Degrading Treatment or Punishment, 1984.

148 Criminal Justice Act 1988, s 134. Grave breaches of the Geneva Conventions and of Additional Protocol I are also contrary to English law, Geneva Conventions Act 1957 (as amended), as are the crimes in Arts 6, 7 and 8 of the Rome Statute 1998, International Criminal Court Act 2001, ss 50(1), 51(1).

149 See the statement of Mr Heath, the Prime Minister, HC Debs 2 March 1972, vol 832, col 744. For discussion of *Ireland v United Kingdom* (1979–80) 2 EHRR 25, see Chapter 7.

150 The Report of the Baha Mousa Inquiry, vol III, [253]–[302]. Compare the difference of view between the deployed Army legal officers in theatre, Report of the Baha Mousa Inquiry, vol III, 1342, [375].

that 'the difficulty [was] that what amounts to inhumane treatment may not always be clear. Military opinion varied on whether hooding was inhumane treatment.'[151] Amongst the different forms of hooding there would seem to be fine distinctions, made more easily in the lecture room than in the real world, where soldiers are fighting against a real enemy, particularly where civilians have taken an active part in the hostilities. It is, perhaps, for this reason that, in April 2003, the British army attempted to ban hooding in a form which involved the covering of the faces of detainees, so as to avoid affects on breathing.[152] This order did not address all the situations in which some form of hooding was adopted. Ministers appeared to be under the impression that the restrictions on hooding only applied to the interrogation process.[153] Indeed, in 2004 a ministerial statement confirmed that 'directions that were issued on 30 September last year that all hooding should cease . . . it was a decision of the Chief of Joint Operations off his own bat . . . if there were examples of hooding, *apart from on arrest*, of course this will be investigated.'[154] The hooding of detainees was to come into the public domain, when, in February 2004, a report from the ICRC concerning 'allegations, amongst other things, of hooding . . . [at a detention centre] was leaked and thus, uncommonly, was in the public domain'.[155] Addressing the issue in May 2004, the Prime Minister told the House of Commons that 'the hooding of prisoners, [referred to in the ICRC report] a practice that had already been stopped by February'.[156]

A British soldier dealing with detainees in 2003 would have received no guidance on this matter from the card outlining arrest procedures,[157] and he could have been forgiven for asking his superior officer whether only some forms of hooding were banned, or whether the practice was banned in all circumstances. The Prime Minister's response to oral questions in the House of Commons appeared to suggest that all forms of hooding had been banned prior to February 2004 (the date of the ICRC report), but he went on to say that 'the practice of hooding prisoners, which is sometimes necessary for security reasons but should not be done for purposes of interrogation'.[158] It is here that policy and the legal

151 *Ibid*, vol III, 1331, [302].

152 For the attempt by the general officer commanding to do so through the giving of verbal orders, see Baha Mousa Report, vol III, 1343, [382]; FRAGO 63, 21 May 2003, 'under no circumstances should their faces be covered as this might impair breathing', Baha Mousa Report, vol III, 930, [10.105].

153 In fact, the ECtHR in *Ireland v United Kingdom* (1979–80) 2 EHRR 25, [96] considered that hooding, which in this case was employed 'except during interrogation' amounted, along with the other five techniques, to inhuman and degrading treatment, [246(3)]. The UK government had given the ECtHR an undertaking that the 'five techniques would not . . . be reintroduced as an aid to interrogation', [4].

154 HL Debs 12 May 2004, vol 661, col 277. Emphasis supplied.

155 Baha Mousa Report, vol III, 1343, [381]. For discussion of the role of the ICRC see Chapter 6.

156 HC Debs 12 May 2004, vol 421, col 347.

157 Baha Mousa Report, vol III, 955, [11.7], 958, [11.15]–[11.16].

158 HC Debs 12 May 2004, vol 421, col 350.

requirements may differ, particularly where there has been considerable media attention given to a particular practice. In 2006 the government continued to draw a distinction between hooding for the purposes of interrogation, which it considered to be unlawful, and for other purposes which, although not unlawful in its view, it decided to ban for policy reasons.[159]

Despite what is likely to have been the intention of the government and the armed forces that hooding should be banned, difficulties with terminology seem to have got in the way. It is easy to see that this policy was intended to cover 'hooding' but what of the use of blacked-out goggles, without any form of hooding, in an appropriate case? This practice was authorised by the Joint Doctrine Publication (2008) when 'transiting through or past military sensitive sites' and it appears not to fall within the policy ban on hooding.[160]

If we leave aside the policy decisions about hooding, and concentrate on the legal principles involved in the placing of blacked-out goggles on a detainee, which appears not to be included within the policy direction, a number of issues are raised. These relate to whether the forcible placing of the goggles on a detainee could amount to any of the following – 'torture, 'inhuman' or 'degrading' treatment, or an assault and battery under English criminal law. In *Ireland v United Kingdom* the ECtHR was concerned with the five techniques (one of which concerned hooding) being applied in combination, and not singly, when it determined that they amounted to inhuman and degrading treatment.[161] On the

159 Joint Committee on Human Rights, *The UN Convention Against Torture*, 19th Report of Session 2005–06, HC 701, Evidence, letter dated 20 April 2006 from Minister of State for the Armed Forces. There was no reference in this letter as to different forms of hooding, or the circumstances which might make what it considered to be lawful hooding, unlawful. See also [83]–[85] and the oral evidence at Q238.

160 Referred to in *Equality and Human Rights Commission v Prime Minister and others; Al-Bazzouni v Prime Minister and others* [2011] EWHC 2401 (Admin), [30]–[32]. The change ordered by the court to the *Consolidated Guidance to Intelligence Officers and Service Personnel on the Detention and Interviewing of Detainees Overseas, and on the Passing and Receipt of Intelligence Relating to Detainees* applied only to the government's policy relating to hooding. The judgment referred to 'hooding' without distinguishing the different forms of sight deprivation. The use of blacked out goggles remains permissible 'as a last resort for the time and extent necessary . . . to preserve operational security', *Joint Doctrine Publication 1–10, Captured Persons (CPERS)* (Ministry of Defence, 2015), [2]–[15].

161 (1979–80) 2 EHRR 25, [167] and see the analysis of the ECtHR jurisprudence set out in the judgment in *Equality and Human Rights Commission v Prime Minister and others; Al-Bazzouni v Prime Minister and others* [2011] EWHC 2401 (Admin), [86]–[89]. In *El-Masri v Former Yugoslav Republic of Macedonia* (2013) 57 EHRR 25 the ECtHR appeared to conclude that the *Ireland v United* Kingdom judgment [167] declared hooding alone sufficient to cause 'at least intense physical and mental suffering to the person subject to it', [209]. It was the imposition of stress positions and hooding which contributed to the death of Baha Mousa, Baha Mousa Report, vol III, 1307, [143]. The prohibition of inhuman treatment is to be found also in Geneva Conventions III and IV, of 1949, Arts 13, 27, respectively. For the meaning of 'treated humanely' in Common Art 3 to the Geneva Conventions, 1949, see *R (Hussein) v Secretary of State for Defence* [2014] EWCA Civ 1087, [60].

other hand, there is no evidence that the ECtHR has ever decided that 'hooding alone might not be unlawful.'[162] It will depend on all the facts so that, for instance, a prisoner of war may consider that being forced to wear blacked out goggles during transit for a short period through military sensitive areas did not amount to 'degrading'[163] treatment, whilst a civilian detainee, unused to military procedures, might reasonable consider it to be so. This is another reason to ensure that all detainees are not treated as a single group.

Since a British soldier is subject to English criminal law wherever he is serving, it might be suggested that to place forcibly blacked-out goggles on a detainee could amount, at least, to an assault.[164] This may be more likely to occur where the soldier is unable to make clear his purpose in a language understood by the detainee. The crucial issue would then become whether, under English law, the soldier had any defence to what might otherwise amount to a criminal offence. Strictly, superior orders could not be prayed in his aid and he would have to rely upon a lawful ground for arresting the detainee, a matter discussed above.[165]

The policy decision banning hooding has at least three advantages. First, it avoids lengthy legal argument as to whether it amounts to inhuman or degrading treatment in different circumstances. Secondly, it avoids the adverse publicity that can be generated by photographs gaining widespread circulation of hooded detainees, and finally, it makes the position so much clearer for the soldier involved with the arrest of suspected insurgents.[166] Some might argue, however, that there is a price to be paid for such a policy. A specialist interrogator might ask: how then can I get information from a detainee that could save the life of a British soldier if it is acted upon? The detainee is unlikely to volunteer to tell soldiers who makes the IEDs, where the parts are stored, or where attacks are planned, but this will, of course, be vital information. To reply that the end justifies the means would be to give a green light to torture and other unlawful practices, and cannot be the right response. It may well be that specialist interrogators

162 *Equality and Human Rights Commission v Prime Minister and others; Al-Bazzouni v Prime Minister and others* [2011] EWHC 2401 (Admin), [85].

163 The definition of 'degrading' treatment was also set out in *Ireland v United Kingdom*, [167] and distinguished from inhuman or degrading treatment in *Al-Nashiri v Poland*, Application No 28761/11, Judgment, 24 July 2014, [508], [511]–[516].

164 This issue was argued in *Equality and Human Rights Commission v Prime Minister and others; Al-Bazzouni v Prime Minister and others* [2011] EWHC 2401 (Admin), [83] but no decision was made on the point.

165 The arrest is likely to involve other forcible measures such as placing plasticuffs on the wrists of the detainee and, perhaps, physically directing his movements. In reality, if the soldier is complying with written orders it is unlikely he would be prosecuted within the military justice system. Although the lawful ground for the soldier's actions may be derived from IHL and not directly from English law, it is suggested that this should give the soldier a defence under the Criminal Law Act 1967, s 3. For the application of IHL to the crime of murder in English law, see Chapter 6.

166 The difficulty of drawing fine distinctions over hooding was one of the reasons given in *R (Al-Bazzouni) v Prime Minister and others* [2011] EWHC 2401 (Admin), for the amendment of the Guidance.

in a war zone will have to accept that the chances of learning anything significant and reliable from civilian detainees is, in practice, remote and that it is just not worth the candle if the policy of the British government is, as it should be, to treat all detainees within the law. The experience of the armed conflicts in Iraq and in Afghanistan shows that it is increasingly difficult either to believe that no one will ever find out, or that, in an armed conflict, the rules somehow fly out of the window.

The way in which civilian detainees are treated is closely linked to the issue of what is to be done to them after any interrogation. If they are to be placed on trial, any statements obtained from them under illegal or any improper pressure could, depending on the law of the territorial state, be inadmissible or unreliable in their subsequent trial. Had, for example, prolonged hooding of a detainee amounted to torture, which had then led to a confession by him, the UK would be precluded from transferring him if this evidence obtained under torture could be used against him in any subsequent trial.[167] The irony of the situation could hardly be overlooked.

viii No-fly zones

The UK had considerable experience of enforcing no-fly zones in Iraq following the Gulf War 1991.[168] It found itself repeating the exercise in 2011 over the skies of Libya. In the case of Libya, the operations, carried out mainly by the RAF, were underpinned by UN Security Council Resolution 1973 (2011), giving a clear legal basis under international law for taking the military action. This resolution authorised member states to 'take all necessary measures . . . to protect civilians and civilian populated areas under threat of attack' and to 'enforce compliance with the ban of flights'.[169] It had also stipulated that there should be no occupation of any part of the territory of Libya, which was interpreted as meaning that there should be no NATO ground forces operating in the territory. Parliament had also approved the deployment of British armed forces for this purpose by a vote of the House of Commons on 21 March 2011.[170]

The requirement to take 'all necessary measures' had, of course, to be interpreted in the light of IHL and so any attack by RAF aircraft on targets on the ground in Libya had to comply with the rules relating to targeting, discussed

167 See *Othman v United Kingdom* (2012) 55 EHRR1, [267] which concluded that it was unnecessary to decide if the same considerations applied in respect of 'ill-treatment which falls short of torture', [267]. For the issue of assurances given by a potential receiving state see above. Evidence obtained by torture would not be admissible in a court in England, *A v Secretary of State for the Home Department* [2005] UKHL 71.

168 The Secretary of State for Defence stated that 'the patrols are justified in international law as a legitimate response to prevent a grave humanitarian crisis', HC Debs 26 February 2001, vol 363, col 620. For discussion of this claimed ground for intervention, see Chapter 2.

169 Operative [4], [8].

170 See Chapter 4.

above. The difficulty faced by the RAF and the other NATO states involved in the operation was that it became necessary to attack targets in heavily populated areas. The use of unmanned aerial vehicles, which could play a significant part in trying to ensure that the risk to innocent civilians was minimised, has been discussed above.

ix Naval operations

Although the Royal Navy may appear to have played a relatively minor role in Britain's wars 2000–2015, the Royal Marines have been active, along with the army and the Royal Air Force Regiment, in the land-based operations in Iraq and Afghanistan. Its warships have also played a supporting role in land and air operations during this period.[171]

171 In the Libya campaign in 2011, RN ships have evacuated civilians from Benghazi and enforced the arms embargo, see HC Select Committee on Defence, *Operations in Libya*, 9th Report, session 2010–12, HC 950, (2012), [113].

10 Conclusion

In keeping with all wars in which the UK has been involved in modern times, the end of a particular conflict brings in its wake the leisure of reflection. The wars fought between 2000 and 2015 were no different, but the emphasis of this book has been on the legal accountability, if any, of those who took part in them, and of the UK itself. Armed conflicts prior to 2002, when the Human Rights Act 1998 came into force, preceded by the International Criminal Court Act 2001, are of limited value as precedents since the legal environment in which they were fought now differs considerably.

The change has, however, not been a smooth one and by the end of 2015 the interpretation of the existing law looks quite dissimilar from its form on 20 March 2003, when British armed forces began military action in Iraq. This process of change led the former chief of the defence staff to comment that 'the Armed Forces are under legal siege'[1] with its attendant connotation that British armed forces were prevented from carrying out their primary role as efficiently or as effectively as they might otherwise have done. It will be argued that this was not the case, although at times it might have felt that it was through the relative lack of certainty of the legal environment and the difficulty of giving and receiving legal advice, which would withstand legal challenge in the courts. The desire to hold the principal actors accountable under the law does, at least, demand a degree of certainty as to the limits of the law applicable to each different form of military action, whilst recognising fully that it will not be the lawyers or judges who will be doing the actual fighting, or making the necessary policy decisions. There must always, therefore, be considerable latitude given by any form of law applicable during the course of an armed conflict to those who are faced with decisions to make during the immediate preparatory stages to, and more particularly during the course of, the conflict.

i Which body of law applies?

This book has attempted to show that the main bodies of law applicable to Britain's wars have ranged from English law, principally, criminal law, the Human

1 Lord Boyce, HL Debs 14 July 2005, vol 673, col 1236. This conclusion was disputed in a ministerial statement, HC Debs 12 December 2005, vol 440, col 1199.

Rights Act 1998 and the law of tort, along with IHL. Within English law, the areas of development between 2003 and 2015 have been the reach of the Human Rights Act, with its attendant application of the ECHR, and the applicability of what would otherwise have been bars to proceedings through state immunity, non-justiciability in its various forms, and combat immunity. In the field of IHL, some significant differences apply, depending on whether the armed conflict is of an international or a non-international character. At various stages of Britain's military involvement both Iraq and Afghanistan were international, and then became non-international armed conflicts, and these changes had profound effects, particularly in terms of the treatment of detainees.

Confusion and uncertainty of the legal consequences of the events of 9/11 in New York and Washington led to the term, the 'war on terror' and a flirtation with the view that, by way of responsive military action, IHL did not apply at all, or that as a body of law it did not fit this form of asymmetric attack. In 2006 the Secretary of State for Defence had even argued that the 'international community . . . need[s] to re-examine these conventions [and also] whether or not further developments in international law in this area [the Geneva Conventions] are necessary' to meet the needs of modern armed conflicts,[2] whilst by 2014 the government position was that IHL should be the *primary* body of law applicable to them.[3] It is, perhaps, fair to conclude that in 2014, IHL was seen by the government and the armed forces as being preferable to the application of the ECHR to the actions of British forces, particularly in Afghanistan. Indeed, the British government maintained a strong line that the ECHR did not apply at all to Afghanistan.[4] The attempt to exclude its application to the activities of British armed forces in Iraq had been lost in 2011, with the decision of the ECtHR in *Al-Skeini v United Kingdom*,[5] certainly in relation to events occurring (at least) during the period of the occupation.[6]

The principal area of confusion as to the appropriate law to apply concerned the treatment of those detained by UK armed forces. Whilst cold war training in the British armed forces would have emphasised the treatment of prisoners of war, very few detainees in Iraq or in Afghanistan came within this category. Again, the protection offered by IHL to civilian internees was not identical with those detained as criminal suspects, although they did share a common requirement, that they be treated humanely.[7] Uncertainty as to the legal regime to be

2 '20th Century Rules, 21st Century Conflict', lecture at the Royal United Services Institute, 3 April 2006, See http://www.responsibilitytoprotect.org/files/UK_SecretaryofState_Speech_Apr_2006.pdf; *The Guardian*, 4 June 2006, http://www.theguardian.com/politics/2006/apr/04/uk.militar. See also the Foreign Affairs Committee, 2nd Report, session 2006–07, *Visit to Guantanamo Bay*, HC 44, [85].

3 Defence Select Committee, 12th Report, session 2013–14, *UK Armed Forces Personnel and the Legal Framework of Future Operations*, HC 931, Government Response, HC 548, 2014, [2].

4 See Chapter 7 for its arguments.

5 (2011) 53 EHRR 18.

6 Although see *Hassan v United Kingdom*, Application No 29750/09, Grand Chamber Judgment, 16 September 2014, discussed in Chapter 7.

7 At least by Common Art 3 to the Geneva Conventions 1949.

applied to any detainee can make it that much more difficult to uphold binding legal obligations.[8]

The importance of sound legal advice to ministers, or senior commanders, can hardly be underestimated, particularly when concentration is placed, as it is in this book, on the requirement of legal accountability. But, particularly in planning military operations, there is a strong argument that the chiefs themselves should have a sound knowledge of the basic principles of the law applicable, rather in the way that British ambassadors are trained for their role.[9] Had they been in this position it is possible to speculate that, for instance, they might have been able to raise questions at a very early stage of the planning stage of the operation against Iraq in 2003, concerning the way in which the armed forces should treat the Iraqi population if an occupation of that territory became inevitable. It would, of course, be for their legal advisers to supply the legal advice and for the Attorney General ultimately to rule on the legal issues involved, but the planning stage would be likely to have been more effectively conducted.[10] In this regard, it is a worrying feature of the National Security Council that its membership does not include the Attorney General, nor a senior legal adviser from the Foreign and Commonwealth Office, to guide the Council through the English law and the international law issues, which might arise at those meetings concerned with taking military action outside the UK.[11]

The difficulties involved in determining an accurate assessment of the appropriate legal environment in which UK armed forces are to take part in an armed conflict are made more complex where they are carrying out military operations with the armed forces of one or more states, whose view on the legal regime may be different. The UK certainly distanced itself from the policy followed by the US government over the detention of individuals at Guantanamo Bay, but allies have to co-operate on the basis that each may be subject to a different legal regime, particularly on their human rights obligations to those whom they detain or wish to transfer.

ii Counter-insurgency

This 'doctrine',[12] which became known as the McChrystal strategy,[13] in relation to Afghanistan, was explored in Chapter 1, where it was also explained why it

8 See Chapters 7 and 9.

9 See the UK Diplomatic Academy, which encompasses a Law Faculty and which opened in 2015, https://www.gov.uk/government/publications/opening-of-new-diplomatic-academy The Academy is open to all diplomatic staff of the Foreign and Commonwealth Office.

10 See the evidence of the Attorney General in 2003, Lord Goldsmith, Iraq Inquiry, 27 January 2010, 224–5.

11 See discussion in Chapter 3.

12 It is also referred to by the acronym, 'COIN'. See generally, Baha Mousa Inquiry, vol II, 526, [6.74], 'Counter Insurgency (COIN) Training for Officers'; J Bailey, R Iron, H Strachan (eds), *British Generals in Blair's Wars* (Ashgate, 2013), 340.

13 It was discussed by the Defence Select Committee, 4th Report, session 2010–12, *Operations in Afghanistan*, HC 554 (2011), [68].

would not be used as a term to describe the activities of the UK armed forces in Iraq or in Afghanistan. It will be argued here that the term 'counter-insurgency' should be consigned to the history of Britain's colonial past and that it has no place as a 'doctrine' in considering Britain's wars between 2000 and 2015.

It was never clear exactly what 'counter-insurgency' meant, nor what it was expected to achieve. General Sir Frank Kitson is often seen as the leading exponent of the 'doctrine' in the UK, largely as a result of his military experience and of his book, *Low Intensity Operations*, published in 1971.[14] The book discusses subversion, insurgency and peacekeeping but Kitson's definition of 'insurgency'[15] is not one with which all would now agree. This is not meant as a criticism but merely as an illustration of the fact that the term, along with that of 'insurgent', is not one with a settled legal (or other) meaning and 'counter-insurgency' must also lack the same qualities. The term begs the question of when it would come into operation. Does it apply, for instance, to a situation short of an armed conflict, such as a riot, or during an occupation of territory,[16] or only during a non-international armed conflict? Or does it apply only when the civilian authorities are unable to function,[17] or only in overseas territory?

There is also uncertainty as to what the 'doctrine' is intended to achieve. Does 'counter-insurgency' refer to a tactical decision as to the way in which military operations are to be conducted, with an emphasis on avoiding civilian casualties, by means of increased troop numbers and more careful targeting? Or does it mean a strategic plan to work with the local armed police, armed forces or civilian agencies, in order to protect the civilian population and to develop ideas of responsible governance of the territory after the insurgents have been defeated?[18] It is likely, in political and military circles, to refer to a combination of these aims, but in reality only as a shorthand way of describing that which is being attempted. In the course of a non-international armed conflict, in particular, British ministers will expect the armed forces not only to perform their military role, but simultaneously also to assist them to achieve their wider political objectives. If this is the case, it would tend to suggest that counter-insurgency should not be a military 'doctrine' at all, although it must be recognised that

14 Faber and Faber, London.

15 At 3. See also terminology discussed in Chapter 1 above.

16 A Alderson, 'Too Busy to Learn: Personal Observations on British Campaigns in Iraq and Afghanistan', in J Bailey, R Iron, H Strachan (eds), *British General's in Blair's Wars* (Ashgate Publishing Ltd, 2013), [283] drew a determined rejection of his view that in Iraq in March 2004 (during the period of occupation) the coalition was facing an insurgency by a US general who is reported as taking the view that it was 'warfighting'.

17 See the suggestion of this in *Mutua and others v Secretary of State for Foreign and Commonwealth Affairs* [2012] EWHC 2678 (QB), [124]. Compare a proclamation by the general officer commanding a district of martial law, discussed in Chapter 3.

18 The Defence Select Committee, 4th Report, session 2010–12, *Operations in Afghanistan*, HC 554 (2011), [71] saw counter-insurgency policy in this light. The Government's response to this Report, HC 1525 (2011) indicated that it 'supports the Committee in welcoming the adoption of the counter-insurgency strategy', [response to recommendation 2].

the armed forces will have to play a greater or lesser part in the wider strategic process.[19]

A formal doctrine based on such a slippery concept is likely to lead, during an armed conflict, to confusion on the part of the soldiers trying to implement it, the politicians both in the UK and where that armed conflict is taking place, along with the general public. Although not inevitable, this confusion could, in turn, lead to breaches of the law, either because the policy does not make it clear that 'counter-insurgency' sits within, and not outside, the law, or because, as Kitson explains,[20] the gathering of intelligence from captured insurgents is the key to its success and the attempts to obtain information, intended for the purpose of saving of the lives of British soldiers and civilians, could possibly lead to the ill-treatment of detainees.[21]

There can be little objection to the use of the term as a means of indicating that UK armed forces were trying to counter the actions of insurgents in Iraq and in Afghanistan, but to elevate it into a defined UK or NATO policy is dangerous. It is dangerous because it attempts to apply a model of military action, stemming (at least) from Ireland in the early 1920s through to Malaya, Kenya and Cyprus, which appears to create a precedent for any new situation, such as in Iraq and Afghanistan, but the reality is that it does not.[22] Sir Hew Strachan summed up the dangers of these earlier claimed precedents when he wrote that 'there was a readiness to use levels of force which would now be deemed unacceptable.'[23] Even in the areas of the world where Britain's 'counter-insurgency' policy was supposedly forged, Malaya and Kenya, alleged incidents have come to light and have become the subject of judicial proceedings.[24] In IHL, the concept of the civilian taking a direct part in hostilities has been developed to such an extent now that it should be able to provide the answer to the armed forces as to who may be targeted and when.[25] By so doing it will be able to provide the

19 See J Wilkinson, 'Using Humanitarian Aid to "Win Hearts and Minds": a Costly Failure?' (2011) 93 IRRC 1035, 1058. For the linkage between military and political activity in Iraq see General Sir Rupert Smith (Interview), (2006) 88 IRRC 719, 722, 725.

20 In his Chapter 6.

21 See, for example, the account given of the effects of Britain's counter-insurgency policy in Kenya, 1954–1959, in *Mutua and others v Secretary of State for Foreign and Commonwealth Affairs* [2012] EWHC 2678 (QB), [124]; H Strachan, 'British Counter-Insurgency from Malaya to Iraq' (2007) 152 RUSI Jo 8, who comments that 'by the end of 1954, there were 77,000 Kikuyu in detention'.

22 See the criticism of it in F Ledwidge, *op cit*, 167–70. H Strachan (note 21 above) concludes that 'the search for a general model of insurgencies proves elusive as each campaign has its own characteristics'. Lt General J Kiszely argued that 'all counter-insurgencies are *sui generis* . . . making problematic the transfer of lessons from one to another', 'Learning About Counter-Insurgency' (2006) 151 RUSI Jo 16, 19.

23 See note 21 above.

24 *Mutua and others v Secretary of State for Foreign and Commonwealth Affairs* [2012] EWHC 2678 (QB); *R (Keyu and others) v Secretary of State for Foreign and Commonwealth Affairs* [2015] UKSC 69. There is no finding, in either case, that the alleged incidents were based on a counter-insurgency policy conducted by the UK.

25 See discussion in Chapter 9.

appropriate circumstances for the foundations of the soldier's RoE and, hence, the link with English criminal law.

The imperative of British soldiers upholding the standards imposed by the law applicable to their military operations, was drawn out clearly by the Baha Mousa and the Al-Sweady public inquiries, along with many cases decided by the courts in London, and it is to those standards that attention should be focused, and not to some vague counter-insurgency doctrine.[26]

iii Did the law hinder UK armed forces during the various armed conflicts?

There has been much concern expressed about the effect of, what has been described as, 'legal siege',[27] 'the fog of law',[28] the 'judicialisation of war', 'lawfare',[29] or the 'weight of law'.[30] The idea has also found expression in the comment that members of the armed forces 'cannot operate effectively with the spectre of the lawyer metaphorically looking over their shoulder'[31] and that that it 'sometimes undermines the willingness of personnel to accept responsibility and to take necessary risks with the consequent impact on operational effectiveness'.[32] These are serious consequences, if the law does actually hinder the armed forces in their difficult task of conducting armed conflict. But is there a real link between this alleged cause and effect, or has a 'straw man' been created, upon whom these verbal attacks are directed?

The 'straw man' is composed largely of four main props. These are the risks of prosecution of commanders,[33] the threat of trial before the ICC at the Hague,[34] the influence of the ECHR, and the end of combat immunity in the combat zone. None of these reflect legal reality. It may be that a combination of a number

26 A 'doctrine' may, or may not, comply with legal requirements. If it does not comply it cannot be raised as a defence to a criminal charge since it would, otherwise, amount to a defence of superior orders. It may, however, be relevant for other purposes, see, for an example, Report of the Baha Mousa Inquiry, HC 1452, Vol 1, 372, [2.1551].

27 See Lord Boyce, note 1 above.

28 T Tugendhat and L Crowe, *The Fog of Law: An Introduction to the Legal Erosion of British Fighting Power* (Policy Exchange, 2013).

29 Discussed in Chapter 1. See also C Waters, 'Beyond Lawfare: Judicial Oversight of Western Militaries' (2009) 46 Alberta Law Rev 885; A Forster, 'British Judicial Engagement and the Juridification of the Armed Forces' (2012) 88 International Affairs 283.

30 Secretary of State for Defence, HC Debs 17 December 2014, vol 589, col 1413.

31 Mr M Ancram, MP, HC Debs 7 November 2005, vol 439, col 23.

32 Defence Select Committee, 12th Report, session 2013–14, *UK Armed Forces Personnel and the Legal Framework of Future Operations*, HC 931, conclusion [6]. The Committee was referring to coroners' inquests and inquiries.

33 See *The Times*, 7 April 2015, letter from former chiefs of the defence staff.

34 See W MacKinlay, 'Perceptions and Misconceptions: How are International and UK Law Perceived to Affect Military Commanders and Their Subordinates on Operations?' (2007) 7 Defence Studies 111, Q 16 in which 58% of all respondents agreed with the statement that they 'could end up in the ICC if we became involved in a serious incident which the UK agrees to prosecute'.

of different factors, such as the intensity of British military activity in Iraq and Afghanistan, the strong desire to support the armed forces, the large number of legal actions and their costs, has driven this argument to the fore. The significance of the legal environment between 2003 and 2015 can, however, easily be lost in the metaphors used to describe its effect but, in reality, the point turns on where the accountability of individual members of the armed forces should lie. Should it be to the law, or to the services disciplinary and other administrative systems, or to both?

It is unlikely that anyone would argue that the British armed forces should be unaccountable for their actions in the conduct of armed conflicts, or indeed, any other action they may take whilst on duty. Their obligation to uphold English law[35] and IHL[36] is well established and under which individuals can be held accountable through judicial procedures, usually through the court martial or other service systems. The same can be said of their obligation to respond to a summons from the coroner to give evidence at an inquest.[37]

What then has been the practical significance of the developing reach of the ECHR into a range of British military activities in Iraq and Afghanistan? It had been conceded by the Secretary of State for Defence in 2005 that it applied to those detained on a British base, the effect of which was that detainees would be entitled to be free from torture, inhuman or degrading treatment, by virtue of Article 3 of the ECHR.[38] But they were entitled to this in any event under Common Article 3 to the Geneva Conventions 1949.[39] The extension of the extra-territorial application of the ECHR to those who were under the authority and control of British armed forces and who were, for example, shot and killed by individual soldiers, led to a substantial increase in the number of investigations, which needed to be compliant with it. This will have increased the burden on the service police, but at a time when the military action, which led to the deaths, had actually been completed. Far from decrying the need for these investigations, the government took the view that they were 'important because by establishing how abuses were allowed to happen, remedial action [could] be taken'.[40] The inability to transfer detainees to the Iraqi or to the Afghan authorities in some cases and the difficulty of doing so in others, is no different, in

35 See Chapter 8.

36 Whether they have an enforceable legal obligation to comply with IHL, in the absence of specific orders to do so, is discussed in Chapter 8. Under IHL there is no general defence of 'military necessity', unless it is specifically referred to in particular provisions.

37 See generally, Chapter 5.

38 *Al-Skeini and others v Secretary of State for Defence* [2005] EWCA Civ 1609, [185].

39 Although Common Art 3 applied, strictly, to non-international armed conflicts it is generally recognised that it reflects customary international law and therefore applicable to international armed conflicts (including periods of occupation).

40 HL Debs 7 November 2013, vol 749, col 413. For the duty to conduct investigations under IHL see discussion in Chapter 6. In the event that the ECHR became inapplicable to British military operations overseas, this duty under IHL to investigate would remain.

principle, from that faced in transferring failed asylum seekers, or those ordered to be deported, from the shores of the UK.[41]

The application of the ECHR to British military operations in Iraq and Afghanistan did have had least two significant potential impacts. The first was the effect it had on British soldiers themselves, who were serving in these zones of armed conflict, not only in respect of the right to the protection of their own life, by the UK authorities,[42] but also in the nature of the coroner's inquest if they died or were killed on duty.[43] The second impact concerned the large number of applications for judicial review brought before the High Court in London by Iraqi and Afghan nationals, to challenge a decision of the Secretary of State not to order an investigation under Article 2 or 3 of the ECHR.[44] Indeed, the numbers kept building, to which were added claims in tort, which led Leggatt J to conclude that 'one of the legacies of the Iraq war is litigation'.[45] The interpretation of the ECHR obligation to protect the lives of (British) soldiers by the Supreme Court in *Smith v Ministry of Defence* (2013) has, however, had little practical impact due to the very limited nature of the decision as set out by the majority in that case[46] and the pursuit of claims in tort against British soldiers is not new.[47] It is possible that, had the Secretary of State taken the view that the ECHR *should*, as a matter of policy, be applied to all British military activities in Iraq and subsequently in Afghanistan, even though there was some doubt prior to 2011 as to whether it did so, the number of claims by Iraqi and Afghan civilians against the British government could have been reduced considerably, with the attendant reduction in costs.

It should not be thought that the resort to the courts has only a negative effect on military actions. The guidance given by the House of Lords in 1977 and in 1985,[48] as to the principles to be applied when opening fire in Northern Ireland can only have had the effect of easing the uncertainty and concern felt by

41 See discussion in Chapter 9. In practice, however, the necessary infracture differs substantially from that existing in the UK.

42 See the discussion of *Smith v Ministry of Defence* [2013] UKSC 41 in Chapter 7.

43 The nature of the 'Art 2 inquest' is discussed in Chapter 5. The giving of evidence by a commander at a coroner's inquest was a matter of some concern expressed by the Defence Select Committee in 2014, see note 32.

44 See further discussion in Chapter 7.

45 *Al-Saadoon and others v Secretary of State for Defence* [2015] EWHC 715, [1].

46 [2013] UKSC 41. See generally, Chapter 7. Lord Hope, who drafted the majority judgment, stated during a debate in the House of Lords that 'those serving in the armed forces . . . are not as vulnerable to legal challenge as some people have been suggesting', HL Debs 7 November 2013, vol 749, col 396.

47 See, *Kelly and others v Ministry of Defence* [1989] NI 341; *Magill v Ministry of Defence* [1987] NI 194; *Lynch v Ministry of Defence* [1983] NI 216; *Farrell v Secretary of State for Defence* [1980] 1 All ER 166; *Bici v Ministry of Defence* [2004] EWHC 786 (relating to shooting by British soldiers of individuals in Kosovo in 1999).

48 *Attorney-General for Northern Ireland's Reference (No 1 of 1975)* [1977] AC 105; *R v Clegg* [1985] 1 AC 482.

commanders on the actions of their young soldiers.[49] Again, the interpretation of the meaning of 'humane' treatment under IHL by the Court of Appeal in 2014,[50] although late in the day, does have the great benefit of explaining what is expected of those guarding detainees, beyond the mere order to treat detainees 'humanely'.

The so-called 'straw man' is really an edifice of misunderstanding about the law applicable to British soldiers conducting military operations during an armed conflict. Soldiers cannot, for instance, be 'prosecuted' under the Human Rights Act 1998, nor is it realistic to believe that a serviceman or woman would be tried by the ICC at The Hague. Although the giving of evidence, whether before a coroner's inquest or in a claim for damages, may not be a pleasant experience,[51] there is much to commend the principle that proper allowance must be, and is, given by judges for operational decisions made in the heat of a battle.[52] It is not an instance of judges 'excusing' what would otherwise be a breach of English law, but it is really a further instance of the respective competences of the judiciary, on the one hand, and of the executive, on the other.[53] It is difficult to accept, at face value, that British commanders, who have the personal qualities to lead others in battle would fear the prospect of giving evidence at a coroner's inquest (or at any other hearing) to such an extent that it 'undermines [their] willingness to accept responsibility and to take *necessary* risks with the consequent impact on operational effectiveness'.[54] They will, in any event, be likely to be subject to service procedures if they have taken *unnecessary* risks, and it is hardly within the scope of the notion of armed forces in a democracy that they should not be liable to be called as a witness to give an account of their actions.

In the light of the discussion above, it is difficult to conclude that the ECHR, applied through the Human Rights Act 1998, or any of the other areas making up the legal environment in which the British armed forces have conducted military operations in the various armed conflicts since 2000, could be said to have hindered, in an unacceptable sense, the military actions of the armed forces. Senior commanders would hardly wish their subordinates to torture or otherwise ill-treat detainees, which in any event could amount to a breach of IHL. It must be recognised, however, that they may wish to have powers to detain for a period

49 See, for example *Attorney-General for Northern Ireland's Reference (No 1 of 1975)* [1977] AC 105, 138.

50 *R (Hussein) v Secretary of State for Defence* [2014] EWCA Civ 1087, [37].

51 See, for example, the situation faced by Major M, in *R (Connor & Allbutt) v Ministry of Defence* [2009] EWHC 3351.

52 This was a significant feature of the majority judgment in *Smith v Ministry of Defence* [2013] UKSC 41.

53 See the discussion of this principle in Chapter 5; *Al-Saadoon v Secretary of State for Defence* [2015] EWHC 715, [111]. See also C Waters, 'Beyond Lawfare: Judicial Oversight of Western Militaries' (2009) 46 Alberta Law Rev 885, 904, who uses the phrase, 'judicial deference to the core military function'.

54 Defence Select Committee, 12th Report, session 2013–14, *UK Armed Forces Personnel and the Legal Framework of Future Operations*, HC 931, conclusions [6]. Emphasis supplied.

longer than 96 hours. The planning of any proposed military action, involving a non-international armed conflict, may need to consider carefully whether the UK would be able to transfer detainees to the territorial state for trial within a 96-hour period and the consequences if it cannot do so, or if circumstances change.

Apart from the concern, expressed from time to time, over service prosecution policy, there is little evidence to suggest that the serviceman, actually engaged in conducting combat activities, is inhibited in performing his or her proper military duties by the metaphorical 'lawyer looking over their shoulder'. It is recognised, however, that some may *believe* this to be the case[55] and this, in itself, is a matter that cannot be ignored.

It has also been suggested that 'in order to distance themselves from "command influence" the military hierarchy were advised to distance themselves from criminal cases, leaving individuals accused of crimes carried out in operational conditions feeling unsupported by their military "family"'.[56] The armed forces are, in fact, good at providing systems in which the chain of command is separated from other functions, such as investigation processes conducted by the service police or through serving on the court martial, each of which has been instigated through much earlier decisions of the ECtHR. It should not therefore be impossible to provide support for soldiers from the military 'family' by service personnel unconnected with the service police or their own chain of command.

It must be recognised that the concern about some of the perceived legal consequences of decisions made during actual combat operations is a serious matter. Those who argue that it does actually hinder military operations will, no doubt, believe sincerely in that which they claim.[57] Whilst it may be a suitable issue to be considered at the highest levels of policy making, the effect of this debate needs to be considered principally on those who are actually engaged on combat operations. It must be in their interests and of the effectiveness of military action, that they are trained on those aspects of the law that impact directly on their military duties. They need, for instance, to know very little about the ECHR requirements on the treatment of detainees which they do not already know from the detail of their RoE (in its various forms) or the criminal law, apart from

55 See the empirical research of Major W MacKinlay, 'Perceptions and Misconceptions: How are International and UK Law Perceived to Affect Military Commanders and Their Subordinates on Operations?' (2007) 7 Defence Studies 111, Q 7, where 50% of British army respondents answered that they believed 'that recent changes to UK law [the International Criminal Court Act 2001 crimes] are damaging the operational effectiveness of units on operations'.

56 Defence Select Committee, 12th Report, session 2013–14, *UK Armed Forces Personnel and the Legal Framework of Future Operations*, HC 931, [35], quoting from evidence supplied to it.

57 See for example, Lord Guthrie, a former chief of the defence staff, HL Debs 7 November 2013, vol 749, col 403. See also the concern expressed by some lawyers having had experience in the armed forces with the issue of civilians taking a direct part in hostilities, discussed in Chapter 9.

the fact that investigations into their conduct may be carried out where there is some evidence of torture, inhuman or degrading treatment, or where a civilian has been killed by them during a non-international armed conflict or a period of occupation.

It does seem an unnecessary distraction for policy makers to add to their complex tasks of engaging in armed conflict of the intensity seen in Iraq and in Afghanistan, a fight against the impact of the law during military operations. It is likely that any future operations of the same type, involving a non-international armed conflict or an occupation of territory, will not experience the same problems as those faced since 2003. Lessons on the treatment of detainees are likely to have been learned, as has the need to provide independent investigations in appropriate cases, and effective processes may well now be in place to achieve the standards required.

It is difficult to believe that the actual effect, in later cases, of the decision of the Supreme Court in *Smith v Ministry of Defence* (2013)[58] will carry the risks to military efficiency claimed for it in relation to those actually carrying out military operations. Even in cases where the Ministry of Defence is sued in negligence for the actions of one of its soldiers the standard of negligence is 'to be measured against the standard to be expected of the reasonable serviceman having similar training, knowledge and experience to the defendant',[59] but it should not be overlooked that combat immunity, in a 'combat situation',[60] is by no means dead.

It has also been argued that the armed forces are treated by the law, in other ways, as would be a civilian employer, particularly in relation to health and safety legislation, an inappropriate position to be in considering the tasks expected of the armed forces during armed conflict.[61] The actual position is, however, that in terms of employment law[62] and health and safety legislation[63] the armed forces are treated differently, in a number of ways, from civilian employers.

The concern about individual servicemen or women having to give evidence at a coroner's court, has been discussed above, with its perceived negative effect on morale, particularly on the part of those who were in command on the ground at the time of the death. If this is considered to be a significant problem the

58 [2013] UKSC 41.

59 *Price v R* [2014] EWCA Crim 229 (death caused at a firing range in peacetime) where the defendant was charged before the court martial with performing a duty negligently under the Army Act 2006, s 15.

60 See *Bici v Ministry of Defence* [2004] EWHC 786, [102]. This case was approved by *Smith v Ministry of Defence* [2013] UKSC 41. It is worth noting that the doctrine of combat immunity did not apply as a defence to actions in tort brought against the Ministry of Defence for the actions of its soldiers during military operations in Northern Ireland, see discussion in Chapter 9. For discussion of combat immunity see Chapter 5.

61 Lord Guthrie, HL Debs 7 November 2013, vol 749, col 403.

62 See further discussion in Chapter 3.

63 See *Halsbury's Laws of England*, vol 3 (LexisNexis, 5th edn, 2011), [339]. See also the Health and Safety Act 1974, s 48(1), although compare s 48(2) relating to persons in the public service of the Crown; Corporate Manslaughter and Corporate Homicide Act 2007, s 4.

process can only be avoided through some form of legislative change. Now that the precedent has been set, and it has become a part of the whole process of the repatriation of British servicemen and women killed during military operations, it will be a bold government that would propose such a change, or invoke the Crown Proceedings (Armed Forces) Act 1987,[64] or derogate from certain articles of the ECHR during British military operations.[65]

As great a degree of certainty of the law is, perhaps, an even greater requirement for the armed forces while conducting military operations, than it would be for other activities in British society and it must surely fall on the ministers at the Ministry of Defence and the service chiefs to ensure that those actually engaged in the combat operations are shielded from the corrosive effects of undue legal speculation, particularly when these are fuelled through the media.[66]

An exclusion, by English law, of the ECHR applying to the actions of British soldiers serving overseas, through a proposed Bill of Rights,[67] could prevent Iraqi and Afghan nationals being able to pursue claims in London and might appear to reduce the impact of the law during British military operations, but at the cost of legal accountability.

It should also be borne in mind that the impact of the law on military operations in Iraq and Afghanistan has occurred during an occupation of territory and non-international armed conflicts. Apart from the period of the occupation of Iraq, the armed conflicts have been of a non-international character, the law applicable to which would have been no different, in principle, had the armed conflicts, of the same type, taken place in the UK at the present time.[68] In this case, however, there would be two policy options available to the British government, which might be much more difficult to achieve during British military participation in a similar conflict in another state. These would be the opportunity to derogate, more easily, from certain obligations under the ECHR and, linked with this, the ability to impose some form of emergency legislation. Were the UK, on the other hand, to become involved in an *international* armed conflict, without occupying territory, the primacy (although not exclusivity) of IHL would be obvious to see.

64 For discussion see Chapter 5.

65 See discussion in Chapter 7.

66 The influence of media coverage of comments made by senior service officers and ministers is explored by MacKinlay, note 55, 113.

67 The proposed Bill of Rights proposes that its reach will be limited to acts occurring in the UK, draft Art 25. The Commission on a Bill of Rights was announced in HC Debs 18 March 2011, vol 525, col 31WS. See generally, House of Lords Library Note, LLN 2013/014, 17 June 2013, and the proposal by the government to repeal the Human Rights Act 1998, HC Debs 26 November 2015, vol 602, cols 1472–3 (Attorney General).

68 For an example of an earlier period, see the campaign in Northern Ireland between 1969 and the Belfast Agreement of 1998, where, although IHL did not apply, see S Haines, 'Northern Ireland 1968–1998' in E Wilmshurst (ed), *International Law and the Classification of Conflicts* (OUP, 2012), 117, 130, the full range of the law of Northern Ireland was applicable, as was the ECHR (although not the Human Rights Act 1998).

iv The role of the House of Commons

The decision of the government in 2003 to give MPs a vote on the proposed action in Iraq should be seen as a first, but not the last, step in involving the House of Commons, if this remains the preferred policy approach, in proposals by the government to take military action overseas. By the time of the Iraq 2014 vote, little had changed in terms of the information supplied by the government to the House, although in 2015 the consideration by the Foreign Affairs Select Committee of possible air strikes in Syria led to a detailed response made by the Prime Minister. Members of Parliament were, however, no more able to explore the strength of the legal grounds advanced than they had been in 2003 and, whilst it is accepted that the Attorney General's advice to the Prime Minister may need to be confidential,[69] there must be a strong case for more in-depth legal analysis to be provided to MPs, in some cases, although not all.[70] A UN Security Council resolution authorising states to take military action will speak largely for itself (as in Libya, 2011) but greater legal analysis would have been helpful to, at least some, MPs in the votes on Iraq (2003), Syria (2013) and Iraq (2014), or the legal justification given for the air strikes by remotely piloted aircraft on 21 August, and on 12 November 2015, over Syria. Members will be aware that any statement about the position in international law will contain a degree of uncertainty greater than there would be in respect of English law since, 'lacking a steady flow of cases [international law] cannot rely heavily on judges to steer the development of the law'.[71] Alternatively, there would seem to be no real reason why the Attorney General should not be expected to speak in the debate, solely on the legal grounds advanced by the government, and to respond to interventions by individual MPs. The need for more detailed legal advice is based, not on legal purism, but on the reflection that individual MPs can expect, at some later date, to be called upon to explain to the public why they voted for or against a particular motion to take military action and, in this sense, there is a form of accountability for the decision each has made, despite the reality of a whipped vote.[72]

In addition, it seems essential that MPs must also be able to know that a full discussion on the legal grounds, amongst the other important issues, has taken place either in the Cabinet, a Cabinet committee, or in the National Security Council, prior to the vote. The minutes of these meetings will not, of course, be available at the time of any particular vote for MPs to see if this has been actually taken place, and possibly not thereafter, although the process,

69 Although see the comment of Lord Bingham, discussed in Chapter 4.
70 See the discussion in Chapter 4.
71 V Lowe, 'The Iraq Crisis: What Now?' (2003) 52 ICLQ 859.
72 See J Gray, MP and M Lomas, QC, *Who Takes Britain to War?* (History Press, 2014), 40, who refer to 'political courage'. The free vote given to Labour MPs on 2 December 2015 can be contrasted with all other relevant votes on this issue.

including whether the legal issue was discussed, may possibly come in to the public domain.[73]

The accountability of MPs for their decision to vote in favour of military action, brings with it a responsibility also to satisfy themselves that they are fully informed as to its progress, objectives, and its conduct. It will be for them to judge whether it is adequate for the discharge of this responsibility that 'both the Prime Minister and the Attorney General are regularly before the House for scrutiny and [MPs] will have an opportunity to put questions to them'.[74] It is difficult to escape the conclusion that the House of Commons, as a body, has very limited opportunity to influence the post-vote military action, compared with the vote itself. The motion in 2015 relating to air strikes on Syria, does, however, specifically refer to the need to 'avoid civilian casualties, using the United Kingdom's particular capabilities' and that the government commits itself to providing 'quarterly progress reports to the House'. This could be seen as a formal acknowledgement that MPs themselves remain seised of the progress of the campaign.

v The problem with intelligence

In the context of this book there were a number of problematic issues with defence intelligence made available to ministers. It was not uncommon to find that it was not sufficiently accurate at crucial stages of a UK military deployment, such as in Iraq 2003 and in Helmand province of Afghanistan in 2006. Even if it was, on other occasions, accurate, it may not have been disclosed to those who had to make important decisions based on it, such as to MPs for a debate and vote to take military action, or it may not have got through to those who were conducting operations on the ground.[75]

When MPs are called upon to vote in support of a decision to take military action overseas they will, generally, have only the contents of the government's proposed motion and any further comments on intelligence information included in the Prime Minister's speech. Even if it is assumed that this is accurate, it is not unreasonable for MPs to be able to look to a small group of other MPs, not holding government positions, who have received a briefing on the intelligence background and who could act, without disclosing details, as a form of objective

73 See the Certificate and Reasons given by the Attorney General for his decision, of 31 July 2012, under the Freedom of Information Act 2000, s 53(2), to prevent disclosure of minutes of the Cabinet on 13 and 17 March 2003 'at which the Attorney General's legal advice concerning military action against Iraq was considered and discussed', https://www.gov.uk/government/publications/attorney-general-vetoes-release-of-cabinet-meeting-minutes. The fact that the Attorney General attended the Cabinet meeting on 17 March 2003 was brought into the public domain through his evidence of 27 January 2010 to the Iraq Inquiry, 214. See further discussion in Chapter 4.

74 Leader of the House of Commons, HC Debs 17 September 2015, vol 599, col 1199.

75 See Brigadier E Butler, oral evidence to the Defence Committee 11th Report, session 2014–15, *Decision-Making and Defence Policy*, HC 682, Q 29.

reassurance to the House of Commons. Such a group could, it has been suggested, be the Intelligence and Security Committee[76] or the Defence Select Committee.[77]

vi Who was in charge, the chiefs or ministers?

The issue is one of considerable constitutional importance, since at its heart lies the question of accountability for the conduct of the various wars discussed in this book. Two well-developed constitutional principles come into play, those of civilian control over the armed forces and of operational decisions being made by the armed forces. The dividing line between them may not, however, be too clear in practice.[78]

In reality, the matter is not one for an allocation of separate areas of decision making between the government on one side, and the most senior armed forces commanders on the other, but it requires an understanding that they will need to work together with clear lines of accountability for particular types of decision. It has been discussed above[79] that government ministers have only one principal source of information on military matters, the senior armed forces commanders, who through the chief of the defence staff, need to be able to provide clear guidance to ministers from the planning to the concluding stages of a particular campaign.[80] Although the government has stated that the chain goes upwards from the chief of the defence staff to the Secretary of State for Defence, there is some evidence that this chain may not be as clear as this in practice, and that military advice may not have been as effective, at times, as might have been expected.[81]

76 See HC Debs 9 September 2015, vol 599, col 400, concerning the attack by a remotely piloted aircraft on 21 August 2015 on two British nationals in Syria.

77 See the suggestion made by Dr K Howells (a former Foreign Office minister), Defence Committee 11th Report, session 2014–15, *Decision-Making and Defence Policy*, HC 682, oral evidence, Q 115.

78 For discussion as to the relationship between defence ministers and the senior military commanders, see Chapter 3; House of Commons Select Committee on Defence, 4th Report, 2010–12, *Operations in Afghanistan*, HC 554, Qs 562, 575, 582 (Lord Browne) and for the relationship between ministers and the chain of command, see *ibid*, Qs 557, 558.

79 See Chapter 3.

80 They will, of course, be assisted by civil servants, the most senior of whom will also be in frequent contact with military commanders. See Sir Sherard Cowper-Coles, Defence Committee 11th report, session 2014–15, *Decision-Making and Defence Policy*, HC 682, Q 15; Mr D Bowen, *ibid*, Q 57. For the suggestion of a 'visible erosion in the confidence and trust between serving officers and the government of the day', see HC Debs 26 January 2006, vol 496, col 516 (Sir Malcolm Rifkind, MP).

81 See Defence Select Committee 4th Report, session 2010–12, *Operations in Afghanistan*, HC 554 (2011), [36]; Defence Committee, 7th Report, session 2014–15, *The Situation in Iraq and Syria and the Response to Al-Dawla al-Islamiya fi al-Iraq al-Sham (DAESH)*, HC 690, 2015, [86]. The Government response, HC 1126, [2] (2015), drew attention to the fact that 'responsibility for such advice to the Defence Secretary does not lie directly with the Service Chiefs [but] . . . through the Chief of the Defence Staff'. *Quaere* whether this answers the point made by the Defence Committee. See also General Lord Richards, Defence Committee 11th Report, session 2014–15, *Decision-Making and Defence Policy*, HC 682, Q 442, 'the single Services answer to the Secretary of State for Defence'.

The comment by the then Secretary of State for Defence, to the Iraq Inquiry in 2010, that 'the advice of the chiefs, which I always take'[82] might suggest that he merely followed their advice, but his statement needs to be read in context. It actually shows that he was not prepared to take the advice conveyed to him concerning the UK's involvement in Helmand Province in 2005–2006 without imposing his own conditions. It did, however lead one retired general to comment that 'you might even conclude that nobody was really in charge'.[83] This view is, however, likely to be challenged by the various secretaries of state for defence who served in that role during the long period when British armed forces were fighting in Iraq and in Afghanistan. Ministers would surely point out that they have had to approve the RoE and, at times, the targeting policy, both of which were put forward by the armed forces, and were key policy issues during the wars between 2000 and 2015.

It may be that the National Security Council, established in 2010, has been able to play a significant part in ensuring not only effective coordination between the chief of the defence staff and ministers, but also accountability within the democratic process.[84] Despite the advantages of this new process, attention might also need to be paid to whether the Armed Forces Committee, has fully analysed the military position prior to any military advice being advanced by the chief of the defence staff at the National Security Council,[85] and to whether its membership should include the Attorney General or a senior legal adviser from the Foreign and Commonwealth Office.[86]

82 Iraq Inquiry, evidence of Dr John Reid, 3 February 2010, 54, 55. It seems plain, however, that ministers 'usually wound up accepting the military advice that they were given [although] [t]hey rarely failed to question it, and rightly so', Lord Stirrup, a former chief of the defence staff, Defence Select Committee 4th Report, session 2010–12, *Operations in Afghanistan* (2011), HC 554, Q 657. *Quaere* whether 'the politicians . . . were in awe of the generals', Sir Sherard Cowper-Coles, Defence Committee 11th Report, session 2014–15, *Decision-Making and Defence Policy*, HC 682, oral evidence, Q 8 and see Dr K Howells (a former Foreign Office minister) who stated that, 'I believe military advice should have been challenged time and again', *ibid*, Q 95.

83 C Elliott, *High Command* (C Hurst and Co, 2015), 82; Defence Committee 11th Report, session 2014–15, *Decision-Making and Defence Policy*, HC 682, [31] , 'no clarity over who was in charge.'

84 For evidence of its role in the Libya campaign in 2011 see discussion in Chapter 3. Its predecessor was the Defence and Oversea Policy Committee of the Cabinet, see Sir Sherard Cowper-Coles, Defence Committee 11th report, session 2014–15, *Decision-Making and Defence Policy*, HC 682, Q 15. That Committee was not convened between 2001 and 2003, Foreign Affairs Committee, *The Decision to go to War*, 9th Report, 2002–03, (2003), [143]. Differences of view between the Prime Minister and the chief of the defence staff can, of course, occur. See, for example, General David Richards, *Taking Command* (Headline Publishing, 2014), 339.

85 See, for example, C Elliott, *High Command: British Military Leadership in the Iraq and Afghanistan Wars* (C Hurst and Co, 2015), 174.

86 The Attorney General was invited to discussions in the National Security Council concerning possible attacks by remotely piloted aircraft on British nationals fighting on behalf of ISIL in Syria, HC Debs 8 September 2015, vol 599, col 26.

It must be an issue of concern, at least in terms of accountability, if the reality of the working relationship between ministers and senior military commanders is such that each group feels inhibited from challenging the other.[87] For the rhetoric of ministers being in charge to be matched by the reality during the actual conduct of military operations, the constitutional arrangements must be such that there can be no perception that 'military commanders [are] not under sufficiently close civilian control'.[88]

vii Legal advice

The legal issues resulting from the decision to engage in military action in Iraq in 2003 and in 2014, and in Afghanistan, from 2006, were a complex blend of English law, along with the impact of the ECHR through the Human Rights Act 1998, and of IHL. The UK had, of course, been engaged in armed conflict before 2003, but the Iraq and Afghanistan wars raised novel legal points that required careful analysis to enable those who were required to play a crucial role, whether it was the House of Commons itself, ministers and civil servants or those serving in the armed forces, to comply with the relevant law. If each group was to be held accountable to the law, each would need sound legal advice to be able to do so. In practice the engine of legal accountability was the English legal system and those who wished to challenge government departments, or the UK itself, also required suitable legal advice. This advice was provided by government lawyers and, where appropriate, by lawyers in private practice, but the difficulties of providing this advice, in a fast-moving legal environment, cannot be underestimated.[89] Where the courts drew conclusions at variance with the legal advice given to ministers the resultant costs and compensation bill has proved to have been substantial. The legal advice given to ministers is not disclosable, even to parliamentary select committees,[90] and so it is not possible to determine whether ministers took a firm line, for example, on the very limited applicability of the Human Rights Act 1998 to Iraq and its non-applicability to Afghanistan, or whether these two separate positions reflected the legal advice they were given.

It may well be that, as discussed above, a much greater knowledge of the legal principles applying to a non-international armed conflict in which the UK may be, or is, engaged, on the part of the service chiefs, could lead to an even stronger

87 See discussion in Chapter 3.

88 See Defence Committee 11th Report, session 2014–15, *Decision-Making and Defence Policy*, HC 682, [115], where the Committee concluded that the various reforms and the creation of the National Security Council in 2010 had 'dealt with perceived problems, particularly in Afghanistan'.

89 For the role of the firms of solicitors, see Chapter 5. As to whether a government's lawyers should play a role more in the nature of independent legal advisers, rather than as in-house lawyers, see *Report of the Dutch Committee of Inquiry on the War in Iraq* (2010) 57 NILR 81, 115.

90 See discussion in Chapter 5.

culture of legal compliance in practice, rather than merely in aspirational terms. This legal knowledge, supported by professional legal advice, could do much to ensure that individual members of the armed forces who actually engage in combat activities, do not fear that the law acts as a hindrance to the performance of their important military functions in planning for, and conducting, an armed conflict.

viii The need for recognition of the increased importance of the law in Britain's wars 2000–2015

From playing a relatively minor publicly visible role in the armed conflicts to which Britain had been a party, the law has, since 2003, found itself thrust into the limelight. The legality, or otherwise, of a particular military intervention is now a subject of considerable public interest, as are reports of the rare occasions when it has been alleged that British soldiers ill-treated detainees. Much of the legal activity occurring in the civil courts in London has gone unnoticed by the public, but is well known by those having executive responsibilities in the area of this activity.

Ministers, service chiefs and their legal advisers have had to try and predict how the courts in England, and in some cases, the ECtHR, will interpret the pre-existing law. This will always be a long drawn-out process and, until a definitive ruling is given, there will be a degree of uncertainty as to how that law should apply to the variety of activities involved in an armed conflict. How could this be speeded up so as to provide a much greater degree of legal certainty for the benefit of ministers and members of the armed forces? One possibility would be to use more frequently the power granted by the Administration of Justice Act 1969, s 12, for an appropriate case to leapfrog to the Supreme Court before its possible progression to the ECtHR.[91] Another would be to establish a law of armed conflict advisory tribunal, chaired by a specialist High Court judge, whose lay members could include a senior member of the armed forces, to provide an advisory, non-binding, opinion on a particular issue. The advantage of such a procedure would be that it could provide to government lawyers and officials, at their option, an independent assessment of how a particular legal issue might be decided if it went to court. The tribunal could permit, for instance, *amicus curiae* briefs and thus hear more than one legal opinion, but it would not replace any existing court structures or causes of action.

A sensible lesson to be drawn from the experience of these armed conflicts is to raise substantially an understanding amongst middle and upper ranking service officers of the requirement to understand the law that they will need to know for the particular military operations in which they are to take part. This understanding, which must reflect more than IHL, should be given the status equivalent to a 'doctrine' and be recognised in importance as being of critical importance in

91 For an example of leapfrog to the Supreme Court, *Al-Waheed v Ministry of Defence* [2014] EWHC 2714.

the career progression of officers. The availability of specialist legal advice will, of course, remain an essential asset for those engaged in the various forms of military operations. Misunderstandings about the reach of the law, and unjustified fears of the legal consequences of action, are likely to have negative impacts on military performance, but they can be ameliorated significantly through a recognition that the proper understanding of the legal principles involved is essential. There is also strong evidence to suggest that service personnel themselves desire, and would benefit from, a much greater knowledge of the legal principles on which they are required to engage in an armed conflict.[92] The great benefit of such training would be able to lessen considerably for them the 'fear of the legal unknown' and to be able to correct misconceptions.

ix Has there been legal accountability?

Few would doubt that in the UK members of the armed forces should be legally accountable for their actions; indeed, the government expressed the same view in 2013.[93] Thus, a very few soldiers have been prosecuted for crimes against English law committed whilst on duty in Iraq and in Afghanistan,[94] and other prosecutions could follow the investigations by IHAT.[95] Others have been called to give evidence before civilian courts, public inquiries,[96] or parliamentary select committees and a medical officer has been required to appear the General Medical Council in relation to his acts or omissions in Iraq. Investigations, particularly in Iraq, of alleged breaches of Articles 2 or 3 of the ECHR, can lead to conclusions that practices need to be changed to provide further protection to detainees or the civilian population, and that the conduct of individuals should be subject to some form of service disciplinary or administrative action.

The measure of success of legal accountability cannot be derived from the numbers of soldiers prosecuted, or otherwise subjected to service disciplinary systems. It must be based on the systems in place to ensure that this form of accountability can be invoked if, and when, the need arises.

The government has borne its own accountability to the law by means of very public processes, particularly in relation to the myriad of cases decided by the

92 W MacKinlay, 'Perceptions and Misconceptions: How are International and UK Law Perceived to Affect Military Commanders and Their Subordinates on Operations?' (2007) 7 Defence Studies 111, 140, where 'more than 50% of those surveyed believed they did not receive adequate legal knowledge', 140.

93 HL Debs 7 November 2013, vol 570, col 413.

94 See Chapter 8.

95 'According to information provided by the Secretary of State, IHAT is currently investigating 153 allegations of unlawful killing and 110 allegations of mistreatment. In total these allegations relate to 263 individuals', *Al-Saadoon v Secretary of State for Defence* [2015] EWHC 715, [26].

96 Discussed in Chapter 5. In the Al-Sweady Inquiry some '507 [military personnel were requested to supply] a full statement [to the Inquiry] . . . around half . . . who provided a written statement also went on to attend the Inquiry to give oral evidence', Report, vol 1, 27, [1.131].

courts, both in London and at the ECtHR. The obligation to conduct investigations has increased the number of them substantially, and where it has been adjudged to have acted unlawfully, it has been required to pay compensation. In addition, a number of claims have been settled out of court, or payments have been made to claimants or their relatives through the Army Goodwill Payments Committee.[97] Where the government is the defendant or respondent to a particular claim, it, rather than individual members of the armed forces, is, in reality, the body held accountable.[98]

It is, however, difficult to accept that ministers, who have made important decisions relating to Britain's wars from 2000 to 2015, have been held legally accountable for their decisions. Some may be willing to support the possibility of requiring ministers, or the most senior civilian officials and service officers, who have been adjudged by a body established by law to have failed in their responsibilities, to re-pay a percentage of their salaries.[99]

There would appear to be a significant degree of legal accountability, but there are factors that can militate against it. Whilst action may, or may not, be taken against individual members of the armed forces, whether through disciplinary or administrative procedures, the relatives of those who have died in British custody or were killed by British forces, may *feel* that there has been no accountability, simply because they are not kept informed of decisions made about their claims.[100] Others may think that the number of British soldiers actually prosecuted is small compared with the number arrested following publicity generated about a particular incident, without realising that proof beyond reasonable doubt is required in a criminal court and this may not, in some cases, be achievable, for reasons based upon the nature of the evidence.

Ironically, the practice of the ICRC in producing confidential reports to states following visits by its delegates to detainees can have the unintended consequence of preventing particular practices or forms of treatment coming to light.[101] Non-disclosure by the government of those parts of the RoE relating to when force may be used may also inhibit transparency and thus accountability.[102] The proposed restriction of legal aid to UK residents only would have meant, if it had applied between 2003 and 2015, that some of the cases that have come before

97 For examples see the details surrounding the claims of the first, second and fourth applicants in *Al-Skeini v United Kingdom* (2011) 53 EHRR 18, [38], [42], [52]. See also FOI, Ministry of Defence releases, 15 December 2014; 26 January 2015, the latter of which refers to the fact that the 'total paid by MOD to [Iraqi] claimants is approximately £19.3 M, representing 321 cases'.

98 See for example, *McCann v United Kingdom* (1996) 21 EHRR 97, in relation to those who planned the operation in Gibraltar compared with those who carried out the shooting dead of the three individuals; *Bici v Ministry of Defence* [2004] EWHC 786.

99 An example of a minister returning half of his pay over a six-month period on a voluntary basis can be found in Japan, see *The Japan Times*, 26 September 2015.

100 An example is given in I Cobain, *Cruel Britannia* (Portobello Books, 2012), 299.

101 See discussion in Chapter 6.

102 HC Debs 14 March 2005, vol 432, col 30W, discussed in Chapter 8.

the English courts, could not have done so. The result would have meant not only that practices that came to light through this litigation would not have done so but also that the accountability to the law for the actions of the British armed forces would have been lessened considerably as a result. The same conclusion, with the same result, would seem to follow if the proposed exclusion of the ECHR to the activities of UK armed forces conducting military operations abroad under a UK Bill of Rights becomes law, or if legislation is passed to nullify the decision of the Supreme Court in *Smith v Ministry of Defence* (2013) in respect of combat immunity.[103]

It is striking how the legal accountability of individuals and of the state itself, have been derived from English law, along with the principles set out in service procedures, such as the RoE, other instructions or orders relating to the treatment of detainees or serious incident report forms,[104] and not directly under IHL. Although the war crimes under the International Criminal Court Act 2001 were, of course, those developed by IHL, there was only one case in which a British soldier was charged with such an offence and that was before a British court-martial.[105] The remainder were the normal criminal or service offences under service law. It is true that a communication was received by the Office of the Prosecutor of the ICC on 10 January 2014 alleging the 'responsibility of officials of the UK for war crimes involving systemic detainee abuse in Iraq from 2003 until 2008' and that the Prosecutor has decided to conduct a preliminary examination into the allegations.[106] In any event, a subsequent trial of a British serviceman or woman would be based on the Armed Forces Act 2006 and not at the ICC, as a result of the principle of complementarity.[107] That the norms of IHL and of the ECHR[108] did provide the environment at the international law level for Britain's wars 2000–2015 cannot be doubted, but it was English law (including the service discipline Acts or the Armed Forces Act 2006) that laid out the actual groundwork of legal accountability.

The actual practice of a state, as compared with what it says it will do in its military manual, is often to be found in its relatively low-level documents, such as the RoE at any one time, or guidance on the treatment of those detained, and through its various processes, whether serious incident reports or investigations, along with activity within its disciplinary system. Many of these documents and processes can be altered relatively quickly, compared with military manuals, to

103 [2013] UKSC 41. See also Defence Select Committee, 12th Report, session 2013–14, *UK Armed Forces Personnel and the Legal Framework of Future Operations*, HC 931, Written Evidence from the Ministry of Defence, [26].

104 See discussion in Chapter 9.

105 *R v Payne* http://www.internationalcrimesdatabase.org/Case/811.

106 The ICC http://www.icc-cpi.int/en_menus/icc/structure%20of%20the%20court/office%20of%20the%20prosecutor/reports%20and%20statements/statement/Pages/otp-statement-iraq-13-05-2014.aspx. The decision was made on 13 May 2014 to re-open the preliminary examination concluded in 2006.

107 Rome Statute of the International Criminal Court 1998, Art 17, see Chapter 6.

108 See also the UN Convention Against Torture 1984 and discussion in Chapter 7.

meet changing conditions.[109] It will be these documents and processes that will be the key drivers to legal accountability of members of the armed forces during combat operations and upon which concentration needs to be placed by service lawyers and by commanders. The primary sources of a legal obligation during an armed conflict, such as IHL, human rights law and English law, become, in effect, the secondary, or even invisible, sources for those who are actually carrying out British government and armed forces policy.

An unusual feature of Britain's wars from 2000 to 2014 has been the practice of the Prime Minister in paying tribute in the House of Commons to individual members of the British armed forces who have been killed in action. It can be seen as a form of accountability that the nation accepts, expressed through the Prime Minister, for at least one of the consequences of the military action undertaken on its behalf. This debt of gratitude led to the development of the Armed Forces Covenant, and although not a legally binding document, it expresses a form of obligation to all members of the armed forces.[110]

It should not be forgotten that five British service personnel lost their lives in Sierra Leone, 178 in the Iraq war, 453 in Afghanistan and one in Libya.[111] Very many more suffered serious or very serious injuries.[112] The many recorded acts of bravery of members of the UK armed forces compel only admiration.

109 The UK Ministry of Defence, *Manual of the Law of Armed Conflict* (OUP) was published in 2004 and has not been updated in this form by the end of 2015. See also Chapter 8.

110 For discussion, see Chapter 3.

111 These figures do not encompass all those who lost their lives during the various campaigns. Those who lost their lives through hostile action were, respectively, 1, 135, 404 and nil, see https://www.gov.uk/government/uploads/system/uploads/attachment_data/file/369400/20141104_UK_Armed_Forces_Operational_deaths_post_World_War_II_O.pdf.

112 The number of those very seriously or seriously injured in Afghanistan 2007-14 was 581, of whom 540 were injured through hostile action, see https://www.gov.uk/government/uploads/system/uploads/attachment_data/file/399080/20150122_Tracking_Oct07_Sep14_SI_VSI_Op_Casualties.pdf.

Select bibliography

Akande D, 'Clearing the Fog of War? The ICRC's Interpretive Guidance on Direct Participation in Hostilities' (2010) 59 ICLQ 180

Annan K, (with Mousavizadeh, N) *Interventions: a Life in War and Peace* (Penguin Books, 2012)

'Attorney General's Advice on the Iraq War: Resolution 1441' (2005) 54 ICLQ 767

Bailey J, Iron R, Strachan H (eds), *British Generals in Blair's Wars* (Ashgate, 2013)

Baxter R, 'The Duty of Obedience to the Belligerent Occupant' (1950) 27 BYBIL 235

———, 'So-Called "Unprivileged Belligerency": Spies, Guerrillas and Saboteurs' (1951) 28 BYBIL 323

Bell C, *Peace Agreements and Human Rights* (OUP, 2000)

Bellinger J III and Haynes W II, 'A US Government Response to the International Committee of the Red Cross Study *Customary International Humanitarian Law*' (2007) 89 IRRC 443

Bingham, Lord, 'The Rule of Law', Sixth Sir David Williams Lecture, 16 November 2006, http://www.cpl.law.cam.ac.uk/Media/THE%20RULE%20OF%20LAW%202006.pdf

Blicke A, 'The Cabinet Manual and the Codification of Conventions' (2014) 67 Parliamentary Affairs 191

Boister N, and Cryer R, *Documents on the Tokyo International Military Tribunal, Charter, Indictments and Judgments* (OUP, 2008)

Boothby W, *The Law of Targeting* (OUP, 2012)

Buckley E, 'Invoking Article 5', NATO Review, 2006, http://www.nato.int/docu/review/2006/issue2/english/art2.html

Cai C, 'New Great Powers and International Law in the 21st Century' (2013) 24 EJIL 755

Campbell A, *The Burden of Power: Countdown to Iraq* (Arrow Books, 2013)

Capps P, 'British Policy on the Recognition of Governments' (Case Comment) [2014] PL 229

Clapham A, *Human Rights Obligations of Non-State* Actors (OUP, 2006)

Clapham A, Gaeta, P, Sassoli M (eds), *The 1949 Geneva Conventions: a Commentary* (OUP, 2015)

Cobain I, *Cruel Britannia*: A Secret History of Torture (Portobello Books, 2012)

Commission on the Responsibility of the Authors of the War and on Enforcement of Penalties' (1920) 14 AJIL 95

Cook R, *The Point of Departure* (Simon & Schuster, 2003)
Cowper-Coles, Sir Sherard, *Ever the Diplomat: Confessions of a Foreign Office Mandarin* (Harper Press, 2012)
de Londras F, 'Revisiting the Five Techniques in the European Court of Human Rights' (12 December 2014) EJIL: Talk!, http://www.ejiltalk.org/revisiting-the-five-techniques-in-the-european-court-of-human-rights/
Dinstein Y, *The International Law of Belligerent Occupation* (CUP, 2009)
Dinstein Y and Tabory M (eds), *War Crimes in International Law* (Nijhoff, 1996)
Elliott C, *High Command: British Military Leadership in the Iraq and Afghanistan Wars* (Hurst & Co, 2015)
Epstein L, Ho D, King G, Segal J, 'The Supreme Court During Crisis: How War Affects only Non-War Cases' (2005) 80 New York University Law Review 1
Farrell T and Gordon S, 'COIN Machine: The British Military in Afghanistan' (2009) 154 RUSI Journal 18
Fear N (lead author), 'What are the Consequences of Deployment to Iraq and Afghanistan on the Mental Health of the Armed Forces?' (2010) 375 The Lancet, No 9728, [1783]
Finer S E, *The Man on Horseback: The Role of the Military in Politics* (Penguin Books, 1962)
Foakes J, *The Position of Heads of State and Senior Officials in International Law* (OUP, 2014)
Forster A, 'British Judicial Engagement and the Juridification of the Armed Forces' (2012) 88 International Affairs 283
Garraway C, 'Direct Participation and the Principle of Distinction: Squaring the Circle' in Harvey C, Summers J and White N (eds), *Contemporary Challenges to the Laws of War* (CUP, 2014)
Gearty C, 'In Praise of Awkwardness: Kadi in the CJEU' (2014) 10 European Constitutional Law Review 15
Gee D, 'Informed Choice? Armed Forces Recruitment Practice in the United Kingdom', http://www.informedchoice.org.uk/informedchoice/informedchoicefull.pdf
Gill T and Fleck D (eds), *The Handbook of the International Law of Military Operations* (OUP, 2010)
Goodwin L and Ronan R, 'PTSD in the Armed Forces: What Have We Learned From the Recent Cohort Studies of Iraq and Afghanistan?' (2013 available at http://www.kcl.ac.uk/kcmhr/pubdb/
Gray C, 'A Crisis of Legitimacy for the UN Collective Security System?' (2007) 56 ICLQ 157
———, *International Law and the Use of Force* (OUP, 3rd edn, 2008)
Gray J, MP and Lomas M, QC, *Who Takes Britain to War?* (The History Press, 2014)
Greenwood C, 'The Concept of War in Modern International Law' (1987) 36 ICLQ 283
———, 'Customary International Law and the First Geneva Protocol of 1977 in the Gulf Conflict' in Rowe P (ed), *The Gulf War 1990–91 in International and English Law* (Routledge, Sweet & Maxwell, 1993)
———, 'International Law and the Pre-emptive Use of Force: Afghanistan, Al-Qaida, and Iraq' (2003) 4 San Diego International Law Journal 7
Gribble R, et al, 'Public Awareness of UK Veterans' Charities' (2014) http://www.kcl.ac.uk/kcmhr/pubdb/
Haines S, 'Northern Ireland 1968–1998' in Wilmshurst E (ed), *International Law and the Classification of Conflicts* (OUP, 2012)

Hampson F, 'Afghanistan 2001–2010' in Wilmshurst E (ed), *International Law and the Classification of Conflicts* (OUP, 2012)
Harvey C, 'The "right to conduct one's own defence in person" and a "fair and expeditious trial" Before the ICTY: An Impossible Balancing Act?' in Harvey C, Summers J and White N (eds), *Contemporary Challenges to the Laws of War* (CUP, 2014)
Heller K, 'Comparing the Trial to International Standards of Due Process,' in Scharf M and McNeal G, *Saddam on Trial: Understanding and Debating the Iraqi High Tribunal* (Carolina Academic Press, 2006)
Henckaerts J-M, 'Customary International Humanitarian Law: a Response to US Comments' (2007) 89 IRRC 473
Henckaerts J-M, and L Doswald-Beck L, *Customary International Humanitarian Law, Volume 1: Rules* (OUP, ICRC 2005)
Henderson C, 'The Bush Doctrine': From Theory to Practice (2004) 9 Jo C & S L 3
——— 'The UK Government's Legal Opinion on Forcible Measures in Response to the Use of Chemical Weapons by the Syria Government' (2015) 64 ICLQ 179
Henriksen A and Schack M, 'The Crisis in Syria and Humanitarian Intervention' (2014) 1 Journal on the Use of Force and International Law 122
Independent International Commission on Kosovo, *Kosovo Report*: Conflict, International Response, Lessons Learned (OUP, 2000)
Jamnejad M and Wood M, 'The Principle of Non-Intervention' (2009) 22 LJIL 345
Juss S Singh, 'Terrorism and the Exclusion of Refugee Status in the UK' (2012) 17 Jo C&SL 465
King A, 'The Afghan War and "Postmodern" Memory: Commemoration and the Dead of Helmand' (2010) 61 British Journal of Sociology 1
King A and Crewe I, *The Blunders of our Governments* (Oneworld Publications, 2014)
Kiszely, Lt General J, 'Learning About Counter-Insurgency' (2006) 151 RUSI Jo 16
Kitson F, *Low Intensity Operations: Subversion, Insurgency, Peace-keeping* (Faber and Faber, 1971)
Krupiy T, 'Of Souls, Spirits and Ghosts: Transposing the Application of the Rules of Targeting to Lethal Autonomous Robots' (2015) 16 MJIL 145
Ledwidge F, *Losing Small Wars: British Military Failure in Iraq and Afghanistan* (Yale University Press, 2012)
Lowe V, 'The Iraq Crisis: What Now?' (2003) 52 ICLQ 859
MacKinlay W, 'Perceptions and Misconceptions: How are International and UK Law Perceived to Affect Military Commanders and Their Subordinates on Operations?' (2007) 7 Defence Studies 111
MacMahon D (lead author), 'Violent Offending by UK Military Personnel Deployed to Iraq and Afghanistan: a Date Linkage Cohort Study' (2013) 381 The Lancet No 9870, [907]
MacManus D, et al, 'The Mental Health of the UK Armed Forces in the 21st Century: Resilience in the Face of Adversity' (2014), www.kcl.ac.uk/kcmhr/pubdb, 3.
The Manual of the Law of Armed Conflict (UK Ministry of Defence, OUP 2004) (also known as the Joint Service Manual)
Marston G, 'Armed Intervention in the 1956 Suez Canal Crisis: The Legal Advice Tendered to the British Government' (1988) 37 ICLQ 773
McConnell M E, 'The International Law of Drones', Insight, ASocIL, Volume 14, 12 November 2010
McLaughlin R, 'The Legal Regime Applicable to Use of Lethal Force When Operating under a United Nations Security Council Chapter VII Mandate Authorising "All Necessary Means"' (2007) 12 Jo C & SL 389

Melzer M, 'Keeping the Balance between Military Necessity and Humanity: A Response to Four Critiques of the ICRC's Interpretive Guidance on the Notion of Direct Participation in Hostilities' (2009–10) 42 New York University Journal of International Law and Politics 831
Melzer M, 'Part IX of the ICRC "Direct Participation in Hostilities" Study: No Mandate, No Expertise, and Legally Incorrect' (2009–10) 42 New York University Journal of International Law and Politics 892
Melzer N, *Targeted Killing in International Law* (OUP, 2008)
Mercer N, 'The Future of Article 5 Tribunals in the Light of Experiences in the Iraq War 2003' in Harvey C, Summers J, White N (eds), *Contemporary Challenges to the Laws of War* (CUP, 2014)
Meyer M, 'The Role of the International Red Cross and Red Crescent Movement: Problems Encountered', in Rowe R (ed), *The Gulf War 1990–91 in International and English Law* (Routledge, Sweet & Maxwell, 1993)
Moir L, *Reappraising the Resort to Force: International Law, Jus ad Bellum and the War on Terror* (Hart Publishing, 2010)
Moorehead C, *Dunant's Dream: War, Switzerland and the History of the Red Cross* (Harper Collins, 1998).
Mullins C, *A View From the Foothills: The Diaries of Chris Mullins* (Profile Books, 2010)
Newton M, 'The Iraqi High Criminal Court: Controversy and Contributions' (2006) 88 IRRC 399
Odello M, 'Commentary on the United Nations High-Level Panel on Threats, Challenges and Change' (2005) 10 Jo C & S Law 231
Orentlicher D, 'Venues for Prosecuting Saddam Hussein: The Legal Framework', American Society of International Law Insights, Vol 8, Issue 30, 30 December 2003
Parks H, 'Part IX of the ICRC "Direct Participation in Hostilities" Study: No Mandate, No Expertise, and Legally Incorrect' (2009–10) 42 New York University Journal of International Law and Politics 769
Payne S, 'War Powers: The War Prerogative and Constitutional Change' Vol 153 (2008) RUSI Jo 28
Peevers C, *The Politics of Justifying Force, The Suez Crisis, the Iraq War, and International Law* (OUP, 2013)
Reid J, '20th Century Rules, 21st Century Conflict', lecture at the Royal United Services Institute, 3 April 2006, http://www.responsibilitytoprotect.org/files/UK_SecretaryofState_Speech_Apr_2006.pdf
'Report of the Dutch Committee of Inquiry on the War in Iraq' (2010) 57 NILR 81
Richards D, *Taking Command* (Headline Publishing Group, 2014)
Roberts A and Guelff R, *Documents on the Laws of War* (OUP, 3rd edn, 2000)
Roberts A, 'The End of Occupation: Iraq 2004' (2005) 54 ICLQ 27
———, 'Transformative Military Occupation: Applying the Laws of War and Human Rights' (2006) 100 AJIL 580
Robinson N, *Live from Downing Street* (Bantam Books, 2012)
Rogers A and McGoldrick D, 'Assassination and Targeted Killing – the Killing of Osama Bin Laden' (2011) 60 ICLQ 778
Rogers A, Risius G, in Harvey C, Summers J, White N (eds), *Contemporary Challenges to the Laws of War* (CUP, 2014)
Rowe P, 'The Rules of Engagement in Occupied Territory: Should They be Published?' (2007) 8 MJIL 327

———, 'Military Misconduct during International Armed Operations: "Bad Apples" or Systemic Failure?' (2008) 13 Jo C&SL 165
———, 'The Criminal Liability of a British Soldier Merely for Participating in the Iraq War 2003: a Response to Chilcot Evidence' [2010] Crim LR 752
Sari A, 'The Conclusion of International Agreements by the European Union in the Context of the ESDP' (2008) 57 ICLQ 53
Sassoli M, 'Legislation and Maintenance of Public Order and Civil Life by Occupying Powers' (2005) 16 EJIL 661, 683
———, 'The International Legal Framework for Stability Operations: When may International Forces Attack or Detain Someone in Afghanistan?' (2009) 39 Israeli Year Book on Human Rights 177
Saul B, *Defining Terrorism in International Law* (OUP, 2006)
Scharf M and McNeal G, *Saddam on Trial: Understanding and Debating the Iraqi High Tribunal* (Carolina Academic Press, 2006)
Schilman S and Strachan H, 'The Town That Weeps: Commemorating Life and Loss in Wootton Bassett' (2010) 155 RUSI Jo 76
Schmitt M, 'Iraq (2003 onwards)' in Wilmshurst E (ed), *International Law and the Classification of Conflicts* (OUP, 2012)
Shaw M, *International Law* (CUP, 7th edn, 2014)
Smith, General Sir Rupert (Interview), (2006) 88 IRRC 719
Strachan H, 'British Counter-Insurgency from Malaya to Iraq' (2007) 152 RUSI Jo 8
Straw J, *Last Man Standing: Memoirs of a Political Survivor* (Macmillan, 2012)
Sumption, Lord, 'Foreign Affairs in the English Courts Since 9/11', Lecture at the Department of Government, London School of Economics, 12 May 2012 https://www.supremecourt.uk/docs/speech_120514.pdf
Talmon S, 'De-Recognition of Colonel Qaddafi as a Head of State of Libya?' (2011) 60 ICLQ 759
———, 'Recognition of Opposition Groups as the Legitimate Representatives of a People' [2013] 12 CJIL 219
Taylor A J P, *English History 1914–45* (Clarendon, 1965)
Tugendhat T and Croft L, *The Fog of Law, An Introduction to the Legal Erosion of British Fighting Power* (Policy Exchange, 2013)
Wallerstein S, 'Why English Law Should Not Incorporate the Defence of Superior Orders' [2010] Crim LR 109
Warbrick C, 'British Policy and the National Transitional Council of Libya' (2012) 61 ICLQ 247
Waters C, 'Beyond Lawfare: Judicial Oversight of Western Militaries' (2008–09) 46 Alberta Law Review 885
Waters C, 'Is the Military Legally Encircled?' (2008) 8 Defence Studies 26
Watkin K, 'Use of Force during Occupation: Law Enforcement and Conduct of Hostilities' (2012) 94 IRRC 267
Weller M, *Iraq and Use of Force in International Law* (OUP, 2010)
White N, *Democracy Goes to War: British Military Deployments Under International Law* (OUP, 2009)
———, 'International Law, the United Kingdom and Decisions to Deploy Troops Overseas' (2010) 59 ICLQ 814
Wilkinson J, 'Using Humanitarian Aid to "Win Hearts and Minds": a Costly Failure?' (2011) 93 IRRC 1035
Wilmshurst E, 'Executive Certificates in Foreign Affairs: the United Kingdom' (1986) 35 ICLQ 157

Woolaver H, 'Pro-Democratic Intervention in Africa and "The Arab Spring"' (2014) 22 African Journal of International and Comparative Law 161
Zahn G, *Chaplains in the RAF: a Study in Role Tension* (Manchester University Press, 1969)
Zegweld L, *The Accountability of Armed Opposition Groups in International Law* (CUP, 2002).

Reports

House of Commons Defence Select Committee

The Iran Hostages Incident: the Lessons Learned, 4th Report, session 2007–08, HC 181 (2007)
Operations in Afghanistan, 4th Report, session 2010–12, HC 554 (2011)
Operations in Libya, 9th Report, session 2010–12, HC 950 (2012); *Operations in Libya: Government Response to the [Defence] Committee's Ninth Report of Session 2010–12*, HC 1952 (2012)
UK Armed Forces Personnel and the Legal Framework, 12th Report, session 2013–14, HC 931 (2014)
Afghanistan, 15th Report, session 2013–14, HC 994 (2014); *Government Response*, Fifth Special Report, session 2014–15, HC 582 (2014), Annex A.
Remote Control: Remotely Piloted Air Systems-Current and Future UK Use, 10th Report of session 2013–14, HC 772 (2014); *Government Response*, session 2014–15, HC 611 (2014)
Intervention: Why, When and How?, 14th Report, session 2013–14, HC 952 (2014)
The Situation in Iraq and Syria and the Response to al-Dawla al-Islamiya fi al-Iraq al-Sham (DAESH), 7th Report 2014–15, HC 690 (2015)
Decision-Making in Defence Policy, 11th Report of 2014–15, HC 682 (2015)

House of Commons Foreign Affairs Select Committee

Kosovo, 4th Report, session 1999–2000, HC 28-I (2000)
Foreign Policy Aspects of the War Against Terrorism, 2nd Report, session 2002–03, HC 196; *Response of the Secretary of State for Foreign and Commonwealth Affairs*, Cm 5739 (2003)
Foreign Policy Aspects of the War Against Terrorism, 4th Report, session 2005–06, HC 573 (2006)
Foreign Policy Aspects of the Detention of Naval Personnel by the Islamic Republic of Iran, 6th Report, session 2006–07, HC 880 (2007)
Visit to Guantanamo Bay, 2nd Report, session 2006–07, HC 44 (2007)
The Extension of Offensive Military Operations to Syria, 2nd Report, session 2015–16, HC 457 (2015)

House of Lords Constitution Select Committee

Waging War: Parliament's Role and Responsibility, 15th Report, session 2005–06, HL paper 236-I (2006)
The Accountability of Civil Servants, 6th Report, session 2012–13, HL paper 61 (2012)

Constitutional Arrangements for the Use of Armed Force, 2nd Report, session 2013–14, HL Paper 46 (2013)

Joint Houses Select Committees

Joint Committee on Human Rights, *The UN Convention Against Torture (UNCAT)*, 19th Report, session 2005–06, HL 185, HC 701 (2006)

Ministry of Justice, *Responding to Human Rights Judgments.* Report to the Joint Committee on Human Rights on the Government Response to Human Rights Judgments 2011–12, Cm 8432 (2012)

House of Commons Library

Franco-British Defence Co-operation, Standard Note SN/1A/5750, 8 November 2010

Military Operations in Libya, Standard Note SN/1A/5909, 24 October 2011

The Crisis in Mali: Current Military Action and Upholding Humanitarian Law, Standard Note SN/06531, 11 March 2013

ISIS: the Military Response in Iraq and Syria, Standard Note SN/IA/6995, 17 October 2014

In Brief: Progress against ISIS December 2014, Standard Note SN/1A/07063, 18 December 2014

Parliamentary Approval for Deploying the Armed Forces: Briefing Paper, 7166, 12 May 2015

Legal Basis for UK Military Action in Syria, HC Briefing Paper 7404, 1 December 2015

Public inquiries

Report of the Baha Mousa Inquiry, Sir William Gage, HC 1452 (2011)

Report of the Al Sweady Inquiry, Sir Thayne Forbes, HC 818 (2014)

Other parliamentary papers

Report of the Inquiry into the Circumstances Surrounding the Death of Dr David Kelly, CMG, HC 247 (2004), Lord Hutton

Review of Intelligence on Weapons of Mass Destruction, HC 898 (2004), Lord Butler; *Review of Intelligence on Weapons of Mass Destruction: Implementation of its Conclusions*, Cm 6492 (2005)

The Governance of Britain-Constitutional Renewal, Cm 7342–1 (2008)

The Nimrod Review: An Independent Review into the Broader Issues Surrounding the Loss of the RAF Nimrod MR2 Aircraft XV230 in Afghanistan in 2006, HC 1025, (2009), C Haddon-Cave QC

The Armed Forces Covenant in Action? Part 1, Military Casualties, 7th Report of Session 2010–12, HC 762 (2011)

House of Commons Select Committee on Political and Constitutional Reform, *Parliament's Role in Conflict Decisions*, An Update, 8th Report, session 2013–14, HC 649 (2013)

Strategic Export Controls. Her Majesty's Government's Annual Report for 2012, Quarterly Reports for 2012 and 2013, and the Government's Policy on Arms Exports and International Arms Control Issues, Cm 8935 (2014)

Political and Constitutional Reform Select Committee, *Parliament's Role in Conflict Decisions: a Way Forward*, 12th Report, session 2013–14, HC 892 (2014)

Former Members of the Armed Forces and the Criminal Justice System: A Review on Behalf of the Secretary of State for Justice (2014), Stephen Phillips, QC, MP

The Iraq Fatality Investigations: Inspector Sir George Newman, Consolidated Report into the Death of Nadheem Abdullah and the Death of Hassan Abbas Said, Cm 9023 (2015)

Ministry of Defence

The Aitken Report, An Investigation into Cases of Deliberate Abuse and Unlawful Killing in Iraq in 2003 and 2004 (2008)

Stop, Search, Question and Detention Operations in the Operation Herrick JOA, J-3-9-2-16

Joint Doctrine Publication 1–10, Captured Persons (CPERS), (2015)

International bodies

A More Secure World: Our Shared Responsibility, Report of the High-Level Panel on Threats, Challenges and Change, UN General Assembly, A/59/565, (2004)

Articles on the Responsibility of States for Internationally Wrongful Acts, 2001, International Law Commission, UN General Assembly A/RES/56/83

Final Report to the Prosecutor by the Committee Established to Review the NATO Bombing Campaign Against the Federal Republic of Yugoslavia, http://www.icty.org/sid/10052

ICRC, *International Humanitarian Law and the Challenges of Contemporary Armed Conflicts*, (2011)

International Law Association, *Final Report on the Meaning of Armed Conflict in International Law* (Hague Conference, 2010)

International Law Commission, *Draft Articles on the Responsibility of International Organizations* (2011)

NATO, *Unmanned Aerial Vehicles: Opportunities and Challenges for the Alliance, Special Report*, 157 STC 12 E rev. 1, November 2012

Report of the Secretary-General on Children in Armed Conflict in Afghanistan, S/2008/695

Report of the Special Rapporteur on Extra-Judicial, Summary or Arbitrary Executions, Philip Alston, A/HRC/14/24/ Add.6, 28 May 2010;

Report of the Special Rapporteur on the Protection of Human Rights and Fundamental Freedoms while Countering Terrorism, Ben Emmerson, A/HRC/25/59, 11 March 2014.

United Nations Assistance Mission in Afghanistan, *Annual Report on Protection of Civilians in Armed Conflict*, 2009 (2010)

UN Secretary-General's Report, *Implementing the Responsibility to Protect*, A/63/677 (2009); A/69/981-S/2015/500 (2015)

Other reports

German War Trials: Report of the Proceedings before the Supreme Court in Leipzig, Cmd. 1450 (1921)

Protocols and Correspondence between the Supreme Council and the Conference of Ambassadors and the German Government and the Peace Delegation between 10 January 1920 and July 17, 1920, Respecting the Execution of the Treaty of Versailles of June 28, 1919, Cmd. 1325 (1921)

Public Commission to Examine the Maritime Incident of 31 May 2010, Second Report: Israel's Mechanisms for Examining and Investigating Complaints and Claims of Violations of the Laws of Armed Conflict According to International Law – The Turkel Commission (2013) (Israel)

Report of the Committee on Alleged German Outrages Appointed by Her Majesty's Government, Viscount Bryce, Cd. 7894 (1915)

Report of the Dutch Committee of Inquiry on the War in Iraq (2010) 57 NILR 81

The Ministerial Code, Cabinet Office, 2010, 2015

The Security Impact of Drones: Challenges and Opportunities for the UK: Birmingham Policy Commission (University of Birmingham, 2014)

Index

For Product Safety Concerns and Information please contact our EU representative GPSR@taylorandfrancis.com
Taylor & Francis Verlag GmbH, Kaufingerstraße 24, 80331 München, Germany

www.ingramcontent.com/pod-product-compliance
Ingram Content Group UK Ltd.
Pitfield, Milton Keynes, MK11 3LW, UK
UKHW020017200926
475702UK00014B/1932
* 9 7 8 1 1 3 8 6 1 3 8 2 9 *